RECLAIMING THE FEDERAL COURTS

Reclaiming the Federal Courts

LARRY W. YACKLE

Harvard University Press
Cambridge, Massachusetts
London, England
1994

Library of Congress Cataloging-in-Publication Data
Yackle, Larry W.
Reclaiming the federal courts / Larry W. Yackle.
p.   cm.
Includes bibliographical references and index.
ISBN 0-674-75007-1 (acid-free paper)
1. Jurisdiction—United States.   2. Locus standi—United States.
3. District courts—United States.   4. Appellate courts—United
States.   I. Title.
KF8858.Y33 1994
347.73'2—dc20
[347.3072]
94-8608
CIP

For the Leavenworth Death Row PAC

Contents

Acknowledgments

My work on this project was underwritten by the general fund for faculty research at Boston University School of Law and was facilitated by a sabbatical leave of absence during the spring term in 1991.

Many friends and colleagues contributed valuable, constructive criticism. They include Ann Althouse, Charles H. Baron, Jack M. Beermann, Clark Byse, Erwin Chemerinsky, Michael G. Collins, Barry Friedman, Wythe Holt, James S. Liebman, Daniel G. MacLeod, Tracey Maclin, Martin H. Redish, Lawrence G. Sager, David J. Seipp, Aviam Soifer, Carol Weisbrod, and Michael Wells. Lisa Ehrmann, Rob Kwon, Tracey J. Norberg, Brad Steiner, and especially Jenifer Magyar rendered excellent research assistance. Kellie Army, Charlotte Gliksman, Ellen Leary, Jesse Lynn, Erika Schneider, and Edith Soloman corrected my clerical errors. Jeanette F. Yackle read proof and offered much-needed encouragement. At Harvard University Press, Michael Aronson's advice was warm and supportive, Nancy Clemente's editing superb.

The material in this volume has not been published before. Occasionally, however, I draw ideas and patches of text from previous work in the *Boston University Law Review,* the *New York University Law Review,* the *New York University Review of Law and Social Change,* the *Southern California Law Review,* and the *University of Michigan Journal of Law Reform.*

The judicial Power of the United States, shall be vested in one supreme Court, and in such inferior Courts as the Congress may from time to time ordain and establish. The Judges, both of the supreme and inferior Courts, shall hold their Offices during good Behaviour, and shall, at stated Times, receive for their Services, a Compensation, which shall not be diminished during their Continuance in Office.

—U.S. Constitution, Article III, Section 1

Introduction

Nationalist leaders hoping to establish Western-style democracies in Eastern Europe, Central and South America, and much of Africa and Asia typically regard the United States as a model. And why not? We in this country are poised to enter our third century with the most successful experiment in democratic self-government in human history. The cornerstones of the American framework define modern political legitimacy. Voters choose their leaders in free and regular elections. Government by the few, for the many, is abandoned. Simultaneously, personal liberty is respected and safeguarded. Independent courts enforce individual rights against majoritarian excesses. Ironically, however, at the very moment we Americans presume to claim victory in the cold war, powerful strains *within* American politics challenge the very institutions that so recommend our system to the rest of the world.

We may take pride in our robust electoral contests, which, for all their manifest flaws, still roughly gauge public attitudes at the polls. The current state of the fundamental liberties logged in our Bill of Rights, the post–Civil War constitutional amendments, and other federal laws is quite a different matter. For twenty years, the Supreme Court has been dominated by justices who consistently favor governmental power over the claims of ordinary citizens. Time and again, in case after case, as the Court narrows the scope of federal rights, it undermines our collective commitment to majoritarian government with *limits*. Moreover, the Supreme Court has thrown up barriers to citizens who wish to take their federal claims to the federal courts. Where once those courts were routinely deployed to curb governmental power, today they are often barred from addressing even the most pressing federal issues. The face the United States turns to emerging democracies elsewhere is therefore duplicitous—promising the essentials of a free society, yet at the same time compromising key features of such a system on our own shores.

In this book, I set to one side the Supreme Court's miserly interpretations of federal rights. Others have traced the diminution of individual liberty that has attended the coming of the Rehnquist Court. I will address the erosion of federal rights indirectly, by exploring the availability of the federal courts to enforce those rights. The kind of court in which rights are adjudicated may appear to be conceptually distinct from the treatment those rights get in some court. Yet I will contend that the full measure of federal rights will be realized only by independent federal tribunals. I will focus on the allocation of federal-question cases between the United States district courts and the courts created and operated by the fifty states. This is the ground over which most of the battles regarding federal jurisdiction are currently fought.[1] My thesis in brief is this. The Supreme Court's decisions in recent years have taken far too much decision-making authority away from the federal courts and given it to the courts of the states. In that process, the federal courts have lost the capacity to check the great power of government in American society. The state courts, for a host of reasons, cannot fill the void. And the fundamental framework of American government is now very much at risk. To meet this threat, Congress should enact a series of new statutes to reclaim the federal courts for their vital role in this constitutional democracy.

The jurisdiction of courts, any courts, is freighted with technical language and ideas, the baggage of history and tradition here and in England. The jurisdiction of the federal courts in the United States is governed by an exceptionally complex system of constitutional principles, explicit statutes and rules, and, most important, malleable policies fashioned by the Supreme Court to mediate the relations between power centers. A rough peace must be established, both between the federal judiciary and Congress and between the federal courts and the courts of the states. This is the stuff of lawyering—the mysterious lore by which professionals baffle average citizens. It is also the stuff of legal academicians, for whom complexity seems at times to be an intrinsic good. American law schools harbor a professoriate that specializes in the law of federal courts and delights in fathoming arguments, considerations, and theoretical constructs of questionable practical value. I warn you now; beware agile minds that make things more difficult than they really have to be. The intricacies that abound in these materials often have the effect, and sometimes the purpose, of restricting access to the federal courts.

Deadly dry and confusing doctrines can mask fundamental differences over values that actually drive arguments about whether the federal courts should be open to adjudicate claims. In the early innings of these chapters, I will offer an internal critique of the tangled affair the law of federal court jurisdiction has become. I promise to be brief in my exegesis and to offer clarification where I can. Borrowing a line from Einstein, however, let me say that I will attempt only to make things as simple as they can be, not simpler. Readers must be patient. There is no escaping some hard work if we are to capture and own this critical field of play. If we do the necessary work, I hasten to say, the jurisdiction of the federal courts can and should be made considerably simpler than it is today. We are not doomed to suffer forever the hardships that spring from historical practices that have no place in the modern order. And certainly we need not accept uncritically the complexities that have been added to the system in recent times. Any doctrines that have the effect of limiting federal rights indirectly by dismantling federal enforcement machinery can be discarded. I also mean, then, to offer an external critique of existing arrangements and an explicit program for reform. That plan is incorporated into a series of concrete legislative proposals.

The time is coming when we Americans will have done with the ideological conservatism that slipped into power when the mainstream liberal consensus collapsed in the mid-1970s. We are not resigned to letting official action go unchallenged. Our respect for rights against governmental power is not moribund. Our appreciation that rights demand effective implementation is not diminished. We know, as the world is beginning to understand, how fragile is our way of life and what dreadful chances we take with it when we trifle with its basic institutions. The time is coming when the reins of power will come again to progressive leaders. On that day, with the guidance of a willing chief executive and on the strength of the legislative power of Congress, we will have reform legislation to set right what has recently gone so terribly wrong. Perhaps what I write here can help identify beginning points for discussion.

In Chapter One, I begin with the arguments supporting a preference for federal courts in cases implicating federal legal questions. Initially,

I address the claim that the federal and state courts are functionally equivalent, such that judicial business can be shifted between the two systems without affecting outcomes. I reject that view and argue, by contrast, that the federal courts are superior to the state courts and thus should be the tribunals of choice in federal-question cases. Next, I explore the way in which the availability of the federal courts is intertwined with the most fundamental elements of American jurisprudence—Legal Formalism, Legal Realism, Legal Process, the Civil Rights Movement, and, of course, the recent conservative retrenchment. I concentrate on Legal Process and its enormous influence on the law of federal courts and trace that influence to current arguments over the optimal allocation of judicial business between the federal and state courts. In particular, I treat a persistent theme within the Legal Process model, which has it that the proper outcome in a case is never plain, that the state courts are capable of reaching acceptable results, and that, so long as the process by which those courts arrive at decisions is adequate, their judgments should be embraced—without involving the federal courts. Where this argument rules, federal court enforcement of federal rights is routinely denied.

I argue in Chapter One that, wherever feasible, the federal courts should be authorized to protect federal rights against the threats posed by majoritarian government. Congress' legislative power should be brought to bear, and the federal courts should be commissioned to do what they do best. If Congress does *its* job well, we will enjoy an appropriate federal judicial power notwithstanding the current Supreme Court's doubts. My emphasis in Chapter One on Congress' responsibility to legislate our future expresses the premise on which the rest of the book proceeds. The federal courts are under siege and can be rescued, and federal rights with them, only by legislation of the kind I propose. In the final section of Chapter One, I address concerns that the federal courts cannot cope with the volume of business the program I advance would contemplate.

Next, I offer four chapters on lawsuits raising federal questions affirmatively in federal court. In Chapter Two, I address the perennial problem that lawyers label "justiciability." Several related ideas fit under this heading. I concentrate on citizens' capacity or "standing" to sue in federal court. In turn, I sketch the elements of modern standing doctrine, the historical and jurisprudential developments behind modern doctrine, the part Congress has played, and the Supreme Court's recent work. The role of Congress is critical, including its widely recognized power to decide whether federal rights may be enforced by citizens in private lawsuits. I probe the reasons the Court gives for denying standing to litigants: the limits fixed by Article III of the Constitution, state prerogatives in a federal system, and the balance of power among the federal courts, Congress, and the presidency within the national government. None of these explanations withstands scrutiny, provided that Congress makes clear its own judgment that the federal courts may properly exercise power in specified instances.

By insisting that its standing doctrine has constitutional roots, the Supreme Court declares that Congress lacks power to make the federal courts available by legislation. I will urge Congress to claim for itself the authority to make policy judgments about who can sue in federal court. In brief, I will contend that citizens concerned enough about the enforcement of federal law to assume the burdens of suit should be able to engage the power of the federal courts. Congress *does* have authority to make the federal courts generally available to Americans, whether or not litigants can claim that their own personal rights are threatened. Herein lies much of the confusion that surrounds many existing jurisdictional statutes and civil rights laws, including the Ku Klux Klan Act of 1871, now codified in 42 U.S.C. §1983—by all accounts one of the most important elements in the package of federal statutes enacted in the Reconstruction period after the Civil War. In a final section of Chapter Two, I recommend specific legislation to resolve most common justiciability problems. Bills supported by President Jimmy Carter in the 1970s provide useful guidance. But the particular proposal I put forward offers a more systematic approach to the general task of opening the federal courts to federal claims. In addition, the legislation I recommend puts Congress' power respecting judicial remedies in its proper place and reconciles the idea of a litigant's right of action with the justiciability doctrines.

In Chapter Three, I take up the formal business of fixing the jurisdiction of the federal courts to entertain justiciable claims from litigants whom Congress permits to seek judicial relief. Article III states that the federal judicial power extends to cases "arising under" federal law, and the Supreme Court has always given the "arising under" category an expansive interpretation. This is as it should be. By reading Article III broadly, we can put constitutional limits on the federal courts' jurisdiction in the background and let statutes enacted by Congress govern the actual, day-to-day work the federal courts can handle. In this vein, Congress is conventionally understood to have given the federal courts some, but not all, of the "arising under" jurisdiction that Article III would permit. This is true notwithstanding that the principal statute in point, 28 U.S.C. §1331, tracks Article III almost verbatim. Some observers quarrel with this status quo, and I will treat their arguments—particularly the claim that Congress has but one choice, either to "ordain and establish" lower federal courts or not, and that, once Congress has chosen to create such courts, those courts are necessarily invested with the full range of authority that Article III contemplates as a constitutional maximum. That position has appeal, but I reject it because of the practical problems it raises. The system benefits from jurisdictional statutes that stop short of the outer boundaries the Constitution itself marks off—even in cases arising under federal law.

I will argue in Chapter Three that Congress should take full and forthright responsibility for the scope of the federal courts' jurisdiction in federal-question cases. We should abandon some judgments embodied in the Supreme Court's interpretations of §1331 and replace those judgments with others that better ensure a day in federal court for all the federal claimants and claims that need one. Most of my suggestions will not be especially controversial, but will build upon ideas advanced by the American Law Institute. I will advocate legislation that specifies more clearly than does §1331 the federal-question jurisdiction the federal courts should have, brings matters that turn substantially on federal law into the federal forum whether or not their federal character appears on the face of a "well-pleaded" complaint, and discards current impediments to actions for a declaration of federal rights. This last proposal contemplates, as well, an adjustment in the law governing a party's ability to transfer or "remove" a civil action begun in state court to the federal forum, namely, the establishment of a right to remove on the basis of a federal defense or counterclaim. By contrast, I will argue against the removal of state criminal prosecutions to federal court. Criminal defendants who raise federal defenses in state court should have access to the federal courts later—by way of federal habeas corpus.

In Chapter Four, I address judicially created doctrines that presuppose the jurisdictional power of the federal courts to adjudicate, but nonetheless reserve the exercise of that power. These doctrines originally came in several forms, but more recently they have been melded together. The rationale is always the same: it is said that federal court action should be postponed or withheld in order to avoid or contain conflicts with the states and the state courts.[2] Initially, I treat the current rule that the federal courts should ordinarily abstain from adjudicating federal constitutional claims when prior state court litigation may resolve uncertain questions of state law in a way that makes treatment of the federal issues unnecessary. I conclude that the postponement of federal adjudication not only creates more practical trouble than it is worth, but also frustrates federal enforcement of federal rights. Next, I grapple with the current rule that the federal courts ordinarily should decline to issue injunctions or declaratory judgments that may interfere with pending state proceedings or the execution of state policies. This form of abstention now routinely channels federal-question litigation out of the federal courts. I explore the principal arguments and considerations in point, explain their implications, and prescribe appropriate reforms. If Congress enacts legislation permitting civil litigants to remove state civil actions on the basis of a federal defense or counterclaim, most instances in which individual citizens seek federal injunctions against pending state proceedings will disappear. Still, carefully crafted rules permitting injunctions against specified criminal prosecutions are needed to ensure that defendants whose federal rights cannot be protected in habeas corpus are not deprived of federal adjudication.

In Chapter Five, I take up the federal courts' authority to entertain habeas corpus petitions from state prisoners raising claims previously presented to the state courts. In ordinary civil cases, losing parties are typically precluded from attacking unfavorable state court judgments "collaterally" in the federal district courts. The exception allowed for habeas petitions on behalf of state prisoners is one of the most complex and controversial aspects of the current law of federal jurisdiction. Yet if readers have come this far with me, the intricacies of habeas corpus should not be daunting. For here again, the federal courts' jurisdiction is complicated in large measure *because* it is controversial. The mysteries that appear on the surface can be solved by digging down to underlying disagreements over values. Recent Supreme Court cases, together with legislative proposals advanced by the Reagan and Bush Administrations, reflect a frank desire to withhold a federal forum for the enforcement of the Bill of Rights and, in the alternative, to submit Bill of Rights claims to the courts of the states. In response, Congress should enact legislation to ensure that federal habeas corpus is available for independent federal consideration of any claims petitioners might have raised in the federal forum in the first instance if they had been permitted to remove the criminal prosecutions against them to federal court on the basis of a federal defense. Habeas corpus for state prisoners is a prime example of the current assault on the federal courts about which I am concerned. In a real sense, I save the best for last. When the value-laden disputes that feed current subtleties are uncovered, and when the availability of the federal courts to consider federal claims arising in state criminal cases is situated within an ideologically coherent framework, the writ's proper place can be understood without great difficulty. Then, and only then, will we be able to clarify and simplify the federal courts' authority through carefully crafted legislation.

CHAPTER ONE

▼

Ordain and Establish

The allocation of jurisdiction between the federal and state courts
in the United States excites a heated ideological debate between those
I will dare call "liberals," who almost always prefer the federal courts
in cases in which federal rights must be determined, and those I will
call "conservatives," who typically urge that the state courts be employed. At first glance, it is unclear why this should be so. One would
think that the serious question in a legal controversy would be the
principle or rule that a court should bring to bear, rather than the
authority of a federal court, as opposed to a state court, to deal with
the dispute. If we must argue about courts at all, it would seem more
sensible to quarrel over *how* a court, any court, should decide a legal
question, rather than over *which* court should draw duty in a case.
Our fascination with jurisdiction seems to subordinate what is vital
in law, the substance of legal rights, to what is comparatively trivial,
the agencies and processes engaged to effectuate rights.

In the machinery of American justice, however, there is a relationship between rights themselves and the courts available to enforce
them. That relationship explains why the yin and yang of American
political alignments are reflected in the debate over the distribution of
judicial authority in federal-question cases. At the outset of this chapter, I must take a few short sections to define terms, to account for the
influence of individual judges' ideology, and to anticipate the claim
that the conservative approach to federal court jurisdiction is
grounded in respect for our decentralized governmental system. Then,
in the body of the chapter, I will explore what is really at stake in
these affairs by following a winding path through the foundational

features of our jurisprudence. The trail begins in the period prior to the emergence of modern constitutional law and meanders through twentieth-century pragmatism before it circles round to current scholarship. Bear with me. I will come to a place where it is possible to pause and address these problems afresh. Then it will become clear that the debate over whether the courts that Congress may "ordain and establish" should determine federal claims touches a profound struggle at the core of American politics. The future of constitutional democracy itself will be placed in the hands of the winners—either mainstream political liberals or the statist conservatives who have dominated the national discourse for the last twenty years.

Labels

American political ideology does not lend itself to neat, convenient classifications. The position one takes on any single issue scarcely weds her to a particular constellation of views respecting other questions. At best, we can only group together general inclinations regarding basic matters—like the optimal size and functions of government, the proper place and scope of individual freedom, and the best means of balancing the two when they conflict—and then assign such groupings rough, shorthand labels. This is unsatisfying intellectually; the labels we use are *very* rough and often misleading. Yet use them we must if we are to generalize at all within the terms of familiar discourse. Party membership is even less exacting, inasmuch as the Democrat and Republican Parties are electoral bodies in the main and accommodate a wide diversity of opinion within their ranks.

In this chapter and those to follow, I use the term "liberal" loosely, in what I think is the conventional way—to connote a general belief in aggressive legislative regulation of economic activity, tempered by rigorous judicial protection of personal affairs. American liberals, by this account, are not libertarians in the classical mold. Liberals do not insist that the exercise of governmental power should be held to a minimum as against individual liberty in all forms. On the contrary, liberals believe that government ought to be used, actively and affirmatively, in search of a better life for society as a whole. In order to meet the material needs of the people at large, liberals promote social welfare legislation that sacrifices the freedom of individuals and corporations to operate in the market as they please. The intellectual challenge facing modern liberals is to justify this distinction between economic liberty, which can and should be subject to regulation in the public interest, and personal liberty, which should and must be accorded judicial protection. Liberals trace their roots to the New Deal and draw their zeal for individual rights from the Supreme Court under Earl Warren, William O. Douglas, and William J. Brennan in the 1960s. By this definition, many Democrats are not liberals. And in a time when this category has lost its appeal in some quarters, many Americans who *are* mainstream liberals within these terms probably would prefer another designation—or none at all. Still, the platform of the national Democratic Party reflects liberal positions on most issues. Lest there be any doubt, I am a liberal.

I also use the term "conservative" in the conventional fashion, at least since the emergence of the American right behind the presidential candidacies of Barry Goldwater and Ronald Reagan. In some respects, American conservatives approach the classical libertarian model, which regards governmental regulation as appropriate primarily to preserve order, internally and externally, so that human affairs can generally be governed by private ordering. Conservatives typically resist governmental regulation of economic activity as an ill-advised attempt to use public power for self-regarding ends of doubtful utility. Conservatives may accept the New Deal as settling the framework of American government, but they draw no comfort from the distributive implications of the regulatory system that Roosevelt ushered into being. *De*regulation and "privatization" are the themes that rally conservatives around a vision of the night-watchman state.

At the same time, and somewhat paradoxically, American conservatives are typically comfortable with the exercise of majoritarian governmental power, particularly executive power, to defeat individual claims touching racial and gender equality, dissident ideology, sexual intimacy, and personal value choices thought to threaten the stability essential to efficient production in a capitalist system. Conservatives often support governmental efforts to enforce selected social and religious mores they regard as constitutive of the bedrock, orderly, and (therefore) desirable status quo. Modern American conservatives thus bear a mirror image of the liberals' burden. Where liberals must justify subjecting economic liberty to social welfare legislation while holding more personal rights inviolate, conservatives must explain why some widely recognized personal rights can be compromised in the name of majoritarian morality and community stability while economic liberty is given a broader field of operation. For conservatives, it is not the

Warren Court's decisions *expanding* personal rights that draw praise, but more recent decisions endorsing the exercise of governmental power and thus *diluting* personal rights—issued by the Nixon and Reagan appointees of the 1970s and 1980s, such as William H. Rehnquist, Sandra Day O'Connor, and Antonin Scalia. Not all Republicans are conservatives, but the platform of the national Republican Party reflects the rough grouping of views this account ascribes to American conservatism.

Parity

I have said that liberals generally prefer the federal courts in federal-question cases. This is so because liberals reject the hypothesis, typically voiced by conservatives, that there is a certain "parity" between the two court systems, such that federal and state courts are essentially interchangeable and equally likely to protect federal rights. If parity is assumed, of course, it would follow that nothing turns on the choice of one set of courts or the other and, accordingly, that we need take no special pains to ensure that litigants have access to the federal courts. Liberals insist, however, that the federal courts offer a much more sympathetic forum for federal rights and thus should be available whenever feasible.

Ideally, we would rely on empirical research to get to the bottom of the dispute over parity—research that demonstrates on the basis of hard data where the better argument lies. Yet this beast is not so easily tamed. Attempts to test the parity hypothesis have been unsuccessful. The methodological difficulties are staggering. Too many assumptions have to be made, too many variables have to be juggled, too many definitions have to be rounded off, and too much value-laden judgment has to be exercised. In one recent study, for example, investigators examined opinions by federal district courts and state appellate courts and, on that basis, concluded that there is no pattern of state court hostility to federal claims.[1] Yet the flaws in that work are everywhere apparent and, in the end, the study has been demolished—along with other reports that rely on simplistic opinion polls and Supreme Court reversal rates to throw light on the predilections and competencies of the federal and state courts.[2]

Empirical evidence being unavailable, the debate over parity focuses on analytic arguments for thinking that the federal courts offer a superior forum. Those arguments, catalogued by Burt Neuborne,[3] are powerful, to say the least. To begin, the judges who sit on our federal courts bring a superior competence to federal-question litigation. The federal judiciary is small, making it comparatively easy to achieve a high level of quality among individual members; the ranks of state judges are legion, making quality control comparatively difficult. Federal judges are underpaid, but still receive significant salaries; state judges are typically less handsomely compensated. Federal court appointments are enormously prestigious; state court positions, at least at the trial level, enjoy less public repute. Federal judges are appointed under a scheme that, for all its faults, takes some account of professional qualifications; state judges often are selected under systems heavily influenced by political patronage. Federal judges are assisted by excellent young law clerks; state judges typically are served by career staff with less rigorous training. Federal judges face a large but tolerable caseload; state judges are swamped with work. Federal judges are generally able to prepare reasoned opinions to guide the public and other courts and to explain results to higher courts; state judges, on the whole, are less proficient. In all these ways, federal judges are more capable of interpreting federal rights generously, provided they choose to do so.

They do so choose. For the extremely capable judges who occupy our federal courts succeed to a special perspective on the federal system, which generates an expansive understanding of federal rights. Federal judges operate within a grand tradition as an elite core of jurists with the duty and responsibility to implement federal law; state judges lack the same tradition and sense of responsibility. Federal judges are located within the bureaucratic structure of the federal judiciary and tend to respond quickly to instructions from above; state judges often behave as though their obligation is merely to avoid straying far from Supreme Court decisions. Federal judges are separated from the local context in which federal issues arise and thus are free from psycholgical pressures that can impede attention to personal rights; state judges typically operate in society's very maw, witness to disturbing routines and patterns of human interaction that can distort the application of abstract ideas.

Most important, federal judges tend to be hospitable to federal rights, because the courts on which they sit are institutionally situated for the very purpose of checking majoritarian governmental power and other societal pressures *on* those rights. In this vein, two points are telling. First, most of the federal rights that require judicial protection in this country are either unpopular in themselves (for example, the rights of criminal defendants) or are asserted by unpopular people (for example, political dissenters). Federal courts have an advantage over state courts in the maintenance of such rights against majoritarian power, because federal judges are appointed with tenure during good behavior and with salaries that cannot be diminished during their service. Those safeguards ensure that the federal courts *as institutions* are sufficiently independent to perform their essentially antimajoritarian duty. State judges, by contrast, are often elected and, even where they are appointed, rarely enjoy the same insulation from political influence. Second, most of the time, anyway, the majoritarian power that threatens individual rights is *state* power. Again, then, federal courts, which owe their existence to the national government, have an obvious advantage over state courts, which depend for their authority on the very state governmental structure that must be held in check.

The Reagan Legacy

In a time when the federal bench has taken a turn to the political right, the notion that the federal courts are likely to enforce personal freedoms aggressively may appear peculiar, even grotesque.[4] Without question, the federal judicial branch is now in the hands of men and (a few) women chosen by Ronald Reagan and George Bush. By the time he left office, President Reagan had named 371 judges—nearly half the number then sitting and far more than any other president since FDR. President Bush, for his part, appointed another 187.[5] Equally clearly, the judges that Reagan and Bush placed on the federal bench are "conservative" in the ordinary sense of that term. Certainly, they are Republicans. When Reagan assumed office, judges who had been members of the Democratic Party held a three-to-two edge over those who had been Republicans; six years later, Republicans held the same proportional edge over Democrats.[6] Moreover, the current federal judiciary is composed almost entirely of white men. Many new appointees are wealthy; more than a third of the judges named by President Bush in his first two years were millionaires. Most are comparatively young; more than a third of Bush's nominees were under forty-five years of age at the time of appointment.[7] Recent presidents have, indeed, packed the federal courts with their own.

Still, it would be a mistake to move from these data to the conclusion that the ability of relatively conservative presidents to name like-minded people to the federal bench outflanks the thesis that the federal courts are likely to be more generous than the state courts toward personal claims of right. Once again, the promise the federal courts offer rests only in part on the capabilities of the individuals who sit on the federal bench. Liberals who look to the federal courts to protect federal rights rely primarily on the institutional advantages those courts enjoy as against the courts of the states, that is, the federal courts' traditions and relative independence from politics. Moreover, concerns that the "Reagan Legacy" of judicial appointments may render the federal courts less sympathetic to federal claims are short-sighted. The practice of appointing federal judges who are ideologically appealing to the sitting president is as old as the republic.[8] At any time in our history, it is easy enough to observe that the ascendant political perspective is busily at work appropriating the judiciary. Sometimes, judicial appointments succeed in advancing a president's agenda. Still, life-tenured judges of whatever ideological stripe share the attributes and institutional posture that render them our best protection against the excesses of the more explicitly political branches. Political fortune, moreover, is a sometime thing. The hegemony gained in one presidency is quickly lost in the next, and over time a corrective balance asserts and reasserts itself. Next to the record of the Reagan and Bush Administrations must be set the previous records of Presidents Johnson and Carter, who named many more liberal judges and, into the bargain, significantly increased the numbers of women and racial minorities on the bench. President Clinton is in a position to adjust the balance once again, by filling new judgeships authorized by Congress in 1990.[9]

This is hardly to discount the significance of the views held by the people who now predominate in the federal courts. Indeed, it is because of the attitudes manifest on the Supreme Court itself that the maintenance of federal remedies for federal rights is now so much at risk. Yet we must remember that, as conservative, white, male, wealthy, and young as many current federal judges may be, they are subject to the same vicissitudes of life as the rest of us. Many will leave office to pursue other careers; some will retire early; all, in any case, are mortal. Things, this is to say, can change—and in a hurry. If anyone doubts this, let her consider what others were thinking in 1951, when President Eisenhower took office and an unsuspecting nation was about to enter its most exciting period of judicial creativity on behalf of individual rights. It is far too early to predict any similar turnabout during the Clinton years. It is equally early, however, to abandon the well-founded expectation that the federal courts will survive as the best institutions we have for enforcing federal rights.

Of course, Americans sometimes choose the state courts for the adjudication of federal claims. Indeed, there are many reasons for doing so. Plaintiffs may simply find the state courthouse closer to home or more convenient for a host of other reasons. In some instances, they may anticipate that they will get a particularly receptive state judge or have the benefit of an especially helpful local precedent. In others, they may want to avoid individual federal judges they believe to be unsympathetic. In still others, litigants may frankly conclude that local courts are willing and able to enforce federal law with enthusiasm. The point here is only that, for the reasons just rehearsed, the federal courts are *in the main* the better tribunals for federal claims. When, then, it is proposed that there are now so many Reagan and Bush appointees on the federal bench that the only hope for civil rights plaintiffs is to seek relief from the state courts, we may prudently pause to ponder. That kind of rhetoric may be more an expression of frustration than a declaration of litigation strategy—in more than a handful of states.

There is, moreover, a chicken-and-egg quality to any argument that the incidence of state court litigation suggests parity between the two judicial systems. It may be that some litigants choose the state courts not because those courts really *are* so likely to be sympathetic, or because litigants *think* they are, but rather because there are now so many procedural barriers to litigation in federal court—the very barriers I will suggest should be removed. Initially, the sheer costs of litigation in federal court are a deterrent. Nobody wants to spend any more resources than necessary to pursue legal claims, and, at some point, the prospect of fighting a series of battles over threshold procedural issues becomes intimidating—even if it appears that the federal courts will be receptive when they finally dispose of procedural problems and get down to deciding the merits of claims. Moreover, litigants must weigh the possibility that, even if they commit the time and effort required to fight procedural battles, they may lose those battles and end up having to back up and start again in state court after all—the very last thing that anyone would wish. If, however, the obstacles now in place were removed, as I mean to suggest, the road to adjudication in the federal courts would be less treacherous—and litigants might be more willing to take it. It is circular, then, to argue that since federal-question litigation is sometimes, or even often, conducted in state court, the state courts must *generally* be as receptive to those claims as are the federal district courts. That phenomenon, to the extent it exists, may only be evidence that increasingly restrictive rules governing access to the federal courts are working—channeling federal questions into state court, irrespective of the response they receive there. Certainly, in any event, liberals may resist any suggestion that *because* the state courts are open for the adjudication of federal claims, and *because* some litigants decide to go there, it follows somehow that the federal courts can and should be closed off.

Federalism

If it would be a mistake to think that the long-term debate over the proper allocation of federal-question cases turns on the ideological character of the federal bench in a given period, it would equally be a mistake to believe that this debate pivots on another ubiquitous factor in the mix of American law and politics: the idea of "federalism." A general inclination to lodge authority at the local level surely must contribute to the debate over the proper distribution of judicial authority.[10] In the main, however, it is doubtful that our differences can be fully explained on the comparatively neutral ground that we are divided over the proper role of the states (and state courts) in American society. The battle is not over the better structure for preserving federal rights that everyone values equally. It is over rights themselves and the scope assigned to rights.

Conventional wisdom tells a familiar story about the demise of federalism as a safeguard for human liberty and its transmutation into a modern basis for the exercise of state power.[11] The early Americans most concerned for individual rights were the Jeffersonians, who envisioned a nation in which yeomen farmers would govern themselves at the local level while the fearful power of the central government of the United States was held at a safe distance. Then, federalism was the language of freedom; governmental power was to be dispersed in order that it not be concentrated at the center and turned to the ends of despotism. Jefferson, the localist, sought to protect individual freedom by keeping government at bay. Hamilton, the nationalist, sought to make government more efficient (and thus potentially a greater threat to liberty). Madison, the statesman, mediated between the two.

The Jeffersonians labored at the Constitutional Convention and the state ratifying conventions both to limit the new national government's power and to establish a series of individual rights, ultimately catalogued in the Bill of Rights, to protect citizens still more. Those rights, moreover, were to be enforced by the courts of the several states, subject to review by the United States Supreme Court. The Constitution itself neither established inferior federal courts nor required Congress to create such courts by statute. In fact, the first Congress erected a system of lower federal courts, but those courts were given no general jurisdiction in federal-question cases for nearly a hundred years.

According to this conventional story, things changed dramatically in the wake of the Civil War. With the adoption of the postwar amendments, particularly the fourteenth, the very structure of American government was revised. Now it was the rebellious southern states that threatened the new federal rights that Americans were to have against state, not national, power. Federalism, previously associated with the protection of individual freedom from the central government, was now offered as a justification for the continued exercise of state authority. Thus did federalism surrender its ties to personal liberty and take up its modern links with assertions of state prerogative. The Reconstruction Congress enrolled the federal courts in this reconceptualization. In 1875, Congress finally conferred on the federal courts a general jurisdiction to entertain civil actions raising federal questions. That statute (now codified in 28 U.S.C. §1331) and others in the same period, including the Ku Klux Klan Act of 1871 (now codified in 42 U.S.C. §1983) and the Habeas Corpus Act of 1867 (28 U.S.C. §2241, et seq.), opened the federal courts to private lawsuits for the vindication of the rights established by the fourteenth amendment.

By this account, it should surprise no one that federalism is today a devil to American liberals and a darling to conservatives. The tables are reversed. Liberals now see state government as the potential evil against which federal rights must be protected, and the courts of choice for enforcement duty are federal courts. Conservatives, by contrast, regard the autonomy that federalism accords to the states as a structural basis for assertions of state authority against personal freedom.[12] Differences over federalism may offer a superficially plausible explanation for the Warren Court's many citations to the realignment brought about by the Civil War and Reconstruction, and for the current Court's competing references to the autonomy and interests of the states.[13] Yet the explanation federalism provides for jurisdictional allocations between the federal and state courts is at best incomplete. Other factors must also be considered, with due weight given to their influence on the distribution of judicial authority. The Supreme Court in the Warren era was actively engaged in the development of federal rights that had not been recognized before. The Court needed a cadre of lower courts that would put those new rights into practice. Since most of the rights that required implementation were rights against state power, the justices who sat on the Supreme Court in the 1960s may well have doubted that the state courts could (or would) handle the difficult work that needed to be done. Instead, they regarded the federal courts as more promising tribunals for enforcing unpopular decisions crafted in Washington. By contrast, the justices sitting today are demonstrably less in need of loyal surrogates to champion individual rights and thus find state court litigation of federal-question cases perfectly satisfying.

In any event, if and when federalism calls for judgment respecting the jurisdiction of the federal and state courts, Congress has broad authority to make the required choices. There was a time when the Supreme Court presumed to second-guess congressional decisions to extend federal power at the expense of the states. Prior to the middle 1930s, the Court invalidated attempts to displace state regulation of private business with uniform national statutes, and for a while in the 1970s the Court invalidated federal supervision of the states themselves.[14] Today, however, there are few limits on congressional power to strike the balance between national and local authority.[15] This is true both with respect to decisions to create federal substantive law and with respect to decisions to make the federal courts available to adjudicate federal issues. The same *should* be true, by the way, regarding another element of American constitutionalism I will take up in due course: the separation of powers within the national government. Someone, to be sure, must prescribe the federal courts' sphere and ensure that they do not trespass into matters better left to the politically accountable branches. Yet if Congress clearly provides for the exercise of judicial authority, it is unpersuasive for the Court to respond that the Constitution prohibits the federal courts from accepting the majoritarian judgment that they can and should comply.[16]

To identify competing agendas for federal rights in decisions about the distribution of judicial power is not to be cynical, but merely to be realistic. It is essential to a fair understanding of what ultimately should be done about these problems that we first understand what actually explains current arrangements. Neither Reconstruction era politics nor a modern appreciation for federalism can provide a sufficient explanation. Nor does the text of the Constitution, the history behind the text, or the structure of the government the text seems to contemplate grind out results in concrete cases. If we are to be serious about these matters, we must recognize that politics plays an important role. Modern liberals typically want federal-question cases to be in federal court, because they believe federal rights will receive a generous interpretation there; conservatives want to funnel such cases to the state courts, because they believe that the state courts will weigh more heavily the arguments that government officials offer in defense of their actions.[17] This is where we will come *out* of this chapter. The way *in* is marked by the winding path we are now equipped to locate and follow.

Four Horsemen

The perspectives associated with modern liberals and conservatives have a common origin in reactions to "Legal Formalism" in American law, which flourished between about 1890 and the middle 1930s.[18] In accord with the teachings of Christopher Columbus Langdell, James Barr Ames, and their colleagues at Harvard Law School, American courts, federal and state, typically regarded and presented law as a logical grid of principles and rules that could be deduced from self-evident propositions. Law was another face of science or mathematics, calling for deductive logic—the application of abstractions to concrete cases. When judges in the Formalist period resolved legal disputes, they claimed they didn't *make* law, but merely *found* it— fully developed in the legal materials available. Courts reputedly existed to safeguard preexisting, private interests against interference by other private citizens. They were neutral referees ensuring that everyone played by unquestioned rules, which depended not on value choices made by flesh-and-blood human beings for the case at hand and other cases like it, but on a vaguely described "common law" of England, which blurred, in turn, with an equally vague sense of the way things just *were*—naturally. Langdell's Formalism found its way into constitutional opinions in the United States Supreme Court, written by four associate justices whom detractors called the "four horsemen." Justices Pierce Butler, James C. McReynolds, George

Sutherland, and Willis Van DeVanter dominated constitutional law for a generation, needing only a single additional vote to have their way in any case. That way, it is now widely agreed, was disastrous for the political order. The four horsemen rode roughshod over American political and economic life, frustrating attempts by the Court's progressive minority to allow Congress and state legislatures more freedom to fashion economic policy. Justice Louis Brandeis, the first great progressive justice, devoted his career to breaking the Court's grip on the economic policies chosen by elected government.

Consider the Formalist approach to the fourteenth amendment, the principal Reconstruction era addition to the Constitution establishing individual rights against state authority. That amendment's due process clause provides: "No State shall . . . deprive any person of life, liberty, or property without due process of law." The Formalists took "liberty" and "property" to denote definite legal categories encompassing a general entitlement to have, keep, and use economic wealth as one pleased.[19] They offered no reasoned explanation for this account; they simply announced that this was what liberty and property *meant*. To be sure, a person could be deprived of such freedom through the traditional (due) procedures known to the common law. But to the Formalists that meant judicial process—as when a court determined that one party had invaded the liberty or property of another (for example, by trespassing on land or breaching a contract) and, for that reason, the court took wherewithal from the wrongdoer and gave it to the wronged as compensation. Since no legislature could supply the kind of process provided by courts at common law, it followed that no legislature could offer the due process of law required constitutionally before a person could be deprived of liberty or property. That meant, in turn, that no legislature could properly affect liberty or property at all. Inasmuch as corporations were deemed to be "persons" within the meaning of the fourteenth amendment, any serious regulation of commercial activity was constitutionally questionable.[20] Sometimes the Court allowed state legislatures to enact "reasonable" regulations designed to protect the public or the health and safety of workers. Yet the Court often concluded that economic constraints interfered too much with corporate freedom and thus were invalid—or, indeed, that restrictions on the way corporate employers dealt with their employees intruded upon *workers'* freedom to agree to their own subjugation. Minimum-wage laws, maximum-hour laws, and sundry other social welfare measures were struck from the books.[21] In the end, the due process clause became an engine of destruction for state regulation of commercial affairs.[22]

Concomitantly, during the Formalist period, the Court broke down jurisdictional barriers to the lower federal courts in fourteenth amendment cases. When state authorities in Nebraska insisted that a petroleum company should be required to ask the state courts to determine the validity of utility rate limits before bringing its due process claim to a federal court, the Supreme Court permitted the company immediate access to the federal forum. When authorities in Los Angeles argued that official conduct in violation of state law could not constitute *state* deprivation of a telephone company's liberty or property, the Court responded that individual officers were sufficiently clothed with state authority to bring the fourteenth amendment into play— whether or not they acted consistent with state law. And when the Minnesota attorney general claimed that the eleventh amendment[23] immunized him from suit in federal court and, accordingly, that Minnesota railroads could not ask a federal court to enjoin his enforcement of a state regulatory scheme, the Court held that the eleventh amendment conferred immunity only on the state itself and not on an individual state officer whose conduct was alleged to violate the Constitution.[24] Those decisions ensured that the giants of American industry would be able to go to the federal courts for relief from allegedly unconstitutional state regulation.

Formalism was nonsense.[25] Abstract principles are vital to legitimate judicial decision-making, but they cannot operate mechanically. As Justice Holmes put it, "[g]eneral propositions do not decide concrete cases."[26] People do that. It is essential to understand that the Formalist period in American law coincided with the ascendancy of Social Darwinism in American thought generally.[27] William Graham Sumner and Herbert Spencer persuaded many prominent Americans, among them (perhaps) the four horsemen, that the same elemental principle that explained biological life (the survival of the fittest) also ruled human political and social life. The attempt by the masses of relatively weak members of society to band together, elect state legislatures, and restrict the capacity of relatively strong members to pursue naked self-interest was regarded as tampering with the natural order of things. To the four horsemen, it was the Court's responsibility to use the Constitution to discourage such dangerous meddling with the physical universe.

To meld laissez faire economic theory with the fourteenth amend-

ment was not to find values in the Constitution, but to bring values
to the Constitution. That, in itself, was neither surprising nor, in principle, objectionable. The Supreme Court always makes value choices
in constitutional law and, indeed, cannot escape such choices in light
of the opaque character of the written Constitution and the country's
evolving needs. We must hope, of course, that the justices will not
routinely implement their personal eccentricities in the guise of law.
But we accord them the authority, indeed the obligation, to draw upon
a variety of sources to fill out the meaning of human freedom in this
constitutional system. Rights don't define themselves. The trouble
with the four horsemen was not that they gave content to federal
rights and enforced those rights against governmental power, but that
they chose the wrong rights to protect: market rights, which could
command only the most precarious support in American culture apart
from the Social Darwinist texts and which, in the end, *had* to surrender to modern social democracy.[28] Moreover, by presenting their work
as no more than simple logical deductions, the four horsemen attempted to conceal what they were actually doing.

Importantly, the "Old" Formalist Court's decisions regarding access
to the federal courts were similarly influenced by the substantive rights
those courts were summoned to enforce. Recall that within the space
of five years, the Court held both that an individual state officer's conduct was state action subject to the fourteenth amendment even
though it violated state law, and that such an officer could not assert
the state's immunity under the eleventh amendment even when he was
attempting to enforce state law. The conjunction of those rulings allowed corporate plaintiffs free access to the federal courts for the litigation of due process claims. This is not to say that the two decisions
could not stand together; they could. Yet they at least appeared to
conflict, and the Court's facile endorsement of both indicates that
"outcome-neutral considerations" were not controlling.[29] The Old
Court's decisions on the jurisdiction of the federal courts were not
neutral at all. They were analogues of the Court's parallel decisions
on the meaning of the fourteenth amendment itself. They guaranteed
federal judicial enforcement machinery while other decisions developed the federal rights to be enforced. It is not too much to suggest
that the Court thought that the lower federal courts could be counted
upon to accept and vindicate federal economic rights, while the state
courts were far less trustworthy on that score. The distribution of authority between the federal and state courts was in this way bound up

with the most potent forces influencing American law. Here again, we should not fault the Old Court for opening the federal forum to federal rights. That Court went wrong only in asking the federal courts to underwrite economic claims. The relationship between expansive federal rights and robust federal enforcement authority was wholly understandable in the Formalist period and equally understandable today—when different kinds of federal rights are at stake. Things could scarcely be otherwise.

A Special Kind of Ought

The Formalist facade ultimately crumbled. Critics like Roscoe Pound ridiculed Formalist orthodoxy as "mechanical jurisprudence" and complained that the Old Court's decisions were out of step with the nation's economic development.[30] Then, accompanying the New Deal, came the Legal Realists at Columbia and Yale—Karl Llewellyn, Thurman Arnold, Morris Cohen, and others.[31] The Realists did not brook Formalist pretentions to neutrality. They launched a vigorous attack on the very notion that law and law-making could be value-free and argued, instead, that judicial decisions inevitably turned on value choices. Indeed, some Realists contended that all law came down to the policy preferences of the decision-makers who forged it; nothing else mattered, least of all the rationalizations that cluttered judicial opinions. The Realist insight that law was driven by value was warmly received in the 1930s, just as it is today. Yet bold claims that law simply *was* value were (and remain) deeply troubling. Arguments of that sort went well beyond criticism of Formalist excesses and threatened the foundational notion that law was distinguishable from raw, self-interested politics. If the Realists were saying that the courts decided cases any way they liked, then they were saying that law was in no way normative and prescriptive, but was only positive and descriptive. Judicial decisions were therefore neither objective, nor neutral, nor even legitimate in a democracy.[32] To use language now in vogue, the Realists threatened the "autonomy" of law, its independent existence apart from social and economic interaction. That, in turn, sounded positively Marxist.[33]

It would not do to let slip the false certainty of Formalism only to slide into the abyss offered by the Realists. The country needed some theoretical explanation for (and check on) judicial behavior that could mediate between these extremes. Conservatives required some safeguard against Realism. Liberals needed a concept of the judicial function that met the needs of the New Deal.[34] The latter was the end in view both for progressives like Brandeis and for developing thinkers like Felix Frankfurter, Brandeis' protégé at Harvard Law School and Roosevelt's chief academic advisor. Frankfurter joined with Henry Hart, James Landis, and others in a series of works on which others continued to build after Frankfurter's appointment to the Supreme Court in 1939. In the 1950s, Hart, Albert Sacks, Alexander Bickel (an erstwhile Frankfurter law clerk), and other academicians at Harvard and Yale developed the "Legal Process" understanding of law and legal institutions, which offered an alternative, pragmatic "process model" to account for what judges do and ought to do.[35]

The challenge at hand was to construct a coherent framework that would permit democratically elected legislatures to operate, allow courts to adjudicate, and control both within intelligible, defensible bounds. Hart and Sacks took the lead in building such a framework on two levels. First, at what I will call the macro level, they disclaimed confrontations over the outcomes produced by various organs of governmental power. Quarrels over results, they insisted, were typically unavailing. By the time government had acted, it was too late to object with any success that an incorrect result had been reached. Indeed, according to Hart and Sacks, it was typically far from clear that there was any real basis for insisting that outcomes were either right or wrong. In most instances of any consequence, the Legal Process theorists saw sound arguments on both sides, such that the particular judgment that government reached could not fairly be the subject of objection *as* an outcome. To complain about such a result was merely to reopen the controversy with which government had grappled in reaching the conclusion it had. In some cases, it might be claimed that government had kicked over the traces and reached a wholly unreasonable result. Most of the time, however, outcomes were disappointing (to the losers), but still within the sphere of tolerance that reason allowed. This was true of legislative policies, which usually reflected some majoritarian compromise among competing interests. It was also true of judicial judgments, which typically struck some balance among contending arguments and the values behind them. Reasonable minds could differ over the principle or rule that should govern a lawsuit, the way in which such a principle or rule should operate, and, certainly, the decision that should be reached in the circumstances of a particular case.

Positing all this, Hart and Sacks counseled that we should set aside complaints about outcomes altogether and focus, instead, on the institutional structure and organization of power—the procedural arrangements by which government as a whole comes to results. As they explained it, "the substance of decision cannot be planned in advance in the form of rules and standards," but the "procedure of decision commonly can be."[36] By controlling the way in which government exercises power, Hart and Sacks hoped to capture and channel the means of governmental decision-making and thereby to establish a procedural apparatus likely to produce good results. They argued that power should be allocated according to institutional competencies. Legislatures, constituted by democratic elections and therefore entitled to make normative value choices, should have responsibility for original policy formulation. Courts, often not elected and thus not entitled to select values for the public, should have responsibility for the "reasoned elaboration" of existing principles and rules necessary to the adjudication of disputes.

Central to the Legal Process approach was the notion that results reached by institutions properly assigned authority for decisions should be accepted without further lament. This was so not because such outcomes *are* right in an absolute sense. Rather, according to what Hart and Sacks called the "principle of institutional settlement," outcomes generated by a procedurally correct means should be *taken* as right, for the pragmatic reason that we have no better measure of the way things *should* turn out. If what the law "is" constitutes the "duly arrived at" result of "duly established procedures," then we may put aside any further discussion of what it "ought" to be. Yet the "is," according to Hart and Sacks, is not an "is" at all, but a "special kind" of "ought."[37] In this way, what might have been confrontations over outcomes are recast as examinations of process.

It was not long before the Legal Process approach to law was invoked with respect to the business in which I am interested: the allocation of jurisdiction between the federal and state courts. In this context, the macro-level phase carries weighty implications. The principle of institutional settlement calls for an analysis of the relative competencies of the institutions available to perform a governmental function. Where the choice is between legislatures and courts, the capacities of political and judicial institutions must be appraised. Equally, where the choice is between two sets of courts, the relative competencies of the two systems must also be judged, so that judicial business may be routed in the proper direction. Some heirs to the Legal Process mantle have explored the question of parity between the federal and state courts. I previously reviewed Burt Neuborne's explanations for the conclusion that the federal courts are institutionally superior to the state courts in federal-question cases.

Next, on what I will call the micro level, the Legal Process thinkers prescribed the same approach for the examination of decision-making by governmental institutions within the spheres assigned to them. For example, it is insufficient that legislatures, acting within their competencies, enact majoritarian policies. They also must proceed according to the procedures appropriate for the exercise of legislative power: elections for choosing representatives, bicameralism (in the federal system), and like arrangements. Similarly, while administrative agencies may combine traditional legislative and judicial functions, they may do so only subject to other procedures, such as those specified (for federal agencies) in the Administrative Procedure Act of 1946. Courts, for their part, can adjudicate disputes, but only by employing "full and fair" procedures for finding facts and determining legal issues. Importantly, the process model at the micro level contemplates not overarching judgments about the relative capacities of an institution generally, but an ad hoc appraisal of the procedures employed by the institution to generate outcomes in individual instances. Applied to the distribution of federal-question cases between the federal and state courts, it invites the judgment that the federal courts should be available only when procedural flaws are discovered behind a specific judgment in state court. Other heirs to Hart and Sacks, notably Paul Bator, have pursued this inquiry. I will come to Bator's arguments below.

The great project of the Legal Process school was to carve out a middle ground between the disingenuous claims of Formalism and the potential nihilism threatened by the most extreme of the Realists. Formalism had placed primary weight on substantive law, said to be a static body of normative propositions drawn from the primordial mist, and on courts as the mechanical instruments by which those norms were implemented in concrete cases. Legal Process inverted the equation, making the process by which judicial decisions were reached the central business of law and assigning substantive value choices to ordinary majoritarian politics.[38] Americans did not have to embrace the results of unrestrained private ordering and take their courts as neutral guardians of private interests known to the common law. Nor did Americans have to regard their public law as so many episodes of decision-makers' personal prejudices masquerading as official, public-regarding policy. By the lights of the process model, private ordering would still be the starting point. Yet policy formulation by legislatures and agencies, augmented by a dynamic, pragmatic adjudicative function performed by courts, would follow close behind. Within this framework, judicial decisions would not be neutral in the naive Formalist sense. They would, however, be constrained by judges' responsibility to engage in the reasoned elaboration of principles and rules rather than simply fastening their own preferences on the country. Hart and Sacks pressed these ideas on their law school classes in widely read teaching materials, made available in mimeo form in 1958.[39] Generations of students at Harvard and elsewhere were offered the process model as the preferred means of contending with governmental power—by allocating its exercise to the institutions best suited to use it wisely and accepting any results reached in a procedurally sound manner.

Interstitial Courts

At the same time he was working with Albert Sacks on the Legal Process materials, Hart established another partnership with Herbert Wechsler at Columbia University, with whom he worked to apply Legal Process thinking to the law of federal courts.[40] In a system in which coordinate sets of courts enjoyed concurrent jurisdiction in most cases involving federal questions, some basis was needed for distributing business between them. Hart and Wechsler's first pass at the challenge was an interpretation of the historical backdrop to the Constitution, the text of Article III, and the structure of the federal system. They noted that the states had existed before the Constitution and the national government it created and that, subject to the Formalist override, local authorities had always been entitled to make public policy in the exercise of the state police power. Indeed, whatever positive law existed for the ordering of human affairs was largely state law. The federal legislative authority, by contrast, was limited to the powers listed in Article I of the Constitution, so that federal law was by nature "interstitial"—consisting of fragments sprinkled over the corpus of state law in places where national standards were needed.[41] In a like manner, the state courts, exercising a general jurisdiction owed to state law, were the routine mechanisms for the resolution of disputes, while the federal courts were available only in the exceptional instances specified in Article III. Viewing the landscape in this way, Hart and Wechsler concluded that the state courts were the primary adjudicative bodies in the United States, even in federal-question cases.

Hart reached the same conclusion by another route in a famous law review article in which he produced a lively dialogue between fictional antagonists, one (a student or colleague) pressing the other (Hart's alter ego) on whether a citizen with a federal claim was entitled by right to proceed in a federal court rather than a state court. That question quickly reduced to whether Congress could constitutionally deny such a litigant a federal forum. Given the explicit text of Article III, a matter I will leave for Chapter Three, Hart found it inescapable that no litigant could claim a federal forum if Congress did not provide one. Hart was equally sure, however, that no litigant could be denied access to *any* court to press a federal claim. The result was that *if* Congress withheld a federal forum, the state courts must be open. "In the scheme of the Constitution," Hart's alter ego declared, the state courts are "the primary guarantors of constitutional rights, and in many cases they may be the ultimate ones."[42] Hart and Wechsler reproduced both their discussion of the interstitial nature of the federal courts and Hart's dialogue in another famous set of teaching materials, published in 1953 and dedicated to Justice Frankfurter, "who first opened our minds to these problems." That book was profoundly influential; it became the basis on which many law professors built their courses on the law of federal courts. The third edition, prepared by Wechsler and others, is used at most national law schools today. The asserted primacy of the state courts is thus deeply embedded in conventional thinking about our judicial system.[43]

Nevertheless, we are not fated to accept the judgment that Hart and Wechsler reached forty years ago. Their view that federal substantive law and the federal courts can only fill the gaps left by state law and the state courts is scarcely compelling. Scores of precedents establish that Congress' enumerated powers are expansive mandates for regulating virtually any subjects Congress wishes to rule. The Supreme Court has held, for example, that Congress itself can determine any internal limits on its power to regulate commerce.[44] The idea that federal law only fills in around the edges of the law of the states is simply wrong. Nor does Hart's dialogue establish that the federal courts by nature take a back seat to the courts of the states in federal-question cases. Inasmuch as Hart came to the (conventional) conclusion that Congress can deny a litigant the chance to be in federal court, it was natural enough that he should offer the state courts as an alternative. Otherwise, substantive federal claims would be left with no forum at all. Having scripted the state courts for an understudy role, however, Hart ended up bringing those courts dramatically to stage center and shouldering the federal courts to the rear. At most, Hart's analysis leads to the conclusion that the availability of the state courts for the adjudication of federal claims is sufficient, constitutionally speaking. Priority for the state courts in federal-question cases within a system in which the federal courts are ready, willing, and able to entertain plaintiffs' lawsuits is quite a different matter.[45]

If a primary role for the courts of the states is not constitutionally compelled, and it isn't, one would have expected Hart and Wechsler to invoke the process model to prescribe the proper orchestration of relations between the two court systems. Yet they failed to ask the question seemingly required at the macro level of their approach to law, namely, whether the federal courts or the state courts were the better tribunals for the adjudication of federal issues. Hart and Wechsler did not consider, then, whether the federal courts might be better situated to safeguard federal rights against encroachment from the other branches of the national government and, more especially, the states. Certainly, they did not answer that question. They merely assumed that the federal and state courts were fungible—as though every court, any court, could offer federal rights the same measure of protection. This was announced, or at least acted upon, in the same way that the Formalists had announced, or acted upon, the notion that liberty and property were inviolate—notwithstanding that the promise of Legal Process had been that answers to hard questions would not be assumed, but rather would be subject to reasoned analysis.

It seems plain that Hart and Wechsler worried that if they acknowledged that the state courts might *not* be the equal of the federal courts in federal-question cases, they risked slipping backward to the Realists' contention that courts of any kind were merely the official cover for judges' personal views.[46] How else to compare the federal and state courts than by examining the judges involved ad hominem? To Hart, an inquiry of that kind meant wholesale surrender of any ambition that judicial law-making could be in some wise controlled. The Realist case could not, however, be met by taking it for granted that there was nothing to choose between the federal and state courts. There *was* something to be explored and decided. Hart and Wechsler ducked the really fundamental question.

Neutral Principles

The implications of the question that Hart and Wechsler put to one side began to take shape as soon as the Supreme Court decided the Segregation Cases in 1954.[47] Once racial segregation in the public schools was outlawed and the lower federal courts began enforcing the principle of racial equality, modern constitutional law was under way—and in earnest. The Warren Court recognized an array of federal rights in various contexts and made sure that litigants would have access to the federal courts to enforce those rights. Just as the Old Court had regarded federal jurisdiction as essential to due process limits on economic regulation, the Warren Court saw federal jurisdiction as equally important to the success of the new, personal rights developing in the 1960s. Barriers to the federal courts came tumbling down once again—this time, however, to provide a sympathetic forum for the enforcement of rights that genuinely *ought* to be enforced against majoritarian power.

In 1961, the year the Court held that evidence seized in violation of the fourth amendment was inadmissible in state criminal trials, the justices also held that the victims of an unlawful search could sue state officers for relief in a federal lawsuit pursuant to the Ku Klux Klan Act (§1983).[48] That previously moribund statute from the Reconstruction era soon became a routine vehicle for gaining access to the federal courts for a wide range of federal claims.[49] In 1963, the year the Court held that the sixth amendment guaranteed lawyers for criminal defendants in state felony trials, the justices also confirmed that state prison inmates could petition the federal courts for a writ of habeas corpus to test the validity of their convictions.[50] In 1965, when the Court was poised to announce a vigorous set of doctrines to safeguard free speech, the justices held that the federal district courts could enjoin state criminal prosecutions if citizens were harassed by prosecutions under state statutes that violated the first amendment.[51] And in a series of other important decisions, the Warren Court declined always to bar federal court consideration of federal claims previously denied in state court and expanded the circumstances in which the states could be said to have waived their immunity to suit under the eleventh amendment.[52]

These developments sent nervous tremors through the Legal Process establishment. In a notorious lecture, Wechsler openly questioned the Court's reasoning in the Segregation Cases.[53] Racial segregation had been struck down, he implied, because the men on the Court believed it was morally wrong, not because they had elaborated a "neutral principle" that would both justify the result in those particular cases and guide judgment in similar cases in the future. Hart, in turn, published a similarly important article, criticizing the Court's handling of habeas corpus cases.[54] To Hart and Wechsler, the Warren Court's work with respect to personal rights looked very much (too much) like the Old Court's pattern regarding economic liberty, even if it was in the service of different and better values that they themselves shared.[55]

It is astonishing that Herbert Wechsler, a man with a solid civil rights record, had such difficulty fitting the Segregation Cases into some formulation of the process model. For if Legal Process could not offer the Supreme Court a defensible justification for invalidating state-sponsored race discrimination, there was something very wrong with that theory. Something *was* wrong with Legal Process as it was practiced at mid-century. The process model's confidence that sound procedural arrangments would generate acceptable results rested on a deep-seated complacency about the existing social and political structure of American government. To put it most charitably, Hart, Wechsler, and the others may honestly have believed that it was better to tolerate racial segregation, unfair criminal trials, and the suppression of free speech in the near term than to undercut a procedural apparatus they hoped and expected would ultimately produce something better. To put it less charitably, they were able, consistent with the principle of institutional settlement, to contemplate what would today be unthinkable—that race discrimination, abusive criminal process, and political oppression had to be accepted, because those things were produced by institutions, that is, state legislatures, courts, and executive officers, that were properly assigned responsibility for fashioning relevant public policies and authoritative judgments.

Legal Process survives today, albeit in different, more flexible variations on the original theme. Liberals certainly appreciate the need for regular procedures if we are to expect even palatable outcomes from governmental decision-making. Yet the single-minded fixation on process that characterized older process-model thinking retains little purchase in modern liberal circles.

The Countermajoritarian Difficulty

None of this is to say that the original brand of Legal Process would never abide Supreme Court decisions declaring state policies unconstitutional. But in Alexander Bickel's famous phrase, the Court could not check a legislature's will without contending with the "countermajoritarian difficulty" that any judicial trump card always presented.[56] The lion's share of scholarship on American constitutional law has been devoted to defending the modern liberal distinction between economic liberty, which liberals are content to see heavily regulated, and other, personal freedoms, which liberals insist the Supreme Court should safeguard against legislative and executive action. I will take time only for a quick and oversimplified statement of the results many liberal academicians have reached.[57]

At first, the anti-majoritarian nature of Supreme Court decisions was vexing. Some observers sought refuge in the Constitution itself, which arguably owed its existence to the people directly. Judicial decisions invalidating policies adopted by legislatures were justified if firmly rooted in the Constitution's text, structure, or historical backdrop. Efforts of that kind were abandoned early on, however, and today most observers have discarded any thought that the Court's decisions interpreting the Constitution or, indeed, the Constitution itself, can be squared with majoritarianism. Neither appeals to literal text, nor inferences from structure, nor "original understanding" can offer real answers. More important, mainstream academics today reject the notion that majoritarianism is an unqualified good and appreciate more fully the importance of restraints on majoritarian power. The first check is republicanism, which is both a practical necessity in a populous nation and a normative device for filtering naked personal preferences. Raw majoritarianism, which chooses policies by a simple show of hands, sacrifices the interests of the politically disadvantaged. Representative bodies can attend to all citizens, fashioning policies for the common good.

The republican form is insufficient standing alone, however. Representative government can degenerate into a bewildering political marketplace dominated by the privileged classes. A further check is therefore required, to be supplied by judges enforcing values identified with or, if you like, read into the Constitution. By the sights of mainstream scholarship today, majority support alone is no longer a sufficient basis for upholding governmental action. Rather, the measure under examination must serve some legitimate objective that takes account of the interests of all citizens. In Ronald Dworkin's influential phrase, legislatures need not treat all citizens equally, but they must treat each citizen "as an equal."[58] When representative government falters, and majorities reach results that disparage political losers out of hostility, courts are empowered to exercise a constitutional veto.

It may seem that judicial action is in this sense consistent with majority rule and can be explained as a means of perfecting majoritarian processes. Yet attempts to defend such an analysis (and the Legal Process orientation on which it rests) have generally been judged unsuccessful.[59] For in performing their constitutional function courts do not enforce ideas that enjoy majority support; they call upon majorities to respect the integrity of all citizens. That mandate needs no majoritarian endorsement and, indeed, holds its own ground in the teeth of majoritarian sentiment. The resulting system, consisting of ordinary policy-making by legislatures subject to judicial review to ensure that all citizens' interests are respected, earns a splendid appellation: American constitutional democracy. The label fits not because the preferences of rank-and-file citizens are aggregated and translated into public policy by majoritarian means, and not because courts force elected officers to adhere to majoritarian preferences, but because all Americans can safely look both to their republican representatives and to their courts to ensure that they are remembered in the councils of government.

American liberals have come a long way from the majoritarian commitments that undergirded the original Legal Process model and restricted its vision. Liberals have embraced both the Warren Court's egalitarianism, displayed so vividly in the Segregation Cases, and other values affirmed more recently. The individual autonomy and personal privacy entitlements on which the Abortion Case[60] rests are obvious illustrations. In short, liberals have drawn the necessary distinction between commercial affairs and personal liberty. What is more, liberals are content with that distinction. This is to make value choices, to be sure; it is to subordinate the values protected by the Formalist Court a half-century ago and to promote, instead, the personal freedoms that form the basis for modern civil rights and civil liberties litigation. And without apology. Liberals no longer delude themselves that constitutional law can be neutral in either the duplicitous fashion of Formalism or the more appealing manner of the original Legal Process school.[61]

Within this mainstream liberal framework, judges are not set free to create and enforce what federal rights they please, when they please. Judges are constrained in the first instance by the narrow base of their power: the resolution of legal questions typically generated by other branches of the national government and the states. In addition, they must treat with one another to marshal votes for their judgments. They must explain their reasoning in persuasive opinions connecting what they do with precedent and other legal materials. They must present the country with results that make sense, both in principle and in practice. They must, in short, win acceptance for their actions in the arena that is American public life. No more than this is expected of them; no less than this is demanded of them.

Appropriate Sensitivity

It is against this theoretical background that the Supreme Court's treatment of federal jurisdiction must be examined. As one might expect, the sentiments expressed in the Court's opinions are inconsistent over time, with the watershed coming in the years when the Warren Court was giving way to new appointees named to the Court by Richard Nixon and Ronald Reagan. Led by Justice Brennan, the Warren Court insisted that the federal courts, not the state courts, had primary responsibility for enforcing federal rights.[62] As I explained previously, the Warren Court typically relied for its decisions on statutes enacted by the Reconstruction Congress. Still, it would be foolish to think that decisions channeling federal question business to the lower federal courts were entirely indifferent respecting the implications for the federal rights at stake. Just as the Warren Court needed the federal district courts to preside over the desegregation of the public schools, it needed those same courts to guarantee procedural safeguards in criminal cases, the freedom of speech and religion, and a battery of other individual rights grounded in the fourteenth amendment. For the Warren Court almost certainly entertained doubts regarding the state courts' capacity and willingness to enforce unpopular decisions restricting state power.[63]

Not long after Chief Justice Warren Burger took the center chair in 1969, the Court's decisions regarding access to the federal courts began to change. The same trend continues today under Chief Justice William Rehnquist. In 1975, Rehnquist summarily rejected the contention that the federal courts must adjudicate federal questions because the state courts will not be "faithful to their constitutional responsibilities."[64] A year later, Justice Lewis Powell bridled at the suggestion that the state courts lack "appropriate sensitivity to constitutional rights."[65] The sea change that has occurred is displayed in two §1983 cases—one in 1972, the other in 1980. In each instance, the majority opinion was signed by Justice Potter Stewart, noted for casting swing votes when he was on the bench. In 1972, Stewart declared that "[t]he very purpose of §1983 was to interpose the federal courts between the States and the people, as guardians of the people's federal rights."[66] In 1980, by contrast, he confirmed the Court's "confidence" in the state courts and flatly denied that litigants with federal claims are entitled to a federal forum: "[N]othing in the language or . . . history of §1983 proves any congressional intent to deny binding effect to a state-court judgment . . . when the state court . . . has shown itself willing and able to protect federal rights."[67] The two cases are distinguishable, and Stewart's results can be defended. Yet there is no mistaking that a remarkable, even revolutionary, shift took place in the space of only eight years.

Where the Warren Court revived §1983 as a vehicle for federal-question litigation in federal court, the Rehnquist Court has erected a series of restrictive doctrines that render §1983 actions markedly less effective for the vindication of federal rights in the federal forum.[68] Where the Warren Court enthusiastically endorsed federal habeas corpus for state prisoners challenging their convictions on federal grounds, the new Court has created numerous substantive and procedural bars to habeas relief.[69] Where the Warren Court permitted the federal courts to enjoin state court proceedings threatening first amendment freedoms, this Court routinely bars federal injunctions against pending state court actions.[70] And where the Warren Court allowed plaintiffs a range of arguments for circumventing the preclusion doctrine and the states' immunity from suit, this Court enforces rigorous preclusion rules and eleventh amendment barriers to claims against the states.[71]

No one thinks that the more conservative justices now sitting are any more driven to their views regarding federal-state relations than the liberals who held the same chairs in the Warren era were dragged kicking and screaming to theirs. A good deal of judgment goes into the allocation of jurisdiction between the federal and state courts, judgment that is not unaffected by the justices' expectations touching what either set of courts will do with the business it receives. The current Court does trust the state courts to cope with federal-question litigation, just as the Court "repeatedly and emphatically" insists it does.[72] Recent decisions encouraging plaintiffs to file §1983 suits in state court only underscore the point.[73] This Court is content with state court litigation, comfortable in the knowledge and belief that the state courts may often permit state interests to defeat federal rights.[74]

To understand and appreciate these developments, it is essential to explore their intellectual underpinnings still further. There have been at least two different scholarly attempts to elaborate the Legal Process model's implications for the proper distribution of business between the federal and state courts. I treat the two lines of academic authority in the next sections and explain the implications of the choice between them.

Full and Fair Adjudication

For an elaboration of the process model that conservatives find appealing, I can find no better source than Paul Bator, whose views flowed readily from the classic Legal Process texts.[75] Bator found it hard to determine whether the results reached by courts are correct in an absolute sense. He insisted that no matter how many times a judgment is reviewed, the possibility remains that the last court to entertain the matter has made some mistake of fact or, equally damning, has identified the wrong legal principle or rule, invoked the right rule but applied it improperly, or failed in some more subtle way. Yet another layer of review may still find fault with the result reached previously. This was true for Bator with respect to all legal issues, including federal questions, and irrespective of the court system in which a case is adjudicated. Justice Robert Jackson's quip about the Supreme Court itself made the point graphically: "We are not final because we are infallible, but we are infallible only because we are final."[76] Setting any forthright evaluation of outcomes to one side, Bator argued that we should focus, instead, on the institutional processes by which results are produced. The goal, according to Bator, should be to establish a "set of arrangements and procedures which provide a *reasoned* and *acceptable* probability that justice will be done." Although he did not refer expressly to the principle of institutional settlement, Bator plainly followed Hart and Sacks in this turn to process.[77]

Bator illustrated the process model by applying it to federal habeas corpus for state prisoners. The lower federal courts' authority to entertain habeas petitions from state prisoners is a complicated affair, the details of which I will leave for Chapter Five. Briefly, a criminal defendant in state court is expected to raise any federal claim she may have as a defense. A typical example is a claim that the state's case depends on a confession that was coerced from the defendant and thus is inadmissible as evidence against her. When such a claim is properly raised, the state trial court considers it routinely. If that court rejects the claim and the prisoner is convicted, the claim can be presented to the state appellate courts on direct review or in further state postconviction proceedings. If the prisoner still is denied relief, she can petition the Supreme Court of the United States to accept her case for direct review. The Supreme Court can no longer undertake review in more than a handful of cases each year, however, and any individual applicant is likely to be turned away.

Importantly, the prisoner has no right to appeal to the lower federal courts; Congress has never granted the inferior federal courts an appellate jurisdiction over state court judgments, even in federal-question cases. Yet if the prisoner is now in some form of custody, the federal courts have jurisdiction to entertain a petition from her for a writ of habeas corpus. In theory, the inquiry in a federal habeas proceeding is limited to the validity of the prisoner's current detention. Since the warden will justify her custody on the basis of the criminal conviction, however, the federal courts will end up reexamining the state courts' treatment of the prisoner's federal claim. If the federal courts conclude that the confession was unconstitutionally used at trial, the conviction is invalid and cannot sustain the detention of which the prisoner complains. Accordingly, the federal court can order state authorities to release her, unless the error is cured in some way—for example, by conducting a new trial from which the invalid confession is excluded.

Invoking the process model in this context, Bator contended that the resulting reexamination of state court outcomes by the lower federal courts cannot be justified as a means of ensuring that the *right* judgment is reached. He argued that, objectively correct outcomes being illusory, an inquiry into the validity of a prisoner's detention should "meaningfully address itself, *at least initially*," to whether the "arrangements and processes which previously determined the facts and applied the law" in state court were "adequate to the task at hand."[78] Bator argued on this basis that the federal courts should defer to previous state court judgments—provided that the processes by which those results were generated furnished the prisoner with a "full and fair opportunity to litigate" her federal claims.[79] Hart and Sacks would have said that outcomes reached in this way not only fix what the law "is," but describe in a "special" way what the law "ought" to be.[80]

Like Hart and Wechsler before him, Bator declined to take up the challenge of the Legal Process model's macro phase and thus to explore the relative competencies of the federal and state courts.[81] He acknowledged that the "full and fair opportunity" idea would make no sense if the state courts could not be trusted to act responsibly. Yet he would not accept that the state courts would fail to respect federal rights.[82] Since the state courts were bound to decide at least some federal issues in at least some instances, it followed, according to Bator, that we should have a system that encourages those courts to "internalize" the sense that they, too, can "speak for the Constitution."[83] In devising an allocation principle, then, Bator effectively assumed that state adjudication may be preferred without jeopardizing "acceptable" results. Bator did, however, engage the inquiry invited by Legal Process in its micro phase. This, indeed, was the point of asking the federal habeas courts to evaluate the process the state courts employ in individual cases. Complaints about flawed state process may be addressed, however, on a case-by-case basis. Bator specified that a full and fair opportunity to litigate federal claims in state court must include some review of initial determinations in the trial courts. Too much is at stake to let a single judge have the final say on the merits of a federal claim. Typically, the states provide the necessary review by way of an appeal to the state appellate courts. When the federal courts get cases thereafter, according to Bator, they should accept judgments reached by the state appellate courts in a proper manner—even if it appears (to the federal courts) that the trial court was wrong initially and that the state appellate courts should have reversed. Given procedurally adequate review in state court, the federal courts should not substitute their different assessments of correct outcomes.

Bator acknowledged that federal law has genuine content, that the state courts may reach incorrect judgments after the most searching process, and that erroneous decisions on federal issues can be upset by the Supreme Court on direct review. In my hypothetical, accordingly, the Supreme Court would reverse the prisoner's conviction on finding that the confession on which it is based was coerced. If, however, such a claim is heard not on direct review in the Supreme Court, but in habeas corpus proceedings in the lower federal courts, Bator insisted that the meaning of due process changes. The federal habeas courts should hold that the state courts provided the process that was "due" if they accorded the prisoner a full and fair opportunity to litigate her federal claim at some point in their procedures. This analysis, if accepted, promises serious implications for micro-level Legal Process in a variety of contexts.

Bator's attachment to process rivaled even the dogged pursuit of neat institutional arrangements I identified in the original work of the Legal Process school. Recall that Herbert Wechsler criticized the Segregation Cases. Bator, for his part, treated another sensitive case in an equally antiseptic way. He noted that the accused had been convicted and sentenced to death in a Georgia state court, that the Georgia Supreme Court had rejected his claim that the trial had been dominated by a mob, and that, given the state supreme court's "independent inquiry" and "careful findings," relief had been denied in federal habeas corpus. Bator praised that result without mentioning that the prisoner was Leo Frank, an almost certainly innocent man whose gross mistreatment and lynching is widely regarded as one of the most notorious episodes of anti-Semitism in modern American history.[84] When Bator recalled the actual circumstances of a celebrated case, he chose the "red light bandit" episode in the 1950s, which saw Caryl Chessman take nine trips to the Supreme Court in an attempt to overturn his death sentence.[85] To Bator, it was the slow pace of criminal cases, particularly capital cases, that was cause for concern—not the ability of the federal courts to protect federal rights.

More important than sterile style, however, was Bator's process-model understanding of "acceptable" judicial outcomes. For liberals, the competence of courts to adjudicate federal-question cases is measured by their receptivity to the claims pressed by individuals against government. Liberals frankly want judges who favor the individual—judges who give federal rights an expansive meaning and, just as important, find facts to support a successful claim in the case at bar. Bator, by contrast, denied that individual rights are entitled to special solicitude. He saw federal values on both sides of cases and assigned no preference to "those that protect the individual from the power of the state" over those, like "separation of powers and federalism," that reflect majoritarian objectives.[86]

Since the early 1970s, the Supreme Court, too, has often declined to rank personal rights more highly than competing governmental interests. Bator's supportive work is often cited with approval.[87] Moreover, this Court does not merely proclaim the ability of the state courts to handle federal questions. When it is possible under existing statutes to do so, the Court is quite prepared to deny the federal courts any warrant in habeas corpus to set at naught state court judgments when the federal courts, examining issues afresh, would reach different results. According to the Chief Justice, there is no reason to doubt state court judgments regarding the Constitution simply because of "their frequent *differences of opinion* as to how that document should be interpreted."[88]

The justices who now command the Supreme Court understand the lessons of Legal Realism and, indeed, constitutional law since the Segregation Cases. Judges have choices to make. Bator's process model offers an attractive vehicle for fostering outcomes favoring governmental authority over the individual. Federal-question cases are funneled to the state courts in the expectation that relief will be denied. If a state court interprets individual rights expansively, the Court can accept direct review and reverse.[89] But in the run of cases, in which the state courts decide cases in government's favor by means of adequate procedure, their results can be summarily affirmed or simply left to stand as authoritative precedents. The lower federal courts are carved out of the picture and are thus unable either to override state court decisions or to force the Supreme Court explicitly to take restrictive positions with respect to federal rights. This is clearly the direction in which federal habeas corpus has been going of late.[90] A similar trend is manifest in other contexts to be examined in this book.

The challenge before liberals is to frame a response to Bator's neutral-sounding, but value-laden, insistence that state court adjudication is close enough for government work. If such a response is not developed, and soon, the federal courts' authority to vindicate federal rights may not be sustained.

The Most Sympathetic Tribunal

Treatments of Legal Process that liberals find more appealing fall into two categories. As I explained previously, Burt Neuborne has taken up the challenge that Hart and Wechsler never accepted as the obliga-

tion of the macro phase of their model: a rigorous examination of the
alleged parity between the federal and state courts. On examination,
the federal courts are clearly superior to the state courts in federal-
question cases.[91] They are more likely to decide in the individual's favor; moreover, they offer institutional advantages, irrespective of outcome. In my view, Neuborne's arguments constitute the best response
to Bator's process model, which, again, erroneously assumes parity
between the federal and state courts.

Other observers despair of resolving the parity controversy satisfactorily. The arguments that liberals marshal, compelling as they are,
have no purchase in conservative quarters. Erwin Chemerinsky argues, accordingly, that we should find some basis for allocating jurisdiction between the federal and state courts that is sufficiently independent of the parity debate to make it unnecessary to declare a
winner. Chemerinsky's own suggestion is that we forbear any blanket
decision about where federal claims should be litigated and, instead,
break forum selection down into individualized decisions on a case-
by-case basis. The choice of forum should simply be delegated to individual litigants advancing federal claims, who should be permitted to
pick the federal or state courts as they see fit.[92] Chemerinsky's hope is
that the resulting litigant-choice principle can satisfy partisans on
both sides of the parity debate. Those who insist that the federal
courts have the comparative advantage should be pleased, because the
litigant-choice device preserves the availability of those courts to willing plaintiffs; those who accept parity can relax in the knowledge that
the state courts retain a role in the system. Moreover, Chemerinsky
insists that the litigant-choice strategy has several other advantages: it
fosters litigants' autonomy, enhances federalism, and "maximizes the
opportunity for protecting constitutional rights."[93]

As a policy prescription for distributing judicial business, the
litigant-choice device is extremely attractive. In due course, I will propose that most of the restrictions on litigant forum-selection that now
exist should be eliminated.[94] As a means of circumventing the parity
question, however, the litigant-choice idea will not do. For it leads
ineluctably in the direction of those who think federal jurisdiction is
essential. Liberals do not argue that plaintiffs who wish to take federal
claims to state court should be prevented from doing so. Rather, conservatives argue that, at least in some circumstances, plaintiffs who
want to be in *federal* court should be denied that option.[95] A rule that
allows litigants to choose for themselves abandons this conservative
position.

Nor do the advantages claimed for the litigant-choice rule suffice to save it. It is unlikely that an individual's autonomy is much at stake in the selection of a court in which to litigate a claim—a selection that, in most instances, will be a strategic choice by counsel.[96] As to federalism, Chemerinsky contends that the litigant-choice principle fits neatly into the idea behind decentralization—which, by his account, is that individual liberty can be enhanced by getting the federal and state courts to compete for business by showing that they will be receptive to federal claims.[97] This understanding of federalism is novel, to say the least. Yet even if we entertain it for purposes of discussion, there are a few things to remember before we let ourselves be carried away by the vision of a vigorous national market for cases in which federal and state courts bid for opportunities to safeguard personal liberty.

In most instances at least, the state courts already have concurrent jurisdiction to entertain federal-question cases, and no one proposes to end that jurisdiction.[98] If the state courts wish to compete for business, they can. But they haven't yet, and they give few signs of wanting to. There is little evidence that many state courts are prepared to give federal rights a more generous interpretation than those rights would receive in the lower federal courts and considerable evidence that most are not.[99] In the one situation in which the federal courts are positioned to review state judgments on federal claims, habeas corpus, it appears that the state courts underprotect federal rights in an appreciable number of cases.[100] Moreover, if any state courts that are disposed to do so interpret federal rights more expansively than the Supreme Court might wish, they have no more capacity than the lower federal courts to insulate their judgments from reversal.[101]

Chemerinsky argues that the litigant-selection principle places responsibility for choosing the forum for litigation with the actors best situated to make sound, reasoned judgments. The obvious candidates are litigants advancing federal claims, because they are positioned to choose the courts that will be most hospitable to their claims, that is, the courts that promise to decide close factual or legal questions in their favor. Far from recommending the litigant-selection plan as neutral in the controversy over parity, this point constitutes the clearest evidence yet that litigant choice does pick a side, and it is the side of the federal courts. For if individuals pressing federal claims make good, self-interested decisions most of the time, they will be the beneficiaries of a general bias in their favor—deliberately built into the system by means of the litigant-choice principle.

An advantage for federal claims does not trouble Chemerinsky, who declares that it is a final recommendation of the litigant-choice scheme that it "maximizes the opportunity to protect constitutional rights" by fostering the selection of the "most sympathetic" tribunal.[102] By his account, federal rights *should* be given an expansive reading, and we *should* adopt a means of allocating judicial business that channels federal claims to the courts most likely to give them that reading. An acknowledged objective to interpret rights generously takes no side in the parity debate, according to Chemerinsky, because just about everybody who participates in that controversy agrees that it is "*desirable* to maximize the likelihood of vindicating such claims."[103] It would be nice if this were true. But it isn't. Proponents of federal court superiority readily embrace the idea that federal rights should be given a generous interpretation. But that sentiment is not so widely shared as Chemerinsky suggests.[104] Bator argued that the desirable end of federal-question litigation is not that individuals should win in close cases, but that courts should reach "acceptable" results. In his view, courts might well find government's assertion of power more persuasive than plaintiffs' ambitious claims of right, even in cases that might be decided either way.[105]

I have devoted considerable space to this critique of Chemerinsky's work not to condemn an admirable contribution to scholarship, but to underscore a point fundamental to all that follows in this book. We can fashion sound rules for the allocation of authority and responsibility between the federal and state courts, and if we do it well we will arrive at substantially the conclusion that Chemerinsky reaches. In the main, citizens advancing federal claims should be able to choose a federal forum. Yet we will come to this result not by evading a judgment about the relative competencies of the two court systems, but by making that judgment in favor of federal jurisdiction. This is the only way to meet the challenge posed by Bator's process model. Rights depend on the courts that enforce them. The federal courts are far better forums for the vindication of rights than are the state courts. Lawyers representing individuals with federal claims almost always want to be in federal court, and government lawyers almost always want to be in state court—and for a reason: to get a "litigating edge."[106]

Legislative Supremacy

The medicine for our maladies is straightforward legislation that both cures problems that have existed for some time and eliminates new difficulties introduced by the Rehnquist Court. I do not mean to suggest that we should turn to legislative solutions on the theory that Congress is institutionally suited to making the right choices regarding the allocation of responsibility for federal-question cases—in the way that the federal courts *are,* I think, institutionally suited to adjudicating those cases when they arise. Legislative reforms are not good simply because they are legislative; they are only good if they make sound, substantive changes. I do contend, however, that Congress has power to enact strong measures to end the erosion of federal judicial authority we have witnessed in recent years. And I contend that Congress should exercise that power.

In the chapters to follow, I will propose specific statutory language to do the work that needs to be done. In every instance, the watchword must be clarity. The Court now sitting in Washington will undoubtedly demand explicit statements from Congress before it will abandon doctrines the Court itself has created. At this juncture, I will suggest only a general, traffic-direction device that, if enacted, would oblige the Court to construe jurisdictional and related statutes most favorably to immediate federal court litigation. The following language should be added to the Judicial Code of the United States:

> Sections of this title shall be construed in a manner most favorable to the immediate adjudication of federal claims in federal court.

If this provision were enacted, the Supreme Court itself, and all the lower federal courts, would be admonished to resolve doubts in favor of litigants seeking access to the federal courts. We should be circumspect in our expectations about such a canon of construction. Devices of this kind are often derided as vapid exhortations that can be respected equally in the breach. Yet courts read statutes in light of "background norms" that do influence judgment at some level. A legislatively prescribed preference for the federal courts in federal-question cases can establish such an expectation in this context.[107]

Moreover, as Bator fairly pointed out, it is infeasible to route all federal questions to the lower federal courts. I will advocate nothing of the kind, but rather that Congress should prefer the federal courts when it is sensible to bring them into play. It follows that new legislation will deliberately install exceptions to a general rule favoring the federal forum and that, here again, the Court will exercise judgment in order to give recognized exceptions authoritative meaning. Indeed, the restrictive, judge-made doctrines now in place are typically defended as attempts to implement exceptions that existing statutes are said to permit. Still, a canon of construction can guide the Court, minimizing the prospect that the justices will substitute their own judgment regarding the proper distribution of judicial business for that of the legislative branch.

Snob Appeal

Before getting down to specific problems, I must acknowledge one last set of questions regarding the orchestration of judicial business in the United States. Crowded dockets in the federal system are sometimes said to justify funneling federal-question litigation to the state courts.[108] There have been many calls for a general overhaul of federal jurisdiction.[109] Indeed, the purpose of this book is to ask yet again for legislation on a wide scale. A fresh appraisal will not, however, justify the surrender of federal-question cases to the states.

The principal commissions organized in recent years to take the federal courts' pulse have uniformly seized upon the increasing volume of lawsuits as a serious, escalating problem. The Study Group on the Caseload of the Supreme Court, better known as the Freund Committee, recommended drastic measures to rescue the Supreme Court itself from the swelling tide of appeals and petitions for discretionary review.[110] The American Law Institute also noted the "special urgency" of the "continually expanding workload of the federal courts."[111] More recently, the Federal Courts Study Committee, a blue-ribbon panel established by the 100th Congress and appointed by Chief Justice Rehnquist, was expressly charged to address the "mounting public and professional concern" with the "expansion" of the federal courts' workload and the accompanying "congestion, delay, [and] expense."[112] True to that mission, the Study Committee's 1990 report concentrates on the "crisis" now facing the federal judicial system and recommends a series of reforms to eliminate entire categories of cases from the federal courts' purview.

When it is proposed to curb federal judicial business, however, several points should be kept in mind. First, fears that the number of cases in the federal courts is approaching the crisis level may be inflated. The overall civil caseload increased less than one half of 1 percent in 1987–88 and 1986–87, and if we go back to 1985–86, we find that civil case filings actually declined, albeit for the first time since

1977. The increases that have raised the alarm recently are found in specialized cases and on the criminal docket.[113]

Second, even if the volume of work warrants concern, the most that sheer numbers can suggest is that we must assess the cases now being heard and determine whether any should be sent elsewhere. That, of course, only raises the question whether some aspects of the federal courts' current jurisdiction should be scaled back or terminated. Certainly, the recognition of increased demand for federal judicial resources does not identify federal-question litigation as either a source of difficulty or a likely candidate for reductions. Indeed, even if the number of federal-question cases has increased in recent years, and it has, the importance of that litigation more than justifies an enlarged share of federal court time. When observers wring their hands over the obvious need to open the federal courts to §1983 actions, but then insist that the pressure on federal dockets demands that those actions be sent stateward, it is time to be suspicious.[114] Federal-question cases should be the last, not the first, to go.

Third, there are many obvious places where the federal caseload can be trimmed before we get to federal-question litigation. Both the American Law Institute and the Federal Courts Study Committee and, indeed, most serious reform groups offer as the primary target the federal courts' jurisdiction to entertain lawsuits over *state*-law claims merely because the parties reside in "diverse" (different) states.[115] Whatever may have been the original basis for "diversity" jurisdiction, it draws its principal modern support from corporations and lawyers who believe their clients benefit from being in federal court for litigation—even when there are no federal issues to decide.[116] It is in response to those powerful political and economic forces, not to any sense of continuing public need, that Congress has repeatedly refused to abolish diversity jurisdiction—which, by the way, accounts for almost one in four of the cases filed in the district courts each year and nearly half the trials those courts conduct.[117]

There are other perennial candidates for cuts. Taxation cases, some bankruptcy matters, and Federal Employers Liability Act claims can safely be redirected to specially charged federal agencies and tribunals. Still other possibilities are more controversial.[118] Within the burgeoning criminal docket, we should note that prosecutions for federal drug offenses have quadrupled over the last decade.[119] It is scarcely surprising that Congress should criminalize the traffic in addictive drugs, that the Justice Department and local United States attorneys should enforce those statutes vigorously, and that drug cases should be advanced on federal district court calendars pursuant to the Speedy Trial Act. Yet the effect on the federal courts' workload must at some point be considered, particularly where the states, too, have an enforcement interest and role. The Federal Courts Study Committee recommends that federal prosecutors funnel as many drug cases as possible to state authorities; that surely is an appropriate, if short, first step.[120]

If there truly is a serious shortfall in federal judicial resources, and if efforts to stem demand prove insufficient, then supply can be increased, at least at the margin. Conventional wisdom opposes an attempt to meet the increasing need for federal judges simply by providing more of them. At its current complement of about nine hundred judges, the federal court system is small by comparison with the aggregate collage of state courts nationwide. And small does have its advantages. At the practical level, more federal judges would accommodate more cases. More cases would generate more differences of opinion and thus more appeals. More appeals would require more appellate judges. More review petitions from more appellate court decisions would bring more pressure to bear on the Supreme Court. And so on. These are serious considerations. But if there really is more work to do, if, this is to say, the federal courts' caseload cannot be reduced by the means I have just surveyed, then it seems inescapable that we must have more judges, magistrates, and clerks.[121] Pressures there will be up and down the judicial hierarchy, but expected dislocations also can and must be managed. They, too, come with the territory.

Finally, we should be wary of the Study Committee's concern that any significant expansion in the federal judiciary would "compromise the quality of federal justice."[122] The thinking here is that the smaller the federal judiciary, the greater the prestige that attaches to federal judgeships, the greater the competition for any individual position, and the greater the effectiveness of the selection system. To summarize, the smaller the federal court system, the easier the task of quality control. To recruit thousands instead of hundreds of federal judges, the argument continues, we would have not only to fish deeper in the talent pool, but also to raise salaries or extend fringe benefits, or both. Moreover, in the Study Committee's colorful description, any single judge might think of herself as "a tiny cog in a vast wheel that would turn at the same speed whatever the judge did" and thus might not "approach the judicial task with the requisite sense that power must be exercised responsibly."[123]

None of us would wish to depreciate the coin that is the federal judiciary. The argument is compelling that federal judges must remain an elite corps of exceptionally talented men and women who are intellectually and psychologically committed to doing federal justice. Still, there are many fine lawyers in the country who respond to incentives other than prestige, money, and power. It is not true that if the job of being a federal judge lost its "snob appeal," we would have to settle for lesser lights.[124] We might just find fewer wealthy middle-aged white men from large law firms queuing up for robes, and more women, racial minorities, and others now rarely represented on the bench. If recent presidents have had difficulty finding candidates to appoint, it has not been because our demand for talent exceeds the supply. Indeed, the native and professional ability of judicial candidates to render service is all too often regarded as only a necessary, not a sufficient, qualification. It is now and always has been true that the political bent of presidential nominees is often what distinguishes them from the field.

I recognize that by dismissing the "talent pool" argument, and certainly by mentioning the politics of federal judicial selection, I conclude this chapter on some superficially discordant notes. I have not forgotten that one of the reasons liberals prefer the federal courts in federal-question cases is that federal judges are extremely capable jurists whose relatively light caseload permits them to give federal issues more and better attention. If this tradition is surrendered to docket congestion, it may fairly be asked whether the superiority of the federal courts on which I rest so much in this book will not also be sacrificed in equal measure. Nor should it satisfy liberals that the federal courts' heavy workload can be ameliorated by expanding the number of judgeships—if those new places may be filled by conservatives. In all candor, however, there really is no serious risk that by modestly increasing the number of federal judges we would jeopardize the advantages they offer. And as I explained at the outset of this chapter, the capacity of presidents to pack the judicial branch is of only passing concern. Mainstream liberals today do not prefer the federal courts in federal-question cases because they think that there still are enough older judges, named by Lyndon Johnson or Jimmy Carter, in office to protect individual rights, or even because they believe that Bill Clinton will add new liberal blood to the breed. Certainly, liberals cannot sensibly switch sides in the parity debate merely because more conservative judges, nominated by Ronald Reagan and George Bush, are in place now and promise to hold their ground for some time to come.

We do not depend entirely on the ideological make-up of individual sitting *judges* to give federal rights a generous interpretation; we also rely, even more fundamentally, on the competence, perspective, and institutional location and structure of the federal *courts*.

This, then, is the story. Realism was a reaction to the duplicity of Formalism, Legal Process was a response to the cynicism of Realism, and the Civil Rights Movement challenged the complacency of Legal Process. At each stage, the allocation of business between the federal and state courts was intimately connected with the larger jurisprudential developments under way. Today, conservatives press Bator's version of the Legal Process perspective as an intelligible explanation for ceding federal business to the state courts, where governmental interests may be weighed more heavily against individual rights. Liberals, charged by the modern civil rights and civil liberties tradition, insist on channeling federal-question cases to the federal courts, where individual claims of right may be greeted more warmly. It remains for me in the rest of this book to identify the most important current barriers to the federal forum and to specify concretely the legislative means by which those barriers can be eliminated.

CHAPTER TWO

▼

Of a Judiciary Nature

Just before Easter in the spring of 1979, the Chamber of Commerce in Rabun County, Georgia, approved a plan to erect a gigantic, electrically lighted cross in Black Rock Mountain State Park. The meaning of the cross was self-evident. It was a religious symbol, pure and simple—constructed with private funds, but placed in a public place and clearly associating state and local government with Christianity. Accordingly, the cross plainly violated the first amendment's establishment clause, which prohibits government from endorsing a sectarian message. One would have thought that the construction of the cross would be a short-lived, tawdry little episode, embarrassing to an increasingly sophisticated and tolerant nation. A quick and easy lawsuit in the local United States District Court by the Georgia affiliate of the American Civil Liberties Union would undoubtedly produce an order requiring local officials to dismantle it. The ACLU affiliate *did* obtain an injunction, but the process was neither quick nor easy.[1]

It was not enough that the ACLU and its members were troubled by a patent violation of the Constitution and, as good citizens who wished to see government comply with the law, brought that violation to the court's attention. Nor was it enough that the plaintiffs were ideologically committed to the separation of church and state. The court could consider the establishment clause issue only because the director of the Georgia ACLU, Gene Guerrero, alleged that he often went camping in local state parks, but would not use the park at Black Rock Mountain while the cross was there. According to Guerrero, the cross was an eyesore, and the glare of its powerful lights illuminated nearby campsites. Guerrero also said that the cross offended his philosophical commitments, but that did little to aid his cause. He would have found it as easy to get into federal court if the cross had been a pile of rubbish.[2]

To the uninitiated, the Rabun County story is nothing short of astonishing. If the federal courts are supposed to enforce the Constitution, it seems senseless that a citizen's ability to get their attention should depend not on his civic respect for the principle at stake, but on his personal interest in sleeping peacefully in a public park, undisturbed by floodlights. Vital as that interest may be to the hikers and campers among us, it scarcely seems even relevant to the compelling need to check the unconstitutional governmental action at hand. Yet this is the law of "justiciability," that is, the law governing *what* claims are adjudicable in federal court, *who* can invoke federal judicial power, and *when* federal court action is timely. Justiciability is a subtle and complex business. Its jurisprudential history is obscure; its theoretical foundations are uncertain; its doctrinal iterations are incoherent. And, as one might have guessed, its political implications are enormous.

Here, then, is the very kind of arcane legalism I have been warning you about: tortured complexity that frustrates the federal courts' ability to implement federal rights. The burden of this chapter is heavy. Initially, I will sketch current doctrines typically listed under the justiciability umbrella, with primary attention to the "standing" of would-be litigants to be in federal court. Standing is, or at least has become, the central issue; other doctrines spin off from standing and the ideas standing reflects. Next, I will trace the history of standing—first to the understandings of law and legal relations in England, then to developments in the period just before and during the New Deal. In doing so, I will revisit familiar themes from private-rights litigation within the Formalist framework. Here again, I will argue that the ability of litigants to gain access to the federal courts is crucial to the preservation of substantive federal rights. I will treat the Warren Court's attempts to break down standing barriers to the federal judicial forum. That history, in turn, will put in context more recent instances in which litigation over "public" rights has been defeated on the ground that would-be litigants lack standing. Returning to current doctrine, I will survey critiques of the Rehnquist Court's recent cases, critiques that expose the intellectual failings and manipulative potential of modern standing rules. I will treat the relevant constitutional themes: the text of Article III, federalism, and the separation of powers. I will discuss the best academic proposals for doctrinal reform, but in the end I will offer carefully constructed legislative measures to resolve standing difficulties.

Justiciability

The justiciability doctrines now in fashion can be stated simply enough. At the outset, some constitutional issues defy judicial resolution altogether. Denoted "political" questions, these issues are assigned by the Constitution itself to the politically accountable (that is, the executive and legislative) branches of the national government. John Marshall is said to have recognized this "political question doctrine" when he disclaimed any judicial authority to inquire into matters about which the president has "discretion."[3] Political questions are few in number, however, and rarely figure in litigation.[4] Other issues can constitutionally be determined by the federal courts, but only when they are presented in the proper posture, by proper litigants, and at the proper time. The federal courts cannot offer "advisory" opinions, but can determine the meaning of the Constitution only if necessary to resolve concrete disputes as they arise.[5] This functional basis for federal judicial power is also conventionally ascribed to Chief Justice Marshall, who relied on it when he asserted the Supreme Court's authority to pass on the constitutionality of congressional enactments.[6] Today, it is widely understood that all courts routinely "make" law, but the federal courts do it only as they resolve disputes.[7]

The adverse parties to justiciable disputes must, in turn, have standing to be in federal court.[8] Standing rules are of two kinds. First, there are primary requirements that must be met in every case. Litigants must demonstrate a "personal stake in the outcome" of a dispute, that is, actual or threatened "injury in fact," caused by the action said to be unlawful and likely to be redressed by a favorable decision. In the lighted-cross case, for example, Gene Guerrero alleged that he was injured "in fact" inasmuch as his enjoyment of the park was spoiled, that his injury was "caused" by the presence of the cross, and that, if the court decided the case in his favor and ordered the cross removed, his injury would be redressed. These primary standing requirements are said to form a constitutional floor. No one who fails to meet them can constitutionally invoke the power of the federal courts.

Second, there are other rules, said to be prudential in nature. These rules are not constitutionally rooted and can be ignored or eliminated as a matter of policy. Where they operate, however, they restrict the standing even of those who satisfy the primary, constitutional requisites. For example, litigants usually will not be allowed to air "generalized grievances" shared by most other people. This is why it was important in the lighted-cross case that Guerrero lived in Georgia, often used the local parks, and alleged that he *would* use the Black Rock Mountain State Park but for the presence of the cross. It was essential that he distinguish himself and his special interest in the case from the great mass of other citizens and their potential complaints about the cross.

Another prudential rule limits the arguments that a litigant can make once he gets into a federal court on the strength of some less generalized injury. Such a plaintiff is typically barred from asserting rights that belong to others not before the court. If, for example, the authorities in Rabun County had required public school children to attend Easter services at the site of the cross, nonbelievers would have had a constitutional right to refuse. The first amendment not only prohibits government from endorsing a particular religion; it guarantees individual citizens the right to exercise the beliefs they choose for themselves, free of governmental coercion to participate in alien religious observances. Gene Guerrero, however, would almost certainly have been denied standing to press such a "free exercise" claim on behalf of children not party to his lawsuit.[9]

Finally, in some instances, plaintiffs who show some specialized injury and who assert no legal rights belonging to others still must bring themselves at least arguably within the zone of interests protected or regulated by the legal standard on which they rely. In establishment clause cases, for example, citizens may complain if taxes are imposed to support religious activities, because at least one purpose of the establishment clause is to prevent government from exacting money from the populace to finance religion.[10] Guerrero's case for standing would have been strengthened in this connection if the Chamber of Commerce had paid for the cross with tax revenues. As it was, the placement of the cross on public property apparently sufficed.

Under two other headings related to standing, the federal courts cannot consider claims that are presented too soon (before they are "ripe" for adjudication) or too late (after they have been resolved by other means and are only hypothetical or "moot" for judicial purposes).[11] If, for example, Gene Guerrero had filed his lawsuit before the Chamber of Commerce had approved the plan for the cross, his action might have been held premature, that is, not ripe for judicial consideration. Likewise, if he had moved away from Georgia while the case was pending and could no longer honestly maintain that he wished to use Black Rock Mountain State Park, the lawsuit might have been dismissed for mootness. These two doctrines governing the timing of federal adjudication focus not on the suitability of litigants to invoke federal judicial power (the province of standing), but on the fitness for adjudication of the issues litigants wish the federal courts to entertain. Nevertheless, recent decisions collapse ripeness and mootness into primary standing rules, thus making these doctrines, too, appear to have constitutional footing.

Stating justiciability doctrines is the easy part. It is quite another matter to apply them consistently and next to impossible to justify them as sensible gate-keeping devices rationing federal judicial power. Understand, however, that these rules often deny access to the federal courts to enforce federal law. This is particularly true of the chief villain of the piece, modern standing doctrine.

Kings and Englishmen

In the beginning (again) were private rights, conceived as aspects of the natural order, embraced by the common law of England, found (not created) by courts, and enforceable against private wrongdoers.[12] The king, reflecting the divine order on earth, was in that sense the *source* of law and by hypothesis could not possibly *violate* it. The courts, moreover, reported to the king and knew no other master. Certainly, the king could not be subject to his own rules; that is, he could not, through his own judges, find himself guilty of violating his own law, such that his victim was entitled to judicial relief. The same went for the king's agents, who enjoyed his immunity from suit so long as they acted on his authority. At some point, however, this foolishness had to end. For there were too many surrogate kings roaming the countryside victimizing the population and, accordingly, much pressure to call those agents to account in court. The answer was to split each of the king's men into two persons, the one sovereign (and still protected from suit as was the king himself), the other private (and subject to suit for offenses against private rights). And in a clever and marvelously convenient twist, the courts declared that agents were acting in their individual, private capacity whenever they violated the private rights of other Englishmen. By this means, it became possible after all to file a lawsuit, the realistic purpose of which was to force the king's agents to conform to the developing common law of England. Royal immunity was skirted as the allegedly unlawful actions of royal officers were said to be undertaken in their private capacity.

In this country, representative government succeeded to the sovereign authority of the crown. American lawsuits took the familiar form of the common law: suits by private citizens (claiming a breach of private rights) against government officials (treated as private citizens who had allegedly violated private rights). And in federal-question lawsuits against government authorities, just as in ordinary cases involving private parties, the function of courts was to resolve disputes over plaintiffs' assertions of private rights. Litigants were entitled to invoke the authority of the federal courts if they alleged violations of such rights, provided that jurisdiction had been conferred on those courts by statute. As I noted earlier, prior to the Civil War, Congress limited federal jurisdiction in cases arising under federal law. When the Reconstruction Congress finally gave the federal courts a general jurisdiction to entertain federal-question cases, the same private-rights model prevailed.

The notion that only litigants with personal, private rights to assert could seek judicial relief was not monolithic, either in England or in America. English courts issued common law "writs," permitting citizens to press the representatives of English government to comply with the law without claiming that some personal legal right had been violated.[13] The English writ practice was well established at the time of the Constitutional Convention on this side of the Atlantic, and our American courts readily issued similar instruments. Early English and American legal history is mired in obscurity, and it is difficult now to say with confidence just how widely the writs opened the courthouse doors. It would be an overstatement to say that the writs recognized no limits at all on suits by parties with no private rights of their own. The record *is* sufficiently clear, however, to say that writs were used without the same insistence on private rights that early decisions in this country typically ascribed to the common law.[14] Nevertheless, the private-rights model of adjudication predominated in the federal courts prior to the New Deal. Indeed, it was part and parcel of the Formalist understanding of law and the judicial function. Recall that the assault on economic regulation launched by the four horsemen was grounded in the notion that preexisting private rights to liberty and property were denied by the agents of government in circumstances that would have entitled plaintiffs to relief at common law.

Public Rights

The private-rights model came under pressure during the New Deal period. Not only did the subjects of regulation (for example, industrialists and corporations) seek judicial protection, but others affected by regulation (for example, workers, consumers, and competitors) sought access to the courts to enforce regulatory measures that promised to shift economic arrangements to their advantage. In some instances, these new plaintiffs argued that government regulators violated new federal statutes or neglected federally prescribed procedures; in other cases, they contended that regulators failed to comply with the very statutes they were supposed to be enforcing. Importantly, however, the new plaintiffs did not always advance claims that could easily be characterized as private rights.[15] Indeed, many were in court to obtain the personal benefits that would flow from forcing the agents of government simply to comply with the Constitution or some federal statute. If rights were at stake in these new cases, they were not personal and private, but "public" rights, that is, the rights of Americans generally to demand that governmental authorities respect federal law.

Louis Jaffe offered a fitting label for these new litigants. One of the great Realists, Wesley Hohfeld, had previously developed an elegant, symmetrical framework in which one party's rights were set over against an opposing party's correlative duties to respect rights.[16] Jaffe proposed that plaintiffs within the conventional, private-rights model of adjudication were "Hohfeldian" in the sense that they sought to litigate some question regarding their own legal status. The new "public" cases, then, must involve "non-Hohfeldian" plaintiffs, who had enough interest in litigation to give them an incentive to sue, but who did not press their own legal rights.[17] Over time, Americans would come to understand that dispute-resolution regarding private rights was not the whole of the judicial function and that "public rights" actions, pursued by non-Hohfeldian individuals and organizations, must also be included in the modern framework.[18] In the near term, however, the Supreme Court refused to modify its conception of adjudication to include the new public-rights cases.

The private-rights model was perfectly satisfying to the Old Court, whose commitment to the protection of economic liberty against regulation I explored in Chapter One.[19] Surprisingly, progressives, too, accepted the private-rights understanding of the judicial function, even though it permitted the subjects of regulation to sue, but denied judicial review to citizens who were otherwise affected by governmental programs. Of course, progressives had no particular sympathy for corporations attacking economic regulation at the hands of the federal administrative agencies established by the New Deal. If they could have put an end to Social Darwinism behind the mask of constitutional law, they would have. Having failed to keep the Old Court from second-guessing regulators on behalf of industrialists and corporations, however, progressives were not about to open regulation to yet another line of judicial attack. Since progressives coalesced with Formalists in support of the private-rights model, the notion that the judicial function was limited to adjudicating private rights was embraced by disparate elements of American jurisprudence.[20]

Locus Standii

Early on, Justice Brandeis invoked the private-rights model to deny access to the federal courts. In an obscure opinion for the Court in 1922, for example, Brandeis declined to consider a taxpayer's claim against a spending program, because the plaintiff's "alleged interest in the question" was insufficient to support the lawsuit.[21] Even then, Brandeis said nothing about "standing." That term probably derives from the Latin phrase *locus standii* (a "place to stand"), used in Britain to describe one's capacity to "stand" before Parliament to address a proposed bill. It had previously appeared in numerous Supreme Court opinions, but it had never been developed into a major constitutional prerequisite for initial access to the federal courts.[22] Felix Frankfurter did not so much as mention standing in his treatise on the federal courts, published in 1928. It was Frankfurter, however, who began building on his mentor's preliminary work when he himself joined the Court. Within a decade, the Court had developed the conventional explanation for the private-rights model and appropriated the term "standing" for modern use.[23]

By Frankfurter's account, litigants had standing to be in federal court only if they asserted a "legal interest," that is, a right, either known to the common law or created by statute or the Constitution itself.[24] That was a bit circular: a litigant had to show that she had a legal claim before she would be allowed into a federal court to present that very claim. Moreover, Frankfurter's approach merged standing, so defined, with the *constitutional* requirements for the exercise of federal judicial power. Pursuant to Article III of the Constitution, the federal courts were empowered only to decide "cases" or "controversies." To Justice Frankfurter, that meant actions brought by litigants with standing, that is, private legal rights to be vindicated in the resolution of disputes. By limiting the federal courts to the resolution of such disputes, according to Frankfurter, Article III ensured that unelected federal judges would not interfere unnecessarily with policies adopted by the other branches of the national government or by the states. This linkage between private-rights standing doctrine and the Constitution was consistent with the Legal Process account of the relationship between courts and democratically elected legislatures, as well as with Frankfurter's objective to accommodate New Deal regulators within the constitutional scheme.[25] Yet it bore dire consequences for the availability of the federal courts to force government officials to comply with federal law when *public* rights were at stake.

Persons Aggrieved

Standing decisions tending to limit judicial oversight of New Deal programs were only partially successful. For Congress, the very body that had legislated regulators into existence, also presumed to prescribe the circumstances in which their actions could be reviewed in the federal courts. For example, the Communications Act of 1934 granted access to the courts to anyone who was "aggrieved" by the actions of the Federal Communications Commission. Other statutes specified similar standing rules regarding other agencies. It would have been possible to read most of those statutes to create new legal rights on the order of the common law rights that sufficed for standing in the Court's framework.[26] Thus standing might have been ceded to persons aggrieved by agency action on the ground that they were enforcing their own statutory rights. After all, Justice Frankfurter had recognized standing grounded not only in common law rights, but also in rights created by statute or the Constitution. Yet observers read such statutes to have a different purpose.

Statutory grants of standing were read not to create new substantive rights, but rather to confer only *litigation* rights on the part of persons aggrieved, that is, standing to sue in the federal courts in order to force government to conform to the law. These plaintiffs would be non-Hohfeldian. They would not have to be enforcing their own rights, but could represent public rights. Another prominent Realist, Judge Jerome Frank, analogized such plaintiffs to the Attorney General of the United States, whom Congress often authorized to represent the public in court.[27] According to Frank, aggrieved persons were *private* attorneys general, entitled to seek judicial help in holding agencies within their lawful powers, but without rights of their own to vindicate. Justice Frankfurter, for his part, seemed to agree—despite his previous insistence that Article III conditioned standing on a litigant's personal, private, substantive rights.[28] Congress' constitutional ability to confer standing on non-Hohfeldian plaintiffs came to a head with the enactment of §10(a) of the Administrative Procedure Act in 1946:

> A person suffering legal wrong because of agency action, or adversely affected or aggrieved by agency action within the meaning of a relevant statute, is entitled to judicial review thereof.[29]

Some observers understood this statute to codify existing standing doctrine.[30] Others read it to recognize standing whenever a complainant was merely "adversely affected" by agency action.[31] The Warren Court split the difference. The Court agreed that litigants asserting common law rights, or rights based on statute or the Constitution, had standing under the "legal wrong" test stated in the first line of §10(a). Since the second line allowed standing on behalf of persons who were merely "adversely affected or aggrieved," however, the Court concluded that Congress had dispensed with previous standing doctrine—which had typically demanded a legal right in every case. No longer must a litigant always claim violation of such a right. Rather, §10(a) conferred standing if the litigant (1) suffered "injury in fact" from the action of which she complained and (2) was "arguably within the zone of interests to be protected or regulated by the statute or constitutional guarantee in question." The first of these requirements (injury in fact) was a constitutional prerequisite. The second (the litigant's obligation to bring her interest within the protection of a statute or constitutional provision) was a discretionary rule established by Congress.[32]

This formulation bristled with implications. The Warren Court was not merely resolving an ambiguity in §10(a) that had divided a few law professors. It was rethinking the entire question of standing as it had developed under the hand of Legal Process theorists like Justice Frankfurter and was using the occasion provided by §10(a) to devise a different analysis more compatible with the role the federal courts were assuming in the 1960s. In contrast to Frankfurter, who feared that loose standing rules might allow citizen suits to undercut the modern regulatory state introduced by the New Deal, the Warren Court recognized that regulators, too, required supervision to ensure that they performed as they should. The complacency of Legal Process was now giving way to a new insistence on federal judicial activism to hold governmental power within bounds. Henceforth, a litigant would be able at least to get into a federal court on the basis of an *injury,* traceable to an alleged violation of a federal statute or constitutional guarantee under which the litigant claimed arguable *protection,* short of a legal *right.*

Note what this general account of standing accomplished. First, the Court recast the assertion of a private right as merely a sufficient, but not a necessary, requirement for standing. In future, the federal courts would still be confined to resolving actual disputes. At least initially, however, those disputes might be over a plaintiff's factual injury—an interest, but not necessarily a legally protected interest. Second, the Court distinguished between the preliminary question whether a litigant would be allowed inside the door and the further question whether, once inside, she would prevail on the merits of some legal claim. Standing, at least in the constitutional sense, now depended on the existence of injury in fact, not on a threshold demonstration of a legal right. In this, standing was conceptualized as a matter of sound judicial methodology: an injured party promised to be a self-interested adversary who could be counted on for zealous advocacy. Third, the Court raised the possibility that a litigant who gained a foothold in federal court on the basis of an injury (rather than a right) might enforce some structural limitation on governmental power, that is, a limitation that could not easily be described as a personal *right* at all— either the plaintiff's right or anybody else's. Finally, the Court marked off the role that Congress could play in the standing drama. Standing doctrine was bifurcated. Only the injury-in-fact element was constitutional; anything beyond that was prudential and thus subject to congressional judgment.

There can be little doubt that the Warren Court expanded citizen access to the federal courts. Justice Frankfurter's more restrictive approach to standing was discarded. In its place, the Warren Court established a new structure that would allow workers, consumers, competitors, and others into federal court to press both statutory and constitutional claims. About the time the Court adopted the bifurcated standing framework in the context of §10(a), it applied the same approach to lawsuits brought by taxpayers seeking to enforce the establishment clause against state officials who used public funds to support religious activities. According to the Warren Court, taxpayers in such cases suffered injury in fact, inasmuch as their pecuniary interest in tax payments was affected. They brought themselves within the zone of interests protected by the establishment clause because, as I mentioned in connection with the lighted-cross case, the chief purpose of that clause was to prohibit the taxation of citizens for the benefit of religion. Previously, the establishment clause had been virtually unenforceable in the federal courts, for want of anyone with a private-rights basis for standing. In the open atmosphere of the 1960s, however, citizens asserting only the largely theoretical financial interest in the portion of their tax bills related to spending for religious purposes were permitted to enforce the Constitution as it never had been enforced before.[33] On this same principle, Gene Guerrero had standing in the lighted-cross case not because he asserted a private right under the establishment clause, but because the cross interfered with (injured in fact) his hiking and camping plans.

During the Warren Court period, the constitutional standing requirement of injury in fact was met by any serious allegation of interest, and the prudential, zone-of-interest test was even less troublesome to would-be litigants. Accordingly, citizens were allowed into the federal forum in order to vindicate not their own private rights, but public rights to the enforcement of federal statutes and, indeed, the Constitution itself.[34] All that changed, however, after the mid-1970s. In the hands of the Warren Court, bifurcated standing doctrine opened the doors of the federal courts to public rights litigation; in the hands of the Nixon and Reagan appointees, by contrast, standing rules tend to close those same doors. Moreover, inasmuch as the newly constituted Court typically rests its decisions on the primary, constitutional elements of standing, this Court reaches results that Congress is said to be unable to affect legislatively.

Right of Action

The notion that standing is partly a constitutional requirement undergirds the Supreme Court's treatment of federal statutes authorizing the enforcement of federal law by means of private lawsuits. When Congress enacts statutes of that kind, it is quite clear that the lawsuits it has in mind will typically be brought in federal court. Nevertheless,

Congress' decision to create a private "cause of action" or "right of action" to enforce federal law is said to be different from a decision to grant standing.[35] Let's pause for a moment over this curious difference between having a right of action to enforce a legal standard through litigation in *some* court and having standing to do so in a *federal* court.

It is well settled that Congress is relatively free to determine the manner in which federal law will be implemented. Henry Hart made this claim in his famous dialogue, and it has been largely unquestioned ever since.[36] With respect to federal statutes, the theory is that since Congress itself enacts legislation, Congress may also control the way in which officials and citizens are forced to conform their behavior to meet a statute's demands. The "greater" power to establish (or to decline to establish) federal statute law is said to include the "lesser" power to specify the means of its enforcement.[37] Of course, congressional authority for choosing enforcement machinery for the Constitution cannot be justified on this ground—for the obvious reason that Congress is not the source of constitutional guarantees. Still, somebody has to decide how the Constitution will be implemented. And since Congress has authority for fixing federal court jurisdiction in constitutional cases, it has long been assumed that the selection of enforcement devices is also a matter of legislative judgment.

A lawsuit by a private citizen asserting that the defendant has violated federal law is only one option. There are others. In addition to private suits, or as an alternative, Congress may establish criminal sanctions or may charge the Attorney General or an administrative agency with responsibility to see that the law is followed. As long as the mechanism selected is roughly as effective as lawsuits would be, the Court insists that Congress' choice will be sustained. This is to say, Congress may provide for the effectuation of federal law by private lawsuits, in which case such lawsuits are clearly permissible. Indeed, with respect to constitutional claims, the Court typically infers a private right of action from the relevant provision. Alternatively, Congress may prohibit private lawsuits, in which case the Court will go along—provided some other, comparable enforcement device is established to take up the slack.[38]

It is also clear that Congress may confer standing on litigants. Everybody who sues in federal court must meet the primary standing requirements the Court ascribes to Article III, but Congress is free either to establish or to sweep aside other standing barriers. The Court conceives of these two legislative powers (the power to authorize private lawsuits to enforce federal law and the power to confer standing to sue in federal court—within constitutional limits) as separate and distinct. The two *are* conceptually different. In the former instance, Congress is making choices from a menu of potential enforcement mechanisms. If it selects private litigation, there is nothing to say (necessarily) that the lawsuits so authorized will be brought in federal rather than state court. In the latter instance, Congress is deciding who, among those with constitutional standing, should be permitted to sue in a federal court. Nevertheless, from Congress' point of view the two choices at hand run into each other. It would make little sense to authorize lawsuits that plaintiffs will typically wish to press in federal court and not, at the same time, to do what Congress can to permit those who are authorized to sue actually to do so in the federal forum. Still, when Congress prescribes private lawsuits as a means of enforcing federal law, the Court draws no inference with respect to the standing of those who are entitled to sue in *some* court.

Take, for example, the Declaratory Judgment Act of 1934, which provides that "[i]n a case of actual controversy within its jurisdiction," a federal court "may declare the rights . . . of any interested party seeking such declaration."[39] The Court has held that the reference to an "actual controversy" signals that the right of action established by the Declaratory Judgment Act assumes that the plaintiff has standing on some independent basis. Moreover, the debates from which the Act emerged reveal that proponents did not conceive of this statute as touching standing. Still, given that litigants seeking to enforce federal law via private lawsuits in federal court must have both a right of action and standing, it is not at all clear how Congress can sensibly have chosen to create the one while remaining wholly indifferent to the other. Indeed, if we did not know the history behind the Declaratory Judgment Act, and if we did not bring to our reading of it the Court's distinction between a right of action and standing, we might well construe this statute to confer on "interested" parties both a right to enforce federal law by suing for a declaratory judgment and standing to do so in federal court.

Or consider the Ku Klux Klan Act, which has appeared in these pages before:

> Every person who, under color of any statute, ordinance, regulation, custom, or usage, of any State or Territory or the District

of Columbia, subjects, or causes to be subjected, any citizen of the United States or other person within the jurisdiction thereof to the deprivation of any rights, privileges, or immunities secured by the Constitution and laws, shall be liable to the party injured in an action at law, suit in equity, or other proper proceeding for redress.

The Court interprets this provision, now 42 U.S.C. §1983, to authorize plaintiffs who claim a deprivation of federal rights at the hands of persons acting under color of state law to sue for relief in either federal or state court.[40] Coming to the matter afresh, one might have thought that such a permission to sue would not only ensure that litigants can enforce federal rights through lawsuits, but would also confer standing on any citizen who fits §1983's specifications for potential plaintiffs. Here again, however, the Supreme Court conceives that litigants who wish to press §1983 actions have two hoops to jump through. They must bring themselves within the precise language of §1983 in order to act on the permission to sue this statute supplies, and they must independently establish standing if they wish to proceed in a federal court.[41]

Why is it that the Court does not acknowledge that these two ideas (a right of action and standing) run together, at least in practice—such that statutes like the Declaratory Judgment Act and §1983 are easily construed to address both? Two possible answers present themselves. First, the Rehnquist Court is deeply suspicious of lawsuits that aim to enforce individual and public rights against governmental power. Accordingly, in any given instance, the justices are loath to conclude that Congress has *either* created a right of action *or* awarded standing. If Congress is crystal clear on these points, the Court will go along, albeit grudgingly. If, however, a statute is ambiguous, the Court will usually choose a construction that minimizes the assistance it provides to potential litigants.[42] Second, the Court wants to remind the legislative branch that its authority with respect to standing is limited. If the Court were easily to read federal statutes to confer standing within their terms, Congress might get the idea that it is free both to authorize what lawsuits it wishes and to confer standing on whom it chooses—even on those who cannot satisfy the primary standing requirements the Court links to Article III. That, in turn, would test the Court's own ability to control access to the federal forum. It is by characterizing some standing rules as constitutional barriers that the

Court maintains its commanding role in this increasingly intricate play.[43]

The Court's qualms to one side, it remains quite clear that Congress can, at one and the same time, establish both a private right of action and standing—up to constitutional limits. Recall, moreover, that the constitutional requirements for standing are no longer tied to the legal arguments that plaintiffs can make once they are allowed into federal court. The usual rules against advancing generalized grievances or rights that belong to others are prudential standing rules, subject to congressional override. It follows that Congress can, if it likes, enact a single statute that empowers anyone with injury-in-fact standing to enforce any federal legal standard, constitutional or statutory, by suing in federal court and making *all* arguments respecting *any* alleged violation—whether or not the plaintiff's own rights are at stake.[44] Congress' conceded power thus to authorize citizens to enforce federal law on behalf of the public at large will figure prominently in the legislative proposal I will offer at the end of this chapter.

Floodgates

Turning now to the damage wrought in the name of standing, I want to emphasize that the Supreme Court has not (yet) developed its own prudential standing rules into difficult barriers to the federal courts.[45] In the main, the Court has built upon primary, constitutional standing rules, namely, that litigants must suffer some injury in fact, caused by the action under attack and likely to be redressed if the court orders relief. What the Court does in standing cases, it typically does in the name of Article III and insists cannot be undone by Congress.[46] In this, the Court has not operated in a vacuum. In the 1960s, Sam Ervin and Wayne Morse introduced bills that would have authorized taxpayers to enforce religious freedom in federal court.[47] And in the 1970s, Senators Edward Kennedy and Howard Metzenbaum proposed more ambitious "citizen standing" bills, supported by the Carter Administration.[48] None of those bills was enacted, but in their wake the Court has increasingly rested its standing decisions on the Constitution—as though to warn Congress to bow out.[49] In form, the three elements of primary standing doctrine (injury in fact, causation, and redressability) seem sensible enough. After all, *some* meaning has to be attached to the constitutional terms "case" and "controversy." On examination, however, these ideas prove to be flawed. In practice, they produce inconsistent, even incomprehensible, results; in principle, they lack persuasive power as interpretations of the Constitution. Let me first explain how primary standing doctrine works in the real world of litigation.

In some instances, the injury-in-fact requirement appears to have the minimal meaning that English grammar would demand. For example, when law students attacked an action by the Interstate Commerce Commission, the Court found it sufficient that the students alleged that the agency's action threatened recreational areas in Washington, D. C., that they used those areas, and that their enjoyment of the outdoors was impaired.[50] Standing, said the Court, is a matter of *fact* to be determined by examining plaintiffs' allegations. If government lawyers thought the students were lying about using the parks in Washington and the effects of the ICC action, they should have said so and asked for judgment on that basis.[51] As might have been expected, however, when the Court reached the merits of the students' claims, all relief was denied.[52] More often, injury in fact is difficult to establish. In another case, for example, the Court found the Sierra Club's allegations of factual injury inadequate. The Club attempted to sue on behalf of its members, but failed to allege that any such member actually used the wilderness area involved in the case. The Court dismissed for want of standing, insisting that no plaintiff appeared to suffer the necessary injury.[53]

Once the Court makes clear what allegations are required, plaintiffs can compensate. On remand, the Sierra Club amended its complaint to allege that particular members did use the area concerned and, on that basis, proceeded with the lawsuit. And recall Gene Guerrero's success in the lighted-cross case in Georgia. Alleging precisely the kind of injury that had been recognized in environmental cases in the Supreme Court, Guererro was able to get his foot in the door to make his establishment clause claim. Still, we should not conclude that the Court readily accepts artful pleading that gets claims into federal court when litigants mean to press vexing public questions.[54] Importantly, the Court refuses to accept as sufficient the one interest that many would think would be the most pertinent: plaintiffs' sincere interest in the observance of federal law. Every citizen can surely claim a legitimate commitment to the enforcement of the law, particularly the Constitution, against government officials who threaten its violation. Yet that kind of psychological or ideological interest is precisely what is insufficient to gain a foothold in federal court. It does not

matter that such injuries are *factual* in the sense that they can be alleged in good faith and demonstrated by evidence. These injuries are
not the kind of factual injuries the Court requires.[55]

In this way, federal calendars are cleansed of politically explosive
cases in which reform-minded plaintiffs advance federal claims. For
example, the Constitution states explicitly that "a regular Statement
and Account of the Receipts and Expenditures of all public Money
shall be published from time to time."[56] Yet citizens who are concerned that the Central Intelligence Agency's budget is never made
public have no sufficient injury in fact on which to base standing to
complain in the federal courts. Allegations that civic-minded people
need this kind of information in order to function politically, even to
vote, are said to be merely assertions of an impersonal concern that
government conform to the law.[57] For the same reason, citizens have
no standing to challenge members of Congress who hold military
commissions in apparent violation of the Constitution, which states
that senators and representatives may not hold "any [other] office under the United States."[58] Cases such as these present ticklish issues for
the Court—issues that are avoided by way of restrictive standing rules.

We should not discount the sentiments on which such decisions
as these probably rest. There is something unappealing about the
meddler who barges in presuming to represent the general public
good. In a society as individualistic as ours, citizens are expected to
be self-sufficient. If they are not themselves complaining of their own
injuries, there may be a good reason for it. Perhaps parties who are
affected more concretely do not see that their lot will be enhanced by
litigation; perhaps they are content with things as they are and, if
asked, would object to interference by officious neighbors. In this
vein, it may be argued that precipitous litigation by interlopers may
produce ill-considered decisions that will frustrate those with more
material interests, if and when they proceed on their own.[59]

Even when *no one* appears to be personally injured in the required
way, the unsolicited volunteer may appear suspicious. The burdens of
litigation are heavy, and when someone is prepared to shoulder them,
something other than sincere altruism may be at work. Ideology may
appear to be an undesirable basis for litigation, even when serious
federal questions cannot otherwise be settled by the courts. In the CIA
and military commission cases, for example, the plaintiffs probably
were motivated not so much by their commitments to the legal claims
they actually presented as by their resistance to the power and influ-

ence of the CIA and the military services. Since many citizens do not share those concerns, the lawsuits could be said to press public rights only insofar as the public is always served when the Constitution is enforced. Of course, we have political institutions for advancing the general public interest in a representative, majoritarian manner. And if our intelligence activities need to be curbed, or our military services have too much influence, perhaps Congress is the body to take action, not the federal courts.[60] Finally, there is the "floodgates" problem. If people with no injuries of their own to redress are permitted to sue, the federal courts may be engulfed by a wave of frivolous lawsuits brought by political activists hoping to use the courts as a forum for their views, by unscrupulous manipulators hoping to obtain a settlement for the nuisance value of a legal action, or by disturbed inhabitants of the lunatic fringe—who may want to be in court for any reason or no reason at all. Our federal courts are valuable resources that we cannot afford to waste.

Understandable as these concerns may be, they offer no substantial justification for restrictive standing rules. If experience is any guide, the reason that citizens with more tangible injuries fail to sue is not that they choose, freely and knowingly, to forgo the pursuit of judicial relief. Far from it. They are discouraged by the costs and other burdens associated with lawsuits, which often outweigh any personal benefits that litigation might bring. Typically, the only litigants likely to press claims are those who respond to psychological and ideological stimuli, quite apart from the prospects of personal gain. The litigants that more generous standing doctrine would empower are not isolated individual dilettantes out for a frolic at the courthouse, but serious, sophisticated, and committed organizations that use litigation as an instrument for restraining governmental power regarding some of the most sensitive aspects of human life. This is true with respect both to individual rights cases and to cases in which structural limitations on governmental power are in issue—for instance, the CIA and military commission examples. As a general proposition, individual liberty is best served if the federal judiciary enforces whatever limits there may be on the authority of the other branches of the national government and the states. For if the judicial branch stands aloof, there will be nothing to check majoritarian excesses. The floodgates problem is grossly overdrawn. We scarcely need restrictive standing doctrine, with all its attendant drawbacks, in order to deal with nuisance litigation. The psychological burdens of suit forestall anything that might be labeled a wave of such lawsuits. Frivolous or abusive actions can be handled on a case-by-case basis.[61]

On a deeper level, concerns about "busybody suits" have their own conservative, ideological roots. Typically, the consequence of denying standing for litigation in the federal courts is to leave the field either to the state courts or (more likely) to private ordering or the politics practiced in the legislative and executive branches of federal or state government. In the latter quarters, public claims of right rarely succeed against private privilege. If, then, the federal courts are unavailable, the status quo will probably be maintained by dint of the forces that produced it in the first instance. That status quo will not often respond on its own even to compelling claims for redress. A catalyst is required. And if we find ourselves reassuring each other that things are just fine, that we should leave well-enough alone, and that we don't need self-appointed champions disrupting our affairs, it may well be time for some serious introspection. Complacency can be the haven of the comfortable. It was not so long ago that apologists for segregation in the Deep South insisted that things would get better if "outside agitators" would only go away.

The second leg of the Court's primary standing doctrine (the requirement that plaintiffs' injuries must be caused by the action under attack) is even more troublesome than the injury-in-fact rule. Originally, this requirement was stated in softer language and tied tightly to the ability of a federal court to do something for the plaintiff if he or she prevails in a lawsuit. Chief Justice Burger said that the only question is whether the injuries asserted for standing "fairly can be traced" to the conduct under challenge. Injuries are fairly traceable, he said, if the court can award relief that provides those injuries some redress.[62] This makes a certain amount of sense. If the root idea is that the federal courts can only decide genuine disputes, it seems necessary that something should turn on the result. Even the Warren Court's insistence that plaintiffs have a personal stake in the outcome conceded this point. A litigant must stand to get something out of a case, or it really isn't a case at all.

Having introduced the notion that injuries must be linked to the defendant's conduct as a matter going to the redressability of a plaintiff's injury, however, the Court has now both stiffened its language and reworked its logic. No longer is it said that injuries must be "traceable to" the conduct under attack. Injuries must, instead, be "caused" by that conduct. Moreover, the Court has torn causation

loose from redressability and now treats the two as independent elements of constitutional standing doctrine. Born as just another way
of making the point that plaintiffs' injuries must be susceptible to judicial *relief* from the federal courts, the causation requirement has
grown up to be an extraordinarily important hurdle for anyone seeking initial *access* to the federal forum.

Sometimes, a sufficient causal chain proves easy enough to find.
Consider again the suit brought by law students in the District of Columbia. The students complained that the ICC had failed to prepare
an environmental impact statement before imposing a surcharge on
railroad rates. In order to get to the merits of that claim, the Court
accepted allegations that the surcharge would keep freight rates high,
which would increase the cost of recycling materials, which would
diminish the use of recycled products in the District, which would
increase the pollution in local parks, which would diminish the students' enjoyment of those facilities. This, of course, was a speculative
exercise—an artful sham for getting through the federal courthouse
door. The Court accepted it in order to reach the merits and, ultimately, to deny relief. In another case, neighbors alleged that the fishing in local lakes would be ruined if the water was heated or polluted
by a nuclear power plant planned for the area. Their claim was not
that the construction of the plant was unlawful, albeit even that argument would have been imaginative. Instead, the plaintiffs claimed that
the Price-Anderson Act, which limited power company liability in the
case of nuclear accident, was unconstitutional. Here is how the causal
linkage necessary for standing was manufactured. But for the Act,
some subcontractors would not agree to work on the plant; but for
the participation of the subcontractors, the plant could not be built;
but for the plant, the lake water would not be heated and radiation
would be normal; but for warmer water and increased emissions, the
fishing would not be affected. The fish would be no less likely to bite
than they had always been. In reality, the lawsuit was brought by environmentalists hoping to get the Act struck down, to increase the risks
associated with nuclear plants, and thus to curb the spread of nuclear
power. It was opposed by developers, who wanted the Act upheld in
order to attract investors. After standing was sustained, the Court rejected the plaintiffs' claims on the merits, thus reassuring the industry.

If it is easy to identify and track questionable causal chains, consider how much easier it is to pick them apart. The obvious way to
accomplish this is to locate a link in the chain that can be broken if

some event does not occur as predicted. Causal chains that are contingent on actions by third parties are always vulnerable. In one recent case, a group of poor people attacked a change in the Internal Revenue Service's regulations governing hospitals. Previously, hospitals had been able to obtain advantageous tax treatment by offering a variety of services to the poor. Under the new ruling, it would be enough to provide only emergency treatment. The plaintiffs' injury was clear: the loss of free medical care. But since it could not be demonstrated (to the Court's satisfaction) that hospitals would respond to the change in the regulation by withdrawing nonemergency services, the causal link between the plaintiffs' injury and the IRS action broke down.[63]

In another illustration, a group of low-income people challenged the validity of a city zoning ordinance that allegedly prevented the construction of multifamily housing projects. The Court acknowledged that the denial of housing might constitute injury in fact, but since the plaintiffs had failed to allege that the ordinance had impeded some particular project to which they were prepared to move, the causal linkage between the ordinance and their injury was too weak.[64] Similarly, in yet another case the Court faulted the causal connection between black children's interest in desegregated public education and the failure on the part of the IRS to adopt effective standards for denying tax exemptions to private schools that discriminate. It wasn't clear (enough) that the IRS policy resulted in the award of sufficient exemptions to segregationst academies to have an effect on the ability of public schools to desegregate.[65]

Cases such as these have generated cynicism in the academic community. It frankly seems that when the Court is hostile to public-rights litigation, it demands exacting proof of causation. Elaborate allegations are not enough if the defendants contest the matter. Hearings are held; evidence is taken. Before long, most of the facts that plaintiffs would have to prove in order to win on the merits of their legal claims are fully explored at the standing stage of litigation—when the only issue is supposed to be injury, albeit injury caused by the defendant's behavior. It is as though the Court is smuggling Justice Frankfurter's model into the causation element of modern standing doctrine, confusing once again the threshold question of standing, which is now supposed to turn on injury alone, with the different question of right, which goes to the merits. Thus the Court may be deciding cases against plaintiffs on the merits of claims, but couching its decisions in the language of standing.[66]

The same is true of the redressability requirement, from which the causation rule emerged, but in which the Court now insists there is an independent barrier to standing. Where causation focuses on the links between a plaintiff's injury and the actions of the defendant claimed to be unlawful, redressability focuses on the connection between the injury and the relief a federal court would be able to provide if the plaintiff should prevail on the merits. Once again, some sort of redressability requirement makes sense. A plaintiff must have some chance to get something out of winning a lawsuit—if that lawsuit is to qualify as a constitutional "case" for the federal courts. Yet in the hands of current justices, redressability demands far more than a "reasonable likelihood" of effective relief; it demands something close to a guarantee. Contingencies that might frustrate a court's ability to cure plaintiffs' injuries if their legal claims prove meritorious quickly develop into reasons for refusing to allow plaintiffs to prove the merits of those claims in the first place.

In one recent case, environmentalists sued to force the Secretary of the Interior to consult with other agency heads regarding the effect of overseas construction projects on endangered species.[67] Assuming that the plaintiffs were right on the merits and that a federal court would decide that consultations were required by federal law, Justice Scalia nevertheless ordered the suit dismissed for want of standing in general and redressability in particular. Even if the court ordered the Secretary to consult with the other agencies, he said, those agencies were not themselves defendants and it was unclear that they would be legally bound to cooperate. Moreover, even if all the federal government's arms agreed to consider the effects of projects on endangered animals, the plaintiffs had failed to prove that officials in the foreign countries involved would pay any heed. The projects might proceed as planned, with the same injurious effects on the crocodiles, elephants, and leopards the plaintiffs claimed an interest in protecting.

On the one hand, this kind of reasoning with respect to redressability is indistinguishable from the reasoning the Court engages regarding causation. In any particular case, standing depends entirely on the choice the Court makes between two speculative exercises: either plaintiffs' predictions of what is likely to happen or defendants' anticipation that some contingency or other will frustrate effective judicial relief. These days, of course, governmental defendants typically enjoy the benefits of the justices' active imaginations. On the other hand, the Court's treatment of redressability reveals two different wrinkles.

First, the Court allows defendants, particularly government agencies, to affect the redressability issue unilaterally. In the case just mentioned, for example, Justice Scalia credited the Solicitor General's position—formed, no doubt, for purposes of the litigation at hand—that other agencies would not be legally obligated to consult with the Secretary, even if the Court ordered the Secretary to consult with *them*. In this way, federal officials were able to cloud the redressability picture by manipulating lines of authority over which they had immediate control. Writ large, Justice Scalia's analysis invites defendants to foil plaintiffs' attempts to gain a federal hearing for their claims simply by confusing the circumstances that will confront the court if it should decide that the plaintiffs are entitled to relief and turn its attention to redressing the injuries they have incurred. Suffice it to say, the country is not well served by a scheme that gives that kind of incentive to the very officials whose behavior is under challenge.

Second, the Court's analysis of redressability imports into standing doctrine an attention to the *form* of relief that plaintiffs hope to obtain from the court. Take another recent case—one involving the Los Angeles Police Department's use of life-threatening "choke holds" to subdue suspects.[68] After sixteen suspects had been killed by choke holds, one who survived sued for an injunction against their use in the future. The Supreme Court conceded that the plaintiff had suffered injury, causally linked to the use of the choke hold. Stopped for driving with a missing tail light, he had been grabbed by the neck and strangled into unconsciousness. On the basis of that episode, the plaintiff had standing to sue for monetary damages—money to compensate him for the physical injury he had already suffered. He lacked standing, however, to sue for an injunction that would prevent the reoccurrence of such episodes. Since, for the moment at least, he was no longer in the officer's death grip and thus did not need the court's assistance to get loose, and since he could not prove that he would be subjected to similar treatment again, the plaintiff asserted no injury that was redressable by the injunctive relief he sought.

Looked at another way, the choke hold case may really have presented a question under the mootness doctrine, the crux of which is that a court must be able to make a difference in the positions of the parties by awarding the relief requested.[69] The prospect of getting an injunction *would* have made a difference in the case, but only if the plaintiff had managed to file his federal lawsuit while the officer's arm was still around his throat. The Chief Justice has expressed doubt that the federal courts are constitutionally barred from treating moot issues.[70] In the wake of the choke hold case, however, the mootness doctrine seems to be another face of injury-in-fact standing under Article III: litigants must have constitutional standing at the outset of litigation and must maintain that standing consistently until their cases are resolved. Mootness is thus standing "set in a time frame."[71]

Primary standing rules overrun not only mootness, but ripeness as well—notwithstanding that the considerations associated with the ripeness requirement would scarcely seem to support the constitutionalization of that doctrine.[72] The idea in ripeness is, first, to avoid premature adjudication on the basis of contingencies that may not occur and, second, to postpone litigation in order that the legal claims that courts ultimately consider are properly presented on a good factual record. Those considerations have little, if anything, to do with the identity and interests of the parties, or even (necessarily) with the existence of actual, adverse disputes. Nevertheless, the Supreme Court treats ripeness as a threshold inquiry into whether plaintiffs present a live case or controversy within the meaning of Article III.[73] Accordingly, not only the form of relief available in federal litigation, but the timing of federal adjudication, is collapsed into primary standing doctrine.[74]

Cases and Controversies

Even if we put aside concerns that standing doctrine seems infinitely manipulable, there are other problems aplenty with which to deal. The Court nowhere explains why some standing rules are deemed primary and constitutional, while others are open to prudential judgment, albeit the justices acknowledge that the values that are supposed to be served by standing are the same at both levels.[75] The constitutional aspects of standing are said to derive from the text of the Constitution, federalism, and the separation of powers. Yet none of these explanations is genuinely satisfying.

The injury/causation/redressability framework is hardly spelled out in Article III, which only limits federal judicial power to "cases" or "controversies." We may concede that federal judges cannot very well come to the office in the way that legislators do (or, at least, can)—sifting through proposals for new law to create in order to advance the public interest as they see fit. The model of adjudication as the resolution of disputes retains a strong hold on contemporary jurisprudence.[76] Even so, the idea of restricting courts to the enforcement and incremental development of existing law, profound as it may be as a matter of political theory, is of little value in the selection of the plaintiffs for whom the federal courts may exercise their power. Article III calls for a "case," but does not itself define a "case" by reference to standing rules.

The history behind Article III is scarcely more useful. As best anyone can tell, very little was said at the Constitutional Convention about the circumstances in which federal courts might act. Historians point to James Madison's statement that the case-or-controversy language in Article III was meant to limit judges to "cases of a Judiciary Nature."[77] But that, again, only restates the question. If Madison intended to incorporate previous experience in England and the American states, his reference cuts against the notion that cases must always involve litigants with personal interests to vindicate. The writ practice in which both English and American courts engaged apparently respected no such rigid limits.

We get no more help from the practices the courts have followed for two hundred years.[78] Many state appellate courts routinely issue advisory opinions and always have. And today the Supreme Court's authority to choose the cases it will decide amounts, in substance, to an ability to set its own agenda. This, one would think, is the very kind of thing that should raise constitutional questions under the Court's standing decisions.[79] Of course, the Court needs discretion regarding its docket in order to perform its crucial function: the final, authoritative declaration of the meaning of federal law. We must not forget, however, that the case-or-controversy requirement the Court purports to be interpreting in the standing cases applies to all federal courts, including the Supreme Court itself.

The Court sometimes offers a functional definition of cases and controversies. By this account, the injury requirement ensures that a litigant has "such a personal stake in the outcome" of a lawsuit "as to assure that concrete adverseness that sharpens the presentation of issues."[80] Only if claims are "framed with the necessary specificity," contested with "the necessary adverseness," and pursued with "the necessary vigor" can we be confident that they will be presented in a "form traditionally thought to be capable of judicial resolution."[81] All this is appealing enough. The federal courts cannot conduct their own investigations and must rely on the parties to present the evidence and arguments on both sides.[82] Yet the kind of injury that is both necessary and sufficient these days does not ensure competent presentation at all. Indeed, if skillful advocacy is the issue, the ideological plaintiffs now excluded by standing doctrine should rather be preferred.[83] The New York–based NAACP Legal Defense and Education Fund is much more likely to build an effective challenge to racial segregation in the public schools in Alabama than is a single local child who suffers personal injury from discrimination.

Some recent decisions appear to rest on federalism, specifically a concern that the federal courts are ill-equipped to deal with local matters. The zoning and housing cases are examples.[84] True, the Court enforces standing rules in the name of federalism primarily when there is no relevant federal statute in view, and thus no evidence that Congress wants litigants to have access to the federal forum. When legislation *is* implicated in a case, the Court steps back a bit and gives Congress substantial room. Still, the Court refuses to defer entirely to the legislative branch and concedes only that Congress can eliminate prudential standing barriers that the Court itself would otherwise adopt in light of its own concerns about federalism. Constitutional standing rules are said still to control. In other contexts, federalism issues are for the legislative branch; if the judgment to be made is whether national, as opposed to state, governmental power should be invoked, that judgment is for Congress. If the states object, they may press their views in the political process. This is true of legislative decisions to displace substantive local rules with national standards; there is no self-evident reason why it is not equally true of decisions to authorize the federal courts to act.[85]

Finally, the Court maintains that its standing doctrine is rooted in the separation-of-powers principle, implied in the Constitution's tripartite structure, the insulation of federal judges from politics, and the threat to democracy when unelected judges second-guess majoritarian policies.[86] We do have a separate federal judicial power, exercised by unelected judges who enjoy life tenure. But the idea that standing is grounded in that structural arrangement marks a sharp departure from precedent. The Warren Court held that standing speaks only to whether would-be litigants are the proper parties to bring suit in federal court and left any concerns that the federal courts may be asked to muck about in the affairs of other branches to the political question doctrine. By contrast, the Court now sitting sees the separation of powers as the "single basic idea" behind *constitutional* standing requirements.[87]

Of course, we might have anticipated that the current Court would see separation-of-powers issues in these cases. This Court recognizes that the federal courts must override isolated actions by the elected branches, at least on occasion. Yet it shrinks from any attempt to use judicial power to make a dramatic difference in the way the federal government conducts itself on a daily basis. The Court resists, accordingly, when plaintiffs sue federal administrative authorities, alleging not only that particular actions are unlawful, but also that the defendants have failed to *take* appropriate action to meet their duties under the Constitution or a federal statute. In such cases, here again we encounter grave suspicions about non-Hohfeldian private attorneys general, who complain not that federal officers are regulating *them* unlawfully, but rather that government is *failing* to regulate *"someone else"* as it ought.[88]

If public-rights cases seeking affirmative governmental action only operated as a check on federal legislative power, there would be a handy response to the separation-of-powers argument. For if Congress expressly authorizes private litigants to invoke judicial power, it scarcely seems persuasive for the Supreme Court to refuse to cooperate on the ground that, by accepting lawsuits so authorized, the federal courts would impermissibly invade the legislative province—barging (by invitation) through an open door. The acceptance of citizen standing in public-rights cases may alter a bit the relations between the judicial and legislative branches. Yet if that is what Congress wishes, it is hard to claim that the justices know better. Just as the Court should defer to Congress with respect to federalism questions, it also should leave the balance of national judicial and legislative powers to political resolution.

The issue is more complex to the extent that public-rights lawsuits threaten federal executive power. In one sense, executive objections to public-rights suits can also be met by the argument from consent. If Congress were to pass a bill purporting to confer standing on citizens in general, it would probably become law only if the president were to sign it—thus, at least formally, approving its content. A truly popular measure can be enacted over presidential veto, however, and in this instance something of that sort might occur. Congress might want to spur the executive branch to implement programs about which the president is not enthusiastic, and thus might wish to foster lawsuits that otherwise would be dismissed for lack of standing. With the potential for some tension between the legislative and executive branches in mind, then, we should not be surprised if the Rehnquist Court deploys primary standing doctrine to protect recalcitrant executive authorities from being called to account in the federal courts. It does just that.[89]

In this, the Court baldly denies Congress the ability to engage judicial power to ensure that the executive *does* execute when there is a duty to do so. For the plaintiffs in public-rights cases do not attempt to force the president's hand in a field in which he enjoys independent constitutional authority to act (or not) as he chooses. Suits that try to do that can be dismissed under the political question doctrine. By contrast, the public-rights lawsuits I have been discussing attempt to force executive officers to carry out legal responsibilities, typically prescribed by Congress. If a federal department or agency is doing its duty, then public-rights plaintiffs will lose on the merits; if not, the courts should demand compliance. Either way, it hardly makes sense to frustrate litigation in the first instance and thus to release the executive from any formal check at all, either by the courts or by Congress. A rule of that kind can be defended only if the executive branch has the prerogative to neglect its legal mandates and answer for its behavior only to the electorate—not to the law. I have little doubt that this is precisely the view that some members of this Court take of the matter. But I dare hope that most of us have less faith in unbridled executive power. Here, too, the Supreme Court simply has no business reading the Constitution to trump a politically accountable congressional decision to authorize the federal courts to accept lawsuits that will ensure that the executive agents of the national government conform their behavior to federal law. It scarcely needs to be added that there is no basis for letting the rigidity the Court exhibits in cases involving federal officials spill over into cases in which citizens challenge the action (or inaction) of state officers. In that context, of course, the prerogatives of the presidency are not implicated.

Finally, even if we give something to the argument that Congress should not be able to consent to suits that threaten executive authority, such a claim could make sense only at a level of generality far removed from the Court's cases. Nothing in the general conception of the separation of powers begets the intricate standing rules the Court has developed. Here, with respect to the current Court's standing doctrine, just as early in this century with respect to the Old Court's economic due process, loosely conceived abstractions do not deliver answers to concrete problems. The justices themselves are responsible for what they do in the name of standing. They do not simply give effect to arid logic; they exercise judgment. When Congress explicitly authorizes the federal courts to settle legal questions, it simply will not do to respond that the separation-of-powers principle establishes the injury/causation/redressability formulation which, in application, forbids those courts to act.[90]

All this talk of constitutional impediments comes to naught. Congress can set the federal courts free to enforce federal law, and it can do so without worrying that it is defiling the Constitution. I must pause a moment over recent appeals for doctrinal reform, but I will shortly return to the legislative path out of this frightful forest.

Rights Again

Some good scholarship has been done of late in hopes of persuading the Supreme Court to alter standing doctrine. The popular idea at the moment is that modern standing analysis should be abandoned and that Justice Frankfurter's rights-based framework should be resurrected in its place. The Court should cease conceiving of standing as a threshold check on federal judicial power, demanding injury in fact, causation, redressability, and perhaps other prerequisites before litigants are permitted in the door. Instead, it is argued, standing and the substance of claims should be united once again. In statutory and constitutional cases alike, every issue should be conceived as part of the merits of the lawsuit, and every such issue on the merits should be determined simply by construing the relevant statute or constitutional provision, together with any additional action by Congress in point, for instance, a statutory grant of standing. In cases in which plaintiffs attempt to enforce federal statutes, whatever Congress prescribes goes. Whoever Congress allows to sue can sue, raising whatever claims and seeking whatever relief Congress permits. The same should hold in constitutional cases, by this account, although Congress should not be allowed to ask the courts to decide political questions or to render advisory opinions.[91]

This approach is attractive, inasmuch as it would introduce a modicum of intellectual integrity into a field where, at the moment, clear thinking is in short supply. The courts would need only to interpret the statutes or constitutional provisions before them. For example, the decisions allowing taxpayers to attack public spending for religious purposes could be reconceived. Now, they are understood to hold that taxpayers have a pecuniary interest in tax payments and come roughly within the zone of protection provided by the establishment clause—and thus can get into federal court to press establishment clause claims. Alternatively, the same decisions might be understood to mean that the establishment clause grants taxpayers not only a right to be free of taxation for the benefit of religion, but also a private right to sue in federal court. The current ambiguity surrounding "right of action" statutes would also be resolved. By this account, all three ideas I have been discussing (standing, a right of action, and the merits) become one.

It is puzzling, however, that anyone should suggest that the explicit revival of the private-rights model of standing would advance the enforcement of federal substantive rights in federal court. How is it, one may ask, that a return to Frankfurter can be advisable, provided only that we acknowledge what Frankfurter himself never would: that if standing is grounded in a private legal right, it must be understood as part of the merits of a lawsuit? The only promising side to this new edition of the private-rights model is that the academicians who propound it would identify ample legal rights in federal statutes and constitutional provisions alike. Just as they would read the establishment clause to embody all the substantive and litigation rights needed to support federal court orders invalidating aid to parochial schools, they would read other statutes and constitutional provisions to confer all the rights necessary for the effective judicial enforcement of federal law generally.

But nobody thinks that the Rehnquist Court would do that. Indeed, proponents concede that the return to Frankfurter they envision would be unlikely to produce results much different from those generated by the Court's current approach. Of course, the primary standing rules the Court has fashioned already amount, in some cases at least, to Frankfurter's framework—notwithstanding that the injury-in-fact requirement is said to flow from the Warren Court's analysis rejecting Frankfurter. The Court's extensive examination of plaintiffs' allegations of injury, causation, and redressability look very much like a search for a private right *before* someone is allowed into federal court. This is why a return to the private-rights explanation of standing would fit existing precedents so well. No, we are not promised better results if standing is reconceptualized along these lines—only clearer arguments and opinions.

It is not enough that judicial opinions might be made more elegant in form. Critics of current standing doctrine would do better to work with what we have. The Court at least says it is concerned about a range of institutional, structural, and methodological considerations: the presentation of issues in an adversary context, federalism, the separation of powers, and so forth. These considerations find expression in the treatment of standing as a threshold question, anterior to the merits. If the Court were to discard the language of standing, plaintiffs still would get unfavorable decisions, but all the background considerations that now go into judgments purporting to dismiss for want of standing would find their way into substantive law. Once that happened, there would be no way for Congress to retrieve anything from this business. Bad results would be locked into bad interpretations of substantive federal rights. If, however, institutional, structural, and methodological considerations continue to be treated under the heading of standing, their ill effects can be ameliorated legislatively. In some instances, Congress can strip them away entirely. If this is done, we still must expect restrictive opinions on the meaning of federal rights from the Supreme Court in the near term. But by marginalizing the concerns that have skewed standing doctrine over the last twenty years, we will have cleared the decks for better things in the future.

Citizens

When Congress fashions a new legislative package regarding justiciability, it would be desirable to include a statement of legislative findings. Such findings do not formally become part of the statute the courts are asked to implement and thus may be played down, even ignored. Again, however, the norms of statutory construction can be influential.[92] Initiatives supported by President Carter in the 1970s employed findings, and a new bill should as well. I suggest some language in a note.[93]

Next, a new section of the Judicial Code should be enacted to address standing problems forthrightly:

(a) Unless excepted by law, any provision of federal law shall be enforceable by private civil action commenced in or removed to a district court of the United States of proper jurisdiction.

(b) In a private civil action of the kind specified in subsection (a), any citizen affected by conduct alleged to violate federal law shall have standing to—

(1) file and maintain the action in the district court and on review in the appropriate court of appeals and the Supreme Court of the United States;

(2) raise, present evidence regarding, and advocate any claim that the conduct complained of violates or will violate federal law, including but not limited to, a claim that the conduct violates or will violate—(i) a federal right of the plaintiff; (ii) a federal right of another not party to the plaintiff's civil action; or (iii) structural limitations on governmental power.

(c) A "citizen affected" under subsection (b) is a citizen of the United States who alleges that he or she has been, is now, or will in the future be affected in fact by the conduct complained of. It shall be sufficient if the citizen alleges that his or her economic, esthetic, health, safety, or other personal interests, or his or her ideological or psychological interests in seeing that conduct conforms to federal law, have been, are, or will be affected, irrespective of whether the same or similar interests are shared by any number of others.

(d) A citizen is affected "by" conduct under subsection (b) if he or she alleges facts which, if true, establish a connection between an interest specified in subsection (c) and the conduct such that, if the plaintiff is successful on the merits, judicial relief is reasonably likely to redress that interest. It shall not be necessary to allege that the conduct caused an injury to such an interest. It shall be sufficient to allege that some form of relief would contribute to remedying or mitigating the injury.

It is apparent that by enacting this proposal, Congress would summon all the power at its disposal to prevent restrictive standing doctrine from thwarting federal adjudication of federal questions. The proposed statute would not create substantive private rights, which can be the basis for standing under the Court's decisions and, indeed, even under the private-rights model that preceded those decisions. This measure would create *litigation* rights only—both the right to enforce federal law through private litigation and standing to do so in federal court. The Carter Administration bill was drafted differently. That bill took the existing body of standing law as the baseline and then sliced off three particularly troubling rules: the causation and

redressability requirements and the usual ban on generalized grievances.[94] Justice Douglas once urged Congress to be more affirmative—
to set the Court's cases to one side and simply to establish a "conclusive presumption" that all citizens who file lawsuits in federal court
have "proper standing."[95] The provision I propose takes the affirmative tack, but deals explicitly with the intricacies of current standing
doctrine. Congress cannot address something as complex and politically sensitive as standing by enacting a single-sentence statute. The
wiser course is not a simple standing statute, but a complicated statute
that will simplify standing.

Subsection (a) establishes a general rule allowing private lawsuits to
enforce federal statutory and constitutional law, but then provides for
separate enactments by which Congress may make exceptions. This
would reverse the current rule with respect to federal statutes, which
has it that private rights of action do *not* exist unless Congress clearly
authorizes them. Congress may wish to establish alternative enforcement machinery for some regulatory measures or to fashion special
rules for private lawsuits as a supplement to the work of administrative agencies or like entities. The private suits this proposal contemplates would not, then, displace the comprehensive schemes now in
place for particularized programs or the timing and other procedural
rules governing judicial review of formal agency action.[96] To ensure
that the federal courts are generally available, however, the default
position should be the reverse of what it is currently.

The blanket authorization for private lawsuits to enforce the Constitution is consistent with current law, which, in turn, reflects our
experience with such suits. In the 1960s, Senator Ervin was unable to
persuade Congress to authorize taxpayer actions raising establishment
claims, in part because it was feared that lawsuits might interfere with
other systems for ensuring that federal money was not spent on religion.[97] Since 1968, when the Warren Court recognized taxpayer
standing in establishment clause cases without the aid of legislation,
we have had substantial experience with private suits in that field.
There is no evidence that the fears expressed over Ervin's bill have been
realized. Not only establishment clause lawsuits, but all constitutional
lawsuits, can properly be approved wholesale by a single provision. In
these cases, unlike cases involving complex federal statutes, there is
no special technical intricacy in the substantive standards to be enforced, such that Congress may think it wise to rely on agency expertise. With respect to constitutional cases, moreover, claims tend to fall

under a few particularly fertile provisions, for example, the Bill of Rights (including the establishment clause) and the fourteenth amendment. Accordingly, private lawsuits can safely be approved en masse and then complemented by official enforcement actions by, for example, the Civil Rights Division of the Justice Department.

Subsection (a) overlaps with §1983, which already authorizes suits against state officers for violations of federal rights, and, in so doing, cleans up some pesky technical difficulties that have troubled §1983 as an enforcement mechanism for federal statutes.[98] Apart from the Declaratory Judgment Act, Congress has never enacted a right-of-action statute similar to §1983 for suits claiming unlawful conduct by federal officers. Inasmuch as subsection (a) is not limited to suits against defendants acting under color of state law, this proposal fills a longstanding statutory gap.[99] Subsection (b), in turn, weds the private rights of action created by subsection (a) to the standing of would-be litigants to press their lawsuits in federal court. If everyone agreed that the existence of a right of action and standing can be merged, the two might be handled in a single paragraph. But since these matters are now held apart, it is better to deal with them in separate provisions—but in such a back-to-back fashion as to make clear that the two hounds do, after all, hunt together. Under this provision, if Congress does not exempt some aspect of federal law from private lawsuits, then any citizen who satisfies the requirements for standing can sue in federal court to enforce that law. Similarly, if a citizen has standing to be a plaintiff in a federal court, it follows (under this proposal) that she has permission from Congress to bring a private civil action.

It is hard to resist the temptation to describe those on whom standing is to be conferred not as "citizens" but as "persons," and thus to include anyone for whom federal law operates—for example, resident aliens. The temptation *should* be resisted, however, inasmuch as the limitation to citizens strengthens the claim that the litigants this proposal envisions have a sufficient commitment to the enforcement of federal law to establish standing in the minimal, factual-injury sense. Aliens, too, may wish the law to be enforced. Yet it is safer to specify only citizens. Recall, too, that the lawsuits this statute will foster are not isolated actions by individuals who want to challenge public officials for their own idiosyncratic reasons. This legislation is not meant to open the floodgates and could not do so even if it had that purpose. Rather, the proposal means to make it substantially easier for public interest groups to press federal claims in the federal courts. The limitation to citizens will have no effect on the ability of the ACLU, the Washington Legal Foundation, or Public Citizen to launch public-rights litigation. Nor will the lawsuits these organizations bring be limited to claims that their own rights, or the rights of their members, are at stake. Subsection (b)(2) confers standing on citizens to proceed as non-Hohfeldian plaintiffs on behalf of the public. These private attorneys general would be able to raise any arguments, including claims that public officials have violated structural legal standards that beget no definite rights in individuals. In this, of course, the proposal sweeps away nonconstitutional standing barriers—just as the Court has said legislation can.

The further limitation of standing to citizens "affected" by the conduct they challenge addresses some of the specifics of current doctrine. Subsection (c) explains that citizens are affected even though their interests are shared by others; this, of course, eliminates the "generalized grievance" restriction to which the Court still occasionally refers. Moreover, the list of factual interests in subsection (c) suggests the kinds of injuries in fact on which standing can rest within the Court's current doctrine. It is important to draft the statute in this way in order to recognize and preserve standing for litigants whom the Court itself would allow into federal court in the absence of legislation. Of course, subsection (c) also specifies interests that the Court does not now accept as sufficient for standing, namely, citizens' unadorned concern that the law be followed. The Court has said that Congress cannot confer standing on such litigants. When Congress insists that it very well *can,* the constitutional issue will be joined. If the Court does not relent, then at least citizens who assert the kinds of interests the Court accepts will be unaffected. Still, once Congress gathers itself to address standing in a deliberate and clear way, fully appreciating the questions at stake, one tends to think that the Court may ultimately accept that what may be required, even by the Constitution, in the absence of congressional judgment is not required when Congress speaks, and speaks clearly, regarding the exercise of federal judicial power.

The proposal makes no explicit provision for taxpayer standing to attack spending measures. Taxpayer suits made important contributions to the development of more flexible standing doctrine during the Warren era. Yet a taxpayer's pecuniary interest in expenditures from the public treasury has always been understood to be remote, even theoretical. Any such economic interest is hardly a guarantee of vigorous advocacy in any event. If we are to make a clean breast of the intellectual embarrassments in current standing law, taxpayer standing, too, must go. Of course, most people who might have sued as taxpayers can equally sue as citizens under subsection (c).

Subsection (d) addresses the further elements of current primary standing doctrine: causation and redressability. Obviously, there must be some relationship between the interest asserted as the basis for standing and the conduct of which a plaintiff complains, even if it is only that a civic-minded citizen is offended by actions she thinks are illegal. This proposal, however, makes it clear that the relationship that must exist need only to be alleged at the standing stage. The actual determination of the facts should await adjudication on the merits.[100] In this, the proposal will avoid the ersatz merits-determinations now rendered in cases in which causation is so thoroughly examined in order to decide the standing question. Next, subsection (d) again rejects current doctrine by separating the relationship between the plaintiff's interest and the conduct under attack (a causal relationship, by the Court's account), on the one hand, and the likelihood that, if the plaintiff is successful on the merits, her injury can be redressed, on the other. The proposal returns to the position the Court itself took at the outset: these two ideas are actually only one. And the name of that idea is not causation, but redressability. What counts for standing is not whether plaintiffs' allegations establish a logical, causal chain linking private injury with public action. It is whether the injuries of which plaintiffs complain are reasonably likely to be redressed by some form of judicial relief.

The causation requirement is now the source of great difficulty. It is critical that new legislation should eliminate that barrier to the federal courts. Subsection (d) achieves this goal legitimately. The key matter really *is* redressability. Behind the standing issue is the requirement of a case or controversy, which, in turn, should turn on whether plaintiffs have something to gain from lawsuits. Of course, it should not be necessary for plaintiffs to negate all the contingencies that might limit the court's ability to provide complete relief or to name precisely the kind of relief that ultimately proves to be needed. The precise form that a judicial remedy may take, say, monetary damages or an injunction, goes not to standing, but to ripeness, mootness, or other concerns beyond the scope of my project.

Once standing is addressed in this way, new legislation should turn to related ideas: political questions, ripeness, and mootness. The following specific language should be adopted:

(e) The existence of a private right of action and standing under this section shall not obligate a court of the United States to decide a question if—

(1) the text of the Constitution commits the question to the judgment of the president or Congress;

(2) the relevant facts have not yet emerged, the postponement of adjudication promises realistically to sharpen the question for judicial resolution, and delay will not work an undue hardship on the parties; or

(3) the question has already been resolved by other means and the court's determination of it can have no effect on the present or future interests of the parties.

Subsection (e) sets these three additional doctrines off from standing and preserves them as independent bases for withholding or postponing federal adjudication. The political question doctrine should be retained inasmuch as it is, in itself, a matter of constitutional law— that is, an interpretation of the Constitution to assign decision-making responsibility to the executive or legislative branches. But recent decisions incorporating ripeness and mootness into standing, and thus constitutionalizing those doctrines as well, should be discarded. Each of the three doctrines is stated in a lean form, which respects the legitimate considerations that warrant hesitation in some instances but discourages manipulation to avoid the merits when non-Hohfeldian plaintiffs pursue public-rights litigation.

Finally, a new statute should include a severability clause that will preserve any individual provision that is not itself declared invalid. This is essential to implement the plan implicit in subsections (c) and (d). Congress should enact this proposal fully expecting that, faced with such a clear declaration from the legislative branch, the Court will cease insisting that its own primary standing rules are inviolate. Yet if the Court holds its ground, the severability clause will preserve standing for private attorneys general who can show injury, causation, and redressability (by the Court's definitions) to enforce federal law in federal court, pressing all available arguments. A simple clause of the following kind will suffice:

(f) If any provision of this Act, on its face or in application to any person or circumstances, is held invalid, the remaining provisions shall not be affected.

▼

The law of justiciability in the federal courts has deep roots in the jurisprudential history examined in Chapter One. Citizens' standing to sue in federal court has followed the ebb and flow of Supreme Court enthusiasm for judicial enforcement of federal substantive law. Early in this century, the private-rights model reserved the federal courts for the adjudication of private rights known to the common law and boxed public-rights cases out of the federal forum. The Warren Court lowered standing barriers, but the justices now in authority have reshaped the Warren Court's work into manipulable rules that often foreclose litigation. Those rules are presented as interpretations of Article III, but the case for their constitutional footing has not been made. We are not bound either to suffer the consequences of antiquated conceptions of the judicial function or to accept the restrictive doctrine that standing has become in recent years. Congress has the power to cut away its ancient roots, its needless complexity, and its disabling effects. Here, as elsewhere, legislation can empower the federal courts to enforce federal rights, public and private. The proposal just discussed would do this critical work.

CHAPTER THREE

▼

Arising Under

*R*ichard Nixon campaigned for the presidency insisting that he had
a secret plan for extricating the nation from Vietnam. After the election, it became clear that, in fact, Nixon hoped finally to win the war
by invading Cambodia. The expansion of the fighting only extended
it, and in the fall of 1970 Richard Steffel had seen enough. He and
some of his friends made up handbills criticizing American involvement in Southeast Asia and began distributing them on a public side-
walk outside a shopping mall in Atlanta. When he was threatened
with prosecution for trespass, Steffel filed a lawsuit pursuant to §1983
and the Declaratory Judgment Act, seeking a declaration that he was
constitutionally entitled to pass out leaflets criticizing Nixon's policies
and that any police interference would violate the first amendment.[1]
Like Gene Guerrero in the lighted-cross case, Steffel had to establish
standing and a right of action. In addition, he was obliged to negotiate
a third threshold barrier that Guerrero also faced, but that I postponed for treatment in this chapter, namely, the federal court's "subject matter" jurisdiction.

Steffel's ability to sue under §1983 and the Declaratory Judgment
Act did not independently establish his ability to do so in *this* court,
a federal district court.[2] For that, he needed another kind of statute—
like §1331 of the Judicial Code, the 1875 law by which Congress
conferred on the lower federal courts a general, subject matter jurisdiction to entertain federal-question cases:

> The district courts shall have original jurisdiction of all civil
> actions arising under the Constitution, laws, or treaties of the
> United States.[3]

Obviously, this language begs the operative question: whether a lawsuit *is* a civil action "arising under" federal law. Steffel's lawsuit was. His complaint stated a federal claim (his alleged right to distribute handbills at the mall without police interference) that had to be adjudicated in order to resolve the dispute. As I will explain in a moment, that conformed to the definition of an action "arising under" federal law. Unfortunately, the Supreme Court decisions in point needlessly confuse matters with outdated jargon and misleading generalizations.

I hasten to say that the Court's interpretations of §1331 reflect few of the machinations I identified in standing doctrine. In the main, liberals and conservatives alike agree that the federal courts should have jurisdiction to entertain federal-question lawsuits brought by litigants with a right of action and standing to proceed in federal court. The task here is to construct a framework that will implement this basic policy: jurisdictional rules that can easily be applied at the outset of litigation to channel cases presenting substantial questions of federal law to the federal forum, while screening out others that should go to state court. I will begin with the specifications of federal judicial power in Article III and survey the principal themes emerging from the constitutional context in which §1331 operates. Then I will turn to the statute itself, its history, and its interpretation in classic Supreme Court opinions. Finally, I will consider substitutes for §1331 and a related jurisdictional statute, 28 U.S.C. §1441, governing litigants' ability to "remove" cases begun in state court to the federal courts for disposition.

Such Exceptions

Mercifully, history has spared us any significant body of evidence touching the formulation of the federal judicial power in Article III of the Constitution. Historians have pieced together a conventional story, relying on inferences from sparse materials from the Constitutional Convention, correspondence, scattered speeches at the state ratifying conventions, and *The Federalist Papers*.[4] This is just as well. More data would only invite another round of futile speculation about "original understanding." As it is, we know precious little, but *what* we know, we *think* we know with some confidence.

All the plans offered at the Convention contemplated a strong central government, with a supreme court sitting atop a third, judicial, branch of that government. The jurisdiction assigned to the judicial branch might cover lots of ground, but, in James Madison's famous

phrase, at least the judiciary's power should extend to "all cases arising under the Natl. laws."[5] Many Jeffersonians opposed a powerful
federal judiciary, perhaps because they feared that national courts
would enforce unpopular war debts left over from the Revolutionary
period.[6] The impasse between federalists, who wanted a complete system of national courts, and anti-federalists, who wanted no lower federal courts at all, was broken by a compromise advanced by Madison:
Article III would itself specify only the Supreme Court and would
leave the creation of any inferior federal courts to the new Congress.[7]
The language employed to express this compromise was malleable,
the better to facilitate the development of the federal courts and their
jurisdiction as a matter of congressional policy.[8] Article III reads as
follows:

> *Section 1:* The judicial Power of the United States, *shall* be
> vested in one supreme Court, and in such inferior Courts as the
> Congress *may,* from time to time, ordain and establish. . . .
>
> *Section 2:* The Judicial Power *shall* extend to *all* Cases . . . aris-
> ing under this Constitution, the Laws of the United States, and
> Treaties made . . . under their authority; to *all* Cases affecting
> Ambassadors . . . ; to *all* Cases of admiralty and maritime juris-
> diction; to Controversies to which the United States shall be a
> party; to Controversies between two or more States, between a
> State and Citizens of another State, between Citizens of differ-
> ent States. . . .
>
> In *all* Cases affecting Ambassadors . . . and those in which a
> State shall be a Party, the supreme Court shall have original Juris-
> diction. In *all* other Cases before mentioned, the supreme Court
> shall have appellate Jurisdiction, both as to Law and Fact, *with
> such Exceptions, and under such Regulations as the Congress
> shall make.*[9]

This language has generated an extraordinarily rich and detailed
literature. The conventional interpretation has it this way.[10] The first
section, again, mandates only the Supreme Court; Congress may, but
need not, establish other federal tribunals. The "cases" and "controversies" described in the second section (some according to subject
matter, most according to the identification of the parties) mark the
outer limits of the jurisdiction that the Supreme Court, or any other
federal court Congress creates, can exercise. A few things are to be
handled by the Supreme Court originally, but most must come up on

appellate review of the judgments reached by other courts.[11] If Congress establishes lower federal courts, some appeals may come from them; if not, all the Supreme Court's appellate cases must come from the state courts. By virtue of the "exceptions" clause in the last line I have quoted from section 2, Congress is free to choose from among the cases and controversies the Supreme Court can constitutionally entertain on appeal and to decide as a matter of policy whether the Court should actually have appellate jurisdiction in all, some, or none of those matters.[12]

The upshot is that Congress is firmly in the driver's seat. At one extreme, it can establish both the Supreme Court and a complete system of inferior federal courts, give the lower federal courts exclusive jurisdiction over all the cases and controversies listed in Article III, and let the Supreme Court take appeals from all lower federal court judgments. In this way, Congress can essentially banish the state courts from the field—preventing them from exercising jurisdiction in any of the cases and controversies that Article III allows federal courts to hear. At the other extreme, Congress can create a Supreme Court, but no other federal courts. The Supreme Court must be entitled to hear the few matters specified for its original jurisdiction,[13] but any cases or controversies the Court may receive on appeal can come from the state courts, and Congress may cut off some or all of those— insulating state court judgments from Supreme Court appellate review and thus making them final. Congress is also free to chart a middle course. It can establish lower federal courts, but give those courts something short of the jurisdiction that Article III would allow.[14] Herein lies another application of the notion that the greater power (to decide whether to create lower federal courts in the first instance) includes the lesser power (to create them but to deny them all the jurisdiction described in Article III).

The literature is filled with attacks on this conventional account. It is not just that academicians are fascinated by the possibilities the text of Article III permits. It is that the consequences of the conventional interpretation are disturbing. If Congress really does have so much authority respecting the very existence and jurisdiction of the federal courts, then the rights those courts now protect are at risk—subject to the political winds that routinely blow through the Capitol. Up to now, Congress has rejected invitations to use its power over federal jurisdiction to limit the courts' ability to decide cases involving school prayer, reapportionment, busing, and abortion.[15] Our luck with respect to such flank attacks on federal rights may run out. Moreover, ostensibly plausible schemes to strip the federal courts of jurisdiction are occasionally offered as neutral mechanisms for dealing with docket congestion and delay. I mentioned this at the end of Chapter One, and I will return to the point in Chapter Five.

It will suffice for present purposes to note the principal assaults on the conventional account of Article III, without an attempt to explore them in depth. Some observers argue that the exceptions clause only authorizes Congress to keep the Supreme Court from second-guessing findings of fact made by juries. Recall in this vein that Article III was drafted before the adoption of the seventh amendment, which guarantees the right of jury trial in common law cases.[16] Others argue that "exceptions" are like "regulations." Congress can decide how many justices we will have, when and where they will meet, and like questions. And regarding the cases and controversies reviewable on appeal, Congress can fix neutral, practical rules—like minimum amounts in controversy. The power to make exceptions is not, by these minimalist accounts, a power to exclude sensitive subjects from the Court's appellate purview.

Still others understand the exceptions clause to establish a zero-sum game. Joseph Story argued that the term "shall" in the first section of Article III (repeated in the second) connotes a mandate that the full judicial power of the United States (all the cases and controversies listed in the second section) must be assigned to *some* federal court.[17] If Congress creates only the Supreme Court, that single tribunal must be able to reach everything, either by exercising original jurisdiction or by taking appeals from the state courts. The power to make exceptions to the Court's appellate jurisdiction is limited, by this account, to allocating business between the Court's original and appellate jurisdictions. Everything must be in one place or the other, with nothing entirely omitted.[18] Zero-sum arguments are easier to make (and accept) if we assume that lower federal courts *do* exist. For example, perhaps Congress can make exceptions to the Supreme Court's appellate jurisdiction if, and only if, what is excepted is channeled either to the Court's original jurisdiction or to the lower federal courts.[19] Alternatively, note that the term "all," which precedes the "cases" listed in the second section of Article III, does not appear before the "controversies" listed thereafter.[20] Perhaps the full federal judicial power need not be vested in some federal tribunal after all; instead, only the "cases" preceded by "all" must be assigned—either to the

Supreme Court's original or appellate jurisdiction, or to the lower federal courts.

Still other commentators suggest different limits on Congress' power. It has been argued, for example, that the legislative branch cannot frustrate the Supreme Court's "essential functions," namely, to ensure that federal law is interpreted in a uniform fashion and held supreme as against state law.[21] In this vein, the salary and tenure safeguards that insulate federal judges from politics may be vital to the independent enforcement of federal rights, such that the exceptions clause may not empower Congress to funnel civil liberties matters to state judges, many of whom are elected.[22] Finally, whatever may be the internal limits of Congress' authority, that power is necessarily subject to external constraints laid down elsewhere in the Constitution. Congress cannot bar the Supreme Court from entertaining appeals on behalf of African Americans, women, or socialists without running afoul of the fifth and first amendments.[23]

The Greater Power

Imaginative arguments regarding Congress' power over the lower federal courts are rare. Justice Story took the view that, notwithstanding the rather clear "may" term in the first sentence of Article III, Congress is obligated to create at least some federal courts other than the Supreme Court. Recall that Story contended that all the cases and controversies listed in Article III must be lodged in some federal court. Inasmuch as a few of those matters arguably cannot be treated originally in the Supreme Court, by Story's account, it follows that there must be at least some lower federal courts to receive that much of the federal judicial power. The case for obligatory inferior courts is fortified by our modern dependence on the courts we have had, in one form or another, for two centuries.[24] Still, most observers surrender to the cold text of Article III: Congress did not have to create the district and circuit courts in the first instance and is constitutionally free, on some mindless day, to discard them.

I hasten to say that one is not logically compelled to accept the view that, having power to take inferior federal courts or leave them, Congress has power to take them *and* to give them something less than the full breadth of jurisdiction that Article III would permit.[25] I have flagged this "greater-power-includes-the-lesser" syllogism before and questioned it.[26] Here, it has no force at all. One can reasonably take the position that the very definition of a federal court within the meaning of Article III is a tribunal with jurisdiction in all the matters listed there. Thus the constitutional plan might well be to give Congress a choice: either to eschew inferior federal courts entirely or to create them and accept that, once established, they will have all the jurisdiction that Article III allows. Perhaps Congress cannot have everything its own way—creating any lower federal courts it wants, but limiting their jurisdiction. Rather, if Congress wishes to have inferior courts at all, it can have them only by accepting that they will come armed with the full range of jurisdiction that, by this account, is theirs constitutionally. At least, the Constitution could fairly be read this way.

Of course, we need not worry that Congress might never have created lower federal courts. One of Congress' first enactments, the Judiciary Act of 1789, did establish a system of lower courts, and we have had such courts ever since. Nor need we worry that Congress might yet jettison the courts now in place. Those courts have been with us too long and have rendered too much service to be put on the block at this late date. Everyone along the political spectrum recognizes some role for the district and circuit courts. Witness the campaign waged to retain diversity jurisdiction. Nor, finally, need we wring our hands over the theoretical question whether Congress is obliged to confer on the federal courts all the jurisdiction that Article III would allow. The reason, however, is not the logical force of the "greater-includes-the-lesser" argument, but the practical demands of the federal system.

If it would be unthinkable to do away with the lower federal courts, it would be equally untenable to give them jurisdiction in all the cases and controversies listed in Article III. Once again, the federal judiciary is relatively small and prestigious, focused primarily on disputes involving federal law. This will remain true even if additional judgeships are established to contend with expanding federal dockets. The weight of litigation rests with the large systems of state courts around the country. If the lower federal courts were given all the authority allowed constitutionally, most judicial business would be shifted from the state to the federal forum. Consider, for example, what it would mean if the diversity jurisdiction were not restricted or eliminated, but, instead, were expanded to its constitutional limits.[27]

Article III's provision for federal jurisdiction in cases arising under federal law harbors equal potential. When Congress created lower federal courts in 1789, it assigned them very little federal-question jurisdiction. Over the next century, jurisdiction was given not in any general form, but in special instances, for example, patent infringements.[28] When, however, Congress conferred broad jurisdiction on the federal courts to hear suits involving the Bank of the United States, John Marshall seized the opportunity to give Article III wide latitude.[29] A case "arises" under federal law for constitutional purposes, he said, if a federal question "forms an ingredient" in the matter—this is to say, if there is so much as a chance that such a question will surface at some point in the litigation.[30] Understand that there is some theoretical, if remote, possibility of a federal issue kicking up in virtually any case. In an ordinary dispute over title to real estate, a party might make an argument touching an original land grant by the federal government; in a rudimentary negligence suit, a party might raise a federal challenge to state rules regarding liability or the measurement of damages. Open-ended as Marshall's interpretation may be, however, no one has questioned it for a long time.[31]

The reason is plain. The constitutional possibilities for federal jurisdiction ought to be far-reaching in order to allow Congress ample maneuvering room in which to fashion workable limits legislatively. We have placed the constitutional bounds of cases arising under federal law at such a distance that they pose no practical question at all. No one would want to extend the federal courts' power (and responsibilities) so far. The subject matter jurisdiction the district courts will have, then, is given over to sound legislative judgment.[32] In this light, the conventional interpretation of Article III is troublesome only if we are concerned that Congress might try to cut back the federal courts' authority to hear important civil liberties cases. It is only to meet that threat that anyone has suggested limits on congressional power. So long as Congress uses its authority to open the federal courthouse doors, those concerns can be set aside. The conventional understanding of Article III is the more convenient in that it is noncontroversial.[33]

We now have what is crucial: congressional power to create lower federal courts and equip them with jurisdiction in federal-question cases. It remains only to examine what Congress has done to date and any improvements that are needed.

No More and No Other

The Reconstruction Congress enacted the precursor to §1331 as an amendment to the Judiciary Act of 1875. The language used in the Act tracked the language appearing in Article III, and there is evidence that the statute was meant to give the lower federal courts the full constitutional range of jurisdiction that Marshall had recognized in the Bank Case.[34] Nevertheless, for the reasons just discussed, §1331 is now understood to confer less jurisdiction than Article III would permit. The power the lower federal courts have is what Congress gives them—"no more and no other."[35]

The jurisdiction conferred by §1331 is not exclusive, but concurrent with that of the state courts. I will explain below that citizens with federal claims for relief can often force opposing parties into the federal forum if they wish. Nevertheless, many civil lawsuits that might be brought in federal court pursuant to §1331 are litigated instead in the courts of the states. Moreover, the judgments reached by the state courts in such cases cannot be appealed to the federal district or circuit courts. Under the federal "full faith and credit" statute, 28 U.S.C. §1738, judgments reached in state court after "full and fair" adjudication are entitled to the respect that the relevant state would accord them in its own courts.[36] Typically, state law forecloses later lawsuits on the same subject matter, between the same parties. Along one branch of conventional doctrine, called "issue preclusion," factual determinations or applications of law to facts may not be relitigated in subsequent proceedings. Along a second branch, denominated "claim preclusion," issues of fact or law-application that might have been, but were not, raised and determined in an initial proceeding cannot be pursued in a later action.[37] These preclusion rules protect the parties' reliance interests and conserve judicial resources. In addition, the credit the lower federal courts lend to state court judgments reduces friction between the two systems.[38]

If the result in a case handled by a state court ultimately turns on a federal question, the state judgment is reviewable by the Supreme Court. Conservatives, who regard the adjudication of federal-question cases in state court as sufficient, typically rely on the Supreme Court's appellate jurisdiction as an adequate backstop against state court errors and abuses. Yet the Supreme Court no longer has the capacity to sit as a court of error in routine cases. It now entertains only about a hundred and fifty cases each year and necessarily restricts its docket to matters of significant national moment.[39] Moreover, in the relatively few instances in which the Court grants review, the justices typically accept state court findings of fact and limit themselves to reviewing determinations of abstract law or the application of law to facts. Accordingly, if an unsympathetic state court slants its factual findings against federal claims, appellate review provides inadequate protection. Liberals who prefer the federal forum in federal-question cases insist there is no substitute for the careful, sensitive, and generous determination of facts offered by the federal district courts.

The function served by §1331 is, therefore, both important and sensitive, namely, to distinguish between civil actions that can be pressed in a federal district court and those that must go to state courts of concurrent jurisdiction, whose judgments will almost always be final—protected from reexamination in the federal district courts by §1738 and unlikely to be revised by the Supreme Court on direct review. The Court's interpretations of §1331 do not always provide a satisfying account of the reasons for sending a case in one direction or the other. The resulting complexity can be frustrating for busy district judges, who need clear guidance in order to deal with the threshold question of their jurisdiction as soon as a complaint is filed.[40] Yet real difficulty is typically avoided by the invocation of two complementary rules.

Initially, there is the terse rule offered by Justice Holmes: "[a] suit arises under the law that creates the cause of action."[41] This is ambiguous. If Holmes is using "cause of action" to mean "right of action" as I did in the last chapter, he seems to be suggesting that a federal court's subject matter jurisdiction turns on the source of a would-be plaintiff's authority to seek judicial relief for the violation of a legal right. That won't work. As I have explained, the question that Congress decides when it establishes jurisdiction, that is, confers power on a federal *court* to entertain a case and resolve it, is conventionally thought to be different from the question Congress decides when it authorizes a *litigant* to enforce a substantive federal claim through litigation.[42] In the latter instance, Congress is merely selecting from a menu of possible enforcement mechanisms that include, but are not limited to, private lawsuits. We may expect that when Congress decides that a right should be enforceable by way of a suit in some tribunal, it will open the federal courts for the purpose. But there is nothing to keep Congress from turning, instead, to the state courts. Accordingly, to make the law (federal or state) under which a case arises for jurisdictional purposes depend on the source (federal or state) of a judicial remedy as an enforcement device is to merge two ideas that settled analysis tries to separate.[43]

The Holmes formulation does work, however, if "cause of action" refers not to the law that authorizes a lawsuit (rather than some other enforcement device), but to the law that establishes the substance of a plaintiff's claim. Thus a suit is sufficiently federal for §1331 jurisdictional purposes if the abstract right the plaintiff asserts against the defendant is federal. Holmes himself may not have sorted things out in this way; indeed, he probably drew no real distinction between an abstract right and an entitlement to enforce it in (some) court—much as Justice Frankfurter conflated legal interests with standing to sue.[44] We have to be more rigorous. Whatever Holmes actually meant, we should *take* "cause of action" within his framework to refer not to the source of a procedural vehicle for enforcing a substantive right, that is, a private lawsuit, but to the source of the substantive right itself. What counts is the "federal nature of the right" the plaintiff seeks to establish, not the "source of the authority to establish it."[45]

This understanding neatly corresponds with another general rule, fashioned by the Supreme Court to help decide whether a claim *is* federal within the Holmes formulation: the "well-pleaded complaint rule." Parties initiating lawsuits in any legal system must generally state in their original complaints the legal rights they mean to press and allege facts that, if true, support their claims that those rights have been violated. Other assertions are not "properly pleaded" or "well-pleaded," but rather are superfluous and may be stricken. In a case in which jurisdiction under §1331 is asserted, the Court insists that the plaintiff must be able to lodge such a "well-pleaded" complaint— showing that the claim the plaintiff advances as the basis for federal jurisdiction includes as one of its elements a "substantial" question of federal law. Note the following points regarding the well-pleaded complaint rule.

First, the adjective "substantial" is here used as a term of art, understood to mean only that a claim cannot be wholly frivolous. Any threshold test of a claim's potential for success necessarily bars the federal courts' doors in the instances in which it is invoked. Yet the exclusion of truly worthless claims is a modest, and largely noncontroversial, check on the demand for federal judicial resources. If frivolous federal claims were sufficient to establish subject matter jurisdiction, precious federal court time and resources might be squandered over litigation that has no "foundation of plausibility."[46] Worse, unscrupulous litigants might trump up federal charges in order to manufacture federal jurisdiction and complicate litigation in hopes of obtaining a settlement by attrition.

Second, a lawsuit can satisfy §1331 even though the issues to be decided are not completely federal in nature and, indeed, even though state-law issues predominate. If there is at least one federal claim, the district court's authority to resolve the parties' dispute is assured. Other state-law claims and issues that arise from a "common nucleus of operative fact" are said to be "pendent" to the federal claim and thus part of the single "case" before the court. As such, they are fully adjudicable in the federal forum, despite their state-law flavor.[47] If the court dismisses the federal claim that triggers federal jurisdiction early on, it may also dismiss pendent state-law claims in its discretion. Jurisdictional *power* to decide any aspect of the case is not, however, in question.

Third, the presence of a federal question alone does not ineluctably lead to an authoritative determination of that question and a resolution of the dispute on that basis. For example, if a decision on a state-law issue can resolve the dispute without reference to the federal question, the court may treat the state issue first and, depending on its determination, perhaps avoid deciding the federal issue. Particularly if the federal claim is constitutional, Supreme Court justices since Brandeis have thought it prudent to skirt it, if possible, and thus to avert the friction that may arise when courts invoke the Constitution to set aside policies adopted by majoritarian means. In this way, the federal question on which a federal court's jurisdiction is grounded sometimes only justifies the exercise of federal judicial power regarding related, state-law claims.[48]

Fourth, and most important for my purposes, the plaintiff must establish federal jurisdiction on the basis of the minimal declarations required to state his federal claim and cannot rely on further, gratuitous assertions. Take, for example, an ordinary tort action for negligence. In the classic formula, the plaintiff must allege that the defendant had a duty of care, that she breached that duty, that her negligence caused the plaintiff's injury, and that the plaintiff was damaged. All this is needed; anything more is excess baggage. Under the Holmes test, such a case does not arise under federal law, because the nature of the right asserted (the right to be free of the defendant's negligence) is grounded in state, not federal, law. Similarly, under the well-pleaded complaint rule, this is not a case arising under federal law, because the plaintiff can assert all that is necessary to state his claim without mentioning anything federal. Now, say the plaintiff anticipates that the defendant will raise a federal defense to the complaint, for example, that a federal statute has preempted state tort law in these circumstances, insulating her from liability. Still, the case is not one arising under federal law, because the plaintiff cannot "properly" refer in the complaint to the defendant's anticipated federal defense. The case ultimately may turn on the validity of that defense and nothing else. Yet since the plaintiff need not mention it in order to state his affirmative state tort claim, it is no part of a well-pleaded complaint and cannot establish federal subject matter jurisdiction.[49]

This illustration of the way the well-pleaded complaint rule operates confirms that what counts for jurisdictional purposes under the Holmes framework is the source of the plaintiff's abstract claim, not the source of his authority to sue. The function of a complaint is to give the defendant and the court due notice of the plaintiff's substantive claim; that is why crucial elements that have to be established can and must be spelled out. That work is hardly finished, or even yet begun, if the plaintiff merely identifies the source of his entitlement to file a lawsuit rather than pursue some other means of getting what he wants. If, this is to say, the law that must be federal to obtain jurisdiction under §1331 were the law that establishes a litigant's ability to sue, rather than the substantive legal claim such a lawsuit is pressed to vindicate, the well-pleaded complaint rule would offer no assistance at all toward screening cases under the Holmes test and, indeed, would be unintelligible for any purpose touching federal-question jurisdiction. Together, the Holmes test and the well-pleaded complaint rule provide fairly clear standards that can be administered effectively by the district courts.[50] In particular, lawsuits against governmental officials fit quite neatly. Typically, there is no state-law theory to mix things up. Nor is there any need to anticipate a federal defense. Yet these rules do filter federal questions out of the federal forum in many instances—chiefly by excluding federal nonconstitutional claims raised by way of defense in disputes between private parties.

The rule against anticipating a federal question in a defendant's answer is typically defended on two grounds. First, at the practical level, the rule ensures that the federal question on which subject matter jurisdiction turns will appear as soon as the original complaint is filed and before the defendant offers an answer or other pleading. Moreover, it avoids the relative uncertainty that would attend the plaintiff's attempt to forecast the defendant's response.[51] Second, at the policy level, the rule incorporates the view that it is most important to make federal jurisdiction available to litigants who themselves advance federal claims. A party who wants to invoke a federal court's jurisdiction on the basis of an anticipated federal defense is not trying to vindicate her own federal claim of right, but rather to defeat a federal claim when it is put forward by an opposing party. Recall Erwin Chemerinsky's argument that parties who are advancing federal claims should always be allowed to choose the forum, because it is in their interest to select the court that will be more sympathetic to those claims.[52] On examination, neither of these explanations is satisfying.

The practical difficulties associated with anticipating a federal defense are grossly exaggerated. As long as a plaintiff is required to set forth specific allegations about what the defendant will do, it is unlikely that the federal court will be misled. Plaintiffs in diversity actions are required to include in their complaints special allegations that the parties reside in different states. Similar allegations of anticipated federal issues could be allowed in federal-question cases—and should be.[53] It may be easier for a trial court to verify assertions regarding citizenship than it is to judge a plaintiff's ability to predict her opponent's litigation strategy.[54] But in modern practice, in which negotiations typically occur before anyone types up a formal complaint, plaintiffs' counsel usually know very well what they are up against before they enter the arena.

The argument that federal jurisdiction should be reserved for citizens who advance federal claims rests on a deeply controversial understanding of human behavior, namely, that people pursue self-interest virtually at all costs and, in turn, that decisions driven by self-interest are efficacious. Even if self-interest is the motivating factor in litigation, a litigant's expectation touching the reception a claim will get in a particular court is only one of many such interests that might influence the choice of a tribunal in which to proceed—including the distance to the courthouse. And even if we assume that litigants tend to select the court in which they think their claims will be warmly received, it is not at all clear that they will actually get what they expect. Plaintiffs who choose the federal courts may be safe enough; that is what the federal courts' victory in the parity debate was all about. But those who think they can identify a sympathetic state judge who will give them relief that the federal courts would deny are on more treacherous ground. The same goes for anyone who chooses state court litigation in order to avoid a Reagan appointee on the federal bench. If we believe that the federal courts are generally superior to the state courts in federal-question cases, we are better off with a system that puts federal questions to them, irrespective of who it is who stands to gain. When a dispute genuinely turns on a question of federal law, the federal courts should be granted subject matter jurisdiction to resolve it correctly, even if the litigant seeking federal review means to contend for a narrow interpretation.[55]

It is also true that the litigant-choice principle is not respected elsewhere. The best illustrations are cases in which citizens who are sued in state court wish to assert federal claims by way of defense and to "remove" or transfer the lawsuits against them to federal court. Under current law, removal on the basis of a federal defense is typically not permitted. In the main, a plaintiff who uses federal law as a "sword" can command a federal forum, but a defendant who uses federal law as a "shield" cannot.[56] In the next few sections, however, I hope to persuade you that existing statutes have it all wrong. Removal should routinely be available in civil actions on the basis of a federal defense.

Any Civil Action

The general removal statute with respect to civil cases, 28 U.S.C. §1441(a), provides as follows:

> Except as otherwise expressly provided by Act of Congress, any civil action brought in a State court of which the district courts of the United States have original jurisdiction, may be removed by the defendant or the defendants, to the district court of the United States for the district and division embracing the place where such action is pending.

This language derives from the same Judiciary Act of 1875 that produced §1331, together with a key amendment in 1887.[57] It allows a party who is named as a defendant in a civil lawsuit in state court to transfer the proceedings to the local federal district court, but only if the *plaintiff's* well-pleaded complaint establishes that the case arises under federal law. In effect, §1441(a) permits a defendant to rebuff a plaintiff's choice to press a federal claim in state court rather than federal court. This surely is surprising. Again, it is plausible to argue (as Chemerinsky does) that if a plaintiff with a federal claim wishes to forgo the opportunity that §1331 provides to litigate in federal court and, instead, to proceed in state court, the choice should be his. That argument proceeds on the theory that a plaintiff advancing a federal right will select the court in which his claim will receive sympathetic treatment. A defendant's desire to be in federal court to contend *against* a federal claim seems unappealing by comparison—suggesting an attempt to reap the benefits of the Reagan Legacy.

More to the point here, the notion that only the character of the plaintiff's claim counts for removal purposes conflicts with the idea that a litigant who advances a federal contention should be able to invoke the federal courts' jurisdiction. Notwithstanding that a citizen is named as a defendant in a lawsuit in state court, if she raises a federal response she fills the role of a plaintiff who presses an affirmative federal claim in an ordinary federal-question lawsuit. Nevertheless, §1441(a) makes no provision for removal on the basis of a federal defense. So if a party with a state-law claim manages to file a lawsuit in state court before the opposing party can lodge a federal-question suit in federal court, both claims will be adjudicated in state court. If Richard Steffel had not been on his toes and filed his declaratory judgment action in federal court when he did, he might have forfeited the opportunity to get to the federal forum at all. The shopping mall operators or local officials might have sued *him* in state court, seeking an injunction against further leafleting. In that instance, Steffel would have had a federal constitutional defense to the action in state court, but he would not have been able to remove the lawsuit against him to federal court on that basis.

Exquisite Obscurity

Current law does allow removal on the basis of a federal defense in a narrow class of "civil rights" cases, which typically turn out to be criminal prosecutions in state court. The Civil Rights Act of 1866, another measure enacted by the Reconstruction Congress, not only established new statutory rights in American citizens, but provided for removal jurisdiction as a means of enforcing those rights. Conventional wisdom has it that Congress was concerned that newly freed African Americans in the South would be sued or prosecuted in state court, where their federal rights would be ignored. Accordingly, they were authorized to transfer at least some state actions against them to federal court in order to ensure that the substantive provisions of the 1866 Act were not frustrated in local proceedings. The modern codification of the Act's removal provisions can be found at 28 U.S.C. §1443:

> Any of the following civil actions or criminal prosecutions, commenced in a State court may be removed by the defendant to

the district court of the United States for the district embracing the place wherein it is pending:

(1) Against any person who is denied or cannot enforce in the courts of such State a right under any law providing for the equal civil rights of citizens of the United States.[58]

This is a "text of exquisite obscurity."[59] In the 1960s, lawyers handling cases in the South insisted that §1443 allowed removal whenever civil rights workers faced prosecution in state court in circumstances suggesting harassment. So understood, §1443 promised to be, and for a time actually was, a potent weapon in the hands of lawyers representing unpopular defendants in hostile territory. The first thing civil rights lawyers did when one of their clients was arrested was to file a removal petition to get the case away from unsympathetic state courts and into the comparatively benevolent arms of local federal district courts. In 1962, only eighteen cases in the entire country were removed from state to federal court pursuant to §1443. In 1965, more than a thousand cases were removed on this basis in the South alone.[60]

The Supreme Court found the trend threatening. Accordingly, the Court rejected arguments for an expansive interpretation of §1443 and, instead, gave this statute an extremely tight construction—so tight, indeed, that removal under §1443 came to a screeching halt. The Court held that the statute authorizes removal on behalf of private citizens only when some state "law of general application" indicates that "specific" federal rights "stated in terms of racial equality" will be denied in state proceedings.[61] It will suffice, for example, if a defendant can point to a state statute or demonstrable state policy denying that African Americans are entitled to be free of race discrimination.[62] This interpretation has serious implications. A citizen who is prosecuted in state court cannot remove under §1443 on the ground that, in her individual case, her federal rights will not be respected— no matter how much evidence she produces to show that state officials, or even the state judge, will not proceed in a fair and proper manner. Rather, the defendant must identify some general feature of state law, like a statute, that makes it clear that the state court proceedings against her will violate "specific" federal rights against racial discrimination. Since most state statutes and policies have now been cleansed of overtly discriminatory language, removal under §1443 is largely a dead letter.[63]

On the one hand, this result seems sensible. We hope, and hope desperately, that the country has progressed since the sad days of the 1960s, when some state courts refused to meet their responsibilities under federal law. We hope, then, that the federal courts need no sweeping jurisdiction inviting removal petitions in every criminal case.[64] On the other hand, there still are cases in which it can fairly be alleged that if defendants are required to suffer prosecution in state court, their federal rights will be frustrated. The parity debate reveals that there are still reasons to be concerned about state processes, at least in some instances.[65]

In one way, allowing removal in criminal cases would provide less federal court protection than federal rights genuinely need. To be sure, federal adjudication offers superior fact-finding and protection from inadequate process in state court. The removal of state prosecutions to federal court would bring those rewards. Yet in some cases the threat to federal rights lies not with state judicial procedures and the possibility of wrongful conviction, but with the basis of prosecution in the first instance and, often, the motivation behind it. When citizens are charged under patently unconstitutional state statutes, harassed by multiple charges that will never produce a valid conviction, or discouraged from exercising federal rights by the mere fact of, or potential for, criminal prosecution—it will do little good to answer that if they are ever actually brought to trial the proceedings can be removed to federal court. The better solution for cases in which federal rights are abused when state officials prefer charges in the first instance is to permit federal injunctions in appropriate instances. I will offer a proper injunction rule in Chapter Four.

In another way, even a narrow removal jurisdiction would provide federal rights with more access to federal court than is warranted in this context. Again, subject matter jurisdiction is a threshold matter. Federal judges need clear standards to follow, standards that can be applied quickly—without significant investment of time and effort. Allowing civil plaintiffs to anticipate a federal defense from the defendant would be one thing. Allowing defendants to offer evidence of the potential for abuse in an individual criminal case would be something else entirely. In order to implement such a rule, the federal court would have to evaluate specific allegations, take evidence, and make a fact-sensitive determination regarding the likelihood that the defendant would be unfairly treated. Moreover, if removal were available on the basis of ad hoc circumstances, criminal defendants might use removal petitions as ploys for making the prosecution of their cases more complex and expensive—in hopes of obtaining concessions from the state. To paint the picture most darkly, a routine entitlement to remove criminal prosecutions, particularly on the basis of facts requiring a hearing to sort out, invites a general breakdown in the state courts' machinery for enforcing local criminal law.

Beyond this, removal in criminal cases can be distinguished from removal in civil actions in two ways, one practical and the other substantive.[66] The practical difference is self-evident. The federal claims available to criminal defendants are typically procedural.[67] Defendants may complain, for example, that evidence against them was obtained unlawfully and cannot be admitted at trial, or that the prosecutor's tactics run afoul of federally guaranteed safeguards. Claims of this kind, and certainly their effect on the proceedings, can often be ascertained only after a prosecution begins and state officials (the prosecutor and the trial judge) have a chance actually to raise federal constitutional issues by their responses to objections. As a practical matter, then, immediate removal of criminal cases will not work. Federal questions should find their way to the federal courts, but only after state proceedings have run their course. This is the province of federal habeas corpus—the topic reserved for Chapter Five.

The substantive difference between criminal and civil cases flows from federalism. In the other instances I have examined, the assignment of cases to the federal courts is only *said* to jeopardize the values associated with the decentralized structure of American government. Those concerns are, in the main, unfounded. Federalism is the Old Reliable of federal jurisdiction, the convenient refrain of conservatives who seek not justifications for the exercise of federal judicial power, but excuses for divesting the federal courts of authority to enforce federal rights. Yet the routine transfer of state criminal cases to federal court for trial genuinely *would* run the risks that other forms of federal jurisdiction are said to present—the very risks, indeed, that drove the Jeffersonians' resistance to a powerful central government two hundred years ago. In this instance, liberals, too, should find perfectly good and articulable reasons for keeping litigation at the local level.

Recall that the Jeffersonians regarded federalism as a bulwark of individual freedom. There was something to that then, and there remains something to it now—provided the idea is not corrupted by tendentious manipulation. There is, if you will, method in the apparent madness of distributing power among multiple layers of government. This stratagem prevents the consolidation of power in the hands of centralized authority, where it might lend itself to abuse. Properly conceived, federalism anticipates that authoritarian forces might come to power in a single state. Yet the practical impossibility of gaining a foothold everywhere at once will preserve the other states and, ultimately, the union itself from oppression.[68] Few instruments of social control can match the making and enforcement of substantive criminal law for sheer coercive capacity. The authority to declare what behavior will be condemned and the form and severity of punishments promises a uniquely effective means for commanding conformity to the will of those in power. Moreover, the authority to fashion substantive standards carries with it an entitlement to establish enforcement machinery—investigators, prosecutors, and courts. The more concentrated the decision-making authority and the more broad-ranging the scope of that authority, the greater the capacity of enforcement officials to demand adherence to substantive policies.[69] It is insufficient that local bodies draft criminal codes and that state officers investigate suspects and prefer charges. The adjudicatory proceedings that follow are crucial to local control of the criminal law. Legislative objectives are identified and given practical meaning when courts implement the criminal law in concrete cases.[70] Only if state courts are allowed to do their assigned work can it be said that the criminal law is safely in the hands of provincial authorities and beyond the effective reach of centralized power. The removal of state criminal prosecutions to the federal forum would tear local policy away from local institutions before it is hammered into shape by the state courts.

These concerns do not attend federal court enforcement of federal procedural safeguards in criminal cases. The purpose of those safeguards is to ensure not only accuracy but fairness—as elaborated in the Bill of Rights. Procedural requirements that benefit criminal defendants can safely be established and orchestrated at the national level and, indeed, should be uniform across the country. It is critical to hold state officials accountable for procedural safeguards in criminal cases. This function can appropriately be given to authorities who have no allegiance to state policies and whose primary responsibility is to protect the individual even if local objectives are nullified. Federal primacy in matters of procedure is thus consistent with, if not compelled by, the framework we have had since Reconstruction.

If, then, the excesses of state officials are to be checked, the federal courts should have the last word regarding procedures in criminal prosecutions. They do. The vehicle by which the federal courts exercise their authority is not, however, removal before trial. It is habeas corpus after trial, when the disruption of proper state functions can be minimized. The critical elements of the criminal law and its processes should be divided. The formulation and implementation of substantive criminal law policy should reside with local authorities, while the final, authoritative enforcement of federal procedural safeguards owed to the accused should be the domain of the federal courts—a domain that is entered later, after state proceedings are complete.

This said regarding removal jurisdiction, let me return to the basic jurisdictional statute, §1331, and explore one more anomaly in current law: the severe constraints on the federal courts' authority to entertain actions for declaratory judgment.

Procedural Only

When the bill containing the Declaratory Judgment Act was introduced in Congress in 1934, the Supreme Court had just begun to float ideas that would develop into modern standing doctrine. The worry in Congress, then, was that if the bill was enacted, the Court might strike it down as an attempt to authorize advisory opinions. That concern is what apparently motivated the drafters to condition the availability of declaratory judgments on the existence of an "actual" controversy between the parties.[71] When the Court took up the validity of the Act, Chief Justice Harlan Fiske Stone read that line to mean that the federal courts were to have authority to issue declaratory judgments only "in respect to controversies . . . in the constitutional sense." The Act, Stone said, was in this way "procedural only."[72] Justice Brandeis joined Stone's opinion.

A dozen years later, Brandeis' protégé turned Stone's words to another purpose, which vexes declaratory judgment actions to this day. In a famous opinion for the Court in 1950, Justice Frankfurter held that since the Declaratory Judgment Act is "procedural only," it adds nothing to a plaintiff's ability to satisfy the well-pleaded complaint rule in a federal-question case. It may be that in order to request a declaration of the parties' rights regarding a federal question, a plaintiff must set that question forth in her complaint. By Frankfurter's account, however, a plaintiff cannot establish jurisdiction so easily. Rather, she must show that she would have had to raise the same federal question if she had sought some coercive form of relief, like an injunction or damages.[73] In effect, Frankfurter held that the well-pleaded complaint rule is not to be applied straightforwardly to the face of a complaint for a declaratory judgment. Instead, the federal court must identify the claim for a more traditional form of relief the plaintiff would have had to advance in the absence of the Declaratory Judgment Act and then apply the well-pleaded complaint rule to the hypothetical complaint the plaintiff might have filed in that kind of lawsuit. This sounds convoluted for a reason. It *is* convoluted. Yet it remains the law of the land.[74]

In most instances, a declaratory plaintiff can easily point to a more traditional complaint for coercive relief that might have been filed and would have satisfied the well-pleaded complaint rule. Certainly, plaintiffs pressing claims against governmental officers need not anticipate that some federal issue will enter their lawsuits by way of defense. Their own claims establish the basis for subject matter jurisdiction. Those claims are properly pleaded, whether they seek only a declaration of rights or some other, coercive relief. The first amendment claim in the shopping mall case is only one of many examples. Trouble is, Frankfurter's gambit has produced overly broad statements of the law that, if taken seriously, promise a great deal of difficulty.

Consider this summary from a leading commentary: "If, but for the availability of the declaratory judgment procedure, the federal claim would arise only as a defense to a state created action, jurisdiction is lacking."[75] This is true enough, but misleading. It leaves the impression that federal claims commonly emerge only as defenses to state-law actions. Yet many plaintiffs are perfectly able to press their federal claims in affirmative lawsuits without waiting for potential defendants to make themselves plaintiffs and attack first on some state-law basis. The first amendment claim in the shopping mall case existed as soon as it was ripe for adjudication. If Steffel had waited until he was arrested, he might have raised his free speech contention as a defense. But he didn't have to wait; his federal claim did not arise *only* as a defense to the potential state prosecution for trespass.

Now consider an account provided by the Supreme Court itself in 1952 and repeated, without equivocation, in 1983: "Where the complaint in an action for declaratory judgment seeks in essence to assert a defense to an impending or threatened state court action, it is the character of the threatened action, and not of the defense, which will determine whether there is federal-question jurisdiction in the District Court." Accordingly, by this account, "[if] the cause of action, which the declaratory defendant threatens to assert, does not itself involve a claim under federal law, it is doubtful if a federal court may entertain an action for a declaratory judgment establishing a defense to that claim."[76] It appears from this that the state-law nature of a threatened lawsuit can keep an immediate declaratory action from being one arising under federal law within the meaning of §1331. Probably, the Court thinks this is so because, under current law, a plaintiff pressing a state-law claim for coercive relief cannot get into federal court by anticipating a federal defense, and because a defendant is not entitled to remove a state-law action against her on the basis of such a federal defense.[77] If the well-pleaded complaint rule, as it applies in other kinds of actions, together with the law of removal as it currently exists, would keep a party out of federal court, it is easy to see how one might get the impression that a different result cannot be obtained under the Declaratory Judgment Act.

But the ability of a citizen like Richard Steffel to turn his own potential federal defense to an anticipated state-law action into an affirmative federal claim for a declaratory judgment in federal court is beyond question—even though it is also true (under current law) that, if he waits until the state-law action has been filed in state court, he will not be able to remove that action to federal court on the basis of his first amendment defense. The very point of an action for declaratory judgment is that a citizen with a federal claim of right, believing himself to be threatened with suit on some state-law theory, need not sit on his hands waiting for the other party to sue first and then raise his federal claim as a defense in state court. Rather, such a citizen can turn his potential federal defense to the state-law action into an affirmative claim for immediate federal declaratory relief, naming the potential plaintiff in state court as the defendant in federal court. Legions of decisions stand for the proposition that declaratory plaintiffs *can* do what the passage I just quoted suggests they *cannot* do.[78]

It would have been harsh, to say the least, to tell Richard Steffel that in order to press his first amendment right to pass out leaflets critical of the Vietnam War, he must flaunt that right before police officers, suffer the indignity of arrest, and accept the risks, expense, and other burdens of criminal prosecution. Faced with that kind of ordeal, many people would surrender their rights without a fight. The judicial system should not tell citizens that "the only way to determine whether [something] is a mushroom or a toadstool is to eat it."[79] The Declaratory Judgment Act offers a practical, straightforward alternative. Steffel and others like him, who believe they are constitutionally entitled to do what they plan, need not put themselves at risk of jail if they are wrong. They can get an authoritative determination of their rights *before* they take any further steps. Current doctrine regarding jurisdiction in declaratory judgment actions is in need of attention.[80]

Minimum Models

It is time now to stop, take stock, and decide precisely what original federal-question jurisdiction the federal courts should have. Several passes have already been made at the question. Henry Hart suggested that we should begin by identifying the least that the federal courts' authority should be and work outward from there. As one might have expected, Hart's notion of the minimum approached zero. So committed was he to his process model that he thought federal rights could be protected, in the main, by initial adjudication in the state courts and appellate review in the Supreme Court.[81] Henry Friendly also formulated a "minimum model," which included suits by and against the federal government, admiralty and maritime cases, bankruptcy, and patent infringement actions.[82] Still, both Hart and Friendly recognized that the country has come a long way from the Judiciary Act of 1789, which created lower federal courts but assigned them no general federal-question jurisdiction. At this stage of our history, according to Judge Friendly, we have near universal agreement that the federal courts should have substantial authority to entertain private suits to enforce federal rights.[83] The American Law Institute is also on the record in this view.[84]

I dare say that agreement would *be* universal were it not for Judge Richard Posner,[85] who would jettison any general power in the district courts to handle federal-question cases and leave this field to the state courts, subject to Supreme Court review.[86] In Posner's view, it is diversity jurisdiction that should be retained (at least in substantial part) to prevent state courts from imposing costs on other states and their citizens. Federal-question jurisdiction is largely unnecessary, according to Posner, because the states internally bear the costs of any errors their own courts make regarding the Bill of Rights. This is not the place for a critique of Posner's position; it will suffice to say that his views have not won wide support. Posner's subcommittee of the Federal Courts Study Committee rejected his "ideal model" of federal jurisdiction and, indeed, disclaimed the notion that there *is* any objectively correct measure of federal jurisdiction. By assigning to Congress the authority to prescribe the role that the inferior federal courts will play in national affairs, Article III makes it clear that the business of fixing jurisdiction has "an unavoidable political dimension." The subcommittee found Posner's prescriptions to be out of step with "common assumptions about when a federal forum is desirable." Assessing those assumptions, the subcommittee concluded that "the area in which federal jurisdiction seems essential turns out to be surprisingly large" and that there is a "consensus" of national opinion that constitutional cases "have a relatively high priority." [87]

When Congress once again sets about legislating with respect to federal-question jurisdiction, the first order of business will be to draft a general statute, applicable in routine instances in which individuals wish to raise affirmative federal claims. Rather than repeating the ambiguous language of §1331, or relying on the equally ambiguous Holmes test and the well-pleaded complaint rule, the new statute should explicitly describe what is required of plaintiffs.[88] Concomitantly, the current problems surrounding declaratory judgment actions should be eliminated. The American Law Institute would give the district courts "original jurisdiction" in "all civil actions, including those for a declaratory judgment," in which "the initial pleading sets forth a substantial claim arising under" federal law. Within this formulation, the reference to declaratory actions is unclear, the well-pleaded complaint rule is too rigid, and the repetition of the "arising under" phrase invites continued confusion with Article III. Let me offer a preferable substitute for §1331 along the following lines:

> The district courts of the United States shall have jurisdiction of any civil action in which it appears that the determination or application of a substantial question of federal law can resolve the dispute between the parties. It shall be sufficient if the complaint—
>   (a) advances a claim for relief in which the federal question is an essential element;
>   (b) requests a declaratory judgment on the federal question; or
>   (c) alleges that the federal question will appear in an answer or other allowable pre-trial pleading or motion.

This proposal would continue the longstanding rule that the federal courts' jurisdiction in federal-question cases is not exclusive, but concurrent with that of the state courts. An argument can be made that if it is so important that federal rights should be determined in the federal forum, and particularly that the federal trial courts be available to determine critical facts, it must follow that parties should be given no choice: all federal-question cases should be routed to the district courts. Yet an exclusive jurisdiction would alter arrangements that have been in place for a very long time and could pose unforeseeable difficulties.[89] I hasten to add that in this provision and in the proposals on removal I will take up below, I eschew Chemerinsky's rule that a party advancing a federal claim should always be able to choose *either* a federal or a state forum.

The reference to a "substantial" federal question marks no change from current law—which, again, finds anything nonfrivolous to suffice. Nor is it controversial that the determination of such a question (or its application to the facts) need not be essential to the resolution of the dispute between the parties, but rather be such that it "can" resolve their differences. As rigid as the current well-pleaded complaint rule concededly is, there still is a tendency to overstate it. No less a jurist than Benjamin Cardozo once wrote that in order to establish jurisdiction under §1331 a federal "right or immunity" must be an "essential" element of the plaintiff's claim.[90] Cardozo meant only to underscore that the federal issue must be essential in the strict pleading sense that it is not surplusage. That, of course, is true enough under current law. Yet his sweeping language is open to the interpretation that the federal claim must be essential in the different sense that the court must decide it in order to dispose of the case. That is not true at all. As I have explained, there may be other issues in the case, the determination of which can resolve matters without the need to reach the federal question on which jurisdiction rests. At the other extreme, use of the term "can" scarcely incorporates the hypothetical possibilities that Chief Justice Marshall's interpretation of Article III itself brings within the federal judicial power. This proposed substitute for §1331 squarely states that the federal question that triggers jurisdiction must actually divide the parties, but at the same time allows for the resolution of disputes on other grounds.

Subsection (a) codifies the well-pleaded complaint rule as it now is understood. Here, the term "essential" is accurate. Departing from the decisional law in point, subsection (b) allows plaintiffs to establish jurisdiction by asking for a declaratory judgment regarding a federal question, whether or not some hypothetical complaint seeking coercive relief would have included that question as an essential element. Frankfurter's treatment of declaratory actions is abandoned. Understand, however, that subsection (b) fits beneath, and is not in addition to, the basic language of the statute. The federal question regarding which a declaratory judgment is sought must still be substantial, and the declaration that the court is asked to make must at least be capable of resolving the dispute.

Subsection (c) permits a plaintiff to anticipate a federal question that does not appear in her affirmative complaint, but will emerge in the defendant's answer or other pre-trial papers. This, too, departs from current law. Yet if plaintiffs are to be permitted to seek a declaratory judgment regarding an anticipated question under subsection (b), it seems only sensible that they should equally be able to anticipate such a question when they seek some coercive form of relief. The American Law Institute considered the change reflected in subsection (c), but decided to endorse the well-pleaded complaint rule as it is currently understood. The ALI offers no explanation for its reticence, and the reasons for it are not self-evident.

In effect, subsection (c) embraces the view that special jurisdictional allegations can be permitted in federal-question cases just as they are now in diversity actions. A simple telephone conversation between counsel, the kind of thing that typically precedes the filing of a complaint in modern practice, will almost always uncover the nature of the parties' opposing claims. In the rare case in which what is predicted does not occur, the court can dismiss without significant effort. A refusal to allow special allegations in this context would be much more burdensome. In a moment, moreover, I am going to propose that either party should be permitted to remove a civil action begun in state court on the basis of a substantial federal defense. A plaintiff who wants to be in federal court and knows he can get there by removal as soon as the defendant files her answer should not be put to the trouble of filing in state court only to transfer the action later. A defendant who wants to be in federal court and who knows that she can get there by removal even if an opposing party sues first in state court will be most unlikely to hide her federal cards, force such a state court lawsuit, and put herself to the trouble of filing a removal petition. Rather, she will acknowledge her federal defense when plaintiff's counsel calls. By allowing parties to cooperate in this way before the plaintiff files in any court, subsection (c) fosters a bit of efficiency in a system that desperately needs as much of that commodity as it can get.

A Federal Defense

For all the reasons I have been through, the federal courts' removal jurisdiction in civil (but not criminal) actions is also due for change.

A proposal offered by the ALI provides a point of departure. Let me first set forth superior language, then explain my differences with the ALI provision. The following statute should be substituted for §1441(a) in existing law:

> Except as otherwise provided by law, a civil action brought in a state court may be removed to the district court of the United States for the district embracing the place where such action is pending:
>
> (1) by any defendant against whom a claim is asserted on which an action might have been brought in a district court under section 1331 of this title; or
>
> (2) by any defendant, or any plaintiff, by or against whom, subsequent to the initial pleading, a substantial federal defense or counterclaim is asserted that can resolve the dispute between the parties.

Taken together, the preamble and paragraph (1) of this proposal incorporate existing law—with minor exceptions that need not detain us.[91] If a plaintiff who is entitled to sue in federal court pursuant to the federal-question jurisdictional statute chooses, instead, to sue in state court, the defendant may remove the action. This provision thus would continue the rule that a defendant may frustrate a plaintiff's choice of the state forum, even though the plaintiff is attempting to vindicate a federal claim of right and the defendant is attempting to defeat it. Chemerinsky's proposal to allow the party advancing a federal claim to choose the forum is again rejected. If we are convinced, as we should be, that the federal courts offer a better place for the adjudication of federal issues, then we should not quickly jettison a longstanding and familiar vehicle for getting such claims into the federal forum, even if it is at the instance of a litigant who is not herself pressing a federal right. The ALI would reach this same conclusion, albeit in slightly different language.[92]

Paragraph (2) would change current law by adding a removal jurisdiction on the basis of a federal defense or counterclaim. The explicit provision for removal by a plaintiff who faces such a defense or counterclaim is consistent with the policy of permitting either party to invoke federal jurisdiction as soon as a dispositive federal issue arises, irrespective of who it is who stands to gain if the federal claim is sustained. Paragraph (2) departs substantively from the ALI proposal in only two respects. In order to discourage litigants from going to federal court in unimportant cases, the ALI would allow removal on the basis of a defense or counterclaim only when at least $10,000 is in controversy. An amount-in-controversy requirement is a blunt instrument for screening cases for federal adjudication. We stand to create a lot of needless difficulty for ourselves and the judicial system if we insist that intrinsically valuable federal rights be quantified in some way to demonstrate their significance. Just as we now require no minimum amount in controversy in §1331 cases, we should require none here.[93] In addition, the ALI would describe the nature of the federal defense or counterclaim that will suffice as one "arising under" the Constitution or other federal law. Again, the "arising under" verbiage from Article III can be confusing. Accordingly, paragraph (2) tracks the parallel wording of my proposed substitute for §1331.[94]

▼

I have covered a lot of ground in this chapter. Yet most of it has been safe and solid, requiring no special care to negotiate. The Constitution empowers Congress to ordain and establish inferior federal courts, and by custom and practice Congress has assumed as well the power to prescribe the subject matter jurisdiction those courts will have—within the outer limits fixed by Article III. The proper interpretation to be placed on Article III has been much debated, and imaginative arguments have been advanced for obligating Congress to provide a federal forum for at least some particularly vital federal claims. Yet if the question is not what Congress *must* do, but what it *can* do when it is moved to behave as it should, constitutional problems drop away and out of sight. We are left with straightforward policy choices regarding the requirements that *should* be established for subject matter jurisdiction in federal-question cases.

To date, Congress, the Court, and most commentators have largely agreed that the federal courts should have broad jurisdiction in federal-question cases. Problems have typically arisen only with respect to the Court's ambiguous interpretations of the basic statute, §1331, the well-pleaded complaint rule's rigidity, removal jurisdiction under §1441(a), and Justice Frankfurter's treatment of declaratory judgment actions. The substitutes for §1331 and §1441(a) just examined promise to resolve those problems, so that I may pass on to the comparatively controversial issues I have deferred for the last two chapters.

CHAPTER FOUR

Our Federalism

The hysteria that gripped the country in the wake of the Russian Revolution produced "criminal syndicalism" statutes in many states—laws prohibiting the advocacy of violence or other unlawful means of effecting political change. In 1927, the Supreme Court upheld California's statute over the objections of Justices Brandeis and Holmes, who argued that the statute punished legitimate expression. Subsequent decisions undercut the Court's initial judgment, and when the Warren Court returned to the syndicalism question later, the Court held that an identical statute in Ohio violated the first amendment. By then, it was settled that the core meaning of free speech in the United States is that citizens are free to advocate political change. To drive the point home, a 1965 opinion for the Court by Justice Brennan approved an injunction, issued by a federal district court in Louisiana, prohibiting state officials from prosecuting civil rights workers under yet another syndicalism law. In this, the Court once again invoked the jurisdiction of the federal courts to enforce federal rights under threat from state authorities.[1]

John Harris took all this seriously. He thought that under the Court's modern decisions he was free to distribute leaflets presenting the Progressive Labor Party's agenda on the streets of Los Angeles. The California syndicalism statute the Court had sustained in 1927 was still on the books, but it seemed clear that he could no longer be prosecuted under it. Harris was quite right in thinking that constitutional law had passed syndicalism statutes by, but he was dead wrong in thinking that the local prosecutor and the state courts would respect his constitutional rights and, more important for present purposes, that if they did not, the federal courts would protect him. When Harris began passing out his handbills, he was arrested and indicted under the syndicalism law. The state trial court, a mid-level appellate court, and the California Supreme Court all refused to bar prosecution.[2] Harris then filed a §1983 suit in the nearest federal district court. That court initially issued an injunction against further state court proceedings—relying on Justice Brennan's recent opinion. But the district attorney appealed to the Supreme Court, where President Nixon's appointees had recently taken their seats. The newly constituted Court held that, however meritorious Harris' first amendment claim might be, the district court should not have enjoined the state criminal prosecution against him. Since he could raise his federal claim as a defense at trial, the federal courts should not interfere with the pending proceedings in state court.[3]

It was not that John Harris lacked standing to invoke the authority of the federal courts, or that Congress had decided that the first amendment should not be enforced in private litigation, or that the federal district court lacked subject matter jurisdiction to entertain the action.[4] The holding in the case was not that the federal courts *could* not hear Harris' claim and award relief, but that they *would* not. In previous chapters, I have tried to demonstrate that the allocation of business between the federal and state courts is generally a matter for Congress. John Marshall declared that the federal courts have "no more right to decline the exercise of jurisdiction which is given, than to usurp that which is not given," and the modern Court insists, at least formally, that Marshall's position continues to be respected.[5] Yet the vagaries of actual cases may require adjustments as jurisdictional statutes are put into practice. To adapt the general jurisdictional scheme that Congress has established to "considerations of convenience, efficiency, and justice," the Supreme Court has often claimed for the federal judiciary an authority to "abstain" from deciding issues and awarding certain forms of relief, notwithstanding clear statutory authority for doing both.[6] Quoting Justice Brennan, the Court has it that abstention is "the exception, not the rule."[7] Still, as a practical matter, the question whether a federal court should exercise jurisdiction in a case is a commonplace feature of federal adjudication.

The validity of abstention has attracted academic attention of late, and I will pause in this chapter to assess the arguments advanced in the literature. In the main, however, what is true in other contexts is equally true here. Theoretical debates about what either branch of the national government can get away with constitutionally are largely irrelevant to pragmatic judgments about the way our judicial system should do business. If abstention is a bad idea, in general or in some particulars, it is not because it offends a conceptual structure that can be inferred from the Constitution, but because it affects matters of vital, practical import—namely, the availability of the federal courts to enforce federal rights. If reforms are needed, the arguments for change need not be hammered into a constitutional challenge to abstention; Congress can deal with our practical problems as a matter of policy and with attention to the real values at stake. The federal courts now decline to exercise their power because they read existing statutes to permit them to do so. If it chooses, Congress can enact more explicit laws that do not brook abstention as it is now practiced.

Reforms plainly are needed, despite the surface appeal of some explanations for abstention I will consider along the way. Occasionally, at least, there are reasons for preferring state court treatment of matters initially (and properly) presented to the federal courts. Some of those reasons are formally neutral, as when federal court action promises to be inefficient or threatens to create needless friction with the state courts or underlying state policies. Yet even considerations touching efficiency and docket management inevitably implicate overarching political judgments regarding the proper distribution of labor between the two court systems. When abstention is undertaken without any apparent objective to route federal-question litigation into state court, that still is the way things typically turn out. Abstention also lends itself to manipulation. After the fashion of its practice in the context of standing doctrine, the Supreme Court tends to find no basis for abstention when it is content that the federal courts should decide federal questions, but to invoke abstention on other occasions in which it prefers to divert litigation to the state courts.

Originally, abstention was not a single doctrine, but several—each with its own rationales. Gradually, however, previous lines of demarcation have been blurred. The "various types of abstention" are no longer "rigid pigeonholes" into which cases must fit, but rather "reflect a complex of considerations designed to soften the tensions inherent in a system that contemplates parallel judicial processes."[8] The result of eliding previously distinct doctrines is not, however, greater insight into the reasons for, or the implications of, abstention. As distant doctrinal cousins have been crowded together under one roof, the specific considerations that produced them have been replaced by an undifferentiated inclination to resolve real or imagined conflicts between the federal and state courts by surrendering federal claims to the latter.

I will begin with some background on abstention generally, focusing on instances in which the federal courts channel cases to the state courts in order to give the state courts an opportunity to pass on questions of state law. It was in this context that abstention first gained currency in this century. On the surface, "state-question" abstention appears harmless enough. My concern is not that the federal courts should adjudicate state-law issues, but that they should treat the claims of federal right for which they are so critical. On examination, however, state-question abstention can threaten federal court authority to decide federal questions indirectly. Next, I will turn to the modern Court's development of the kind of abstention at work in the syndicalism case—"federal-question" abstention that deliberately funnels federal questions to the state courts. Finally, I will explore legislative solutions. To be effective, the system requires not only the changes in removal jurisdiction proposed in the last chapter, but also new statutory guidelines for cases in which the federal courts now decline to act in federal-question cases.

Scrupulous Regard

The notion that the federal courts have discretion to withhold the exercise of jurisdiction to decide state-law issues surfaced early.[9] Yet it was Justice Frankfurter who nursed the idea of federal deference to the state courts into an important doctrine of general applicability. Recall that a plaintiff may assert both a federal claim sufficient to establish jurisdiction under §1331 and a "pendent" state-law claim— that is, a state-law claim that arises from the same circumstances and thus forms part of the same "case" for jurisdictional purposes.[10] In an opinion for the Court in 1941, Justice Frankfurter said that when a plaintiff seeks injunctive relief both on federal constitutional grounds and on alternative state-law grounds, a federal district court is not obliged to respond immediately. In some situations, the federal court should defer judgment on either claim until the plaintiff has sought relief in state court.[11]

Initially, Frankfurter said that litigants have no right to injunctive relief, whatever the merits of their claims, and that, instead, requests for an injunction are addressed to the "sound discretion" of the court.[12] For that, he relied on the traditions of the central courts in England, in which "equitable" remedies like injunctions were available only from the king's chancellor, not from the courts of the common law—and then only if the remedy the "law" courts might provide, typically money damages, was "inadequate" to spare complaining parties "irreparable" harm.[13] In this country, we have discarded the distinction between "chancery" or "equity" courts on the one hand and "law" courts on the other. Nevertheless, the special character of injunctive relief remains intact. It follows, according to Justice Frankfurter, that in cases in which injunctions are sought, the district courts are not bound to take up the merits, but may exercise discretion with an eye to sound administrative policy.

Next, Frankfurter recalled Justice Brandeis' admonition that the federal courts should decide constitutional questions only when it is necessary to do so.[14] On that reasoning, he said, federal courts faced with alternative claims should address state-law claims first—in hopes that disputes can be resolved on a state-law basis without broaching constitutional issues. Turning to state-law questions, however, Justice Frankfurter noted that there, too, the federal courts may get themselves into trouble by reaching premature decisions. Despite the federal courts' undoubted power to decide state issues, any judgment reached cannot be authoritative beyond the case at hand. The state courts have responsibility for the interpretation of state law, and in some future instance those courts may well come to a different resolution of the same issue. This means, in Frankfurter's telling, that a federal court's judgment is not really a "determination" at all, but only a "forecast" of what the state courts will do with a question when they address it. If a "tentative" federal court ruling "may be displaced tomorrow by a state adjudication," the federal court's action appears both wasteful and potentially offensive to the state courts. Moreover, until an erroneous federal court decision on a state-law issue is corrected by the state courts, it may needlessly interfere with a "sensitive area of social policy" within the state concerned. Accordingly, if the state provides "an easy and ample means" of resolving state-law issues, further proceedings in federal court should be postponed.[15]

The doctrine that emerges from all this is a mouthful: When (1) a plaintiff in federal court asserts both a federal constitutional claim and a state-law claim for equitable relief; (2) the resolution of the state-law claim might dispose of the case without recourse to the constitutional claim on which the federal court's jurisdiction is based; (3)

the state-law question is unsettled, such that there is a serious chance that the federal court may fail to predict the way in which the state courts would decide it; and (4) the state courts offer an effective means of obtaining an authoritative judgment on the state-law issue—then the federal district court should postpone a decision on either claim pending state court adjudication of the state claim.[16] We have seen this sort of thing before from Justice Frankfurter: plausible policy objectives reflecting the Legal Process school's attention to institutional competencies, accompanied by doctrinal intricacy to further those objectives. Recall, for example, Frankfurter's treatment of subject matter jurisdiction in declaratory judgment actions.[17] The complexity for which he contended in the abstention context has proved to be no more feasible than the complexity he insisted on there. State-question abstention was invoked "occasionally" in the 1940s and 1950s, rarely during the Warren Court period, and then much more often "when the character of the [Supreme] Court began to change in the late 1960s."[18] Along the way, slippage has occurred regarding each element of the doctrine that Frankfurter described.

Justice Frankfurter's reliance on the conventions of equity to support state-question abstention has been largely ignored.[19] In place of "equitable discretion," we now see general references to comity and federalism, what Frankfurter himself called "scrupulous regard for the rightful independence of the state governments."[20] Nor is it essential that the state-law issues referred to the state courts must be dispositive. Abstention is now invoked when it is quite plain that the resolution of state questions will not obviate the need to decide a related federal issue—that is, when state-law issues are only complicated, when relevant state policies require elaboration, or when state court litigation can develop the factual context of a dispute.[21] When abstention is invoked for reasons such as these, the federal courts merely get the state courts to clean up messy cases.[22] Finally, the degree of uncertainty regarding state law that warrants abstention has been articulated and applied inconsistently.[23]

Judged by experience, the really vital flaw in state-question abstention is that the procedural burdens it imposes on plaintiffs operate, in effect, to defeat federal judicial authority to enforce federal rights. Inasmuch as the rationale for this kind of abstention is that premature federal judgments should be avoided, the district courts do not dismiss actions entirely, but rather stay their own proceedings until the state courts have determined state-law issues. Some states facilitate matters by inviting the federal courts to "certify" questions to the state's highest court for expedited treatment. Where certification is available, litigants can get prompt answers to state-law questions without jeopardizing federal adjudication of federal claims once state-law issues are cleared up.[24] Elsewhere, the only "easy and ample" mechanisms available are new lawsuits in the state trial courts, followed by appeals to the state appellate courts. Years can go by before plaintiffs obtain answers to the state-law questions that triggered abstention.[25]

Most people can pursue time-consuming and expensive litigation only once. That, after all, is why plaintiffs try in the first instance to join federal and state claims in a single lawsuit in federal court. When the federal courts abstain and force litigation in state court on state-law issues, plaintiffs face powerful economic incentives to commit to the state courts both state and federal claims and to accept the state courts' judgments with respect to both.[26] Justice Brennan recognized that if things run this course, the practical ability of plaintiffs with federal claims to seek relief from the federal courts, seemingly assured by §1331, is put in grave jeopardy. In an important opinion for the Court in 1964, he held that if litigants who are sent to state court for the adjudication of state-law claims make it clear to the state courts that they intend to return to federal court for the treatment of federal claims, they are free to do so—even if, during the course of state proceedings, the state courts pass on the federal issues.[27] This rule prevents a decision by a federal court to hold a case in abeyance pending state litigation from developing into a complete abdication of jurisdiction to determine federal claims.[28] Still, one must question the practical value of the option Brennan's rule makes available to plaintiffs. Most litigants still may forgo the lengthy, burdensome, and redundant litigation necessary to preserve the federal forum to which they are entitled.[29]

Many commentators conclude that state-question abstention is too reminiscent of *Bleak House* to be tolerated.[30] The American Law Institute would retain it only when it is *very* difficult for the federal courts to decide state-law issues, when there is clearly an effective means by which authoritative state court judgments can be obtained, say, a certification scheme, and, most important, when it appears that federal rights can be adequately protected by litigation in state court, subject to direct review in the Supreme Court.[31] Stronger medicine is needed. Congress should give the federal courts explicit authority to stay federal proceedings for a short time while state-law questions are

certified to a state's highest court. Otherwise, state-question abstention should be abandoned.

Blind Deference

In the syndicalism case, the Supreme Court did not defer to the state
courts regarding any unsettled questions of state law, but rather declined to enjoin a state criminal prosecution that John Harris claimed
would violate the first amendment. That result was not explained as
an interpretation of any statute enacted by Congress. The Anti-
Injunction Act, 28 U.S.C. §2283, might have been brought into play.
That statute, initially enacted in 1793, bars federal injunctions against
proceedings in state court—except when "necessary in aid of [federal]
jurisdiction," to "protect or effectuate" federal judgments, or when
injunctions are "expressly authorized" by Congress. But since the statute under which Harris filed suit, §1983, *is* an express exception to
the Anti-Injunction Act, the abstention ordered in the syndicalism case
could not be ascribed to Congress.[32] It was the Court's doing.

On first blush, the Court's policy appears quite sound. For even if
the Anti-Injunction Act is inapplicable when plaintiffs sue in federal
court under §1983, the federal courts should hesitate to disrupt pending state proceedings by injunction. After all, we do have two sets of
courts in the United States, each with jurisdiction in federal-question
cases. And litigants often believe (with reason) that one set of courts
or the other offers a more sympathetic forum for their positions. Once
negotiations founder, the parties to a dispute may break and run to
different courts—one side heading for federal court, the other side
making for state court. It does not necessarily follow from the mere
existence of this race to the courthouse door(s) that the winner should
choose the forum in which a dispute will be litigated. Yet by ceding
the day to the fleet afoot, the Court may avoid the spectacle of leaving
the federal and state courts to "fight each other for control of a . . .
case" at the finish line.[33]

Even so, the explanation provided for the decision in the syndicalism case left much to be desired. According to Justice Hugo Black's
opinion for the Court, a federal-question abstention doctrine, which
forbids the federal courts to enjoin state criminal proceedings once
they begin, can be justified much in the way that Justice Frankfurter
justified the federal courts' discretion to withhold federal court action
in state-question cases. It is a "basic doctrine of equity jurisprudence,"

Black said, that courts "should not . . . restrain a criminal prosecution" when the complaining party has an "adequate remedy at law" and will suffer no "irreparable" injury if an injunction is denied.[34] As I have pointed out, however, the preference for "legal" (as opposed to "equitable") relief emerges from the development of the central courts in England. Transported to this country, where equity and law have been merged, and deployed in a debate over whether the federal courts should interfere with state proceedings, that history is of questionable value. It would be the purest accident if rules developed to govern the relations between Chancery and Common Pleas in England could substitute for reasoned judgment regarding whether and when the federal courts in the United States should be open to resolve federal claims.[35]

Sensing, perhaps, the need for firmer support, Justice Black declared that the equity basis for federal-question abstention is reinforced by "an even more vital" consideration: "comity." Abstention rests on "a proper respect for state functions" and a "belief" that the nation "will fare best if the States and their institutions are left free to perform their separate functions in their separate ways." Black gave this notion a name, "Our Federalism," which in his telling means not that the federal courts should accord "blind deference" to "States' Rights," but that the national government, "anxious though it may be to vindicate . . . federal rights," should always seek to do so in a manner that does not "unduly interfere with the legitimate activities of the States." Thus "the normal thing to do" when the federal courts are asked to enjoin state criminal proceedings is "not to issue such injunctions."[36]

Here again, federal adjudication of federal rights is blocked on the basis of a "patriotic hymn" to federalism.[37] The abstention doctrine threatens to be precisely what Justice Black denied, that is, "blind deference" to the states in federal-question cases. State-question abstention is one thing; in that context the federal courts respect both state responsibility for local law and state court authority for elaborating that law. Federal-question abstention is quite another matter. Federalism can neither explain nor justify relinquishing the federal courts' power to adjudicate federal-question cases properly initiated in the federal forum. In this context, federalism is a "slogan," useful and used to extend abstention "beyond its rationale"—which, you will recall, was to prevent the federal courts from interfering with state court adjudication of federal-question cases already under way when a federal injunction is sought.[38] No one doubts either that the states have significance as governmental units or that decentralized power serves values that warrant consideration when authority is distributed between the national and state courts. I surveyed those values in the last chapter when I explored the reasons why state criminal prosecutions should not be removable to federal court on the basis of a federal defense.[39] Yet in Justice Black's opinion in the syndicalism case, and even more obviously in the Court's subsequent elaborations of federal-question abstention, federalism is invoked much more loosely to rationalize a general "devolution of judicial power" to the states.[40]

The Widest Latitude

Martin Redish isolates four independent values that federal-question abstention may further: avoiding attacks on the state courts' ability and willingness to respect federal rights, preventing the disruption of state judicial proceedings, avoiding interference with state policies, and preserving the discretion of local officials.[41] Each of the four can claim some footing in Supreme Court decisions, but none offers a consistent, and consistently satisfying, justification for the Court's results.[42] At the threshold, abstention in the syndicalism case and cases like it surely does avoid charging the state courts with insensitivity to federal rights. Rather than deciding federal questions themselves, the federal courts explicitly defer to the state courts for the adjudication of constitutional questions. In this way, however, abstention plainly rests on the assumption of parity between the federal and state courts—and lays itself open to all the counters to that assumption I canvassed in Chapter One.

Federal-question abstention also avoids disrupting state judicial proceedings. Recall that John Harris had been formally indicted and was about to be taken to trial in state court. The pendency of the criminal prosecution distinguished his case from the shopping mall case in Chapter Three, in which Richard Steffel sought a declaratory judgment from the federal courts on the basis of a (well-established) anticipation that he would be charged in state court in the future. Justice Brennan explained in that case that the federal forum was open to Steffel because equity, comity, and federalism "have little force in the absence of a pending state proceeding."[43] On essentially the same reasoning, the syndicalism case contemplated that the federal courts would consider Harris' claim after state court proceedings had ended. True, Justice Black did not instruct the district court to hold the case on its docket while the state prosecution continued—after the fashion of the procedure in state-question abstention cases. Instead, he ordered outright dismissal. But since the proceeding in state court was criminal, it was entirely possible that if the state courts rejected Harris' first amendment claim, he would be able to present it to the federal courts later in a petition for a writ of habeas corpus.[44] The potential availability of habeas corpus as a mechanism for federal adjudication of the federal issue made abstention in the syndicalism case itself a matter of postponing federal jurisdiction, not relinquishing it entirely and forever to the state courts.

More recently, however, the Court has invoked federal-question abstention when there is no pending state court action with which the federal courts can interfere. Even if a would-be federal plaintiff like John Harris files an action in federal court before being named as a defendant in a state prosecution, the federal court will abstain if, at the time the state court action is initiated, the federal court has not yet undertaken any proceedings "of substance on the merits."[45] According to the Supreme Court, any other result would allow a litigant with a potential federal defense to a prosecution in state court to turn that defense into an affirmative claim for injunctive relief in federal court—as long as he gets to federal court before the prosecutor gets to state court. The Court insists that such a result would "trivialize" the interests served by abstention. If that is so, however, then the values the Court itself ascribes to abstention threaten to override Congress' judgment regarding the proper jurisdiction of the federal courts in federal-question cases—the judgment reflected in §1331. By refusing to allow the federal courts to adjudicate federal-question lawsuits over which they plainly have subject matter jurisdiction even when there are no pending state court proceedings that might be affected, the Court does not merely resolve conflicts between competing courts of concurrent jurisdiction when they arise, but simply prefers the state courts in the first instance in the teeth of Congress' contrary judgment. This being so, it seems that the availability of the federal courts for federal litigation, displayed so vividly in the shopping mall case, is now very much at risk.[46]

In addition, the Court has extended federal-question abstention beyond the criminal context in which it was born to at least some civil actions in state court and, indeed, some state administrative proceedings deemed to be "judicial in nature."[47] The consequence is that the rule of postponement invoked in the syndicalism case has now become a rule of surrender. For habeas corpus is available only in the criminal context. Remember that under current law a defendant in a civil lawsuit in state court cannot remove the action to federal court on the basis of a federal defense, and state court decisions in civil cases ordinarily preclude further litigation in federal court regarding issues that were, or might have been, determined in state court.[48] It follows that a litigant who files an action in federal court in the absence of a state proceeding may be diverted to state court nevertheless—and held there until the state courts render a judgment that is entitled to preclusive effect.[49]

As long as abstention was limited to criminal cases, the third value associated with abstention (avoiding interference with substantive state policies) carried some weight. Powerful state interests are reflected in substantive criminal law. And for all the reasons we would not want criminal defendants to be able to remove state criminal prosecutions to federal court for trial, we would not want them to be able to obtain federal injunctions against state criminal proceedings once they are under way. Here, too, the federal courts should not upset the making and enforcement of local criminal law policy. On a practical level, moreover, the criminal/noncriminal distinction formerly provided a criterion delineating which state proceedings should be immune from federal interference and which should not. Now that the Court has abandoned the special concerns of the criminal law, we know only that abstention is appropriate with respect to some, but not all, state proceedings. The Court neglects any *federal* interest either in the enforcement of federal rights or in the maintenance of a healthy federal system.[50] Instead, the Court invokes federal-question abstention with respect to a range of state proceedings, whether formally identified as judicial or administrative, which are thought to be sufficiently judicial in character and sufficiently important (to the states) to warrant federal deference.[51]

More than this, the Court has pressed federal-question abstention beyond any purpose to avoid interfering with state proceedings of any sort. Abstention has become, instead, a more generally available basis for refusing to entertain lawsuits properly within the federal courts' jurisdiction—if, in some manner, federal court action may affect other kinds of state interests. The perplexing results of this further shift are vividly clear in cases in which the Court appears to rest on the last value said to be served by abstention: preserving the discretion of local police and prosecutors.[52] In a series of notorious cases, citizens' groups have sought federal declaratory and injunctive relief against law enforcement officials and agencies alleged to have engaged in egregious, typically racist, practices on the streets. In each instance, the Court has invoked abstention in order to allow local officials the "widest latitude" in the performance of their duties.[53] Used in this way, abstention threatens to degenerate into a general abdication of responsibility for the vindication of federal rights. For the extension of abstention beyond any concern for state judicial proceedings has been undertaken without an account of the limits, if any there are, to the Court's willingness to leave the superintendence of state officials to the state courts.[54]

In this sense, federal-question abstention has become a legal amoeba, originating in one context but oozing across doctrinal lines to befuddle federal adjudication in a variety of federal-question cases. The pattern continues. Chief Justice Rehnquist has announced that he would hold that all §1983 actions filed in federal court should be dismissed unless and until the plaintiffs concerned have exhausted any avenues available for litigating their federal claims in state court.[55] A rule of that kind could not be adopted without overruling existing precedents,[56] but the Court may be prepared to do that before long. If and when it happens, we can expect that decisions from the abstention field will be cited in support. Abstention now rivals standing doctrine as a device for closing the federal courthouse doors. I must devote the next two sections to the specifics of current doctrine in order to get straight precisely what the rules regarding abstention are at present and, therefore, the shape that reform legislation should take. Then, I promise to get down to the difficult business of fashioning concrete proposals for change.[57]

A Fair Opportunity

Recall that Justice Black initially articulated federal-question abstention in the language of equity. The general rule, again, is that, in ordinary circumstances, citizens who have federal defenses against criminal charges in state court are not entitled to seek a federal injunction that will derail pending state prosecutions. The burdens of mounting such a defense, however terrible for the individual, do not amount to "irreparable" harm both "great and immediate." Those same equitable considerations, however, provide a basis for making an exception to the general rule against injunctions. If plaintiffs show that they face not "a single prosecution brought in good faith," but "repeated" prosecutions pursued in "bad faith," Justice Black conceded that the situation is quite different. The irreparable injury required for an injunction is established by a demonstration of "bad faith and harassment."[58]

The general rationale goes like this. In ordinary cases, citizens can protect their federal rights well enough by raising them as defenses in state court. The state courts, by this account, are ready, willing, and able to enforce federal rights fairly—and will do so even on behalf of criminal defendants. Indeed, since most of the provisions of the Bill of Rights are procedural safeguards in criminal prosecutions, this is the way the system contemplates that such claims will be handled in the ordinary course. There are (rare) cases, however, in which state authorities do not engage the criminal process in a good faith attempt to secure valid convictions, but rather prosecute in bad faith, that is, without any such intention or expectation. Multiple criminal charges, filed and withdrawn on the eve of trial, may be used by police and prosecutors merely to harass citizens. In the 1965 Louisiana case in which Justice Brennan approved a federal injunction, for example, local officials were using multiple charges under an unconstitutional statute to discourage civil rights organizations from carrying on their work. When criminal proceedings are brought in bad faith, the citizens affected may not be able to vindicate their federal claims by raising them in defense in state court. The injury to defendants is "not simply a conviction under an illegal statute," but illegal charges in the first instance.[59] Accordingly, irreparable harm is implicated, there is no adequate remedy for federal claims in state court, and a federal injunction can be issued.[60]

Stated abstractly, the "bad faith" test appears plausible. If we examine it carefully, however, it proves dissatisfying—for two reasons. First, the standard is impractical even as far as it goes. Because of the evidentiary barriers facing litigants charged to demonstrate bad faith, the lower federal courts do not often find occasion actually to invoke this exception to abstention. The Supreme Court itself has never done so.[61] Second, and more important, the standard does not go nearly far enough. In many instances, federal rights cannot be adequately safeguarded in state court even if state authorities act in good faith and the state courts properly treat federal claims when they are raised in defense. The very most that a successful criminal defendant can obtain is the dismissal of charges or, perhaps, an acquittal. Much more than that is needed in cases in which citizens are beset by patterns of official misbehavior that affect entire populations, not just individuals singled out for criminal charges. If, for example, African Americans in Los Angeles suffer repeatedly from police brutality, it is scarcely an answer to propose that if a confession is coerced from an individual in a single episode, the defendant can attack the police conduct as unconstitutional when his statement is introduced at trial. General practices that deny federal rights require prospective, injunctive relief that is unavailable from state courts presiding over individual criminal cases.[62] Just as restrictive standing doctrine frustrates the federal courts' authority to enforce public rights, the abstention doctrine thwarts the federal courts' ability to protect classes of citizens from patterns of official misconduct.[63]

Other exceptions to abstention are equally unavailing. For example, the federal courts can enjoin state proceedings if the state statute concerned is "flagrantly" unconstitutional in its "every clause, sentence and paragraph" and in "whatever manner and against whomever" it is invoked.[64] Evidently, the Court wants to spare citizens the trouble of arduous criminal trials when it is clear that, if convicted, they can easily win reversal on appeal. Yet there are not many statutes like this around (one hopes!); making them an exception to the general rule against injunctions gives away very little. Justice Stevens has learned this the hard way—by trying, unsuccessfully, to authorize the federal courts to act when plaintiffs press federal claims against the very state procedures they must employ if abstention is invoked.[65] Moreover, a refusal to abstain in cases involving such patently invalid state laws seems inconsistent with the Court's rationale in abstention. If the state courts can protect federal rights in ordinary cases, surely they can do so when they come upon a statute that so reeks of unconstitutionality.[66] The Court concedes that "other unusual situations calling for federal intervention" may arise. But the only illustration under this heading to date is a case in which the state tribunal to which the federal courts were asked to defer was biased.[67]

More recently, the Supreme Court has assimilated the original exceptions to federal-question abstention behind a single, generally stated exception to the otherwise blanket rule against injunctions. Now, abstention is improper when, and apparently only when, "extraordinary circumstances" render the state courts incapable of "fully and fairly adjudicating" the individual's federal claims.[68] The question in every case is whether, if the federal courts abstain, would-be federal plaintiffs will have an "opportunity" to litigate their federal claims in state proceedings, either pending already or initiated before substantial effort on the merits in federal court.[69] This, too, we have seen before. At least in description, the Court's framework in federal-question abstention cases embraces Paul Bator's process model: the federal courts should not exercise jurisdiction unless there is a genuine breakdown in state court machinery.[70]

The Court is much taken with Bator's extension of the Legal Process tradition and the intellectual basis his analysis offers for distributing federal-question business—usually in the state courts' direction. Abstention is merely another doctrinal iteration of a familiar theme. The Court recognizes that there are cases in which the federal courts are needed—and thus occasions when the general inclination to abstain should be resisted. The practical result of relying on the process model to identify those occasions, however, is that abstention is invoked in all but the most egregious cases. According to recent decisions, plaintiffs can get the federal courts to act only by demonstrating that there is no feasible way in which the state courts can consider their federal claims.[71]

Not only does Bator's process model force plaintiffs with federal claims to litigate in the first instance in state court. It also cuts off federal adjudication at the other end—after the state proceedings to which the federal courts defer are complete. I pointed out in the last chapter that when parties litigate federal questions in state court, they must generally accept the judgments the state courts give them.[72] Direct review in the Supreme Court is only a theoretical possibilty, nothing to count on as a serious vehicle for federal redress. The lower federal courts have no appellate jurisdiction to examine state judgments for error, and habeas corpus is reserved, in the main, for criminal cases. In the routine civil case, then, a state decision regarding a federal claim is entitled to preclusive effect. If disappointed litigants try to sue later in federal court, the federal courts will dismiss on the basis of previous proceedings in state court. Here, too, the exception to the general rule against federal court action is stated in process-model terms. A state judgment may be denied preclusive effect, but only if it is reached through process that fails to provide a "full and fair opportunity" to litigate federal claims.[73]

There is a certain symmetry in this that may seem appealing at first glance. Parties with federal claims are routed to state court, unless the state courts offer no "full and fair opportunity" to litigate those claims; if such an opportunity is provided, resulting state judgments are insulated from later attack in federal court. Yet if we look closely at the decisions on preclusion, we find that the measure of process deemed to be "full and fair" so as to ensure the preclusive effect of state judgments is fundamental fairness in the constitutional sense.[74] The federal courts cannot consider federal issues that were, or might have been, adjudicated previously in state court, unless the processes in state court were *so* bad as to have been *unconstitutionally* bad. This, by the way, also tracks with Bator's program for habeas corpus, by which the lower federal courts would be restricted to considering whether the procedures used to adjudicate due process claims in state court were themselves consistent with due process.[75]

When Congress enacts legislation to address federal-question abstention, there will be occasion for making federal injunctions available in criminal cases when state processes break down. But the standard written into statute law should not be solely the "full and fair" adjudication test now employed by the Supreme Court. Nor can the measure of inadequate state procedure seek the constitutional floor, as would Bator's framework. Congress should discard the Court's abstention precedents, then specify clearly when it is that the federal courts should enjoin pending state proceedings. Injunctions should be available when, for explicitly stated reasons, state processes are insufficient to protect litigants' federal rights.

Majoritarian Branches

In urging Congress to write new statutes respecting abstention, I set aside arguments that the Constitution itself occupies this field. Others disagree, both with me and among themselves. On one side, Martin Redish argues that the judge-made doctrines now in place amount to a refusal by the federal courts to comply with statutes like §1331 and thus constitute a breach of the separation-of-powers principle.[76] By Redish's account, that structural principle reflects our American commitment to democracy. For when the elected Congress of the United States has prescribed jurisdiction for the federal courts, we can "logically" allow the courts to decline that jurisdiction only if we "place little value on judicial adherence to majoritarian-based policy choices."[77] On the other side, Barry Friedman contends that neither Congress nor the Court has plenary responsibility for federal court jurisdiction. Rather, the two branches share authority—to be excrcised in a dialogic give and take, with neither branch having the final word. To Redish, the judge-drawn abstention doctrines we now have are unconstitutional; to Friedman, what we have now is constitutionally *grounded,* and it would be unconstitutional for Congress to try to change it without regard for the Court's independent role.[78]

These polar positions rely on (competing) interpretations of the separation-of-powers idea, which, I am afraid, invite us to imbide another draught of Formalism—at least the notion that we can derive answers to specific constitutional questions by reference to general constitutional propositions. Redish insists that the Constitution identifies some functions that are by nature legislative and thus to be performed only by Congress; that the determination of federal court jurisdiction is one such legislative function; that Congress has, in fact, wielded its exclusive power by enacting the jurisdictional statutes now on the books; and that any refusal by the courts to exercise the jurisdiction so granted is an invalid usurpation. Friedman, for his part, responds with a different understanding of "the constitutional plan," which, if accepted, makes the separation-of-powers "problem" disappear. Together, Redish and Friedman pick their way over familiar ground, taking opposite sides as they go along.

No step in Redish's deductive scheme is without its shortcomings. Initially, the precedents we have on the separation of powers largely disclaim the notion that the national government is divided into three tightly sealed spheres in which different organs of power function independently.[79] Granted a separation-of-powers principle of some stripe, the proposition that the Constitution assigns absolute power over federal court jurisdiction to Congress is also problematic. The text does not bestow this power on the legislative branch in so many words; Article III, indeed, says nothing at all (explicitly) regarding authority over jurisdiction.[80] The argument, then, must rest on Supreme Court decisions holding that Congress' explicit power to create lower federal courts "logically implies" the "lesser" power to prescribe the jurisdiction of the courts so created.[81] But if extant judicial precedents are acceptable as the basis for congressional authority for fixing the subject matter jurisdiction of the federal courts, it is anything but clear why they are unacceptable as the basis of current abstention doctrine. The answer cannot be that in the one instance Congress has not spoken, and in the other it has. For Congress' practical ability to speak depends initially on the Court's decisions.[82]

These circularity problems are exacerbated by the difficulty of showing that the Supreme Court has made unwarranted exceptions to the statutes currently in place. We have a lot of experience with (effective) judicial discretion to decline jurisdiction conferred by Congress,[83] and it is too pat merely to say that the record only shows that we have tolerated judicial lawlessness for a long time.[84] Tradition and experience count for something in American law; Congress' silence in the face of the Court's decisions cannot be discounted as the product of inattention or inertia.[85] Moreover, as Friedman fairly points out, the courts are positioned to adapt their own jurisdiction to changing circumstances. It is entirely plausible to argue that Congress has implicitly delegated to the courts the flexibility required to tailor their work to current needs. Nor is it clear that when the Court construes existing statutes to allow for abstention, it reaches results that defy the plain meaning of the statutes involved. Many of the statutes we now have are not perfectly plain; those that *are* ostensibly clear are that way because they are written in sweeping terms and set forth no explicit exceptions. In cases involving ambiguous statutes, one may argue that the Court has come out the wrong way. Redish himself has often done so.[86] A further argument, to the effect that *by* coming out the wrong way the Court violates the Constitution, is largely of rhetorical value.

Nor, certainly, is it helpful to complain that the Supreme Court's opinions in abstention cases candidly rest on the Court's own sense of sound judicial policy rather than on the language of the relevant statute or "congressional intent."[87] The Court sometimes couches opinions as simply an exegesis of statutory text, read in light of its legislative history. But opinions of that kind are typically the *least* helpful in understanding the Court's true analysis. Given a choice between opinions that explain results in frank policy terms and opinions that purport to rely only on the express language of statutes and on strained inferences from historical materials, most of us would choose the former. Honest opinions not only clarify what the Court actually does, but also recognize (honestly) that the results reached are, in fact, the Court's responsibility.[88]

Finally, Redish's appeal to democracy may prove too much. In his general analysis of federal jurisdiction, he recognizes (and defends) the idea that the American "constitutional" democracy contemplates a judicial check on the politically sensitive branches. In his specific analysis of abstention, however, he places great emphasis on unadorned majoritarianism—suggesting to some critics that he thinks it is always objectionable for the Court to confront majoritarian policies. That, of course, Redish does not mean to argue. By contrast, and

for all his insistence that the Court should bow to legislatively drawn
jurisdictional lines, Redish recognizes that the Court cannot and
should not defer equally to majoritarian policies against which individuals claim constitutional rights. Still, it is not at all clear from his
work precisely where illegitimate judicial overreaching ends and legitimate judicial review begins.[89]

Friedman, too, has an uphill battle to wage. He attempts to win
support for his position by contending that a broad congressional
power to determine the jurisdiction of the federal courts would work
in both directions. If it is true that Congress can require the exercise
of federal jurisdiction despite the Supreme Court's objections, it must
also be true that Congress can restrict federal jurisdiction—as drastically as it likes and even in constitutional cases.[90] More than this will
be needed, however, if we are to be drawn to Friedman's revisionist
account out of fear that, if we resist, we must make our peace with
plenary congressional power to channel constitutional cases to the
state courts. On the contrary, one can take both the position that Congress can protect federal rights by making the federal courts available
and, in so doing, eliminating judicially created restrictions, and the
position that, for the reasons covered in Chapter Three, Congress cannot frustrate federal rights by depriving them of a federal forum.[91]

Even if broad congressional power to extend jurisdiction implies
equally broad power to restrict federal judicial power, Friedman will
not scare readers familiar with the record. Recall that Congress has
consistently rejected attempts to strip the federal courts of authority
in controversial cases.[92] It may be a little worrisome that the availability of the federal courts to enforce citizens' rights should turn on
choices made by a majoritarian body. But, here again, the record is
hard to ignore. It is the judge-made abstention doctrine that poses the
current danger. With the judicial wolf at the gate, this hardly seems
the time to worry that the legislative dog standing by to safeguard the
household may one day itself get hungry. In the end, Friedman's attempt to constitutionalize a role for the Court in orchestrating the
federal courts' jurisdiction is no more successful than Redish's attempt
to constitutionalize a ban on the Court's participation, given existing
statutes.

The result that Redish would reach is the right one. But the straightforward, policy-oriented arguments I explored previously offer better
reasons for focusing on congressional authority than does the constitutional analysis he offers. If existing statutes have not discouraged

the Court from withholding federal judicial power, then more explicit legislation is in order. The legislative course faces the daunting task of obtaining help from the political tumult that is Congress. Yet there comes a time when academic arguments about democracy should be abandoned in favor of forthright attempts to engage the machinery of American politics to produce needed change. If more exacting statutes are put in place, the Supreme Court will be obliged to comply with their terms or be charged with much more flagrant resistance to congressional authority than is reflected in current abstention doctrine. There is circularity in this position, too. Since the Court will also be the judge of what new statutes mean, the justices will be positioned to limit the effect of those statutes on existing arrangements—without formally acknowledging any failure to keep faith with congressional will. Yet new legislation, drafted with existing law in mind, will permit Congress to hold the Court's feet rather closer to the fire.

Competency

The drafting task at hand is difficult. The variety of circumstances that can arise, coupled with the inability of abstract statutory language always to give instructions with specificity, augers for a system in which Congress at least takes advice from judges on the way in which the federal judicial power should be implemented. In some minds, indeed, the scheme we now have, complete with abstention, is the product of a sensible accommodation of comparative competencies, albeit not one necessarily mandated constitutionally: Congress writes baseline statutes that enable the federal courts to take cases, while the Court fashions more refined rules regarding the timing of federal adjudication and the form of relief that should be available.[93]

We have seen this antiseptic, Legal Process thinking before. The objective appears to be an elegant, symmetrical framework in which institutions are assigned the duties for which they have a comparative advantage: a place for every case and every case in its place. And never a really serious appraisal of the consequences for federal claims driven into the waiting arms of potentially unsympathetic state courts. Indeed, it is because the commentators who take the Legal Process perspective sometimes ignore the parity debate that they can so easily construct a system that routinely directs cases in one direction or another on the basis of ostensibly neutral considerations—for example, administrative costs.[94] The stakes for federal rights are too high to let the allocation of jurisdiction turn on matters such as these. There is a difference between the federal and state courts in federal-question cases, and if we neglect the value judgments that difference demands we risk falling victim to the dangerous sterility that has attended the process model for nearly forty years.

As to the merits of the "competency" question, the case for deferring to the Supreme Court is much weaker than is often supposed. The exercise of federal jurisdiction may well need to be tempered in practice, and it may be impossible to anticipate all contingencies and provide for them beforehand. But new statutes can be written against an ample background of experience with the actual problems that have arisen under existing law. Thus far, those problems have been resolved by the Court. Congress need only focus on the same issues, substituting different judgments for those of the justices. Likewise, the capacity of language to convey precise meaning is scarcely an issue confined to, or especially important in, the business of writing jurisdictional legislation. A legal text is rarely so intrinsically clear as to admit of no debate whatever regarding its meaning. This, again, is one of the lessons of Legal Realism. Yet unless we are to abandon legislation of any kind, indeed, unless we are prepared to discard any attempt to put any kind of law down on paper, we have to put some stock in the ability of drafters to get across ideas with a measure of clarity.

Finally, let me say again that I do not for a moment propose that Congress is inherently good (better than the Supreme Court) at developing either sound policies regarding the work of the federal courts and their relations with state courts, or precise statutory language for implementing such policies. I do not mean to argue that since we are dissatisfied with judge-crafted abstention doctrines, we should simply urge Congress to vanquish what the justices have done and cross our fingers in hopes that elected representatives will get it right. I want to offer specific prescriptive remedies and ask Congress to use the great power at its disposal to effect change that, for reasons I have just discussed, is needed to restore the federal courts' ability to enforce federal rights. The statutes now in place are not doing the job. We can do a lot better. And we should.

No Wholly Satisfactory Answer

The proposal discussed in the last chapter to allow removal on the basis of a federal defense would go a long way toward eliminating the problems with federal-question abstention. If that change were made, one who is named as a defendant in a civil action in state court would no longer need to seek injunctive relief from a federal court, but, instead, would be entitled to remove the action to the local district court. Once in the federal forum, moreover, the litigant would be able to counterclaim for any prospective injunctive or declaratory relief needed to vindicate his federal rights. Removal would both ensure that the litigant's federal rights are adjudicated properly and fully in the better forum, and head off potential unfairness in state proceedings—without requiring any special showing of misconduct by state officials or, for that matter, the state courts themselves. The resulting scheme would be not only efficient, but likely to minimize friction between the two court systems.

Even if removal becomes available in civil cases on the basis of a federal defense or counterclaim, however, new statutes will be needed. In the absence of new legislation, the existing judicial precedents on which abstention depends would remain in place, albeit the Supreme Court would presumably find it necessary or appropriate to make adjustments to accommodate the enlargement of removal. Certainly when actions are commenced in federal court, we will need some legislative limit on abstention if the present state of affairs is to be altered. But even in cases that reach the federal courts by way of the new removal statute, similar limits will be necessary to keep litigants from being forced back to state court on the basis of judge-made abstention rules. The model provisions prepared by the American Law Institute and bills introduced during the Carter Administration again offer points of departure, respecting both state-question and federal-question abstention.[95]

Regarding the former, the ALI finds "no wholly satisfactory answer" to the competing concerns that Justice Frankfurter identified.[96] If cases involving both federal and state issues are litigated entirely in federal court, the costs that Frankfurter noted must be engaged. If, instead, "mixed-issue" cases are channeled entirely to the state courts, litigants with federal claims will be denied the benefits of trial-level adjudication in the federal district courts. The current scheme, in which cases are shuttled back and forth between the two court systems, may be the worst of both worlds. Federal-question cases are litigated piecemeal in both sets of courts, and final resolution is unduly delayed. Faced with a difficult situation, the ALI suggests a rough set of compromises. To avoid excessive friction with the states, the ALI proposes to retain state-question abstention in those situations in which the values it serves are most evident and can be respected with minimal "delay, confusion, and inconvenience."[97] By the ALI's reckoning, these are cases in which issues of state law "cannot be satisfactorily determined" in light of existing state authorities; in which abstention can avoid a decision on a "substantial question of federal constitutional law" or the "serious danger" of frustrating state policies; in which there is a "plain, speedy, and efficient remedy" available in state court; and in which related federal claims can be "adequately protected" by appellate review of any state court judgment in the United States Supreme Court.[98]

In essence, then, the ALI would restrict state-question abstention to cases in which it is acceptable for the federal courts to relinquish jurisdiction entirely in order to achieve competing objectives. In cases in which state-question abstention is ordered under this plan, the state courts would determine all issues, subject to appellate review in the Supreme Court. The rule announced by Justice Brennan thirty years ago, which allows litigants who are sent to state court for the adjudication of state-law issues to reserve an ability to return to federal court later for federal questions, is judged to be too cumbersome and time-consuming to be maintained. In this, the ALI would transmute state-question abstention, when it occurs, from a doctrine contemplating the postponement of federal jurisdiction to a doctrine mandating the total surrender of judicial authority to the states. To its credit, the ALI candidly owns up to a significant policy judgment with crucial implications for the allocation of judicial power in the United States. Searching for an imperfect but acceptable set of compromises, the ALI would place apparent efficiency ahead of the preservation of the federal forum for the determination of federal rights.

Within the class of cases in which state-question abstention would be retained, the ALI proposes two ways of mitigating the effects of delay. First, state certification schemes should be regarded as fitting occasions for abstention, and the federal courts should be encouraged to take the opportunity those schemes offer to obtain authoritative judgments on state-law issues from the state courts. A bill offered by Charles Mathias and Edward Brooke in 1977 included the ALI's proposal regarding certification almost verbatim.[99] Second, the ALI would authorize the federal district courts to monitor proceedings in state court in order to protect litigants from state processes that look "plain, speedy, and efficient" enough when abstention is ordered, but that turn out to be ineffective. Under this latter authority, the district courts would be able to issue any procedural or "ancillary" orders needed to protect litigants in state court and, when necessary, to vacate original stays of federal proceedings and resume responsibility for cases.

Finally, as a qualified bow to the special value of federal jurisdiction in some instances, the ALI recommends that certain kinds of cases should be exempted entirely from state-question abstention—namely, cases involving the right to vote or the right to equal protection of the laws. In the late 1960s, when the ALI plan was developed, those exceptions seemed to capture the situations in which prompt federal adjudication was most important and in which the delays, inefficiencies, and potential inadequacies of state court litigation were outweighed by the "strong national interest" in a federal forum.[100] Still, according to the ALI, if all "civil rights" cases were exempted from abstention, the list of exceptions would swallow the general rule continuing abstention—within the confines set forth above.

The American Law Institute's plan constitutes the best effort ever made to address the flaws in state-question abstention, while retaining the doctrine and the advantages said to attach to it. The attempt is unsuccessful. The wiser course is outright rejection of state-question abstention, subject to a circumscribed provision for stays when genuinely unsettled questions of state law can quickly be answered by way of a certification scheme. We need a statute like this one:

(a) Except as provided in subsection (b), no court of the United States shall stay any action commenced in or removed to a district court under this title for the purpose of obtaining a decision regarding a question of state law from a state court.

(b) A court of the United States may stay an action, otherwise properly commenced in or removed to a district court under this title, in order to certify to the highest court of a state a question of state law, if—

(1) the state has a procedure by which its highest court may answer the question;

(2) the question of state law can resolve the dispute between the parties and cannot satisfactorily be determined in light of existing state authorities; and

(3) the court expressly finds that certification will not cause undue delay or prejudice to the parties.

(c) In all cases in which a question of state law is certified under subsection (b), the court shall retain jurisdiction and may enter any appropriate ancillary orders. If the state certification proceeding fails to produce a prompt determination of the state law question, the court shall vacate the stay.

Since there is no existing section of the Judicial Code governing state-question abstention, I offer this proposal as a new, free-standing statute. Subsection (a) would establish an explicit prohibition on the kind of abstention that Justice Frankfurter developed. Subsection (b) would allow an exception for any case, irrespective of the nature of the federal claims involved, if the state concerned offers a certification procedure that will produce an authoritative answer to an unsettled question of state law in a prompt and efficacious manner. Here, I track the relevant ALI position, also incorporated in the Mathias-Brooke bill. Since this new proposal would not authorize abstention in favor of ordinary state court litigation as would the ALI model, it need not include the conditions suggested by the ALI to limit the incidence of abstention generally. Instead, a straightforward authority to certify questions to the state appellate courts can stand alone. As long as the three conditions specified in subsection (b) are met, abstention should present no substantial barrier to federal adjudication of federal claims. Employed wisely, certification can ameliorate friction with the state courts and should be available for that purpose. Under this provision, the state courts will determine only questions of state law. If necessary, the litigants will promptly be back in federal court for the treatment of federal issues. This proposal, too, eliminates the rule by which litigants now reserve federal claims from state court judgment, but only because reservations of that kind are unnecessary when the only kind of state-question abstention available is by way of certification. Subsection (c) is substantially the monitoring provision that appears in the ALI plan.[101]

Some Circumstances

The ALI's proposal regarding federal-question abstention was drafted before the syndicalism case was decided and, accordingly, does not fully address the Supreme Court's recent decisions. Consistent with the Anti-Injunction Act, the ALI would largely bar federal injunctions against civil proceedings in state court, but would permit injunctions against criminal prosecutions in two situations: when state officials attempt to enforce statutes that are facially invalid, and when local proceedings are so "plainly discriminatory as to amount to a denial of the equal protection of the laws."[102] The first of these two possibilities tracks Justice Brennan's 1965 opinion for the Court, later undercut by the decision in the syndicalism case;[103] the second once again reflects the ALI's preoccupation with race discrimination in the 1960s. The ALI's model is noteworthy in two ways: it assumes that the federal courts should not ordinarily interfere with any kind of judicial proceedings already pending in state court, and it contemplates that troubling criminal cases should be handled not by expanding removal jurisdiction, but by making injunctions available in "some circumstances."[104] The Mathias-Brooke bill would have codified the holding in the syndicalism case, but would have overruled the most disturbing extension of abstention that had been announced when the bill was introduced, namely, the rule that a federal court must decline jurisdiction if a state prosecution is initiated after a federal action is begun, but before the federal court has taken serious action.[105]

Backing up and beginning again, it is essential that we set in place legislation directing the federal courts to exercise the jurisdiction they have to decide federal questions and to award prevailing parties any appropriate relief. Abstention should no longer be recognized as a general excuse for refusing to exercise federal judicial power in deference to an array of state interests, real or imagined. Instead, abstention should be collapsed back into the comparatively narrow circumstances that gave it birth, namely, cases in which federal plaintiffs seek injunctions against state judicial proceedings already under way. Injunctions against pending civil proceedings in state court should almost always be prohibited. Parties to civil actions should ordinarily deal with any concerns they have about litigating in state court by removing their actions to federal court on the basis of a federal defense or counterclaim—under the proposal offered in Chapter Three.

For the reasons I have given, removal should not be permitted in criminal cases.[106] Since injunctions against pending prosecutions can have the same untoward impact on local control of the criminal law, injunctions, too, should be hard to get. In this sense, the syndicalism case was correctly decided, but for the wrong reasons. The difficulties surrounding federal-question abstention flow not from what this form of abstention was at the outset, but from the development it has seen in recent years: its extension to criminal proceedings not yet begun, to civil cases (without the possibility of removal), and to situations in which injunctions are said to interfere with the administration of state policies, for example, law enforcement by local police departments.

New legislation should establish a general rule against injunctions running to pending state criminal prosecutions, subject to exceptions for cases in which federal rights cannot be protected in state court—cases, that is, in which federal rights may well be violated by the mere fact of prosecution, as opposed to a wrongful conviction that can be remedied later in federal habeas corpus. To be specific, Congress should enact the following substitute for the Anti-Injunction Act:

(a) Except as provided in subsection (b), in any civil action commenced in or removed to a court of the United states of proper jurisdiction, the court shall exercise jurisdiction and shall award any relief warranted to redress meritorious claims, without regard to the effect the exercise of federal jurisdiction or the award of federal relief may have on proceedings in a state court or administrative agency, state policies, or the execution of state policies by state officials.

(b) No court of the United States shall enjoin a judicial proceeding pending in a state court, unless—

(1) in the case of a civil proceeding in state court, the court finds that an injunction is necessary either to protect its jurisdiction or to effectuate its judgments; or

(2) in the case of a criminal prosecution in state court, the court finds that—

(A) the statute under which the state prosecution was brought is constitutionally invalid on its face;

(B) the state prosecution was initiated without an objective to obtain a valid conviction;

(C) the state prosecution has an effect on the exercise of a federal right that cannot be eliminated by the presentation of a claim based on that right by an individual criminal defendant; or

(D) the proceedings in state court otherwise fail to provide an opportunity for full and fair adjudication of a federal claim.

(c) For purposes of subsection (b), a proceeding is pending in a state court only if the complaint, indictment, information, or other initiating or charging instrument was filed in state court before the complaint or removal petition was filed in the federal civil action in which the injunction is sought.

Initially, this proposal appears to produce precisely what should rather be denied: routinely available injunctions against pending state proceedings, civil *or* criminal. Far from establishing a blanket prohibition, subsection (a) goes to some lengths to say that the federal courts "shall" grant appropriate relief whenever the claims in issue are meritorious, irrespective of the effects on state judicial proceedings, state policies, or the administration of state affairs generally. The provision must begin this way, however, in order to contend with existing abstention decisions. Recall that the Court has exempted §1983 actions from the reach of the Anti-Injunction Act on the ground that §1983 is an act of Congress that expressly authorizes injunctions against state proceedings.[107] That decision frees many federal-question cases from any existing statutory restriction on injunctions and substitutes the Court's own abstention rules. Those rules, in turn, transform abstention into a sweeping denial of federal adjudication in a host of circumstances in which there is no threat of federal interference with pending judicial proceedings.

All this makes it infeasible to deal with federal-question abstention by tinkering with existing statutory language. The better way to proceed is to begin with a general rule allowing, indeed, requiring injunctive and other relief when it is merited. In this way, we ensure that in the run of cases, in which federal interference with pending state judicial proceedings is not in issue, the federal courts will exercise the jurisdiction they surely have in federal-question cases. Then, we can retrieve that (small) part of abstention that should be preserved, that is, a ban on (most) injunctions against pending state judicial proceedings. When the parties to a civil action in state court forgo removal to federal court, we (usually) do not want the federal courts to interfere with the resulting state proceedings by coercive injunction. Similarly, when state criminal prosecutions are under way, we (usually) do not want the federal courts to be involved—until later, when habeas corpus becomes available. Otherwise, in the great mass of cases in which the federal courts' adjudication of federal questions does not disrupt pending state judicial proceedings of any kind, abstention should be abolished.

Paragraph (b)(1) codifies the substance of §2283 as that statute now stands—minus a reference to exceptions specially enacted by Congress. If there is good reason to short-circuit state court litigation in some civil case or set of cases, the means to that end should not be an exception to the general rule against federal injunctions, but a more generous opportunity for removal to federal court, that is, removal on the basis of a federal defense or counterclaim.[108] Paragraph (b)(2) enacts the elements of federal-question abstention that should be preserved. Under this provision, the federal courts would be barred from issuing injunctions against pending state criminal proceedings in all but the rare instances I have identified.[109] Subparagraph (b)(2)(A) captures the situation in Justice Brennan's 1965 decision regarding a state criminal prosecution under a statute that violates the Constitution on its face. Subparagraph (b)(2)(B) covers cases in which state prosecutors pursue charges merely to harass defendants. Rather than use words like "harassment" or "bad faith," this paragraph spells out the kind of prosecution it means to reach. Subparagraph (b)(2)(C) captures the other cases about which I have been concerned, in which citizens need injunctive relief that will safeguard their rights prospectively. Finally, subparagraph (b)(2)(D) establishes a safety net for cases in which federal injunctions should be available, but in which none of the circumstances specified in subparagraphs (b)(2)(A–C) obtain. Here, it is safe to employ the "full and fair" adjudication standard as a general category—not to describe all the instances in which the federal courts should be free to act, but to provide authority for injunctions in additional situations not explicitly covered previously. Finally, subsection (c) ensures that injunctions will not be withheld when state authorities initiate state proceedings only after a party files suit in federal court. Recall that existing precedents *do* bar the exercise of federal jurisdiction in cases of that kind, so long as state officials act before the federal court gets very far. Subsection (c) protects the result in the shopping mall case, where Justice Brennan's opinion allowed a declaratory judgment action when a state criminal prosecution had not yet been initiated.

I do not suggest that the cases identified in subsection (b) will always be easy to spot, or that the federal courts will not have to expend scarce resources to separate cases that warrant injunctions from those that do not. In the main, however, it seems unlikely that the availability of injunctions in circumstances described this narrowly will cause great mischief—for either the federal or the state courts.

▼

In this chapter, I have surveyed the history and asserted justifications for the Supreme Court's multifaceted abstention doctrines, pursuant to which the federal courts decline, in effect, to exercise jurisdiction in federal-question cases. I began with state-question abstention as it was initially articulated by Justice Frankfurter. Under that doctrine, litigants who assert both federal and state claims for relief may be channeled to the state courts for an authoritative adjudication of uncertain state-law questions. While would-be federal plaintiffs are entitled to reserve a chance to return to federal court if need be for the consideration of federal claims, the practical consequence of state-question abstention can often be the commitment of both state and federal issues to the state courts. On reflection, the state-question abstention doctrine is more trouble than it is worth, sacrificing the federal adjudication of federal claims in a misguided attempt to avoid friction between the federal and state courts. Accordingly, that doctrine should be restricted to narrow circumstances in which a state certification scheme ensures prompt state court action on state issues alone.

The federal-question abstention doctrine illustrated by the syndicalism case presents an even more serious threat to plaintiffs seeking access to the federal courts. For under that doctrine the federal courts deliberately direct would-be federal litigants to press federal claims in state court. Early on, federal-question abstention was limited to cases in which the federal courts were asked to enjoin pending state criminal prosecutions. If the doctrine had been held within those limits, it would have been acceptable, even desirable, in most instances. It would have prevented the federal courts from interfering with local authorities' control of criminal law enforcement while preserving the federal courts' authority to consider federal constitutional claims later in habeas corpus. But the Court has extended federal-question abstention beyond the criminal context to cases in which habeas corpus will not be available, thus channeling federal-question litigation into the state courts when the judgments those courts reach will have preclusive effect. Moreover, the Court has invoked this same abstention doctrine to defer not only to state judicial proceedings, but to state executive functions against which citizens have federal claims.

Reform legislation should abolish federal-question abstention as a free-wheeling excuse for withholding federal court jurisdiction in a variety of contexts. In place of the Court's decisions, Congress should do two things. First, Congress should establish a right to remove state civil actions on the basis of a federal defense or counterclaim. That change in existing law, proposed in Chapter Three, would eliminate the felt need on the part of defendants in state civil lawsuits to seek injunctions from the federal courts. Second, Congress should bar most federal injunctions against pending civil and criminal proceedings in state court—provided that, in the special circumstances I have discussed, the federal courts should be authorized to enjoin state criminal prosecutions in which federal rights are at risk and cannot be secured by habeas corpus after state proceedings have come to a close.

CHAPTER FIVE

▼

In Custody

One night in September 1919, African American tenant farmers gathered in a church near Hoop Spur, Arkansas, to talk to lawyers associated with the Progressive Farmers and Household Union of America. The purpose of the meeting was to explore legal means by which local white landowners might be forced to lower the excessive rents they charged blacks for the privilege of tilling their lands. According to reports,[1] the group at the church was attacked by a gang of armed white men employed by the landowners. In disturbances lasting for days thereafter, as many as two whites and two hundred blacks were killed. The police arrested numerous black suspects and charged five of them with murder.

The arrests ignited events that were extraordinary even for the rural South in the wake of World War I. The governor formed a committee to investigate what he called a black "insurrection"; newspapers published inflammatory articles; a lynch mob of whites marched on the jail where the defendants were held—to be turned away by federal troops and a "solemn promise" from the governor's committee that "the law" would be "carried out."[2] The committee reportedly made good on its promise by torturing black witnesses into testifying against the defendants. The trial, such as it was, took place a few weeks later amid a mob threatening "dangerous consequences" for anyone interfering with the "desired result." The judge appointed a single lawyer to represent all five defendants. That lawyer did not consult with his clients. He filed no motions, called no witnesses, and declined to put the defendants on the witness stand to tell their side of the story. The trial lasted forty-five minutes; the all-white jury took just five minutes more to return guilty verdicts and death sentences for all. On appeal to the Arkansas Supreme Court, the convicted men insisted that they had been convicted and sentenced in violation of the Constitution. The state supreme court refused to credit those claims, however, and the governor set a date for the executions.

On all too many occasions in our history, African Americans have gone to their deaths in circumstances like those at Hoop Spur, the innocent victims of grossly unfair and racist proceedings in state court. This time, however, one of the Union lawyers filed a petition for a writ of habeas corpus in the U. S. District Court for the Eastern District of Arkansas. At the time, it was not clear that citizens whose constitutional claims had been rejected on appeal in state court could seek a reexamination of those claims by way of habeas corpus in federal court. The petition in the tenant farmer case thus offered the Supreme Court a vehicle for developing the "Great Writ" as a federal remedy for the federal rights of criminal defendants in state court.

Initially, it appeared that federal adjudication might be denied. The district court discharged the petition,[3] and in the Supreme Court, Justice McReynolds, one of the Old Court's four horsemen, tried to persuade his colleagues that the precedent they had recently set in Leo Frank's case should be the guide.[4] McReynolds recognized that the Supreme Court itself had jurisdiction to review a judgment rendered by a state's highest court. Accordingly, if this case had come to the U. S. Supreme Court directly from the Arkansas Supreme Court, the state court's decision would have been "voidable," that is, reversible, if found to be erroneous. McReynolds insisted, however, that the federal district court that had received the prisoners' petition had no such direct appellate jurisdiction to review the Arkansas Supreme Court's judgment for error. Since the case had arisen in habeas corpus, he contended that the petitioners could be granted relief only if the state judgment was not merely "voidable," but "void," that is, the outcome of an appellate process so fundamentally flawed as not to be entitled to respect as a judicial proceeding at all. According to McReynolds, federal habeas corpus was available only if the state supreme court had exceeded its jurisdiction—if, in other words, it had ceased to act *as a court.* Since in this instance the Arkansas Supreme Court had treated the prisoners according to "established modes of procedure" under state law (including an opportunity to raise their claims that their constitutional rights had been violated at trial), subsequent litigation in federal court should be barred.

Justice McReynolds acknowledged that the federal courts had authority to issue the writ of habeas corpus on behalf of prisoners held in state custody in violation of the fourteenth amendment's due process clause. But in his view these petitioners had received the process that was "due" when the state supreme court provided "corrective process" for any "irregularities" at their trial.[5] Paul Bator would have said that, in habeas corpus, due process required only "full and fair" adjudication in state court: the state courts need only have employed sound *procedures,* whether or not they arrived at the correct *outcome* in the eyes of federal judges looking on.[6] As I have explained, the process model that McReynolds and Bator would have invoked in habeas corpus amounted to the doctrine of preclusion, which ordinarily limits litigants' ability to obtain federal adjudication of issues that were or might have been tested in previous proceedings in state court.

Fortunately for the five black prisoners, the full Court saw things differently. Writing for the majority, Justice Holmes rejected McReynolds' contention that federal adjudication was foreclosed in light of prior state proceedings. In so doing, Holmes both vindicated his dissent in Leo Frank's case and laid the groundwork for the development of federal habeas corpus as a means by which state prisoners now obtain access to the federal courts for the consideration of federal claims the state courts have previously rejected. Holmes agreed (for the moment) that the federal district court could not grant habeas corpus relief whenever a petitioner showed federal error in a state criminal trial. Yet when it appeared that the "whole proceeding" in state court was a "mask," that "counsel, jury and judge were swept to the fatal end by an irresistible wave of public passion," and that the Arkansas Supreme Court had "failed to correct the wrong," then "perfection in the machinery for correction [of trial error]" could not keep the federal courts from "securing" federal rights. State adjudication, however "full and fair" in *form,* could not insulate invalid convictions from reconsideration by way of habeas corpus in federal court.[7]

In the tenant farmer case, Justice Holmes concluded that the form of state process might, indeed, have been an empty shell. The alleged errors at trial were glaring. The petitioners claimed that blacks had been excluded from both the grand jury that had indicted them and the trial jury that had convicted them, and that the domination of the trial by angry whites had robbed the proceedings of any hint of fairness. The state supreme court had brushed aside the race-discrimination claims, because the petitioners' assigned counsel had not objected soon enough. As to the mob-domination claim, the state court had said only that the evidence did not "necessarily" show that the petitioners had been denied a fair trial. In the main, the state court said only that the trial had been conducted "according to law," that the jury had been "correctly charged," and that the evidence had been "legally sufficient." Holmes was forced to agree with Justice McReynolds. This case from Arkansas, involving African American defendants railroaded by an angry, racist mob, looked very much like Leo Frank's case from Georgia—involving a Jewish defendant facing an equally angry, anti-Semitic gang. To Holmes, however, the similarity of the two cases suggested not that the sterile approach in Frank's case should be followed yet again, but rather that the process model that had permitted injustice in the past should be abandoned. Justice Holmes remanded the tenant farmer case for a hearing on the prisoners' federal claims.

The writ of habeas corpus has a long and distinguished history in Anglo-American law. In this chapter, I begin with a brief sketch of that history in order to put in context the role the writ plays (or should play) in the structure of federal jurisdiction today. We must reach beyond the pioneering work by Justice Holmes in the tenant farmer case to Justice Frankfurter's contributions at mid-century and the arrangements established by Chief Justice Warren and Justice Brennan in the 1960s. The first question on the table is the justification for exempting federal habeas corpus from ordinary preclusion rules. The conventional answer is that a citizen's interest in being free from unlawful "custody" justifies resort to the federal courts. That will not do. Habeas corpus is better understood as a mechanism for ensuring that citizens subject to criminal prosecution in state court have access to a federal court for the adjudication of their federal claims. Since state criminal defendants are unable to obtain such a federal forum initially by removing their cases to federal court for trial, they are (or should be) entitled to obtain federal adjudication later in habeas corpus—after the state courts have completed their work.

I bear down on this intensely controversial aspect of modern habeas corpus: the availability of federal jurisdiction as a sequel to state court adjudication. I will explore the values and interests at stake and consider current challenges to the very core of the Warren Court's framework. Legislative initiatives by the Reagan and Bush Administrations would have installed preclusion in habeas corpus explicitly. Recent

Supreme Court decisions threaten to transmute various habeas doctrines into preclusion rules by another name. As in prior chapters, I will survey the responses that have been proposed to date and then identify better ideas for legislative action to preserve habeas corpus as a vital federal remedy for federal rights. In this instance, we need legislation that gives petitioners an opportunity to litigate their federal claims in federal court that is roughly equivalent to the opportunity they would have had if they had been permitted to remove the state prosecutions against them to federal court under §1441. I promise a concrete proposal toward that end. Finally, in four brief sections, I will discuss the implications of that proposal for some procedural questions that have attracted attention in recent years: the state proceedings a prisoner must engage before seeking a federal writ of habeas corpus; the time a prisoner should have to marshal his or her arguments and file a federal petition; the effect the federal court should give to a prisoner's failure to raise a claim in state court at the time and in the manner prescribed by state law; and the circumstances in which a prisoner may file multiple federal petitions.[8]

The Law of the Land

The English common law writ of habeas corpus may strike the uninitiated as an unlikely means of access to American federal courts. When it first appeared late in the twelfth century, the habeas writ did not itself initiate a lawsuit, but rather was one of several ancillary writs, employed as an adjunct to more familiar actions when it was necessary to have the "body" of a person before the court.[9] Over the next six centuries, however, habeas emerged as an independent basis of jurisdiction for the king's courts at Westminster.[10] Importantly, the central courts used the writ, first, to draw judicial business away from manorial and franchise courts operated by local barons and, second, to fight among themselves for authority to decide cases. For example, the Court of Chancery might resolve a dispute and issue an injunction ordering the defendant to take some action. If the defendant refused, Chancery might hold him in contempt and send him to the Tower of London. At that point, King's Bench might grant the imprisoned man a writ of habeas corpus, setting him free to pursue his claims in the law courts.[11]

In due course, the courts at Westminster invoked habeas corpus against royal power itself. When the king or his council sent Englishmen to the Tower without first following the procedures developed by the courts for criminal trials, both King's Bench and Common Pleas responded by issuing the writ to set free those whom the king condemned without trial. The result was confrontation between two emerging segments of English government. A third new body, the English Parliament, soon sided with the courts—by tying habeas corpus to the thirty-ninth chapter of Magna Carta, said to guarantee that no Englishman could be detained against his will except by the "law of the land." Parliament declared that the mere command of the king was an insufficient basis for imprisonment, that Magna Carta required a trial under common law procedures, and that habeas corpus was available to anyone jailed without the process that was due in such a trial. The record shows that Parliament, too, occasionally denigrated due process, and habeas corpus into the bargain, by suspending the writ in order to deny trials to political dissenters.[12] In the main, however, habeas corpus provided a procedural vehicle by which English courts could enforce individual rights against governmental power.

The American colonists also linked habeas corpus with due process and thus laid claim to the writ as one of the rights they enjoyed as English citizens. Yet we have only sparse evidence regarding the uses to which habeas was put in this country. By some accounts, the writ could be sought only to contest detention before or, better said, without trial; by other accounts, habeas was available after trial as a means by which some courts reviewed the work of others.[13] Suffice it to say that all the early American states recognized habeas corpus of *some* dimension. Moreover, the new U. S. Constitution in 1787 specifically provided that the writ could not be "suspended" except in "Cases of Rebellion or Invasion." The Judiciary Act of 1789 authorized both the Supreme Court and the lower federal courts to issue the writ on behalf of prisoners held in the custody of federal officers in violation of federal law. And one of the most significant enactments of the Reconstruction era, the Habeas Corpus Act of 1867, extended that jurisdiction to cases in which petitioners claimed they were unlawfully held by state officials. The modern version of the 1789 and 1867 Acts conferring basic, subject matter jurisdiction on the federal courts in habeas corpus is 28 U.S.C. §2241:

> (a) Writs of habeas corpus may be granted by the Supreme Court, any justice thereof, the district courts and any circuit judge within their respective jurisdictions. . . .

(c) The writ of habeas corpus shall not extend to a prisoner unless—. . . .

(3) He is in custody in violation of the Constitution or laws or treaties of the United States. . . .

An important additional statute, enacted in 1966, underscores the federal courts' authority to entertain petitions from state prisoners held in custody on the basis of criminal convictions and sentences imposed by the state courts. Section 2254(a) reads this way:

(a) The Supreme Court, a Justice thereof, a circuit judge, or a district court shall entertain an application for a writ of habeas corpus in behalf of a person in custody pursuant to the judgment of a State court only on the ground that he is in custody in violation of the Constitution or laws or treaties of the United States.

Habeas corpus, in sum, has been the Great Writ of Liberty, both in England and in the United States, for a very long time. Its uses have evolved in surprising, but salutary, ways. Indeed, the writ's development has not ceased even now.

Conventional Notions

In law, as in life generally, it is usually best and almost always efficient to do things well the first time and thereafter to leave well-enough alone. This, at any rate, is the working idea behind preclusion doctrine, which (via the full faith and credit statute, 28 U.S.C. §1738) typically cuts off federal court consideration of claims that were or might have been "fully and fairly" adjudicated in previous state court proceedings.[14] Nevertheless, the federal courts' jurisdiction to entertain applications for the writ of habeas corpus has historically enjoyed an exemption from §1738. Petitioners *can* apply for the federal writ on grounds that were, or might have been, raised and determined in state court.[15] In habeas, the effect of prior state litigation is governed by statutes, rules, and judge-made doctrines that respond to values associated with preclusion, but are not neatly congruent with the preclusion standards that would control ordinary civil actions.

Under the common law of England, prisoners were permitted to go "first to the judge of a court, and, on being refused, to a court itself, and on being refused by one court, to . . . another court."[16] In this way, they could "proceed from court to court until [they] obtained [their] liberty."[17] Just why this was so is unclear, and the origins of the similar understanding in this country have been debated.[18] The modern explanation focuses on the detention of which prisoners complain. The subject matter jurisdiction of the federal courts is limited to petitions from applicants who allege "custody" in violation of federal law. This custody requirement also has ancient roots, bearing a correlative relation to the function of the writ in the seventeenth century: to secure the release of persons who were wrongfully confined. Petitioners had to be in some form of detention from which they could be discharged. Custody, accordingly, is no mere artificial prerequisite to a habeas action. It is intrinsic to what habeas corpus is—what it means or, at least, what it has been and meant traditionally.[19]

By conventional account, the link between habeas corpus and custody supplies a gate-keeping device for the federal courts: it screens cases according to the nature of the interests at stake, limiting access to petitioners who allege unlawful restraints on liberty. For example, petitioners who complain only of unlawful fines are excluded. Likewise, the custody requirement screens petitions according to the timing of applicants' attempts to enter the federal courts: only petitioners who are in custody at the time they file their petitions are heard. Those who are not yet threatened with custody or who have been discharged from past restraints are not entitled to pursue the writ.[20] By this account, moreover, custody also provides a normative justification for allowing some litigants into federal court despite prior litigation in state court, but excluding others. A petitioner's interest in freedom from unlawful detention is said to warrant another look at claims that were or might have been considered previously in state court. In ordinary litigation in which the parties vie for economic advantage, "conventional notions of finality" reflected in preclusion rules have their place.[21] In habeas corpus, by contrast, in which prisoners contend for their very life or liberty, the practical interests served by preclusion are outweighed by the paramount concern that unlawful custody should be terminated. Both the architects of the modern framework, such as Justice Brennan, and loyal detractors, such as Justice Harlan, met on this common ground. The "role and function" of habeas corpus depends on an exemption from preclusion; "[t]he consequences of injustice—loss of liberty and sometimes loss of life—[are] far too great to permit the automatic application of an entire body of technical rules whose primary relevance [is] in the area of civil litigation."[22]

In the end, custody is said to offer, on a nonconstitutional level, something akin to what primary standing rules provide on a constitutional level.[23] Standing doctrine identifies litigants who can invoke the power of the federal courts generally; the custody requirement divides cases that are justiciable under Article III into two further categories. In one category are cases in which litigants are not in custody and thus can get into federal court only for original adjudication of their federal claims, for example, by filing an action in a district court under a statute like §1331 and somehow avoiding abstention.[24] In cases in this first category, litigants who find themselves initially in state court will usually be precluded from approaching the federal courts later in hopes of upsetting an unfavorable judgment by the state courts. In the second category are cases in which litigants do complain of unlawful custody and thus can seek federal litigation of their federal claims in habeas corpus, notwithstanding prior state court proceedings.

Surrogates

The explanation the custody requirement provides for allowing convicts to file federal habeas corpus petitions is no more satisfying than the explanation primary standing doctrine supplies for allowing any litigants to be in federal court at all. The interests at stake in a habeas action, important as they are, do not fully explain why state prisoners are entitled to relitigate claims in federal court. For one thing, even as the Court makes custody a jurisdictional prerequisite, the justices allow comparatively weak restraints to suffice. Not only prisoners who are physically incarcerated may apply for relief, but also probationers, parolees, and others facing even less severe restrictions of their liberty.[25] The more expansive the definition of custody for habeas corpus purposes, of course, the less serious is the custody requirement as a screening device.

More fundamentally, custody fails to explain why the relitigation of claims, if warranted at all, should be undertaken in federal rather than state court. Trying to make custody do service as a means of distributing business between the federal and state courts in the habeas context is rather like trying to make the maxims of equity perform a similar function in the abstention context.[26] Neither effort is successful. The real explanation for the writ's exemption from preclusion is simply that citizens subject to criminal prosecution in state court should have an opportunity to raise any federal claims they may have in federal court—after state court proceedings have been completed. The explanation for that, in turn, is to "effectuate the purposes" of the modern writ, namely, to vindicate federal rights in federal court.[27] Once again, to appreciate the general framework of federal jurisdiction, we must take account of the substantive claims that the federal courts may be asked to enforce.

The development of federal habeas corpus for state prisoners tracks the development of constitutional safeguards in state criminal cases, which began about the time of the tenant farmer case, gradually gained momentum in the period following World War II, and then blossomed in the Warren Court period. Within that movement, the Court's elaboration of the very meaning of the Constitution went hand in hand with the establishment of federal habeas corpus as an integral part of the machinery by which the Constitution was, and would be, enforced on a daily basis. Even Justice Frankfurter participated in these developments. In a classic opinion in 1953, Frankfurter declared that federal habeas was available for all federal claims arising from state prosecutions ending in custody. Previous state court judgments on federal rights were not entitled to preclusive effect.[28] For if federal habeas corpus were not free from ordinary preclusion rules and, indeed, the full faith and credit statute, the writ could not serve as a routinely available federal remedy for federal rights. The writ of habeas corpus, long a weapon in battles among courts for jurisdiction, was once again unsheathed to transfer power from local courts to national tribunals.

Ten years later, a trilogy of cases orchestrated by Chief Justice Warren and Justice Brennan built on the formative work done by Holmes, Frankfurter, and sympathetic academicians.[29] The Warren Court employed habeas corpus to implement its innovations in criminal procedure, most prominently the application of the Bill of Rights to the states. This was scarcely a brazen grab for power, but only another instance in which the Supreme Court summoned the lower federal courts to enforce constitutional rights currently in favor. Where the Old Court enlisted the federal courts in the cause of protecting corporations from economic regulation, the Warren Court recruited them to enforce the procedural rights owed to criminal defendants in state court. The justices could not superintend fifty state supreme courts by means of direct review and therefore turned to the federal district and circuit courts as surrogates.

The Rights of a Human Being

If custody does not explain the exemption habeas corpus enjoys from preclusion, and if the genuine explanation for federal adjudication after judgment in state court is the preservation of the federal courts' authority to vindicate federal rights, then habeas provides yet another arena in which to rehearse the parity debate I reviewed in Chapter One.[30] In this context, however, one who insists that the federal courts should be available has a heavier burden than usual. It must be contended not merely that litigants who wish to go to federal court rather than state court should be allowed to do so, but also that parties who have once *been* to state court should be permitted to litigate *again* in the federal forum. Predictably, the proposition that the federal courts should operate in tandem with the state courts produces yet another layer of arguments and counterarguments between the liberal and conservative camps.

For conservatives, federal habeas corpus is the paradigm of all that was *wrong* with the Warren Court, namely, that Court's distrust of the states and state courts and its failure to appreciate the societal threat posed by crime. To these critics, habeas is a constant irritant: an expensive, time-consuming, and repetitive enterprise that frustrates law enforcement by needlessly injecting the federal courts into matters better left to the states. Conservatives charge that federal habeas corpus for state prisoners generates friction between the two court systems. State judges are offended by the award of habeas relief to prisoners whose federal claims were found wanting in state court and resent the very idea that federal, trial-level courts accept petitions from state prisoners and thus presume to second-guess judgments that may have been affirmed by the states' highest courts. The delays associated with habeas corpus are said to undercut the finality of state judgments and, particularly in death penalty cases, to frustrate state attempts to carry out valid sentencing policies. Finally, it is alleged that most habeas corpus petitions are frivolous anyway and thus needlessly clog federal dockets. The concentration of effort on so many trivial claims may hamper the vindication of the very federal rights habeas is supposed to protect. As Justice Jackson once warned, "[i]t must prejudice the occasional meritorious application to be buried in a flood of worthless ones. He who must search a haystack for a needle is likely to end up with the attitude that the needle is not worth the search."[31]

To liberals, by contrast, habeas makes perfect sense. The authority of the federal courts to entertain constitutional challenges to state criminal convictions is the embodiment of all that was *right* about the Warren Court and the vision that Court offered of a meaningful system of American liberty, underwritten by independent federal tribunals willing and able to check the coercive power of government. Supporters of habeas corpus for state prisoners meet critics' charges forthrightly. It is said, for example, that if the state courts are offended by the federal courts' involvement, they have their own poor record in federal-question cases to blame. There are competing considerations to weigh against the states' interest in the finality of criminal judgments. The institutional settings in which state and federal courts operate make it imperative that the federal courts have the final word on federal issues. In habeas corpus, the federal courts can consider federal questions in isolation from state procedural rules and the inevitable focus in state court on the guilt or innocence of the accused. Although habeas corpus takes time and may cause the postponement of criminal sanctions, the treatment of substantial federal claims should not be frustrated by an unseemly rush to judgment—particularly in capital cases. By this account, the ostensible redundancy of federal habeas corpus is a positive thing, producing a fruitful dialogue between the state and federal courts.[32]

In addition, habeas supporters contend that the federal courts need their current habeas corpus jurisdiction in order to address claims that counsel failed to raise in state court or that otherwise escaped notice previously. As to the relative merit of habeas petitions, habeas supporters point out that petitioners in death penalty cases are successful in federal court nearly 40 percent of the time. The success rate in noncapital cases is much lower (about 4 percent), but even that figure is significant inasmuch as the federal courts consider claims only after the state courts have had an opportunity to treat them. Moreover, if the state courts avoid errors in most cases, it may be in part because they know the federal courts are waiting in the wings. Responding to Justice Jackson, Judge Walter Schaefer once remarked that "it is not a needle we are looking for in these stacks of paper, but the rights of a human being."[33]

In light of the controversy that seems always to swirl around habeas corpus, it is small wonder that Bator chose habeas as the vehicle for elaborating his process model.[34] Since he was convinced that the pursuit of objectively correct outcomes was misguided, since he saw no reason to prefer the judgments of federal courts to those of the state courts, and since he was content to accept state decisions that preferred governmental interests over individual claims of right, Bator found it troubling that federal habeas corpus should even exist as a mechanism for reexamining issues that were, or might have been, determined by the state courts. His model thus adopted the language of preclusion to express the circumstances in which the federal courts should accept petitions notwithstanding prior state court proceedings. In Bator's view, federal habeas corpus should be open only if the state courts failed to offer an opportunity for "full and fair" adjudication of a prisoner's federal claims. Recent legislative initiatives and Supreme Court decisions partake of Bator's approach, in some form or other.

In habeas corpus, as elsewhere, the process model seriously undervalues the federal forum. In liberal circles, the arguments for preserving federal habeas are regarded as far more persuasive than critics' cost/benefit analysis suggesting curbs on the writ. At a more fundamental level, however, habeas corpus following state proceedings in criminal cases should be available, irrespective of the attendant costs. If citizens with federal claims are generally to have an opportunity to litigate those claims in federal court, litigants who are haled into state court in the first instance to respond to criminal charges must also be allowed some access to the federal forum. For the reasons examined in Chapter Three, that access cannot come by way of removal before trial.[35] It must be achieved later, in habeas corpus, after the state courts have implemented state criminal law policy. The goal is to provide state criminal defendants with an opportunity for federal litigation of federal claims that approximates the adjudication they would have had if they had been in a position to raise those claims in affirmative civil lawsuits pursuant to statutes like §1331, or by way of removal. It is insufficient, then, to limit habeas corpus to the role that Bator's model contemplates.

Similarly, it would be inadequate to refashion the writ into an appellate review mechanism, as some observers have suggested. True, a federal habeas corpus court addresses a prisoner's federal claims after the state courts have rejected them; true, the usual occasion for reexamination of this kind arises when one court has appellate jurisdiction to review another court's judgments for error. Yet an appellate model for habeas would suggest that the federal district courts should typically accept the facts developed in state court and concentrate on any mistakes of law—or, at least, that the federal courts should give serious weight to what the state courts have already concluded regarding the merits of federal claims. Optimally, however, the function performed by federal courts in habeas corpus should be more like the fresh, independent adjudication we associate with ordinary civil actions pursuant to §1331, albeit without the usual preclusive implications.[36] The federal courts should begin anew—determining the historical facts underlying prisoners' claims, ascertaining the pertinent legal standards, and applying those standards to the facts. In habeas as in §1331 cases, Chief Justice Warren once explained, "[i]t is the typical, not the rare, case in which constitutional claims turn upon the resolution of factual issues." Subject to some qualifications I will explore in a moment, petitioners should be entitled to thoroughgoing trial-level treatment of their federal claims in the federal forum.[37]

Effective Assistance

The proper form and function of habeas corpus is especially complicated—for two reasons. First, most would-be habeas corpus petitioners are financially unable to obtain counsel to speak on their behalf, either in state or in federal court. Inadequate representation of the poor is a constant in the American legal system, bedeviling ordinary civil litigation of the kind discussed in previous chapters, as well as habeas corpus. The problem is acute here, however, in that most habeas applicants are indigent prison inmates pressing their own, individualized claims rather than generalized issues touching the public interest, which are typically more likely to attract support from organizations and volunteer lawyers. While defendants in serious criminal cases enjoy a constitutional right to the "effective assistance" of counsel at trial and on direct appeal, the representation indigents actually get is often inferior.[38] Moreover, federal questions destined for habeas corpus are typically raised initially in state "postconviction proceedings," which take place after the state appellate process is complete. There is no constitutional entitlement to professional representation in those proceedings. Nor is there a general right to counsel in federal habeas corpus.[39]

Congress has established a statutory right to counsel in death penalty habeas cases in federal court, and current bills would encourage the states to do so at all stages of capital cases in their own courts. Moreover, most state courts and all federal district courts have discretionary authority to appoint counsel when prisoners' claims apparently have merit.[40] Still, the supply of competent legal services to prisoners scarcely meets the demand. In the run of cases, the pursuit of postconviction relief, in either state or federal court, is all too often left to prison inmates who cannot represent themselves competently and may well be denied the relief they deserve—and would receive if they had advocates to advance their claims. The value of qualified counsel at all stages can hardly be denied. Professional representation in federal court is the single best predictor of success.[41]

The second complicating factor is the linkage in public debates between habeas corpus and the many failings of the criminal justice system. Crime is a potent political issue. Inasmuch as effective preventive measures are both elusive and expensive, the temptation is strong to find other, simpler (but often illusory) answers. So it is that conservatives typically insist that the federal courts are preoccupied with protecting outsized individual rights at the expense of public order and thus contribute, in their way, to the rising problem of crime in the streets. When Richard Nixon campaigned for the presidency, he promised to name justices to the bench who would support law enforcement authorities in criminal cases.[42] More to the point here, when the Reagan Administration initially proposed legislation to restrict habeas corpus, it was as one of a series of recommendations offered by the Attorney General's Task Force on Violent Crime.[43]

It was the purest demagoguery to suggest that the federal courts were in any way responsible for criminal violence and that street crime would seriously be reduced by altering those courts' jurisdiction to enforce the Bill of Rights. Nevertheless, the Department of Justice, first under Nixon and Reagan and then under President Bush, exhibited an intense, ideological antipathy to the Warren Court's innovations in criminal procedure. That antipathy often took the form of repeated attempts to circumscribe federal habeas corpus—in many ways the centerpiece of the Warren Court's framework for expansive individual rights safeguarded by independent federal courts. Certainly the Bush Administration regarded habeas corpus as a key target of its efforts to expedite the processing of criminal cases. The program that Bush advocated for habeas corpus was consistently tucked into omnibus bills containing a range of anti-crime measures.[44]

In a similar vein, habeas corpus is linked in public debates with the death penalty. At first glance, one would expect that both proponents and opponents of capital punishment would insist on an energetic federal jurisdiction in habeas corpus to ensure that prisoners are not executed in violation of federal law. Yet some death penalty proponents complain that, like the civil rights workers who once used the civil rights removal statute as a means of frustrating criminal prosecutions in state court,[45] death row prisoners now pursue habeas corpus in order to hinder state efforts to carry out authorized sentences. Prison-

ers are said not to use, but to abuse, habeas corpus for the sole purpose of extending litigation. Accordingly, reform proposals that stop
short of the wholesale elimination of habeas corpus are regarded as
duplicitous attempts by the opponents of capital punishment actually
to foster time-consuming federal litigation as a flank attack on the
death penalty.[46]

The Supreme Court itself often expresses impatience with habeas
corpus in death penalty cases. When the Court has restricted the availability of the writ in recent years, it has often done so in capital cases
or, at least, with the effect of its actions on capital cases well in mind.[47]
In 1988, Chief Justice Rehnquist appointed an ad hoc committee of
the Judicial Conference of the United States to investigate "delay" in
the federal courts' handling of death penalty cases. That committee
of senior federal judges, chaired by former Justice Powell, presented a
report to the full Judicial Conference in the fall of 1989. The committee identified inadequate counsel in state postconviction proceedings
as a principal cause of confusion and delay. Rather than recommending that death penalty states be required to appoint counsel for indigents at that stage, however, the committee suggested that the states
be offered procedural advantages in federal habeas corpus as incentives to provide counsel voluntarily. The full Judicial Conference
adopted the Powell Committee Report, with amendments.[48] At about
the same time, the American Bar Association published its own recommendations.[49]

The federal government has little ability to promote capital punishment. Aside from authorizing executions for federal crimes, a tactic
of little practical significance, Congress can lend its support to the
death penalty only by cutting away perceived impediments to its use
in the states in which it is available. In some circles, federal habeas
corpus is deemed to be such an impediment. Accordingly, if reforms
that open the federal courts more widely will be difficult to obtain
regarding standing, subject matter jurisdiction, and abstention, they
will be doubly difficult to achieve respecting habeas corpus.

Limitations

In habeas corpus as in related contexts I have canvassed, the Supreme
Court has abandoned the Warren Court's commitment to the federal
adjudication of federal rights.[50] Chief Justice Rehnquist in particular
has complained that the current system permits "a single federal

judge" to "overturn the judgment of the highest court of a State."[51] Other Nixon and Reagan appointees have expressed similar views.[52] In an effort to deal with the building controversy in the mid-1970s, the Judicial Conference promulgated a special set of rules to stream-line the processing of cases.[53] Nevertheless, recent decisions reflect a relentless campaign to establish more, and more significant, limits on the federal courts' authority to issue the writ.

Meanwhile, the executive branch of the national government has pursued a parallel strategy. The Nixon Administration proposed drastic limitations on the writ, and the Reagan Administration advanced a package of proposals for similar restrictions in both capital and non-capital cases.[54] In his own anti-crime program, President Bush adopted Reagan's plan for general revisions of habeas corpus, as well as the Powell Committee's recommendations for capital cases. First and fore-most, however, the Reagan and Bush Administrations proposed that the federal courts should be barred from considering claims that were "fully and fairly adjudicated" in state court.[55] That idea, borrowed from Paul Bator and the Legal Process tradition on which he drew, has dominated the national debate over habeas corpus ever since—notwithstanding the election of President Clinton. Numerous bills have been advanced to make it law; numerous alternatives have been offered to disclaim it, explicitly or implicitly. Needless to say, the en-actment of the full-and-fair proposal would force the federal courts to give preclusive effect (in some measure) to previous state court judg-ments on federal claims.

I will discuss these developments in the sections to follow. In each instance, current law is flawed—both as it appears in statutes and rules and as it has been interpreted by the Supreme Court. A legislative response is required, but it should scarcely be the full-and-fair pro-gram. Nor should it be the alternative proposals put forward to date. We need, instead, legislation that guarantees the maintenance of ha-beas corpus as the alternative to removal we should conceive the writ to be.

The Constable Blundered

In the wake of the tenant farmer case, habeas corpus developed into a general federal remedy for federal rights. The writ's freedom from preclusion was controversial—then as now. Yet at least after Justice Frankfurter's great opinion in 1953, and certainly during the Warren

Court era, the role assigned to habeas corpus within the system of federal jurisdiction seemed secure.[56] More recently, the Rehnquist Court has questioned the federal courts' use of the writ to entertain *all* federal claims that were, or might have been, adjudicated previously in state court.

Consider, for example, claims based on the "exclusionary rule," which prohibits the states from using evidence obtained by unreasonable searches in violation of the fourth amendment to obtain criminal convictions. While the conceptual basis of the exclusionary rule can be debated, the Court has held in recent years that the rule is not itself a constitutional right, but a judge-made rule of evidence meant to enforce the fourth amendment by deterring illegal police behavior. The loss of reliable evidence is a high price to pay for getting the police to follow the Constitution: the criminal goes free, because "the constable blundered."[57] Accordingly, it has long been argued that the federal courts should not consider habeas petitions that seek relief solely on the basis of the exclusionary rule—for any or all of three reasons: because the rule is not constitutionally grounded (and is thus easier to adjust as the justices see fit); because (unlike most other safeguards) the rule does not enable the trial court to distinguish the innocent from the guilty; or because the deterrent effect of the rule is diminished by the time a case reaches the federal courts in habeas corpus (in some instances years after the unlawful search was conducted).[58]

In 1976, the Supreme Court adopted at least some of these arguments. Importantly, however, Justice Powell's majority opinion expressed the Court's holding in the process-model terms conventionally associated with preclusion. The federal courts were told that they may consider a claim that a prisoner was convicted on the basis of illegally seized evidence only if the state courts failed to provide an "opportunity" for "full and fair" adjudication of that claim.[59] By making critical the mere "opportunity" for state adjudication, rather than actual adjudication, Justice Powell declared that the federal courts should rebuff not only claims previously treated and rejected in state court, but also claims that were not, but might have been, adjudicated there. The new formulation thus introduced both "issue" and "claim" preclusion into habeas cases involving exclusionary rule claims. Now, if the state courts consider a prisoner's fourth amendment claim and find it wanting, a prisoner is typically barred from attempting to relitigate that claim in federal court. If the state courts offer a prisoner a procedure for raising an exclusionary rule claim and she does not seize that "opportunity," the federal courts are equally closed. The consequences have been dramatic. The enforcement of the exclusionary rule in habeas corpus has ground to a halt. New legislation will be required to put the federal courts back in the fourth amendment business.

The turn to preclusion in fourth amendment cases prompted speculation that other claims, too, would soon receive the same treatment. In some minds, indeed, it seemed inevitable that, even without a formal change in §2241 and §2254, the Court would soon jettison entirely the exemption that habeas corpus had always enjoyed from preclusion. While they remained on the bench, Justice Powell himself and Chief Justice Burger urged precisely that course. More recently, Justices Antonin Scalia and Clarence Thomas have taken up the same cause.[60] The full Court, however, regards the fourth amendment exclusionary rule case not as a decision about the scope of the federal courts' jurisdiction in habeas corpus, but rather as a decision about the scope of the exclusionary rule itself. That rule of federal substantive law is of such a character that it is routinely applicable only when its purposes are adequately served. And that, it turns out, is at trial or on direct review, but not in federal habeas corpus. On this conception, the federal habeas courts retain power to consider federal claims generally and, indeed, may consider even an exclusionary rule claim in a case in which the state courts fail to offer an adequate opportunity for adjudicating such a claim. But in ordinary circumstances (in which prisoners do get a fair chance to press fourth amendment claims in state court) the likelihood that the enforcement of the exclusionary rule in habeas corpus will deter future police misconduct is insufficient to justify the costs.

The process-model language the Court used in the fourth amendment case is not to be read as the principal focus in that case. The Court attached significance to whether the prisoner had received an opportunity for "full and fair" adjudication in state court only insofar as it held that the absence of such an opportunity would establish an exception to its primary holding that, ordinarily, the fourth amendment exclusionary rule is inapplicable in habeas. Such an exception was necessary in order to give state authorities themselves an incentive to enforce the exclusionary rule at trial and on appeal. The foundation of the Court's decision, however, was the nature of the fourth amendment exclusionary rule. There is nothing about habeas corpus that excludes a fourth amendment exclusionary rule claim from a federal court's purview simply because the state courts previously determined such a claim against the prisoner; rather, there is something about the fourth amendment exclusionary rule that makes its enforcement in federal habeas corpus unnecessary.

It seems unlikely that other claims can similarly be understood to include as one of their elements a specification of the judicial proceedings in which they should routinely be invoked, that is, claims which by their nature are applicable at trial and on appeal, but (usually) not in habeas corpus.[61] Nevertheless, given the hydraulic pressures for restricting the federal courts' field of operation, and the persistence of some justices on this point, we may yet find the Court extending the reach of its reasoning in the fourth amendment case to other quarters. The matter is far from settled, and when Congress enacts new legislation it should establish a framework that will both bring fourth amendment claims back to habeas corpus and also ensure that other claims do not go on the block in the future.

Facts

The Court has undercut the federal courts' authority with respect to other claims by capitalizing on an instance in which current law explicitly employs the process model in habeas corpus: the standard governing the treatment that should be accorded to state court findings of fact. I said previously that the federal habeas courts should have plenary power to hold their own hearings, examine documentary evidence, listen to witnesses, and make independent determinations of the facts bearing on petitioners' federal claims. Under the precedents, however, a federal hearing is required only if there was some "vital flaw" in the process used in state court, such that the hearing there was not "full and fair."[62] Moreover, by the terms of another provision in §2254, subsection (d), the federal courts must presume the accuracy of particular state findings of fact, so long as those findings were reached in a procedurally sound manner. Once that presumption is engaged, it can be rebutted only by "convincing" evidence that the state courts got the facts wrong, despite using adequate procedures.[63]

The upshot is that §2254(d) recognizes a kind of "issue" preclusion with respect to state findings of *fact*, as distinct from conclusions of *law*. Previously, I identified and examined various mechanisms by which the Supreme Court or Congress distributes judicial authority to handle entire cases. This, by contrast, is a mechanism by which

Congress allocates authority for particular issues within a single case. Lawyers and judges are used to distinguishing between factual issues on the one hand and legal questions on the other. Under §2254(d), the characterization of a question as factual or legal determines the court that will have primary decision-making responsibility for it: facts are typically left to the state courts, while legal issues are decided independently by the federal courts.

The fact/law distinction employed by §2254(d) draws on a well-developed set of definitions articulated by Justice Frankfurter in his general elaboration of habeas corpus in 1953. Facts are the "primary" and "basic" elements of a historical episode "in the sense of a recital of . . . events and the credibility of their narrators."[64] Thus when a court sets about to determine facts, it engages in a "case-specific inquiry into *what happened here.*"[65] If, for example, a petitioner claims that the police coerced an "involuntary" confession from her, the underlying factual questions include such matters as: Where did the interrogation take place? How long did it last? Who said what to whom? Litigants typically dispute historical facts such as these, and when they do a court must take evidence, appraise witnesses' demeanor, and decide who is telling the truth.

As I have noted, the fact-finding function is critical to the development of a complete and accurate record on which to base judicial determinations of federal rights. It is in part because the federal courts offer superior fact-finding capability that I have insisted that parties with federal claims should ordinarily be able to take their cases to federal court for initial consideration—either by filing original complaints in the district courts or by removing federal-question litigation begun in state court. As Chief Justice Warren made clear, finding the historical facts can also be crucial in habeas corpus.[66] Nevertheless, there is some sense to the current rule that the federal courts should credit at least some factual findings made in state court, rather than setting off to find all the facts underlying all the federal claims in all habeas cases.

In ordinary civil actions pursuant to §1331, federal-question business is channeled to the federal courts as an original matter; the state courts are out of the picture. In habeas corpus, by contrast, state criminal defendants are prosecuted in state court and cannot remove the actions against them to federal court for disposition. Accordingly, the state courts are very much *in* the picture. They are initially positioned to find the essential facts, both with respect to guilt or innocence and with respect to any federal defenses an accused person may assert. Thus by the time a prisoner passes through the state system and seeks habeas corpus relief from the federal courts, the state courts have typically already heard what the witnesses have to say and have chosen to believe one version of the story over another. The point is not just that one set of courts has already found the facts, and it seems arguably wasteful or potentially frictious for another set of courts to start over from scratch. The passage of time since the critical events occurred may frustrate another round of fact-finding: witnesses may be unavailable, memories may be faded, physical evidence may be lost. The federal courts might try to make independent findings on the basis of the record in state court. Yet the state judge who saw witnesses first-hand was probably in a better position to sort truth from falsehood. Federal court factual determinations based only on the transcript of witnesses' testimony in state court may not be superior at all. Accordingly, §2254(d) establishes a presumption in favor of any facts actually found by the state courts in a procedurally adequate way.[67]

Questions of law, by contrast, are answered not by building an accurate record of historical events, but by identifying and elaborating the standards by which society judges human behavior. Legal standards in their pure form can be articulated in the abstract, without reference to the facts found to exist in any particular instance. In a confession case, for example, the purely legal question is the constitutional standard for the admissibility of a defendant's statement. The answer is that the due process clause allows the prosecution to use only "voluntary" confessions. The very point of exempting federal habeas corpus from preclusion is to allow the federal courts to make their own, independent determinations of the law applicable to prisoners' claims. The presumption in §2254(d) thus clearly does not extend to state declarations of legal standards.[68]

Similarly, §2254(d) has always been understood to be inapplicable to questions at the intersection of primary facts and legal principles. At some point in every case, it becomes necessary to determine the legal significance of historical events—to bring a legal principle or rule to bear on the facts. This hybrid issue is called a "mixed" question of law and fact, that is, the "application of a legal standard to . . . historical-fact determinations."[69] To state such a mixed question, a court must refer both to the primary facts of a case and to the abstract legal standards deemed to be applicable. And in joining the facts and the law bearing on a claim, the court actually *decides* whether the claim has merit. Mixed questions are the crux of legal judgment. If a federal court's independent authority were limited to announcing the abstract voluntariness standard in a confession case, and state applications of that standard were presumed to be correct under §2254(d), federal habeas corpus would forfeit its freedom from preclusion respecting state decisions in confession cases. Accordingly, the federal court must exercise independent judgment in deciding whether, given the facts found by the state courts, the confession in a particular case was voluntary within the meaning of the due process clause.[70]

Here again, the statute reflects Justice Frankfurter's understanding of the allocation of authority between the federal and state courts. Frankfurter insisted that while "[a]ll that has gone before is not to be ignored," a previous state court determination of a federal claim "cannot foreclose consideration of such a claim" in federal habeas corpus, "else the State court would have the final say which Congress, by the Act of 1867, provided it should not have." In cases calling not merely for "ascertainment of the . . . facts" but for "interpretation of the legal significance of . . . facts," the federal judge entertaining a petition "must exercise his own judgment on this blend of facts and their legal values." Specifically, Justice Frankfurter said that "so-called mixed questions or the application of constitutional principles to the facts as found leave the duty of adjudication with the federal judge."[71]

In apparent recognition that §2254(d) draws these same distinctions, the Rehnquist Court has acknowledged that the presumption in favor of state findings of primary fact does not extend either to state judgments on purely legal issues or to state court applications of legal standards to the facts of individual cases.[72] Yet the Court's record with respect to mixed questions is itself mixed. The justices have held (correctly) that the "voluntariness" of a confession and the "effectiveness" of defense counsel are mixed issues to which §2254(d) is inapplicable. But they have also held (incorrectly) that the "partiality" or "bias" of jurors and the "competency" of defendants to stand trial are questions of primary fact—to which the statutory presumption applies.[73] To explain why it treats issues that seem plainly to be mixed as, instead, factual, the Court candidly offers that when it decides to put an issue in one pigeonhole or the other, it does so on the basis of its own judgment regarding the best allocation of judicial authority.[74] Since this Court is inclined to think that most issues should be decided in state court, it strains to characterize state decisions as findings of fact, rather than applications of law to fact, and thus invokes the statutory presumption in favor of the result reached in state court.

Given this backdrop, it probably should not have been so surprising as it was when, in an otherwise unremarkable case in 1992, the Court asked the parties to prepare arguments regarding a general question of federal law the justices had developed on their own: "In determining whether to grant a petition for a writ of habeas corpus by a person in custody pursuant to the judgment of a state court, should a federal court give deference to the state court's application of law to the specific facts of the petitioner's case or should it review the state court's determination *de novo?*"[75] On its face, this question challenged the very fact/law distinction drawn in §2254(d). The Court thus appeared to be poised to discard that distinction, to overrule the precedents depending on it, and to hold, after all, that the federal courts must defer to the state courts with respect to mixed questions. The prisoner, supported by friend-of-the-court briefs by other interested individuals and groups, insisted that §2254(d) bars federal court deference to the state courts regarding mixed issues.[76] Entering the mixed-question case on behalf of the Bush Administration, the Solicitor General of the United States argued that it is indefensible to maintain the allocation of authority contemplated by the statute.[77] In the end, none of the justices purported to resolve the mixed-question issue, one way or the other. The episode suggests, however, that the Court may yet declare that the federal courts should treat mixed issues in the way they treat issues of primary fact.

One would not expect the Rehnquist Court to overlook the forum-allocation implications of the fact/law distinction built into §2254(d). Nor would one expect that the justices now sitting would set those implications aside and decide whether a question is one of fact, law, or a combination of the two, as a hollow matter of semantics. The Court ought to appreciate the practical implications of the doctrines it employs and should bear in mind the purposes and functions of legal ideas when it puts them into effect. Yet the Court cannot legitimately skew conventional understandings of these categories in order to promote its own ideas about where issues should be decided—in the teeth of Congress' contrary judgment. Here, too, new legislation will be required to preserve the federal courts' ability to adjudicate federal claims.[78]

The Intended Sense

President Reagan's legislative plan for habeas corpus appeared within a few years of the decision in the exclusionary rule case and contemporaneously with the cases on state fact-finding prior to the mixed-question case in 1992. It is scarcely surprising, then, that his plan built on the Court's work. Once again, under the Reagan proposal, later adopted by President Bush, the federal courts would be prohibited from granting federal habeas corpus relief on the basis of any claim that was "fully and fairly adjudicated" in state court. This is to say: if the Court hesitates in the teeth of §2241 and §2254 to invoke preclusion with respect to all federal claims raised in habeas corpus, and with respect to all factual, legal, and mixed issues that must be determined to dispose of those claims, Congress should amend existing statutes as necessary.

Proponents of the full-and-fair program typically deny that it would simply extend the Court's treatment of the exclusionary rule to all aspects of all claims, and there are differences worth noting.[79] For example, in its current legislative form, the full-and-fair plan is limited to "issue" preclusion and does not embrace "claim" preclusion. The federal courts would be barred from addressing a claim that *was* "fully and fairly" adjudicated in state court, but not a claim that was *not,* but might have been, considered there.[80] Moreover, the full-and-fair legislative program would not restrict the federal courts to an appraisal of the procedures employed in state court—as would be their function under Bator's process model and ordinary "issue" preclusion rules. Instead, proponents explain that the plan includes an element of substantive judgment: adjudication would not be "full and fair" in the "intended sense" if the decision reached in state court failed to meet a "minimum standard of reasonableness."[81] Thus the *outcome* in state court must "reflect a reasonable interpretation of Federal law, a reasonable view of the facts in light of the evidence presented to the State court, and a reasonable disposition in light of the facts found and the rule of law applied."[82] Nevertheless, the full-and-fair program plainly would abolish habeas corpus for state prisoners as we know it. Federal relief would not be available even if (in the view of the federal courts) the state courts were wrong in rejecting a prisoner's federal claim; it would only be available if the state courts were *unreasonably* wrong.[83]

The full-and-fair plan does not conceive of the writ as a generally available basis of federal jurisdiction for the independent determination of federal questions arising in state criminal prosecutions. Rather, the state courts are assumed to have responsibility for processing criminal cases and for attending to any federal questions that may come up. Indeed, the state courts are assumed to do an acceptable job most of the time, so that we need no routine mechanism for litigation in the federal courts. Under the full-and-fair plan, habeas corpus would be merely a safety net, situated (well) behind the state courts in order to catch the rare case in which those courts commit egregious error. The federal courts would serve only to keep the state courts within bounds by remaining vigilant against intolerable injustice. Liberals, too, claim this role for the federal courts. The difference is that the full-and-fair scheme recognizes no other role.

At the descriptive level, the full-and-fair plan appears to be the predictable product of the Legal Process tradition on which it rests and the preclusion language in which it is expressed. The plan posits that there is rarely any objectively right answer to a question; instead, there is some number of "reasonably" right answers—right enough to be *accepted* as right if produced by the appropriate decision-making body in a procedurally satisfying manner. Yet at the functional level the full-and-fair program recalls the extravagances of the most radical of the Legal Realists: understandings of law and jurisprudence usually associated with the left wing of American academia rather than the councils of American conservatism.[84] Law is taken to be indeterminate, subject to an elastic list of possibilities limited only by the imaginations of lawyers contending for their conclusions. Inasmuch as there are almost always plausible arguments on both sides of cases, virtually any result a state court reaches with respect to a federal claim would seem to be reasonable—and thus immune from federal examination in habeas corpus.

The full-and-fair plan does concede that courts can arrive at answers that are unacceptable. But an answer given by a state court is sufficiently wrong to warrant habeas corpus relief not when it departs from the answer that other courts, most courts, or, certainly, a federal court would reach, but only when it is *so* off the mark that no reasonable court acting in good faith could produce it. Within this framework, the federal courts are not to evaluate competing "reasonable" results and choose the one that seems, if you will, the *most* reasonable and therefore the best interpretation of federal rights. By contrast, the state courts are free to pick any marginally defensible result they like and to insulate that result from oversight. The federal courts do not superintend the exercise of judgment under the constitutional rules by which the adjudication game is to be played; they can only police the most flagrant violations of those rules.[85]

The justices are divided over the advisability of the full-and-fair formula. Justice O'Connor has endorsed it as a sound basis for legislative reform; the Chief Justice has said that legislative proposals to jettison habeas corpus in favor of "full and fair" adjudication in state court are premature at this time.[86] In Chief Justice Rehnquist's view, however, the system now in place is flawed and "verges on the chaotic" in its handling of capital litigation.[87] Particularly in death penalty cases, the Chief Justice complains that habeas corpus is used to upset state convictions and sentences on the basis of changes in the law that the state courts could not reasonably have foreseen. By his account, habeas only rarely vindicates meritorious claims; usually it simply prevents the implementation of the death penalty—even when state authorities honored the federal rights that capital defendants were known to have when their cases were considered in state court.[88] Some state's attorneys echo this charge.[89] The concern that the federal courts evade the execution of the guilty by changing the rules of the game after cases leave state court animates another line of recent decisions, in which the Court has broached essentially the full-and-fair plan from a different direction.

New Rules

In an opinion for the Court in 1989, Justice O'Connor discarded the Warren Court's approach to the problems associated with shifting legal standards and substituted a variation on themes advocated by Justice Harlan's dissents from the Warren Court's decisions.[90] More recently, the Court has elaborated on this approach and, in the process, has twisted the law governing the "retroactive" effect of "new rules" of law into a means of curbing, and curbing drastically, the substantive scope of the habeas jurisdiction—enacting the full-and-fair program by indirection.[91] It was these decisions, as well as the earlier cases on what counts as a mixed question of law and fact, on which the Bush Administration built its argument in the mixed-question case for the proposition that the federal courts should generally defer to previous state court decisions on the merits of federal claims. To explain how all this fits together, I must pause to sketch the history of "retroactivity" analysis.

There was a time when the Supreme Court indulged the simplistic understanding of the judicial function associated with Legal Formalism.[92] Since judges did not *make* law, but merely *found* it in preexisting materials, any interpretation of the Constitution the Court embraced and enforced could not be the justices' own "new" creation. If something was the law on one day, it must have been the law on every preceding day—even if the Court had not previously discovered it. There was, then, no basis for failing to apply a rule of constitutional law, both to the case at bar and to other pending cases in which it might figure—including cases in which other courts had arrived at results on the basis of a different understanding of the Constitution. That kind of thinking was absurd, of course, and in the early 1930s the Court candidly conceded that it sometimes changed prior constitutional interpretations and that, when it did so, it had to decide whether to apply its "new rules" retrospectively to all cases or, instead, only prospectively to cases begun in the future.[93]

The retroactivity issue took on special importance in the 1960s, when the Warren Court began interpreting constitutional safeguards in criminal cases in plainly innovative ways—unquestionably departing from precedent. There was pressure to apply such "new rules" only to future cases and thus to deny any retroactive effect on past events and judgments already in place. For if all "new rules" were routinely applied retroactively, the entire system might be disrupted. That, moreover, would almost certainly discourage the justices from making the changes they otherwise would. The Court thus rejected the notion that all its new constitutional rules must be given retrospective effect and adopted a more flexible analysis with respect to rules that, when viewed realistically, clearly broke with the past.[94] If such an innovative rule did not protect against convicting the innocent, and if its application would upset reliance interests and disturb the administration of justice, the Court denied its benefits to prisoners whose claims rested on prior events or judgments.[95]

There was no serious argument about the retroactive effect of a rule unless it constituted a genuine change in the law, and when that was true the Court determined retroactivity on a case-by-case basis. Since the decision extending the fourth amendment exclusionary rule to state prosecutions clearly broke with the past, and since it did not advance the accuracy of criminal judgments but might disrupt settled arrangements, the Court concluded that the new decision would control only the particular case at bar and future cases. Similarly, the decision requiring the police to warn suspects of their rights before interrogation, was given only prospective effect. By contrast, the Warren Court decided that its "new rule" requiring the states to appoint counsel for indigents in felony cases was so vital to fairness that prisoners who had already been tried should have the benefit of the new decision.[96]

Justice Harlan objected to the Warren Court's work and proposed instead a different model that drew a sharp distinction between cases heard in the Supreme Court on direct (appellate) review and cases reaching the Court by way of federal habeas corpus. In all direct review cases, according to Justice Harlan, the Court's role as a court of error demanded that it should announce and apply the rule of law on which the justices were agreed at the time of decision. Any "new rule" established in such a case should be applicable to the case at bar, to all future cases, *and* to all cases then pending at trial or on direct review—including cases in which a state court had already rejected such a claim in light of prior precedents, but in which the state judgment was still subject to direct review in the Supreme Court. On direct review, this is to say, the Court should return to the practice of giving "new rules" retroactive effect, without exception.[97]

When, however, cases arose by way of habeas corpus, Justice Harlan regarded the federal courts' role as entirely different. To Harlan, the purpose of habeas corpus was not to release state prisoners from custody in violation of federal law as it was when a case reached federal court, but to deter the state courts from neglecting the federal legal standards that were in place when they acted. Therefore, according to Harlan, a petitioner whose conviction and sentence had previously been approved on direct review in the state appellate courts should not be heard to claim relief on the basis of a "new rule," established more recently. Rather, such a petitioner should ordinarily be entitled to relief only if his claim was shown to be meritorious in light of the law prevailing when the case was still in state court. Justice Harlan recommended two exceptions to this general prohibition on the retrospective application of "new rules" in habeas corpus: a "new rule" should be enforced if it either placed "certain kinds of primary . . . individual conduct beyond the power of the criminal lawmaking authority to proscribe" or required "the observance of procedures . . . 'implicit in the concept of ordered liberty.'"[98]

The approach the Rehnquist Court takes regarding these problems borrows from Harlan, but departs from him in critical respects. The Court embraces Harlan's crucial distinction between direct review cases on the one hand and habeas corpus cases on the other. On direct review, the Court follows Harlan conscientiously. The retroactivity issue simply does not arise; a "new rule" automatically applies—both

to the case in which it is announced and to all other cases still subject
to direct review in the Supreme Court. Similarly, this Court accepts
Harlan's view that "new rules" ordinarily should *not* be announced
or applied in habeas corpus and his recommendation that certain exceptions should be recognized.[99] Yet the Rehnquist Court defines both
"new rules" and the exceptional circumstances in which they should
be invoked in its own, quite different, way.

The circumstances in which this Court will allow the federal habeas
courts to apply "new rules" are extremely narrow. The justices accept
Justice Harlan's view that "new rules" should be enforced if they render petitioners immune from prosecution altogether. But they reject
Harlan's argument that the federal courts should also invoke "new
rules" that establish safeguards essential to the "fairness" of criminal
trials. Instead, this Court insists that only "new rules" that bear on
the "accuracy" of the verdict in state court are sufficient to warrant
federal attention. Thus the federal courts may announce and apply
only "new rules" without which "the likelihood of an accurate conviction is seriously diminished."[100]

The Court's conception of "new rules" is, by contrast, extremely
broad. Justice Harlan recognized that the key issue within his framework was whether the rule on which a petitioner grounded her claim
was genuinely "new," so that it would trigger the general bar and redi-
rect attention to whether the rule nonetheless fit one of the two exceptions. Harlan thought the decision on the novelty of a rule would
often be close. In his view, the "content" of constitutional principles
rarely changed "dramatically from year to year," but rather was "altered slowly and subtly." Thus a rule was not "really" to be judged
"new" unless it could be said "with assurance" that the Supreme
Court would have *rejected* a prisoner's claim at the time a case was in
state court, but that, by the time the case reached federal habeas corpus, the Court had changed its mind and was prepared to sustain it.
Moreover, what might appear on first glance to be the announcement
of a "new rule" could instead be "simply" the application of a "well-
established constitutional principle" to a "closely analogous" case.
According to Justice Harlan, the courts did change constitutional law,
but not every time they decided mixed questions—applying established legal standards to different sets of historical facts.[101]

In her initial opinion, Justice O'Connor conceded that it is often
difficult to recognize a "new rule" when you see one and thus declined
to offer a definition for all seasons. As a general matter, however, she

said that a "case" establishes a "new rule" when it "breaks new ground or imposes a new obligation" on the government.[102] In the case at bar, for example, Justice O'Connor explained that since the Court had previously said that racial groups need not be proportionately represented on juries, a rule requiring juries to reflect the racial make-up of the community would be "new." That conception of "new rules" was consistent with Justice Harlan's thinking: a judicial decision creates "new" substantive law when it adopts an innovative legal standard that makes demands of state authorities that previously did not exist—roughly the kind of thing the Warren Court seems to have had in mind when it referred to a "new rule" as a "clear break" from the past.[103]

Within a few months, however, in another opinion for the Court purporting to expand on Justice O'Connor's beginning, Justice Kennedy said that not only "clear breaks" constitute "new rules," but also "gradual developments in the law over which reasonable jurists may disagree."[104] This, of course, is precisely what Justice Harlan denied. Where Harlan insisted that a rule was not "new" unless, at the time a case was in state court, the Supreme Court would have *rejected* the legal standard on which a prisoner relied, Justice Kennedy has it that a rule is "new" unless it can be said that, when the case was in state court, the Supreme Court would have *accepted* the prisoner's argument—and the state courts unaccountably failed to comprehend as much.[105] Thus the kind of evolutionary development that Justice Harlan thought was *not* the announcement of an entirely "new" rule would *be* such a "new rule" within Justice Kennedy's formulation. Even if a rule of constitutional law was plainly foreshadowed in earlier cases, so that many, or even most, lawyers and judges saw it coming, still the decision in which the development is explicitly acknowledged would establish a "new rule" if *some* "reasonable" state judge might have thought the law was maturing differently.[106]

Other statements in the Rehnquist Court's cases indicate that "new rules" are created not only when the content of legal rules emerges in a gradual way, but also when settled rules do not change at all, but are merely applied to the facts of particular cases. In this, the Court suggests that the resolution of an ordinary mixed question establishes "new" constitutional law. Immediately following her statement that decisions create "new rules" if they impose "new obligations" on the states, Justice O'Connor offered that "[t]o put it differently," a "case" announces a "new rule" if "the result was not *dictated* by precedent" when the prisoner's conviction was affirmed in state court.[107] That, taken literally, was a non sequitur. Having said that a federal decision establishes a "new rule" when it alters the content of a legal standard, O'Connor hardly said the same thing in another way by declaring that a federal court announces a "new rule" of law whenever the "result" it reaches on the facts of an individual case would not have been logically compelled when the prisoner was in state court.[108]

Here, too, the Court has followed up Justice O'Connor's start with further accounts of "new rules," which, taken literally, collapse the general matter of announcing entirely new legal standards into the case-specific business of deciding mixed issues. Justice Kennedy has suggested that the "application" of a settled rule to the facts of an analogous case may well "involve a new rule of law."[109] The Chief Justice, meanwhile, has said that a "new rule" is any judgment regarding the proper resolution of a particular case that could reasonably have been debated previously. Even if the Supreme Court itself declares that a decision is within the "logical compass" of past precedents or, indeed, is "controlled" by those precedents, a decision establishes a "new rule" if the "outcome" was "susceptible to debate among reasonable minds" before a habeas petitioner's sentence became final.[110] If these accounts are read for all they are worth, a prisoner would seem to be barred from federal habeas corpus even if she merely asks a federal court to decide that the facts in her case warrant relief in light of established law—that is, the same legal standard that controlled when her case was in state court and that continues to control when the federal court takes up her claim. No two cases are identical. By hypothesis, then, even if there are lots of cases in which others have obtained relief in similar circumstances, no one has ever succeeded on the basis of *precisely* the same fact pattern. Under Chief Justice Rehnquist's test, the prisoner therefore would seem to be seeking a "new rule" for the particular circumstances of her own case. In contrast to Justice Harlan, this Court apparently thinks that the federal courts *do* change federal law every time they apply settled legal standards to analogous cases.

Taken together, the Court's various descriptions of "new rules" would seem to capture all claims raised in habeas corpus—claims seeking incremental developments in the content of legal standards and claims seeking the application of settled standards to different facts. Both questions of law and mixed questions of law and fact appear to be surrendered to the state courts—subject to federal examination only for minimal rationality. A petitioner who relies on a decision handed down *after* his sentence became final must demonstrate that the new case *had* to be decided as it was in light of precedents in place *before* he left state court. If the case could have gone the other way, if any reasonable judge could have decided it differently, then it announced a "new" rule that, except in narrow circumstances, cannot be applied in habeas corpus. Similarly, a prisoner who simply advances an argument, not grounded in any particular recent precedent, is required to show that his argument *must* be accepted by any reasonable judge considering it in light of the precedents on the books when his sentence became final. If a reasonable judge could reject the argument, the prisoner is seeking the establishment of a "new rule" of law, which, again, cannot be applied in habeas corpus save in special circumstances.[111] Finally, a petitioner who merely asks the federal courts to apply an established and unchanged legal standard to the particular facts of his case is also foreclosed, unless the state courts acted unreasonably when they applied that standard to the facts and found the prisoner's claim without merit. For if the state courts were merely wrong, but not unreasonably wrong, in their judgment regarding the mixed question in the case, the federal court cannot reach a different decision without creating a "new rule" of law—which, again, usually cannot be applied in federal habeas corpus. As though to underscore this last, the Court has said that the very purpose of its "new rule" formulations is to "validate reasonable, good-faith" decisions by the state courts regarding the merits of federal claims.[112]

Small wonder that these decisions came quickly to mind in the mixed-question case, when the Court invited briefs on whether the federal courts should routinely defer to state court applications of federal legal standards.[113] The prisoner contended that the habeas jurisdiction conferred by Congress cannot be ignored and that, accordingly, the Court's decisions on "new rules" must be limited to situations in which legal rules are genuinely altered.[114] By contrast, the state insisted that these same decisions had already established a general deference rule in habeas corpus, albeit indirectly. According to the state, Justice O'Connor's initial decision stands for the proposition that any "reasonable" disagreement between the federal habeas courts and the state courts regarding the legal standard applicable to a case must now be resolved in the state courts' favor. By this account, a "reasonable" state judgment fixes the baseline of then-prevailing federal law, from which the departure contemplated by a "new rule" can be measured; such a state judgment serves, in effect, as a *correct* judgment, so that a federal habeas court must change the law in order to reach a different result. It follows, then, that "reasonable, good-faith" state court decisions regarding "pure law" issues are now free from independent examination by the federal courts. Next, according to the state, the more recent opinions by the Chief Justice and Justice Kennedy have "extend[ed]" O'Connor's reasoning beyond the retro-activity context to ordinary cases in which "settled law" is applied to a "given set of facts." Finally, by virtue of §2254(d), Congress itself demands deference to state court findings of primary fact. In the end, then, the federal courts must presume the accuracy of *"all"* state court conclusions—"legal, factual, and mixed." Speaking for the Bush Ad-ministration, the Solicitor General added only that if the "new rule" cases have not already eliminated the federal courts' authority inde-pendently to apply settled law to the facts of individual cases, the Court ought to finish the job.[115]

The justices balked. As I explained previously, they failed to decide the question they themselves had put to the parties. Parsing the opin-ions, one concludes that the Chief Justice, together with Justices Thomas and Scalia, would now adopt a deference rule for all the is-sues in habeas corpus cases and would rely on the "new rule" deci-sions for support.[116] Others are more cautious and, in the cause of caution, offer more limited interpretations of the "new rule" cases. Justice O'Connor rejects the argument that the "new rule" decisions have already established a deferential "standard of review" for exam-ining the work of the state courts, such that habeas relief is now avail-able only if the state courts reached an unreasonable result when they applied the law then available to them. She is crystal clear that the federal habeas courts are to ensure that the state courts reached results that the federal courts themselves deem to have been *correct,* based on the legal standards controlling at the time. Indeed, she is adamant that "a state court's *incorrect* legal determination" has never "been allowed to stand because it was *reasonable.*"[117] Justice O'Connor's po-sition, then, is formally straightforward: state judicial decisions are not correct because they are reasonable; they are reasonable because they are correct.

Justice Kennedy also denies that the "new rule" cases are on a "col-lision course" with the federal courts' authority to decide ordinary mixed issues independently. He explains that the Court's decisions are tethered to the purpose that drives them—the desire to respect state judgments rendered in accordance with the precedents that prevailed when the state courts acted. Like Justice O'Connor, he insists that he means only to spare the states from a regime in which their judgments are upset by "changing a rule" of law "once thought *correct* but now understood to be deficient in its own terms."[118] That purpose would be thwarted if the federal courts were to defer to state judgments said to be minimally rational. Justice Souter, for his part, also seems to think that the very idea that some rules are "new" (and thus are largely excluded from federal habeas corpus) must concede that others are not "new" (and thus are applicable in federal court).[119] And there are, moreover, several recent instances in which the Court has considered the merits of claims in habeas corpus and, in so doing, has indicated, explicitly or implicitly, that not every decision is a "new rule" decision after all.[120]

Nevertheless, there remains a building tension between the Court's literal descriptions of "new rules" and the federal courts' authority independently to judge the merits of prisoners' claims. The justices who now seem ready to adopt a general deference rule clearly have it that the "new rule" cases mean, at least in effect, that the federal courts must accept "reasonable" state judgments across the board. And even the justices who now refuse to shape the "new rule" cases into a general rule of deference may reach the same result on a case-by-case basis.[121] Worse, the "new rule" cases may turn out to offer a loose (and extremely convenient) means by which the justices can dispatch claims they deem to be questionable without committing themselves (as a body) on the merits. Even if five votes cannot be found to reject a claim on the merits, it may be possible to get a majority to hold that, valid or invalid by current standards, the claim depends on a "new rule" that cannot be considered in habeas.

None of the justices appears willing to restrict the definition of a "new rule" to a genuine change in the content of the legal standard applicable to a case—a new *rule,* this is to say, rather than a new *application* of an old rule. Justice O'Connor begins in a promising way, arguing that a rule is "new" only if it can be "meaningfully distinguished from that established by binding precedent" when a case was in state court. Yet in the next breath she shifts back to a case-specific formulation, now saying that a federal court announces a "new rule" if it awards relief in a case in which there is some "factual distinction" that alters the "force with which . . . [an] underlying principle applies."[122] For his part, Justice Kennedy thinks that the federal courts are barred from invoking both "new rules" and "old rule[s] in a novel setting."[123] The threat to the federal courts' longstanding jurisdiction thus looms over each habeas corpus case that reaches this Court. For every such case offers another opportunity to bring habeas corpus for state prisoners effectively to an end.

Beyond a Reasonable Doubt

If the cases on what count as questions of "fact" or "new rules" are not enough, the Rehnquist Court has seized upon yet another strategy for forcing the federal courts to defer to prior state judgments. It has long been settled that some violations of constitutional rights in state trials may be overlooked if the state proves, beyond a reasonable doubt, that they were harmless.[124] For years, the Court applied that traditional standard in habeas corpus just as on direct review.[125] Recently, however, the Court has shifted to a much less rigorous test for harmless error in habeas cases. In an opinion by the Chief Justice himself, the Court has held that state prisoners who demonstrate constitutional error at trial in state court can obtain federal habeas relief only if the error had a "substantial and injurious effect" on the verdict.[126] This, the Chief Justice explains, means "actual prejudice."[127] Such a diluted standard for harmless error has all the devastating potential of the general rule of deference to state decisions that we narrowly escaped in the mixed-question case.[128] This decision, too, threatens to circumnavigate the Habeas Corpus Act—but from yet another direction.

There is, of course, a conceptual distinction between the general deference rule the Court deflected in the mixed-question case (under which a federal court would defer to a state judgment the federal court thinks is erroneous) and the relaxed standard for harmless error (under which a federal court can reach the decision it believes to be correct, but must withhold federal relief unless the violation had a sufficient effect on the determination of guilt in state court). Yet both roads lead to the same Rome: the denial of federal habeas relief to citizens the federal courts judge to be in custody in violation of the Constitution. It takes little imagination to anticipate that the district courts may now make it their practice to consider the relative harmfulness of an error at the threshold—and fail to reach the merits unless they first conclude that a claim, if found to *be* meritorious, could bring relief.[129]

The relaxed standard for harmless error is hostile to the very nature of the federal courts' jurisdiction in habeas corpus. The federal courts are supposed to protect citizens from detention in violation of the Bill of Rights.[130] In most circumstances, if a constitutional error played *no* part in the conviction on which the state relies for a prisoner's custody, then the conviction is not unjust and habeas relief can be denied consistent with the Act. The same cannot be said, however, if an error may have had some effect, albeit not a demonstrably prejudicial effect, on the verdict. The adoption of a diluted harmless error standard thus evades the federal habeas courts' core obligation within their congressionally prescribed jurisdiction. That obligation is to determine properly preserved claims on the merits and to set free anyone whose incarceration is based, in large or small part, on unconstitutional grounds.

Nor should we miss the reversal of fortune the idea of "reasonable doubt" has undergone in the run of habeas cases from this Court. Look at it this way. The traditional "beyond a reasonable doubt" standard for harmless error was demanding. And deliberately so. For if there is a reasonable doubt about whether constitutional error influenced a criminal conviction, we have long thought that the individual should have the benefit of that doubt. That sentiment has now been abandoned in habeas corpus, displaced by a standard for harmless error whose plain and unvarnished purpose is to shift comparatively more of the risk of constitutional mistakes to the individual in the dock. At the same time, via the "new rule" cases, this Court gives *state courts* the benefit of any reasonable doubt regarding the accuracy of their determinations of constitutional claims.

Chief Justice Rehnquist candidly acknowledges that his treatment of harmless error is wholly a creature of his own policy predilections. He insists that Congress has been "silent" on this issue and dismisses the argument that legislative silence should be taken as an implicit approval of the familiar "beyond a reasonable doubt" test.[131] As usual, when the Chief Justice is able to find any daylight in §2241 or §2254, he fills what he takes to be a void with his own cost/benefit analysis—which inevitably sacrifices prisoners' access to the federal courts. If it is for the Court to identify the standard for harmless error, and Chief Justice Rehnquist declares that it is, then federal habeas corpus for state prisoners must sustain another setback.[132]

I hasten to say that there may be some hope to be found in what Justice Stevens has to say in a separate opinion—for his vote in the principal case is essential to Chief Justice Rehnquist's five-member majority. Stevens works hard to reassure us that the diluted standard for harmless error is not the dragon it appears to be. If the district courts proceed as they ought, according to Justice Stevens, they will not engage in any "single-minded focus on how [an] error may . . . have affected the . . . verdict."[133] Instead, they will continue to exercise independent judgment on the merits of claims and then review the "entire record" to discern "all the ways that error can infect the course of a trial."[134] Moreover, Justice Stevens departs from the Chief Justice regarding what may be the crucial issue in close cases: who bears the burden of persuasion with respect to the harmless error question? Chief Justice Rehnquist intimates that habeas petitioners must show that error *did* affect the verdict, while Justice Stevens insists that the prosecution must prove no such effect.[135]

Even if Justice Stevens is successful in assigning the burden of persuasion to the prosecution, I am afraid that he may have handed the Chief Justice yet another way to skin the habeas cat. The relaxed harmless error rule may yet function as a general rule of deference to state judgments. Under either label, the federal courts will stay their hand in all but the most outrageous cases.

A Treacherous Course

Let me sum up. At the outset, recognizing the conventional distinction between questions of historical fact, on the one hand, and legal or mixed questions, on the other, the Rehnquist Court places an outsized number in the former category and thus diverts a large portion of judicial business to the state courts. Next, with respect to questions that are undeniably legal or mixed, and thus ostensibly subject to independent federal adjudication, the Court distinguishes between claims that rest on clearly established principles and those that call for the announcement of "new rules"—and sends many, if not most, claims to the latter category. In the typical case, then, a prisoner seeking a writ of habeas corpus must negotiate a treacherous course. The issue he wants to litigate in federal court must demand enough legal judgment that it cannot be considered "factual," such that an unfavorable conclusion reached by the state courts will be presumed correct under §2254(d). But at the same time, the issue cannot demand so much judgment that it falls within the definition of a "new rule." To get a federal court to look at a legal or mixed question, the petitioner must demonstrate that reasonable minds, passing on the claim in light of the precedents existing when the state courts acted, could *not* have disagreed over the correct answer and *had* to arrive at the result for which the petitioner now contends.[136] Finally, by dint of a relaxed standard for harmless error in habeas corpus, petitioners now face yet another, analytically distinct but functionally similar, obstacle to federal relief.[137]

The parallel with the full-and-fair plan is clear.[138] Even if a question that looks like a legal or mixed issue is not treated as a question of fact and thus left to the state courts under §2254(d), a petitioner can obtain federal adjudication of the question only by establishing that the answer the state courts gave was not only wrong, but *unreasonably* wrong. The Court's interpretations of §2254(d), brigaded with its definitions of "new rules" for retroactivity purposes and its diluted standard for harmless error, now threaten to do by judicial decision what the full-and-fair program would do by legislation. Quite different legislative reforms will be required to wrestle with this seething morass of counterintuitive rhetoric—legislation, I might add, that will seem delightfully simple and straightforward by comparison.

Clear Breaks

In light of the developments at the Court, some members of Congress have concluded that in order to preserve habeas corpus at all, it is insufficient merely to defeat the full-and-fair program when it is offered in legislative bills. In addition, affirmative congressional action is needed to disclaim that plan explicitly, to overrule the Court's treatment of fourth amendment claims, to clear up the problems that have developed with §2254(d), to redefine "new rules" for retroactivity purposes, and at least to mitigate the effect of the relaxed test for harmless error.

Senators Gaylord Nelson and Charles Mathias once introduced a bill that would have renounced the notion that the federal courts should dismiss *any* claim on the ground that a prisoner had previously received a "full and fair" opportunity to litigate in state court.[139] More recent bills address the retroactivity problem.[140] A provision in H. R. 5269, an omnibus crime bill reported from the House Judiciary Committee in the 101st Congress, would have added this provision to the habeas chapter of the United States Code:[141]

(a) Except as provided in subsection (b) of this section, each claim under this chapter shall be governed by the law existing on the date the court determines the claim.

(b) In determining whether to apply a new rule, the court shall consider—(1) the purpose to be served by the new rule; (2) the extent of the reliance by law enforcement authorities on a different rule; and (3) the effect on the administration of justice of the application of the new rule.

(c) For purposes of this section, the term "new rule" means a sharp break from precedent announced by the Supreme Court of the United States that explicitly and substantially changes the law from that governing at the time the claimant's sentence became final. A rule is not new merely because, based on precedent existing before the rule's announcement, it was susceptible to debate among reasonable minds. . . .

This provision elides the intellectual framework advanced by Justice Harlan with the standards for judging the retroactive effect of genuine changes in the law employed by the Warren Court. The baseline established by subsection (a) puts cases reaching the federal courts in habeas corpus on the same footing as cases reaching the Supreme Court on direct review: in both instances, the rule to be applied is the current rule—even if that rule is "new" in the sense that it departs, incrementally or radically, from what went before. In this, subsection (a) embraces Harlan's position that currently prevailing law should always be enforced on direct review.[142] The similar treatment of habeas corpus cases departs from Harlan, of course, but the exception recognized in subsection (b) immediately retrieves his view that "new rules" should not always be applied in habeas. Together, subsections (a) and (b) make it plain that the question whether a change in the law should be recognized and applied arises only in habeas corpus.

Next, subsection (b) incorporates the standards employed by the Warren Court for determining when "new rules" should be available to habeas petitioners. Applying these standards, that Court sometimes, but rarely, gave retrospective effect to genuine changes in the law. Functionally, the standards do the work now performed by the two narrow exceptions to the current Court's blanket prohibition on the announcement or application of "new rules" in habeas corpus.[143] The vital matter, of course, lies in subsection (c), which tracks the understanding of "new rules" appearing in cases prior to 1989.[144] The last line of subsection (c) expressly negates the formulation offered by Chief Justice Rehnquist. Since the "sharp break" definition in subsection (c) is plainly inconsistent with Rehnquist's position, an explicit rejection of his account of "new rules" would be unnecessary in ordinary circumstances. In this instance, however, the drafters thought it essential to commit Congress to a different course in the most exacting manner.[145]

An alternative proposal can be found in H. R. 3371, another major crime bill passed by the House in the 102d Congress:[146]

> In an action filed under this chapter, the court shall not apply a new rule. For purposes of this section, the term "new rule" means a clear break from precedent, announced by the Supreme Court of the United States, that could not reasonably have been anticipated at the time the claimant's sentence became final in State court.

This constitutes a surgical strike at the heart of the Court's "new rule" decisions. It is very much the product of the politically charged atmosphere in which it was drafted and defended in debate. The first sentence draws Harlan's distinction between direct review and habeas cases, and then, in draconian fashion, absolutely forbids the federal courts to invoke "new rules" in habeas corpus. In this, H. R. 3371 refuses to admit even the two exceptions recognized by Justice Harlan and, after a fashion, by the Rehnquist Court itself. The result is harsh, but it enabled proponents to insist that they had answered the charge that the federal courts now upset state judgments on the basis of changes in the law. This bill, according to Rep. Don Edwards, "prohibits new rules of law from applying retroactively in any case."[147] Inasmuch as the Court's current exceptions are extremely narrow anyway, the drafters concluded that the strategic value of a rigid, unforgiving prohibition was worth the sacrifice. Even written in this stark way, this provision passed the House by only a slim margin.[148]

The reason lies, of course, in the second sentence, which defines "new rules" much in the manner of H. R. 5269. Here again, there is evidence of strategic maneuvering. The shift from a "sharp" to a "clear" break ties the proposal tightly to the terms of art previously employed by the Supreme Court, a move thought to enhance the chances of attracting conservative support.[149] In a similar vein, this provision drops the explicit reference to Chief Justice Rehnquist's definition of "new rules" contained in H. R. 5269—the better to avoid an open, arguably gratuitous, and strategically ill-advised conflict with a jurist who is demonstrably popular among conservatives. The essential task, the elimination of the Court's expansive descriptions of "new rules," is accomplished by the "clear break" definition.

On its face, the reference to rules the state courts could not reasonably anticipate tightens the meaning of "new rules" even more than does the initial, "clear break" formulation. The Supreme Court never does anything without at least some warning. Even when the Court flatly and explicitly overrules prior cases, its decisions are almost always adumbrated in comments in majority opinions, separate opinions by individual justices, other state and federal court decisions, or, at the very least, speculation in the legal literature. So careful observers can always "reasonably" anticipate what the Court is about to do, and it is never *unreasonable* to predict that the Court is about to chart the course the Court ultimately takes. In effect, H. R. 3371 embraces the Rehnquist Court's duplicitous use of the "reasonableness" label, but reverses the direction in which it operates. Under the Court's recent cases, a rule is "new" unless the *state courts* acted unreasonably in failing to recognize and enforce it; under H. R. 3371, a rule would be "new" only if the *Supreme Court* acts unreasonably in announcing it.[150]

Despite its logical implications, however, H. R. 3371's reference to rules that "could not reasonably" have been anticipated was offered by the drafters, and by its proponents in the floor debates, not as a means of narrowing the definition of "new rules," but, paradoxically, as a redundant flourish that added nothing to the threshold, "clear break" definition. If, this is to say, conservative critics were genuinely worried that the "clear break" definition of "new rules" would allow the federal courts to surprise the state courts by departing from the precedents existing at the time, then this clause should lay those concerns to rest. A change in the law that "could not reasonably" have been anticipated by the state courts would never again be used to upset a state judgment in habeas corpus.

All this confusion flows, of course, from the misleading arguments employed to explain and defend the Rehnquist Court's recent cases. The Court insists that it was justified in adopting Justice Harlan's approach to retroactivity in order to keep the federal courts from trumping state decisions on the basis of changes in the law the state courts could not foresee. House Democrats simply accepted that political rhetoric on its face—and put it in their bill. Sophisticated observers understand, however, that the Court's definitions of "new rules" are closer to *Animal Farm* than common usage. Taken literally, they bar the federal courts from vindicating not only federal constitutional rights the state courts could not have recognized, but also (and much more important) rights those courts could have recognized, and very well ought to have recognized, when prisoners' cases were before them. Indeed, as I have pointed out, the "new rule" cases, taken literally, threaten to foreclose federal habeas petitions seeking only the application of unchanged legal standards to the facts of particular cases.

A third bill, introduced by Senator Joseph Biden as S. 1441 in the 103rd Congress, attempted to refocus attention on a change in the content of an abstract legal rule—and away from the notion that "new" law is created when a settled rule is applied to a case whose facts differ from the facts of the case in which the rule was initially established:[151]

> (c) As used in this section, a "new rule" is a rule that changes the constitutional or statutory standards that prevailed at the time the petitioner's conviction became final.

This simple "change in the legal standard" definition of "new rules" is intellectually sensible, even refreshing, in that it goes forthrightly to the real issue in retroactivity cases, namely, whether abstract legal rules actually shift between state and federal court. Nevertheless, this formulation lacks the rhetorical punch that the "break" metaphor in H. R. 5269 and H. R. 3371 brings to bear. Accordingly, in an apparent effort to clarify its purpose to overrule the Court's decisions, S. 1441 includes another section, which specifies that the federal courts are to exercise fresh judgment when they review state rulings on questions of federal law, "including the application of Federal law to facts," and that it makes no difference whether the state courts previously gave prisoners' claims a "full and fair hearing." That explicit disclaimer of deference to prior state judgments, and, indeed, the full-and-fair program for habeas corpus, plainly reinforces the bill's chances of getting the Court's attention. The aim is rather clear, namely, to tell the justices that they are not to use a capacious understanding of "new rules" to defeat the federal habeas courts' general authority to determine the merits of ordinary federal claims.[152]

S. 1441 is mute with respect to the standard for harmless constitutional error and thus fails (expressly) to revive the traditional, "beyond a reasonable doubt" test. This bill does, however, assign the burden of proving harmless error to the state. H. R. 5269 and H. R. 3371 were written before the mixed-question and harmless error cases were

decided and thus do not address those developments and their implications for the writ's future.

Current Law

It is obvious by now that even the most basic question that can be
asked about federal habeas corpus—what claims the federal courts
can consider—is problematic. In habeas corpus, perhaps more vividly
than in any other aspect of the law of federal jurisdiction, complexity
and subtlety mask an underlying debate over whether citizens with
federal claims should have access to the federal courts. It is time now
to cut away the confusion and propose a sensible legislative solution.
We must cease trying to decide as a matter of logic whether a "new
rule" has been established; rather we should determine as a matter of
policy whether the novelty of a legal claim should affect the choice
of a particular response to it—for example, relief in habeas corpus.
Abstract debates over when and whether the law changes only confuse
matters, as my discussion of the competing definitions of "new rules"
plainly demonstrates.[153] Just as an argument over whether a question
is one of fact or law is a proxy for an underlying argument over
whether the state courts or the federal courts should have primary
authority to decide it, the "new rule" controversy is a proxy for an
underlying debate about the general availability of the federal courts
to entertain federal claims as a sequel to state court litigation.

The proper scope of the issues cognizable in habeas corpus depends
on the function the federal courts perform. On this point, the full-
and-fair plan's attempt to introduce "issue" preclusion into habeas is
due some credit. That program incorporates the view that the state
courts should enforce the Constitution in criminal cases and the federal courts should have only a marginal, backstop role. While we can
complain that proponents understate the severity of the restrictions
the full-and-fair plan would bring about, we cannot complain that the
plan lacks a clear conception of what federal habeas corpus should
be. The same cannot be said for the Supreme Court's definitions of
"facts" and "new rules," which, as I have shown, may lead to the same
result. Yet to the extent the Court openly decides whether a question
is factual, legal, or mixed by reference to its own judgment regarding
forum-allocation, it does concede what is actually afoot. And to the
extent the Court embraces Justice Harlan's views regarding retroactivity, it again acknowledges the underpinnings of what it is doing.

Harlan was in no way disingenuous. He bluntly criticized the availability of habeas corpus after prisoners had had a "fair opportunity" to air their claims in state court and candidly admitted that his framework for retroactivity was a second-best means of restoring habeas corpus to the limited role it had before the tenant farmer case.[154] Under Harlan's view, as under the full-and-fair program, the federal courts should step in only when necessary to deter the state courts from neglecting federal rights. The approach to retroactivity the Rehnquist Court now employs, then, is in the service of this same vision. The flaw in the Court's work is not so much that the justices conceal their own value choices or that they fail to identify and implement a consistent understanding of the federal courts' role in habeas corpus. It is rather that they have in mind the wrong role. The purpose of habeas corpus is not to deter the state courts from ignoring federal rights, so that, assuming the state courts usually can be relied upon to enforce the Constitution, the federal courts should not routinely be open to entertain prisoners' claims.

Harlan was wrong. The federal habeas courts are not in the business of looking back at state judgments and *reviewing* them at all, serving *either* as ordinary appellate courts of error *or* as figurative safety nets to catch the occasional egregious case. Federal habeas corpus is an independent basis for adjudicating federal claims arising in state criminal cases. Criminal defendants cannot be permitted to remove their prosecutions to federal court in the first instance.[155] Accordingly, if the system is to provide citizens with at least one chance to litigate federal claims in the federal forum, there must be some vehicle for federal adjudication after the state courts have completed their work. Habeas corpus is that vehicle.

The implications of this different understanding of the role habeas plays in the federal judicial system are plain. Since the very point is that the federal courts should be open after state adjudication to address claims they could not treat earlier, the application of preclusion rules in habeas corpus is inadmissible. The full-and-fair program would introduce preclusion and therefore should be rejected. Similarly, the Court's manipulations of the meaning of primary "facts" and "new rules" have no place in habeas corpus, properly conceived. Habeas is not a backstop against outrageous injustice, but a routine means by which federal claims, both conventional and creative, can be considered in the ordinary course of business. Certainly, there is no warrant for reconceptualizing the very nature of constitutional law in a transparent effort to drain the blood from the writ. There is a sensible difference between factual questions on the one hand and legal or mixed issues on the other. There is also is a difference between the incremental development of legal principles over time and abrupt disruptions in the normal continuity of things. Justice Harlan was right about one thing. Constitutional law is a gradually evolving body of thinking about an ever-changing social landscape. It is not, as the current Court implies, a series of lurching leaps from unquestionable propositions to "new rules."

The legislation needed, then, is not of the kind contemplated by H. R. 5269, H. R. 3371, or S. 1441. Those bills engage the notion that habeas corpus is a mechanism for reviewing state judgments and attempt to make the ambit of that review considerably wider than the full-and-fair program or the Court's decisions would allow.[156] Given the current state of affairs, it does seem necessary to prescribe the effect, short of preclusive effect, the federal courts should give to prior state judgments. But we require more. With respect to the fact/law distinction, we should not patch up §2254(d) in an attempt to get the Court back on track. In a perverse way, the Bush Administration was right in the mixed-question case. The attempt to divide authority for deciding different issues within a single case is troublesome. This scarcely means, however, that we should simply route all issues to the state courts. To ensure that litigants get from habeas corpus the rough equivalent of the removal jurisdiction they were denied prior to trial, Congress should repeal §2254(d), and with it the current *requirement* that state court factual findings must ordinarily be accepted as correct. Starting again, Congress should enact a new statute that confirms the federal courts' power to determine all the issues necessary to resolve a federal claim—questions of law, mixed questions, and, as well, questions of primary fact. Respecting facts, however, the statute should permit the federal courts to rely on state findings when fresh investigation in federal court would be impractical or wasteful.

Congress should also specify that the federal courts have the authority and obligation to announce and apply whatever legal standards are needed to determine a claim correctly. In ordinary civil actions under §1331, the federal courts independently determine the facts and all legal or mixed issues that bear on the merits of federal claims, and they do so in light of current law. They should do the same in habeas corpus. Furthermore, they should entertain all the claims, including fourth amendment exclusionary rule claims, that would have been cognizable at trial (in federal court) if removal had been available. Finally, of course, the same standards for harmless error that guide judgment on direct review should also govern in federal habeas corpus. If a prisoner demonstrates that his constitutional rights were violated at trial, he should be entitled to habeas corpus relief—unless the state shows, beyond a reasonable doubt, that the error did not affect the judgment.

It will be said that the reforms I have in mind will not do. For the reasons I have acknowledged, the federal courts do not always offer superior fact-finding capacity. Accordingly, it will be said that the federal courts should continue to defer at least to the primary facts already found in state court. Moreover, the content of legal standards *does* change abruptly, at least on occasion. Accordingly, it will be said that the federal courts should decline to enforce genuine breaks with the past, lest every prisoner whose case admits of a claim under new constitutional interpretations be free to file another habeas petition. The states have a legitimate interest in the finality of state judgments, and, it will be said, criminal cases should not be subject to redundant factual investigations and repeated litigation over the effects of shifting legal rules.

Yet a framework in which habeas corpus provides state prisoners with the rough equivalent of what they might have had originally by removal presents neither of these difficulties—necessarily. A federal authority to develop the facts fully and accurately would not always squander resources. Nor would an authority to enforce current law necessarily generate repetitious litigation. Other aspects of habeas law produce those problems—namely, the absence of a statute of limitations for federal petitions and the potential for multiple petitions on behalf of a single prisoner. Those elements of current law can and should be altered (in the manner discussed below) in order to construct a system in which citizens with federal claims touching state criminal prosecutions are entitled to one, but usually only one, bite at the federal apple.

In this spirit, the following provision should be enacted as a substitute for §2254(a):

(a) A petitioner may apply for a writ of habeas corpus under this chapter if the custody of which the petitioner complains is based on a criminal sentence imposed by a state court. In such an action—

(1) the court in which the action is filed shall have jurisdiction to determine any federal claim that would have been cognizable in federal court if the original proceedings in state court had been removable and removed under §1441 of this title and shall:

(A) exercise independent judgment on the merits of the claim, including finding the facts and determining the legal significance of the facts in light of the federal legal standards prevailing at the time the court considers the claim; and

(B) grant appropriate relief if—(i) the claim is meritorious; and (ii) in the case of a violation of federal law that can be harmless, the respondent fails to show that the error was harmless beyond a reasonable doubt; and

(2) a previous state court conclusion of federal law, finding of fact, or determination of the legal significance of facts under federal law shall not be entitled to deference, but shall be considered for whatever persuasive power it may have.

This provision, like the current version of §2254(a), proceeds on the premise that the federal courts have subject matter jurisdiction to entertain petitions from state convicts pursuant to the basic statute, §2241. It dispenses, however, with the current statute's recitation of the federal grounds that must be asserted to invoke that jurisdiction, which also appear in §2241 and need not be repeated. Subsection (a) locates a district court's authority to entertain habeas corpus petitions on behalf of state prisoners within the general, overarching structure of federal jurisdiction. Specifically, habeas corpus after state criminal proceedings is a substitute for the removal jurisdiction that would have been available under 28 U.S.C. §1441 (as amended by the proposal in Chapter Three) if the original proceedings in state court had been civil in nature.[157] Paragraph (1) fixes the reach of the federal court's power by reference to the claims that would have been available to the petitioner if the case had been removable and, in fact, removed to federal court for trial. Rejecting the Supreme Court's current position, paragraph (1) would treat fourth amendment exclusionary rule claims equally with all other claims typically raised at criminal trials. Subparagraph (A) specifies that the federal court is to make its own independent findings of fact—subject to the proviso in paragraph (2) that previous findings by the state courts can be taken into account.

Subparagraph (A) also specifies that the federal court is to exercise independent judgment on mixed issues and, critically, to invoke the current legal standard—not the standard prevailing at the time the state courts acted. This brings habeas cases into line with cases arising on direct review in the Supreme Court.[158] Under this provision, a district court in habeas corpus would have the authority and responsibility, equally with the Supreme Court itself in a direct review case, to announce and apply any rules of federal law needed to decide a case correctly. The federal court would not be concerned that the state courts reached a different result at a time when arguably different legal rules were in place.[159] Concerns about exposing state decisions to repetitive attacks whenever constitutional safeguards evolve can be addressed by establishing time limits for habeas petitions and restricting multiple applications for federal relief. More on those options below. Of course, subparagraph (B) revives the traditional standard for harmless constitutional error.

Paragraph (2) explicitly disclaims any deference to (and therefore any preclusive effect for) prior state determinations of the facts underlying a prisoner's claim or the federal legal basis for it. As to questions of fact, the existing requirement in §2254(d) that the federal courts presume that state findings are correct is abandoned. In its place, paragraph (2) substitutes a general permission to use state fact-finding appropriately. This flexible scheme would permit a federal court to accept facts found in state court when there is sufficient reason to think they are reliable and it would be impractical or wasteful for the federal court to begin anew—either by holding another hearing or by basing different findings on an independent appraisal of the state record. As to questions of law and law-application, existing precedents already have it that the federal courts are to exercise fresh, independent judgment. Yet the Court's treatment of fourth amendment claims, its interpretations of §2254(d), its definitions of "new rules," and the relaxed standard for harmless error in habeas corpus, together with the persistence of the full-and-fair program, make it essential that Congress reconfirm its commitment to the independent adjudication of federal rights in federal court.

Once the role played by habeas corpus is properly framed, subsidiary elements of the federal courts' jurisdiction to issue the writ fall readily into place. In the remaining sections of this chapter, I will explore the implications of what I have said for the procedural issues mentioned at the outset: the exhaustion of state judicial remedies prior to the commencement of federal habeas corpus proceedings; the timing of federal petitions after the completion of state court action; the effect to be given any failure to raise claims properly in state court; and multiple federal petitions from a single prisoner.

Exhaustion

Before seeking a federal writ of habeas corpus, state prisoners are generally required to "exhaust" currently available state court opportunities to litigate federal claims. In theory, the "exhaustion doctrine" is a rule of timing. The federal courts have power to entertain a petition whenever it is filed, but find it imprudent to do so before the state courts have finished with the case.[160] In practice, the doctrine often frustrates federal adjudication altogether. For it saps the strength and tries the patience of prisoners, lawyers, and judges alike. Prisoners attempt to meet the doctrine's exacting standards, but they are repeatedly sent back to the state courts with instructions to invoke some further state procedure, to articulate their federal claims more clearly, or to offer the state courts more evidence regarding the primary facts.[161] In some minds, the federal courts expend more effort explaining why the exhaustion doctrine prevents them from considering prisoners' claims than they ever would devote to the adjudication of those claims on the merits. As Chief Justice Warren once lamented, we seem at times to forget that it is state remedies that are to be exhausted, not state prisoners.[162]

Concerns about the efficacy and costs of the exhaustion doctrine have spawned reform proposals pointing in different directions. To expedite habeas litigation, the Reagan and Bush Administrations proposed that the district courts be given authority to *ignore* the availability of state remedies when claims are frivolous and can be dismissed summarily on the merits. Senators Strom Thurmond and Arlen Specter have suggested that prisoners on death row should be released from any obligation to pursue state postconviction remedies after state appeals have run their course. At least, according to Specter, prisoners under a death sentence should have to choose between state postconviction remedies and federal habeas corpus. In his view, a prisoner who invokes state postconviction procedures should not be given time to complete those procedures and still apply for federal relief.[163] By contrast, the Powell Committee would foster the use of state postconviction procedures in capital cases by suspending a proposed statute of limitations while state relief is being sought.[164] None of these plans starts from the correct theoretical premise; none, accordingly, is satisfying.

The delays and inefficiencies occasioned by the exhaustion requirement are typically justified on two grounds: first, earlier federal adjudication would disrupt orderly state processes in criminal cases; second, the state courts should have the first opportunity to pass on federal claims in order to participate along with the federal courts in the elaboration and enforcement of federal rights.[165] If we posit (as we should) that litigants with federal claims are entitled to choose a federal forum for the litigation of those claims, and that federal habeas corpus is the means by which litigants who cannot remove state prosecutions to federal court are able to obtain federal adjudication later, we should find only the first of these justifications to be legitimate. The only proper basis for delaying federal litigation until after state prosecutions are complete is the justification for disallowing removal before trial, namely, to avoid disturbing state responsibility for the making and enforcement of substantive criminal law.[166]

By this (the proper) account of habeas corpus and the timing of federal court availability, there is no justification for forcing prisoners to raise *any* federal claim in state court, even at trial or on direct appeal. Criminal defendants may well think it wise to press their federal claims on the state courts while they have the chance, in hopes of winning relief from those courts and obviating the need to go to federal court later. In some instances, it will be necessary to object to what happens in state proceedings in order to elicit a reaction from the state courts, which then can be the basis of a federal claim. And prisoners may litigate federal claims of all kinds in state court merely to build a record for direct review in the Supreme Court. Yet the availability of habeas corpus in the federal district courts after state authorities have finished their work is indifferent to the issues raised in state court. Federal adjudication is postponed not to give the state courts the first crack at federal claims, but only to avoid interference with state processes for prosecuting criminal offenders under local law.

What we need is not a rule requiring petitioners to present federal claims to the state courts, but rather a rule preventing the federal courts from accepting a petition until a prisoner's conviction and accompanying sentence have been affirmed on direct appellate review in state court.[167] Other state procedures for addressing federal claims are beside the point. To be specific, the availability of federal habeas corpus before, during, or in place of state postconviction proceedings threatens no disruption of law enforcement and, therefore, should be permitted. The fact of the matter is that state postconviction remedies have become little more than an obstacle course for unrepresented prison inmates attempting to satisfy the exhaustion doctrine and get into federal court, but actually only committing procedural errors that *bar* federal adjudication—as I will demonstrate in a moment. Prisoners who wish to pursue state postconviction relief should be allowed to do so, but anyone who prefers to go straight to federal habeas corpus after direct review in the state appellate courts should be welcome.[168]

Temporary Victories

Under current law, prisoners have no obligation to seek federal habeas corpus relief within a specified time period.[169] Since the complaint in federal habeas is theoretically focused on the alleged invalidity of current custody, rather than the state criminal judgment that forms the basis for that custody, it is thought to be troublesome to require prisoners to act within a fixed time after the conclusion of state proceedings—which are only indirectly implicated in a habeas corpus action. In addition, at a practical level, would-be petitioners are, again, typically indigent and unable to find lawyers willing and able to prepare their claims for expeditious federal adjudication. Rule 9(a) of the federal habeas corpus rules permits the district courts to dismiss petitions that are unduly delayed on a showing of prejudice to the state's ability to respond to prisoners' claims. Liberal supporters of habeas corpus contend that nothing further is needed to deal with tardy petitions, because citizens who are denied their liberty have every incentive to act as soon as they can.[170] Critics complain, however, that the absence of filing deadlines allows prisoners to put off federal litigation for strategic purposes—until the record is stale, witnesses and other evidence are unavailable, and, if relief is awarded, the state may be unable to cure error in another trial.[171]

Various bills introduced in recent years would impose fixed filing deadlines for federal habeas petitions. The Attorney General's Task Force appointed by President Reagan proposed a three-year statute of limitations, running (with exceptions) from the date of the criminal conviction in state court. Other bills would give prisoners only one year, running from the exhaustion of state remedies. Senator Biden's proposal would allow only six months from the conclusion of direct review—but with enough exceptions to give most would-be petitioners a year to get into federal court.[172] The pressure for change is most intense in death penalty cases, in which the Chief Justice insists the ordinary incentives for prompt litigation do not operate: a death row prisoner "does not need to prevail on the merits in order to accomplish his purpose; he wins temporary victories by postponing a final adjudication."[173] On this ground, President Bush embraced the Powell Committee's recommendation that a six-month deadline be adopted for capital cases. The American Bar Association and the National District Attorneys Association propose a one-year period for death penalty cases. In one of their initiatives, Senators Thurmond and Specter have recommended that habeas petitions in capital cases be dismissed if filed more than sixty days after the conclusion of direct review.[174]

Rule 9(a) almost certainly provides a sufficient guard against belated petitions.[175] Precise filing deadlines are not, however, either theoretically objectionable or (necessarily) practically unworkable or unfair. Ordinary §1331 lawsuits are subject to time requirements that force plaintiffs to press their claims before the circumstances that gave rise to them become stale. By the same token, prisoners can properly be required to file habeas petitions within a similar time period. It is true that habeas corpus is theoretically focused on a prisoner's current detention. Yet it is only realistic to acknowledge that the gravamen of a habeas action is the constitutional harm allegedly done to the petitioner when a criminal prosecution was being processed by state authorities. The proper date from which a fixed time limit should run may be open to question in some instances, but a general rule that chooses the conclusion of appellate review makes some sense. If prisoners are assured of competent counsel to marshal their claims, a statute of limitations can and should be enacted.[176]

Sandbagging

Once a petitioner exhausts currently available state court opportunities for litigation and files a federal petition without undue delay, yet another procedural barrier may frustrate adjudication of a claim on the merits. While there may be no *current* state opportunity to litigate the claim, it is often true that such an opportunity existed at some point in the past, that the prisoner failed to take advantage of it, and that it is because of the prisoner's "default" that the state courts are no longer willing to consider the claim. The exhaustion doctrine is satisfied, this is to say, only because the prisoner neglected to apply for relief in state court at the time and in the manner required by state law. The federal courts have power to ignore default in state court; the question is whether that power should be exercised.[177] The Warren Court insisted on a general rule favoring adjudication on the merits despite default, subject to an exception if a prisoner's failure to raise a claim in state court constituted a "deliberate bypass" of state procedures, that is, a *waiver* of the opportunity to litigate the claim in state court.[178] The Rehnquist Court, by contrast, largely bars the federal adjudication of a claim that might have been, but was not, raised seasonably in state court. If the state courts refuse to entertain the claim because of default, the claim is *forfeited* in federal court—unless the case falls within narrow exceptions to a general rule *against* federal consideration of the merits. Specifically, the prisoner must either demonstrate both "cause" for his failure to raise the claim at the proper time and "prejudice" flowing from the federal wrong that went uncorrected in state court, or show that federal treatment of the merits is necessary to avoid a "fundamental miscarriage of justice."[179] Under this same forfeiture standard, the Court cuts off attempts to develop the primary facts supporting a federal claim—if the evidence the prisoner wishes to present might have been, but was not, offered to the state courts.[180]

The forfeiture rule for procedural default in state court introduces yet another version of "claim" preclusion into habeas corpus: issues that were not, but might have been, raised and litigated in state court are foreclosed in federal court. As it interlocks with the exhaustion doctrine, moreover, the forfeiture rule wastes all manner of resources in circular litigation, both frustrating and fruitless. A familiar sequence is repeated again and again. A prisoner who seeks to litigate a federal claim in federal court is met by a boilerplate motion to dismiss for failure to exhaust state remedies. The prisoner resists dismissal on that basis, contending that there is no currently available mechanism for putting the claim to the state courts—not because the state courts have already rejected the claim on the merits and will not reconsider, but because the prisoner failed to raise the claim at trial in state court and, for that reason, the state courts will not consider it at all. The district court finds the record ambiguous and notes that the state courts might yet entertain the claim in postconviction proceedings. The court thus decides the exhaustion question against the petitioner and dismisses without prejudice to another federal habeas petition after that state remedy has been tried. The petitioner returns to state court to press the claim in local postconviction proceedings, which become the vehicle by which the state courts explicitly hold that the prisoner committed default at trial and, for that reason, cannot now raise the claim in state court by any means.

Having established that the state courts are currently closed to his claim, the prisoner has met the exhaustion requirement and may return to federal court. But, of course, the very basis upon which state procedures can be said to be exhausted triggers the forfeiture rule for default. The prisoner will almost certainly suffer dismissal yet again, this time with no chance to try back later. Things are no different if, in the first instance, the petitioner avoids dismissal for want of exhaustion on the theory that, because of his default at trial, state postconviction procedures are unavailable. In that case, the petitioner's federal action may be dismissed with prejudice immediately. Either way, a prisoner who escapes the exhaustion doctrine's frying pan falls irretrievably into the default doctrine's fire. Federal claims are defeated on procedural grounds, irrespective of their merit.[181] For when a claim is forfeited because of procedural default in state court, *no* court (state or federal) ever decides whether a prisoner's federal rights have been violated.

None of the justifications typically offered for this state of affairs is entitled to credit. Initially, we can set aside the argument that some sort of procedural bar is necessary in order to respect and protect state interests in the orderly consideration of federal claims. Again, federal habeas corpus is deferred until state criminal prosecutions have come to an end not to allow the state courts to pass on federal claims, but to maintain local control of state criminal law. Likewise, we can dismiss any thought that a procedural bar is needed to enforce the exhaustion doctrine, that is, to keep a state criminal defendant from circumventing the exhaustion requirement simply by failing to raise a claim in state court at the proper time, inviting the state courts to resist further state litigation on that basis, and then pleading that as a consequence there is no currently available state opportunity to litigate the claim. Here again, federal adjudication in habeas corpus should be postponed not to allow the state courts an initial chance to address federal claims, but only to avoid disrupting the prosecution of state criminal cases under local substantive law.

Nor is there anything to the persistent argument that a tough forfeiture rule is essential to combat "sandbagging" in state court. That misguided argument is typically illustrated by a jury trial case in which counsel is aware of a federal claim regarding evidence offered by the prosecution. A timely objection will give the state trial judge an opportunity to evaluate the claim immediately, avoiding error if the claim is sustained and creating a record for appeal or postconviction proceedings if it is rejected. If counsel anticipates that the defendant may escape conviction notwithstanding the offending evidence, so the "sandbagging" argument goes, she may sit silent. If the defendant is acquitted, the presence of federal error will make no difference. If the defendant is convicted, the error strategically inserted in the record by procedural default can be raised later—in federal habeas corpus. In 1977, when he substituted a forfeiture rule for the Warren Court's waiver rule in default cases, then-Justice Rehnquist explicitly stated that stronger medicine was needed to combat this kind of manipulation.[182]

Within a framework in which habeas corpus provides an opportunity for federal adjudication of federal claims roughly equivalent to what might have been achieved by removal prior to trial, the states have no purchase on the adjudication of federal claims for their own sake. The states do, however, have a significant interest in seeing that the judgments they reach in the enforcement of local criminal law are not needlessly upset because federal issues are not raised as soon as they might be. Nevertheless, the vision the "sandbagging" argument conjures up is wholly unrealistic. A criminal defendant's immediate objective is to succeed, or at least to avoid heavy losses, at the trial level in state court. Accordingly, counsel has powerful incentives to raise any claims of which she is aware at the time those claims offer the most promise of protecting against conviction, that is, before the case goes to the jury. To propose that counsel may knowingly withhold potentially meritorious claims at trial is to propose that she may reasonably choose an increased risk of conviction in order to hold out a claim on which to attack an unfavorable judgment later. That is not the way trial lawyers think.

It would be nonsense for a defense attorney to hold a claim in reserve during trial, when the underlying facts and attendant arguments can be spread on the record and when the claim may prevent the defendant's conviction, in order to call it into service after conviction—when the claim will suffer from inadequate development and, even then, can be useful only to attack a verdict already in place. Only if other evidence is so damning that conviction is inevitable would counsel entertain such a strategy. And in circumstances of that kind, the potential gain would be illusory. If claims held in reserve were successful later and the conviction were upset, the client would simply be reconvicted on the basis of the same (untainted) evidence. Indeed, for that very reason, any error found after conviction would be dismissed as harmless—even under the "beyond a reasonable doubt" standard.[183]

In almost all cases in which federal claims are not raised at trial, the explanation lies not in any artful plot by skillful trial lawyers, but rather in counsel's ignorance of a claim or the factual basis for it.[184] Here again, the sad state of the criminal defense bar frustrates a rational incentive system. Underpaid, overworked, and ill-prepared lawyers simply overlook federal claims. Defense lawyers do not "sandbag" the state courts in an attempt to manipulate the judicial system for their clients' benefit. They squander their clients' federal rights by committing default out of ignorance, neglect, insufficient time and resources, or rank incompetence. In these circumstances, a forfeiture rule that cuts off federal habeas corpus because of default in state court makes little sense. A lawyer who is aware of a claim in time to raise it at trial will almost certainly do so and needs no threat of losing federal habeas corpus as an additional incentive. A lawyer who is unaware of a claim cannot raise it, irrespective of the consequences. On this point, not even the Warren Court's waiver standard is justified as a spur to action. Certainly, if the objective is to encourage lawyers to raise known claims, we need go no further than a waiver rule.

The current Court's forfeiture standard is gross overkill. In truth, it is the doctrinal reflection of underlying value judgments. To be sure, this Court wishes to avoid interjurisdictional conflicts of the kind that can occur if the federal courts treat claims the state courts declined to consider. More fundamentally, however, the Court doubts that the federal courts are essential to the enforcement of federal rights in criminal cases and places heavy weight on the states' asserted interest in the finality of criminal judgments. The Court's treatment of default in state court thus impedes the flow of federal petitions for procedural reasons unrelated to the merits. That, after all, is the meaning of a forfeiture rule: an individual loses something of value not out of personal choice, but in light of competing interests judged to be of greater importance.[185] The forfeiture standard does not establish a serious incentive to comply with state procedures for raising federal claims; the waiver rule would have sufficed for that. Instead, the forfeiture standard simply prevents the federal courts from enforcing federal rights.

The Nelson-Mathias bill would have rejected the forfeiture rule in procedural default cases and restored the Warren Court's waiver standard. Recent initiatives touching default either would work a rough peace with the forfeiture framework or would establish an even more stringent test for access to the federal courts.[186] The proper way to proceed, however, is to dispense with any procedural bar at all and, instead, to fortify state systems for delivering competent legal services to criminal defendants—so that professionals can respond to the incentives already in place at the state level.

Inexcusable Neglect

Finally, I come to the vexing problem of multiple federal petitions from a single prisoner. Formally, the traditional exemption habeas corpus enjoys from preclusion covers not only a state prisoner's initial application for habeas relief, but second or successive petitions as well.[187] Yet prisoners who file more than one petition for federal relief face substantial barriers to adjudication on the merits. Until recently, the rules governing multiple petitions had remained constant for a quarter century. Both the controlling statute, §2244(b), and the applicable rule of federal court practice, Rule 9(b), had been read to codify previous guidelines established by the Warren Court.[188] A petitioner presenting the same claim in a second or successive petition had to persuade the court either that the claim had not been determined on the merits in the prior proceeding or that the "ends of justice" would be served by taking it up again.[189] A petitioner pressing a claim omitted from a prior petition had to refute the charge that he had "abused the writ" by failing to raise the claim at the earliest practicable time. The test for an "abuse of the writ" was the "deliberate bypass" standard borrowed from the Warren Court's cases on procedural default in state court.[190]

In the 1980s, however, the current Supreme Court made it clear that in future the "ends of justice" would be harder to serve and that an "abuse" of the writ would be easier to find.[191] Especially in death penalty cases, in which it was feared that condemned prisoners might litigate claims piecemeal in order to postpone final resolution of their cases, the Court sometimes refused to reach the merits of claims that were or might have been put forward in a prior petition—if the omission could be ascribed to a prisoner's "inexcusable neglect."[192] Ultimately, the Court abandoned incrementalism respecting successive petitions and substituted revisionism. In the teeth of §2244(b) and Rule 9(b), the Court now has it that a second or successive habeas petition raising a claim that was not, but might have been, included in a previous petition can and should be dismissed even if it is quite clear that the prisoner did not deliberately withhold the claim from the earlier application. Just as the Rehnquist Court has jettisoned the Warren Court's waiver rule in the default context, this Court has also discarded that rule in the successive petition context. A forfeiture standard now governs equally when prisoners fail to raise claims in *state* court and when they fail to present claims in initial habeas corpus petitions in *federal* court.[193]

Even this further tightening of restrictions on multiple petitions has failed to silence critics calling for ever more drastic limits. The Bush Administration endorsed the Powell Committee's recommendation for capital cases. By that account, the federal courts should refuse to entertain a second or successive application unless the petitioner raises a different claim, not previously presented in either state or federal court. If such a claim is raised, the merits still should not be treated—unless the claim was omitted because of state action in violation of federal law, is based on a new Supreme Court decision with retroactive effect, or depends on facts that could not have been discovered earlier. If the claim meets one of these criteria, it still should not be considered, according to the Powell Committee, unless the supporting facts, if proved, would undermine confidence in the prisoner's guilt of the offense for which the death penalty was imposed. Rejecting the Powell Committee's proposal on this last point, the Judicial Conference recommended that successive petitions be allowed if a prisoner's claim goes *either* to guilt or innocence, *or* to the validity of a death sentence.[194] Nevertheless, the Bush Administration persisted in sponsoring the original committee position, and most other bills since have included similar proposals. Senator Biden's bill would install an approximation of the Judicial Conference recommendation—for both capital and noncapital cases.[195]

The federal courts' doors *should* be closed to all but the most compelling successive applications for federal habeas corpus relief. Just as the custody requirement fails to explain why habeas is available after state criminal proceedings, it also fails to explain why the federal courts should hear multiple federal petitions from a single prisoner.

We do not have federal habeas corpus for state prisoners because we think that as a general matter of social policy criminal convictions should be subject to repeated reexamination as long as the convicts affected are serving their sentences. We have, and ought to have, federal habeas corpus for state prisoners because we deny, and ought to deny, criminal defendants in state court the ability to remove their prosecutions to federal court for original adjudication. The writ's function is to allocate authority between the federal and state courts in criminal cases—leaving responsibility for the making and enforcement of state criminal law with the states and the state courts, but ensuring that citizens with federal claims have access to the federal courts after state authorities have completed their work. Once that function has been served, ordinary preclusion rules may properly be invoked. Plaintiffs who unsuccessfully pursue federal claims in civil actions under §1983 and §1331 are generally precluded from filing additional lawsuits in an attempt to relitigate issues that were or might have been decided against them. Equally, then, competently represented habeas corpus petitioners who obtain one opportunity to litigate in federal court in an initial petition may fairly be denied additional chances.

In the cases in which multiple petitions have raised the greatest controversy, those in which applicants are under sentence of death, the availability of *more* than one chance should turn on the singular nature of capital punishment—not the nature of criminal sanctions generally or, certainly, the nature of federal habeas corpus, properly conceived. In my view, it would be nothing short of monstrous to elevate efficiency above rights in death penalty cases—and thus to send citizens to the gas chamber without pausing to consider second or successive habeas corpus petitions claiming that their convictions were obtained, or their sentences were imposed, in violation of the Constitution. I think that, however, because I think that if prisoners are to be executed at all, it surely should be only after we are assured that all procedural safeguards have been scrupulously observed—not because I think that limiting even death row prisoners to one petition for the federal writ is inconsistent with the model of habeas corpus for which I have argued in this chapter.

▼

Nowhere else in all the law of federal jurisdiction is the thesis of this book so graphically illustrated as it is in the arcane lore of federal habeas corpus for state prisoners. We require effective federal judicial machinery for the enforcement of federal rights. But we don't have it. Instead, we have doctrinal intricacy, which may be of enormous interest to academicians, but which operates on a daily basis to cripple the pursuit of our goals. We have lost touch with the spendid traditions that previously attended the Great Writ of Liberty—from its obscure origins in medieval England, through its American development in powerful opinions by Holmes and Frankfurter, to its emergence in the Warren Court years as a vital instrument by which the federal courts might enforce the Bill of Rights. Moreover, we have failed to keep pace with the many ingenious strategies that conservative justices and presidents alike have pressed in hopes of forcing the federal courts from the field, directly or indirectly. We can get what we need and want legislatively, however, if we examine afresh the relevant values and interests at stake and fashion reforms accordingly. A statute of the kind I have proposed will do the essential work in an honest, forthright manner.

Epilogue

When I was a student, I spent many afternoons in the visiting room at the United States Penitentiary at Leavenworth. It was, as I recall, a large rectangular chamber, accessible to outsiders only through a series of sally ports and steel doors. At first, I was chilled when I heard those doors clank shut and lock behind me. Yet after frequent visits I became as hardened to the doors, the bars, and the rest of the prison environment as the others who came that way—the inmates, the families, the guards. I presented myself at the gate, rattled off the routine disavowals (no weapons, no food, no magazines), named the inmates on my list, and then passed through those dreadful doors to meet my "clients"—many of whom had received no other visitors for years. I had two reasons for being there. As far as the prisoners were concerned, I was supposed to be helping them prepare federal habeas corpus petitions seeking their release from Leavenworth on constitutional grounds. They had no money to pay lawyers, and they graciously accepted any modest assistance they could get from a young man with more enthusiasm than expertise. According to the aspirations of my professors, I was also supposed to be learning something about constitutional law, about the federal courts, and about flesh-and-blood people who very much needed both. I don't know whether I ever genuinely advanced any prisoner's cause, but I did learn one lesson that has remained with me ever since.

One might have expected the prisoners at Leavenworth to be among the last Americans to have any particular regard for courts. After all, they had been convicted in courts and had been sentenced by courts; they had suffered at the hands of courts—however properly and fairly, and with whatever measure of compassion. I was frankly confounded, then, by their incorruptible conviction that if nobody else was still prepared to listen to their claims, the courts remained open. And not just any courts, but the federal courts—the courts ordained and established by Congress to exercise the federal judicial power. Those federal convicts at Leavenworth, and equally the inmates at the state penitentiary a few miles away, believed as they believed nothing else that the federal courts *were* still listening. I understood perfectly well that very few of them had meritorious claims. And if the truth be told, I suspect that they, too, recognized that the chances of success were remote. Still, I did not discount those men and their abundant confidence that the federal courts were there to see that federal rights were respected. Don't you discount them, either. I am not telling you a tragic story about miserable men clinging to desperate dreams. The lesson I learned at Leavenworth is that the federal courts are special. They are the most splendid institutions for the maintenance of governmental order and individual liberty that humankind has ever conceived. They work, you see. And they ensure that the rest of the framework we call constitutional democracy also works. On them we have built the system we have; without them, we would have another system—the fundamental character of which we can only guess (and mostly fear).

The federal courts are not merely additional tribunals created to help the courts of the states resolve disputes over federal questions. The federal courts are structured, equipped, and positioned to be more than that. They are not procedural devices for implementing substantive federal law at all. They are integral to that law; they are part and parcel of it. If you go in search of the Constitution today, you must look beyond the pages of a little book that Justice Black used to carry around in his vest pocket. You must go to the courthouse and see what the judges are actually *doing*. That is the Constitution. The Old Court surely understood as much and thus recruited the federal courts to enforce Formalist limits on governmental regulation of the economy. The Realists resisted the Formalist facade, exposing the federal courts' great capacity. The Legal Process model tried to capture and confine that capacity, but modern liberals have realized its magnificent potential to check governmental power and consequent threats to liberty in all manner of situations apart from markets. The convicts at Leavenworth understood this in their own way. Gene Guerrero did, too—as did Richard Steffel, John Harris, and the five African Americans who would have died at Hoop Spur if the federal courts had not secured their civil rights.

The current conservative retrenchment has diverted the country, to be sure, but we have not yet lost our way entirely. The legislative proposals I have offered in these pages may yet guide us back to the proper path. I do not insist that federal-question cases must be channeled into the federal courts in precisely the way I have suggested or, for that matter, that access to the federal forum must be pursued as relentlessly as my recommendations contemplate. There are undoubtedly cases in which federal issues figure only modestly and in which matters of local concern so predominate that Congress may wisely prefer state court litigation. There may even be circumstances in which Congress may sensibly wish to enforce federal law exclusively through criminal prosecutions or actions by the Department of Justice, administrative agencies, or other instrumentalities—rather than through ordinary civil lawsuits by concerned citizens. I am content to leave the identification of such cases to specialists in the fields in which they arise. I have advanced pristine proposals in order to make the crucial point that we should begin with a system in which the federal courts are broadly open for the adjudication of federal-question cases and then make special exceptions from that baseline. In the end, my message is only this. The federal courts have restrained governmental power in this society for a very long time, and they promise to serve equally well in the future—if we recognize the growing threat to their survival and set about reclaiming them.

NOTES

INDEX

Notes

Introduction

1. I also set aside a range of other issues of obvious significance: the identification of defendants in federal litigation; the defenses and immunities to which defendants may repair; the nature and scope of federal judicial relief; the assignment of federal claims to one of the federal administrative agencies or "legislative" courts; general rules regarding the preclusive effect of state court judgments in federal court; and the Supreme Court's jurisdiction. Nor will I treat related problems in the current system, such as the means by which judges are selected and the inability of poor and middle-income citizens to obtain good lawyers to present their claims. I have examined some aspects of judicial selection elsewhere. Larry W. Yackle, "Choosing Judges the Democratic Way," 69 *B.U. L. Rev.* 273 (1989).

2. I will not treat doctrines that establish similar, but less significant, barriers to immediate federal adjudication, e.g., rules demanding the "exhaustion" of state judicial or administrative remedies prior to federal court action.

One. Ordain and Establish

1. Michael E. Solimine & James L. Walker, "Constitutional Litigation in Federal and State Courts: An Empirical Analysis of Judicial Parity," 10 *Hastings Const. L.Q.* 213 (1983).

2. Erwin Chemerinsky notes, first, that by examining only state *appellate* opinions, Solimine and Walker took no account of the possibility that, because plaintiffs perceive that state *trial* courts are unsympathetic, federal-question cases may not be pursued in state court in the first instance or, when pressed initially, may be settled sooner than they would be in federal court. If cases tend to settle sooner at the trial level in state court, claims that reach the state appellate courts may be comparatively strong—as against claims resolved by opinion in the federal

district courts. Second, the federal courts studied by Solimine and Walker probably determined claims when they were advanced by plaintiffs, while the state courts treated them when they arose in defense. That difference can have a range of implications. Third, state court determinations of federal claims in criminal cases can often be reexamined in the federal district courts on habeas corpus. That being true, the state court decisions that Solimine and Walker counted as sympathetic to claims of federal right may have derived, in part, from the knowledge that the federal courts were waiting in the wings. Erwin Chemerinsky, "Parity Reconsidered: Defining a Role for the Federal Judiciary," 36 *UCLA L. Rev.* 233, 260 (1988). Cf. Thomas B. Marvell, "The Rationales for Federal Question Jurisdiction: An Empirical Examination of Student Rights Litigation," 1984 *Wis. L. Rev.* 1315, 1351 (offering poll data).

3. Burt Neuborne, "The Myth of Parity," 90 *Harv. L. Rev.* 1105 (1977). See Erwin Chemerinsky, "Federal Courts, State Courts, and the Constitution: A Rejoinder to Professor Redish," 36 *UCLA L. Rev.* 369, 370–375 (1988). The argument on behalf of federal courts is made with respect to cases in which plaintiffs press claims under *federal* law. Cases in which litigants have claims under *state* law are of a different order. The state courts are authoritative regarding questions of local law, and plaintiffs who seek relief under that law typically find it advisable, even necessary, to be in state court. When controlling state statutes or constitutional provisions track the corresponding provisions of federal law, state courts often interpret their own law to be coextensive with federal law—in which case state-law theories of suit are rendered practically redundant. E. g., People v. Holland, 520 N.E.2d 270 (Ill. 1987); State v. Lang, 672 P.2d 561 (Idaho 1983). Even when state and federal provisions are identical, however, a state court is free to give the former an independent meaning. There are, then, cases in which state courts have read their own constitutions to protect individual interests in ways the federal Constitution does not. Ronald K. L. Collins & John Kincaid et al., "State High Courts, State Constitutions, and Individual Rights Litigation since 1980: A Judicial Survey," 13 *Hastings Const. L.Q.* 599 (1986); "Developments in the Law—The Interpretation of State Constitutional Rights," 95 *Harv. L. Rev.* 1324 (1982); see generally Robert F. Williams, *State Constitutional Law* (1993).

Of course, local decisions protecting personal liberty operate only in the state in which they are rendered and thus lack the broad, national significance carried by similarly expansive interpretations of federal rights. Nevertheless, state court decisions of this kind have generated a certain amount of excitement over the potential for a new age of litigation in state court, which both exploits the possibilities for vindicating personal rights under state law and renders the pursuit of federal theories (in either the federal or state courts) unnecessary. E. g., Charles H. Baron, "The Supreme Judicial Court in Its Fourth Century: Meeting the Challenge of the New Constitutional Revolution," 77 *Mass. L. Rev.* 35 (1992); Charles G. Douglas III, "State Judicial Activism—The New Role for State Bills of Rights," 12 *Suffolk U. L. Rev.* 1123 (1978); Hans A. Linde, "First Things First: Rediscovering the State's Bill of Rights," 9 *U. Baltimore L. Rev.* 379 (1980); Robert F. Williams, "State Constitutional Law: Teaching and Scholarship," 41 *J. Legal*

Educ. 243 (1991). For if plaintiffs can win under state law something they cannot achieve under federal law, state court litigation on state-law theories can effectively evade the current Supreme Court's more restrictive decisions respecting federal rights—within the states concerned. E. g., Commonwealth v. Upton, 476 N.E.2d 548 (Mass. 1985); State v. Opperman, 247 N.W.2d 673 (S.D. 1976); see Shirley S. Abrahamson, "Criminal Law and State Constitutions: The Emergence of State Constitutional Law," 63 *Tex. L. Rev.* 1141 (1985); A. E. Dick Howard, "State Courts and Constitutional Rights in the Day of the Burger Court," 62 *Va. L. Rev.* 873 (1976); Donald E. Wilkes, Jr., "The New Federalism in Criminal Procedure: State Court Evasion of the Burger Court," 62 *Ky. L.J.* 421 (1974). Justice Brennan has urged litigators (and state courts) to capitalize on these possibilities. E. g., William J. Brennan, Jr., "State Constitutions and the Protection of Individual Rights," 90 *Harv. L. Rev.* 489 (1977); William J. Brennan, Jr., "The Bill of Rights and the States: The Revival of State Constitutions as Guardians of Individual Rights," 61 *N.Y.U. L. Rev.* 535 (1986). Professor Neuborne, too, has recognized the same potential. Burt Neuborne, "Foreword: State Constitutions and the Evolution of Positive Rights," 20 *Rutgers L.J.* 881 (1989).

Specialists are divided over the extent to which state court litigation on state-law theories offers a legitimate, promising avenue for vindicating personal liberty. An inquiry into the specifics of those arguments is well beyond my current project. See generally Ronald K. L. Collins, "Foreword: The Once New Judicial Federalism and Its Critics," 64 *Wash. L. Rev.* 5 (1989). It is pertinent, however, to consider whether the willingness of some state courts to protect individuals via local law proves that the state courts are generally hospitable to personal liberty claims or, indeed, refutes the argument that the federal courts' institutional advantages in personal liberty cases render them better tribunals for the adjudication of *federal* claims. Cf. Gary L. McDowell, "Foreword: Rediscovering Federalism? State Constitutional Law and the Restoration of State Sovereignty," 21 *Rutgers L.J.* 797 (1990).

On examination, the evidence is insufficient to support either conclusion. After all, we would expect that state-law claims would be vindicated by the state courts, for the self-evident reason that those are the courts with responsibility for giving state claims definitive treatment. Moreover, generous readings of state law do not necessarily signal equally generous readings of federal law. State courts may have any number of local reasons for reading their own law as they do—reasons that do not extend to cases controlled by federal law alone. One tends to suspect, for example, that the recent spate of state court decisions invalidating local schemes for financing public schools has as much to do with logjams in local legislatures as with an enthusiasm for giving state constitutional provisions a capacious reading. See Edgewood Ind. School Dist. v. Kirby, 777 S.W.2d 391 (Tex. 1989). It is questionable at best, then, whether state court enforcement of individual liberty under state-law theories throws significant light on the parity debate.

4. E.g., Erwin Chemerinsky, "Ending the Parity Debate," 71 *B.U. L. Rev.* 593, 594 (1991).

5. See Neil A. Lewis, "Unmaking the GOP Court Legacy," *N.Y. Times* (Aug.

23, 1993); see also Neil A. Lewis, "Selection of Conservative Judges Guards Part of Bush's Legacy," *N.Y. Times* (July 1, 1992); Ruth Marcus, "Bush Quietly Fosters Conservative Trend in Courts," *Washington Post* (Feb. 18, 1991).

6. Herman Schwartz, *Packing the Courts* 58 (1988). See Sheldon Goldman, "Reorganizing the Judiciary: The First Term Appointments," 68 *Judicature* 313 (1985); Note, "All the President's Men? A Study of Ronald Reagan's Appointments to the U. S. Courts of Appeals," 87 *Colum. L. Rev.* 766 (1987); Robert A. Carp et al., "The Voting Behavior of Judges Appointed by President Bush," 76 *Judicature* 298 (1993) (reporting empirical evidence that the "Bush judicial cohort has been relatively conservative"). Mark Tushnet contends that "[o]ne could account for perhaps ninety percent of Chief Justice Rehnquist's bottom-line results by looking, not at anything in the *United States Reports,* but rather at the platforms of the Republican Party." Mark V. Tushnet, "A Republican Chief Justice," 88 *Mich. L. Rev.* 1326, 1328 (1990).

7. People for the American Way, *Judicial Nominees in the First Two Years of the Bush Administration: White, Male, and Wealthy* (1990); Terrence Moran, "In His Own Image," *Legal Times* (Dec. 31, 1990). But see Sheldon Goldman, "Bush's Judicial Legacy: The Final Imprint," 76 *Judicature* 282 (1993) (reporting that Bush named higher percentages of women and people of color in his final two years).

8. I collect the standard references in Larry W. Yackle, "Choosing Judges the Democratic Way," 69 *B.U. L. Rev.* 273 (1989).

9. See George Kassouf, "Clinton Picks Up Pace in Naming Judges," 27 *Alliance for Justice Pipeline* 4 (1993) (reporting that Clinton's initial nominees reflect "unprecedented . . . diversity"). On the Johnson and Carter records, see Larry C. Berkson & Susan B. Carbon, *Federal Judicial Selection during the Carter Administration* (1979); Neil McFeeley, *Appointment of Judges: The Johnson Presidency* (1987); Sheldon Goldman, "Carter's Judicial Appointments: A Lasting Legacy," 64 *Judicature* 344 (1981). On the new judgeships, see Federal Judgeship Act of 1990, 104 Stat. 5099 (Dec. 1, 1990); Lewis, "Unmaking," supra note 5. But see Goldman, "Final Imprint," supra note 7 (reporting that President Bush increasingly named women and people of color to the bench as his presidency wore on).

10. For an elaboration, see Richard H. Fallon, Jr., "The Ideologies of Federal Courts Law," 74 *Va. L. Rev.* 1141 (1988).

11. See Zwickler v. Koota, 389 U. S. 241, 245–249 (1967), and the standard sources cited therein. E. g., Felix Frankfurter & James M. Landis, *The Business of the Supreme Court: A Study in the Federal Judicial System* (1928); Felix Frankfurter, "Distribution of Judicial Power between the United States and State Courts," 13 *Cornell L.Q.* 499 (1928); Charles Warren, "New Light on the History of the Federal Judiciary Act of 1789," 37 *Harv. L. Rev.* 49 (1923).

12. *The Status of Federalism in America: A Report of the Working Group on Federalism of the Domestic Policy Council* (1986).

13. The Rehnquist Court's decisions favoring jurisdiction in the state courts invoke not only federalism but the "comity" owed the states. That term is borrowed from international law, where it refers to arrangements that ameliorate

conflicts between nations. See Hilton v. Guyot, 159 U. S. 113, 164 (1895). On the genuine contributions of federalism to modern analysis, see Aviam Soifer, "Truisms That Never Will Be True: The Tenth Amendment and the Spending Power," 57 *U. Colo. L. Rev.* 793 (1986).

14. See the text accompanying notes 18–24 infra; National League of Cities v. Usery, 426 U. S. 833 (1976) (enforcing "federalism" limits on Congress' power to regulate the states themselves).

15. E.g., Garcia v. San Antonio Metro. Trans. Auth., 469 U. S. 528 (1985) (overruling *National League of Cities*). At least if Congress makes its meaning clear—see Gregory v. Ashcroft, 111 S.Ct. 2395 (1991)—the Court almost always recognizes legislative power to order state affairs. The only recent exception is New York v. United States, 112 S.Ct. 2408 (1992), in which the Court invalidated a federal statute directing the states to regulate in a particular manner, undermining the accountability of local officials.

16. See Chapter Two, notes 86–90 and the accompanying text. The Court has occasionally warned that the constitutionally prescribed separation of powers cannot be altered by the consent of the "governmental unit whose domain is . . . narrowed." New York v. United States, 112 S.Ct. 2408, 2432 (1992). That general proposition is only abstract formalism, which contributes little to the practical adjudication of actual cases. There are, moreover, situations in which the Court seems to tolerate what might otherwise violate structural constitutional norms— *if* the party affected consents to the arrangement under attack. For example, Congress can authorize a state to regulate commercial activity in a way that would violate the commerce clause absent such consent. Prudential Ins. Co. v. Benjamin, 328 U. S. 408 (1946). I will not say that the Court is plainly inconsistent. In the commerce clause instance, Congress probably can consent only to local regulations that Congress itself might have imposed directly. Yet if we leaf through the reports, we find that the presence (or absence) of consent or waiver does arguably make a difference, at least at the margin. For example, in the cases in which Congress assigns disputes to "legislative" tribunals rather than to federal courts organized under Article III, the Supreme Court recognizes two different constitutional concerns: the private litigants' interest in being in an Article III court and the public interest in keeping legislative courts from usurping the basic functions of the federal judicial branch. The Court concedes that the first of these can be waived by a private litigant, but insists that the second goes to structural matters that private parties "cannot be expected to protect." Commodity Futures Trading Comm. v. Schor, 478 U. S. 833, 851 (1986). Nevertheless, once a private party has, indeed, consented, the Court seems clearly to be less worried that the arrangement genuinely threatens structural values. See, e.g., Peretz v. United States, 111 S.Ct. 2661 (1991). Cf. Northern Pipeline Const. Co. v. Marathon Pipe Line Co., 458 U. S. 50, 91 (1982) (Rehnquist & O'Connor, J. J., concurring) (agreeing that use of a legislative court violated the separation-of-powers principle reflected in Article III and giving as part of the reason that the private company involved had been forced into that court "against its will"). So when the justices make the separation-of-powers principle sound so rigid, so impervious to the policies that

Congress wishes in its wisdom to advance, we can reasonably be suspicious. It's all a little too convenient. But see Martin H. Redish, "Abstention, Separation of Powers, and the Limits of the Judicial Function," 94 *Yale L.J.* 71 (1984). See also Chapter Four, the text accompanying notes 76–92.

17. Michael Wells, "Rhetoric and Reality in the Law of Federal Courts: Professor Fallon's Faulty Premise," 6 *Const. Commentary* 367, 372 (1989). See also Michael Wells, "The Impact of Substantive Interests on the Law of Federal Courts," 30 *Wm. & Mary L. Rev.* 499 (1989).

18. In this section, I follow William N. Eskridge & Gary Peller, "The New Public Law Movement: Moderation as a Postmodern Cultural Form," 89 *Mich. L. Rev.* 707 (1991). See also Gary Peller, "Classical Theory of Law," 73 *Cornell L. Rev.* 300 (1988); Thomas C. Grey, "Langdell's Orthodoxy," 45 *U. Pitt. L. Rev.* 1 (1983); Richard A. Posner, "Legal Formalism, Legal Realism, and the Interpretation of Statutes and the Constitution," 37 *Case W. Res. L. Rev.* 179 (1987); Richard A. Posner, "Jurisprudential Responses to Legal Realism," 73 *Cornell L. Rev.* 326 (1988); Frederick Schauer, "Formalism," 97 *Yale L.J.* 509 (1988); Ernest J. Weinrib, "Legal Formalism: On the Immanent Rationality of Law," 97 *Yale L.J.* 949 (1988).

19. See Charles Warren, "The New 'Liberty' under the Fourteenth Amendment," 39 *Harv. L. Rev.* 431 (1926). For a modern treatment, see C. Edwin Baker, "Property and Its Relation to Constitutionally Protected Liberty," 134 *U. Pa. L. Rev.* 741 (1986).

20. Santa Clara County v. Southern Pac. R. R., 118 U. S. 394 (1886) (holding that corporations could be "persons"); Allgeyer v. Louisiana, 165 U. S. 578 (1897) (invoking the due process clause on behalf of economic liberty broadly conceived). For classic commentaries, see Howard J. Graham, "Justice Field and the Fourteenth Amendment," 52 *Yale L.J.* 851 (1943); Howard J. Graham, "The 'Conspiracy Theory' of the Fourteenth Amendment," 47 *Yale L.J.* 371 (1938); John Dewey, "The Historical Background of Corporate Legal Personality," 36 *Yale L.J.* 655 (1926). For a fresh, insightful account, see Morton J. Horwitz, *The Transformation of American Law, 1870–1960* (1992).

21. E.g., New State Ice Co. v. Liebmann, 285 U. S. 262 (1932); Adkins v. Children's Hosp., 261 U. S. 525 (1923); Lochner v. New York, 198 U. S. 45 (1905); Coppage v. Kansas, 236 U. S. 1 (1915).

22. In fairness, I should say that some recent scholarship is a bit more charitable—explaining the Old Court's rejection of certain economic measures as, in truth, the rejection of "class" legislation, which furthered no general public value, but rather favored some citizens at the expense of others. See, e.g., Howard Gillman, *The Constitution Besieged* 6–8 (1993) (collecting other authorities). Of course, virtually any attempt to regulate economic affairs treats market participants unequally, for the very reason that the legislature deems it to be in the public interest to shift economic wealth around. Moreover, the Old Court also typically faulted federal statutes on other ostensible grounds, namely, the internal limits on Congress' power to regulate commerce and the "nondelegation" doctrine. E. g., Carter v. Carter Coal Co., 298 U. S. 238 (1936); A. L. A. Schechter Poultry Corp.

v. United States, 295 U. S. 495 (1935). It does seem fair to say that the Old Court had little patience with raw, pluralistic politics, in which the many simply take from the few for no better reason than that they have the votes. Indeed, in that attitude about the way politics should work lies the core of some of our most widely admired modern doctrines. See generally Cass R. Sunstein, *The Partial Constitution* (1993).

23. The eleventh amendment has conventionally been read to provide the states with immunity against suit in federal court.

24. Smyth v. Ames, 169 U. S. 466 (1898) (the Nebraska case); Home Tel. & Tel. Co. v. City of Los Angeles, 227 U. S. 278 (1913) (the Los Angeles case); Ex parte Young, 209 U. S. 123 (1908) (the Minnesota case). See Neuborne, "Myth," supra note 3, at 1107–08 (citing these illustrations).

25. Felix S. Cohen, "Transcendental Nonsense and the Functional Approach," 35 *Colum. L. Rev.* 809 (1935).

26. Lochner v. New York, 198 U. S. 45, 76 (1905) (Holmes, J., dissenting).

27. Richard Hofstadter, *Social Darwinism in American Thought* (1955); see Edward A. Purcell, *The Crisis of Democratic Theory* (1973).

28. See Ira C. Lupu, "Untangling the Strands of the Fourteenth Amendment," 77 *Mich. L. Rev.* 981, 989 (1979). Even Justice Holmes, who was personally much taken with laissez faire economic theory, conceded that nothing in the fourteenth amendment condemned state statutes reflecting a different economic policy. Lochner v. New York, 198 U. S. 45, 75 (1905) (dissenting opinion). In the end, Holmes and Brandeis won out. Today, the Supreme Court rarely invalidates statutes regulating business. See Williamson v. Lee Optical, 348 U. S. 483, 488 (1955). Only genuinely radical modern conservatives advocate a return to economic due process. E. g., Richard A. Epstein, *Takings: Private Property and the Power of Eminent Domain* (1985); Bernard H. Siegan, *Economic Liberties and the Constitution* (1980). Formalism still rears its head on occasion, notably in the Court's decisions on the separation of powers. E. g., Bowsher v. Synar, 478 U. S. 714 (1986); INS v. Chadha, 462 U. S. 919 (1983). See Erwin Chemerinsky, "A Paradox without a Principle: A Comment on the Burger Court's Jurisprudence in Separation of Powers Cases," 60 *So. Calif. L. Rev.* 1083 (1987); Philip B. Kurland, "The Rise and Fall of the 'Doctrine' of Separation of Powers," 85 *Mich. L. Rev.* 592 (1986). But only Justice Scalia purports to take seriously the notion that the Court can deny that it "creates" law. See Chapter Five, note 99. Scalia is a devotee of Formalist separation-of-powers categories. E. g., Morrison v. Olson, 487 U. S. 654, 697–699 (1988) (Scalia, J., dissenting).

29. Neuborne, "Myth," supra note 3, at 1107–08.

30. Roscoe Pound, "Mechanical Jurisprudence," 8 *Colum. L. Rev.* 605 (1908); Roscoe Pound, "Common Law and Legislation," 21 *Harv. L. Rev.* 383 (1908). See also John C. Gray, *The Nature and Sources of the Law* (1909). Previously, James Thayer had pleaded for judicial restraint respecting democratic policy-making. James B. Thayer, "The Origin and Scope of the American Doctrine of Constitutional Law," 7 *Harv. L. Rev.* 129 (1893). See Frank M. Coffin, *The Ways of a Judge* 206–249 (1980).

31. The Realist movement had many sides to it, and historians debate which of its themes is entitled to definitional significance. For classic works, see Karl N. Llewellyn, *The Bramble Bush: Some Lectures on Law and Its Study* (1930); Karl N. Llewellyn, "Some Realism about Realism," 44 *Harv. L. Rev.* 1222 (1931); Felix S. Cohen, "The Ethical Basis of Legal Criticism," 41 *Yale L.J.* 201 (1931). Just who fits the Legal Realist category historically is often a matter of dispute. See Horwitz, *Transformation,* supra note 20; Laura Kalman, *Legal Realism at Yale* (1986); Joseph W. Singer, "Legal Realism Now," 76 *Calif. L. Rev.* 465 (1988); G. Edward White, "From Sociological Jurisprudence to Realism: Jurisprudence and Social Change in Early Twentieth-Century America," 58 *Va. L. Rev.* 999 (1972).

32. Eskridge & Peller, "New Public Law," supra note 18, at 715.

33. See Hugh Collins, *Marxism and Law* (1982). Or fascist. Eskridge and Peller suggest that Pound and another major academic figure of his generation, Lon Fuller, worried that the Realists meant so to divorce law from objective morality that the American system would be rendered no more legitimate than the power-driven directives issued in Nazi Germany. Eskridge & Peller, "New Public Law," supra note 18, at 716 n.11.

34. See Eskridge & Peller, "New Public Law," supra note 18, at 723. For an insightful treatment of the course of substantive constitutional law in the New Deal period, and particularly the realization that government was largely responsible for the status quo, see Sunstein, *Partial,* supra note 22.

35. Here again, commentators differ over the range of themes embodied in the Legal Process school. In addition to Eskridge and Peller, see Bruce A. Ackerman, *Reconstructing American Law* (1984); Grant Gilmore, *The Ages of American Law* (1979); G. Edward White, *The American Judicial Tradition* (1978); William N. Eskridge & Philip P. Frickey, "Legislation Scholarship and Pedagogy in the Post-Legal Process Era," 48 *U. Pitt. L. Rev.* 691 (1987); G. Edward White, "The Evolution of Reasoned Elaboration: Jurisprudential Criticism and Social Change," 59 *Va. L. Rev.* 279 (1973). Eskridge and Peller link Legal Process with contemporaneous developments in political philosophy. See, e.g., John Dewey, *Freedom and Culture* (1939); Purcell, *Crisis,* supra note 27. Both Eskridge and Peller have written separately on the problem. William N. Eskridge, "Metaprocedure," 98 *Yale L.J.* 945 (1989); Gary Peller, "Neutral Principles in the 1950's," 21 *U. Mich. J. L. Ref.* 561 (1988). See generally Morton G. White, *Social Thought in America: The Revolt against Formalism* (1947). Edward Levi's essays, published virtually contemporaneously with the Legal Process texts I am about to discuss, were also influential. Edward H. Levi, "An Introduction to Legal Reasoning," 15 *U. Chi. L. Rev.* 501 (1948). See Jan Vetter, "Postwar Legal Scholarship on Judicial Decision-Making," 33 *J. Legal Educ.* 412, 413–417 (1983). For Frankfurter's early work, see, e.g., Felix Frankfurter & Henry M. Hart, Jr., "The Business of the Supreme Court at October Term, 1934," 49 *Harv. L. Rev.* 68 (1935); Felix Frankfurter & J. Forrester Davison, *Cases and Other Materials on Administrative Law* (1932); Frankfurter & Landis, *Business,* supra note 11.

36. Henry M. Hart, Jr. & Albert M. Sacks, *The Legal Process: Basic Problems in the Making and Application of Law* 173 (tent. ed. 1958).

37. Id. at 4.

38. I owe this insight to Grey, "Orthodoxy," supra note 18, at 47–48.

39. For another statement of Legal Process, see Lon L. Fuller, "The Forms and Limits of Adjudication," 92 *Harv. L. Rev.* 353 (1978).

40. Henry M. Hart, Jr. & Herbert Wechsler, *The Federal Courts and the Federal System* (1953).

41. Id. at 435.

42. Henry M. Hart, Jr., "The Power of Congress to Limit the Jurisdiction of the Federal Courts: An Exercise in Dialectic," 66 *Harv. L. Rev.* 1362, 1401 (1953). On the Article III analysis, see Chapter Three, the text accompanying notes 10–39.

43. See Akhil R. Amar, "Law Story," 102 *Harv. L. Rev.* 688 (1989).

44. Garcia v. San Antonio Metro. Trans. Auth., 469 U. S. 528 (1985).

45. Bator understood Hart to have argued that *if* Congress withholds a federal forum, the state courts can ignore any similar attempt to limit their jurisidiction. Paul M. Bator, "The State Courts and Federal Constitutional Litigation," 22 *Wm. & Mary L. Rev.* 605, 628 n.58 (1981).

46. Michael Wells, "Behind the Parity Debate: The Decline of the Legal Process Tradition in the Law of Federal Courts," 71 *B.U. L. Rev.* 609, 619–623 (1991).

47. Brown v. Bd. of Educ., 347 U. S. 483 (1954).

48. Mapp v. Ohio, 367 U. S. 643 (1961) (establishing the fourth amendment exclusionary rule in state cases); Monroe v. Pape, 365 U. S. 167 (1961) (revitalizing §1983).

49. See generally "Developments in the Law—Section 1983 and Federalism," 90 *Harv. L. Rev.* 1133 (1977).

50. Gideon v. Wainwright, 372 U. S. 335 (1963) (recognizing the right to counsel in state felony prosecutions); Fay v. Noia, 372 U. S. 391 (1963) (developing habeas corpus for state prisoners).

51. E.g., Brandenburg v. Ohio, 395 U. S. 444 (1969) (establishing protective doctrine for speech); Dombrowski v. Pfister, 380 U. S. 479 (1965) (allowing an injunction).

52. England v. Louisiana State Bd. of Medical Examiners, 375 U. S. 411 (1964) (allowing an exemption from ordinary preclusion doctrine in some abstention cases); Parden v. Terminal Ry. of Alabama State Docks Dep't, 377 U. S. 184 (1964) (finding an implied waiver of eleventh amendment immunity).

53. Herbert Wechsler, "Toward Neutral Principles of Constitutional Law," 73 *Harv. L. Rev.* 1 (1959).

54. Henry M. Hart, Jr., "The Supreme Court, 1958 Term—Foreword: The Time Chart of the Justices," 73 *Harv. L. Rev.* 84 (1959).

55. See Peller, "Neutral Principles," supra note 35.

56. Alexander M. Bickel, *The Least Dangerous Branch: The Supreme Court at the Bar of Politics* 16 (1962).

57. This summary is a lightly edited loan from Yackle, "Choosing," supra note 8, at 273–275. Among others, the summary draws on Bruce A. Ackerman, "Constitutional Politics / Constitutional Law," 99 *Yale L.J.* 457 (1989); Bruce A. Ackerman, "The Storrs Lectures: Discovering the Constitution," 93 *Yale L.J.* 1013 (1984); Frank I. Michelman, "Law's Republic," 97 *Yale L.J.* 1493 (1988); Cass R. Sunstein, "Interest Groups in American Law," 38 *Stan. L. Rev.* 29 (1985); Cass R. Sunstein, "Naked Preferences and the Constitution," 84 *Colum. L. Rev.* 1689 (1984); Laurence H. Tribe, "The Puzzling Persistence of Process-Based Constitutional Theories," 89 *Yale L.J.* 1063 (1980); and especially Lawrence G. Sager, "The Incorrigible Constitution," 65 *N.Y.U. L. Rev.* 893 (1990) (an early draft of which was available to me).

58. Ronald M. Dworkin, *Law's Empire* 376, 381 (1986).

59. Sager, "Incorrigible," supra note 57, reviewing John H. Ely, *Democracy and Distrust: A Theory of Judicial Review* (1980).

60. Roe v. Wade, 410 U. S. 113 (1973).

61. Accord William N. Eskridge, "Public Values in Statutory Interpretation," 137 *U. Pa. L. Rev.* 1007, 1015 (1989); Morton J. Horwitz, "The Warren Court: Rediscovering the Link between Law and Culture," 55 *U. Chi. L. Rev.* 450, 455 (1988).

62. Steffel v. Thompson, 415 U. S. 452, 464 (1974). Accord Dombrowski v. Pfister, 380 U. S. 479 (1965); England v. Louisiana State Bd. of Medical Examiners, 375 U. S. 411 (1964); Fay v. Noia, 372 U. S. 391 (1963); Zwickler v. Koota, 389 U. S. 241 (1967)—all Brennan opinions for the Court.

63. Michael Wells, "Is Disparity a Problem?" 22 *Ga. L. Rev.* 283, 298 (1988).

64. Huffman v. Pursue, Ltd., 420 U. S. 592, 611 (1975).

65. Stone v. Powell, 428 U. S. 465, 494 n.35 (1976).

66. Mitchum v. Foster, 407 U. S. 225, 238–242 (1972).

67. Allen v. McCurry, 449 U. S. 90, 103–105 (1980).

68. See Chapter Four.

69. See Chapter Five.

70. See Chapter Four.

71. E.g., Allen v. McCurry, 449 U. S. 90 (1980) (refusing to exempt §1983 actions from issue preclusion doctrine); Migra v. Warren City School Dist., 465 U. S. 75 (1984) (invoking claim preclusion in a §1983 action); Edelman v. Jordan, 415 U. S. 651 (1974) (recognizing eleventh amendment immunity in §1983 actions for backward-looking relief); Quern v. Jordan, 440 U. S. 332 (1979) (declining to read §1983 to override the eleventh amendment). But see Pennsylvania v. Union Gas Co., 491 U. S. 1 (1989) (opinion for the Court by Brennan, J.) (holding that Congress can abrogate eleventh amendment immunity by legislation enacted under the authority of the commerce clause).

72. Moore v. Sims, 442 U. S. 415, 430 (1979).

73. E.g., Maine v. Thiboutot, 448 U. S. 1 (1980); Howlett v. Rose, 496 U. S. 356 (1990).

74. The Rehnquist Court does not appear to be engaged in a campaign to *extend* federal rights, either economic or personal, such that we might predict

that the Court means to shift litigation regarding those rights to the court system thought to be the more cooperative. But see Hugh C. Macgill, "The Role of the District Courts in a Changing Political Climate," 56 *Conn. B.J.* 222 (1982) (worrying that extremists hope to resurrect some version of the old economic due process and that recent decisions sending cases to state court play a role in that plan).

75. Paul M. Bator, "Finality in Criminal Law and Federal Habeas Corpus for State Prisoners," 76 *Harv. L. Rev.* 441 (1963).

76. Brown v. Allen, 344 U. S. 443, 540 (1953) (concurring opinion).

77. Bator, "Finality," supra note 75, at 448 (emphasis supplied). Bator *did* cite Louis Jaffe, who had proposed that the question is not whether an outcome is correct in some "absolute sense," but whether it supplies a "sufficient moral predicate" such that "society will accept it." Louis L. Jaffe, "Judicial Review: Question of Law," 69 *Harv. L. Rev.* 239, 244 (1955), quoted in Bator, "Finality" at 448. See also Louis L. Jaffe, "Judicial Review: Constitutional and Jurisdictional Fact," 70 *Harv. L. Rev.* 953, 966 (1957) (observing that a court "cannot any more than any other human agency break down the barrier between appearance and reality"), quoted in Bator, "Finality" at 447; Herbert L. A. Hart, *The Concept of Law* 139 (1961) (insisting that it is "impossible to provide by rule for the correction of the breach of every rule"), quoted in Bator, "Finality" at 448 n.12.

78. Bator, "Finality," supra note 75, at 449 (emphasis in original).

79. Id. at 462.

80. See the text accompanying note 37 supra.

81. See the text accompanying note 45 supra.

82. Bator, "Finality," supra note 75, at 625.

83. Id. at 625–626.

84. Id. at 484; Frank v. Mangum, 237 U. S. 309 (1915). See Leonard Dinnerstein, *The Leo Frank Case* (1968).

85. Bator, "Finality," supra note 75, at 506. See Frank J. Parker, *Caryl Chessman: The Redlight Bandit* (1975).

86. Bator, "Finality," supra note 75, at 631–633.

87. The Hart & Wechsler casebook, for which Paul Bator was an editor until his death, is an even more ubiquitous citation in the Court's opinions on federal jurisdiction. Bator served as Deputy Solicitor General in the Reagan Administration.

88. Sumner v. Mata, 449 U. S. 539, 549 (1981) (emphasis supplied).

89. Michigan v. Long, 463 U. S. 1032 (1983).

90. See Chapter Five. On the Rehnquist Court's apparent acceptance of an extreme version of the Realist creed, see John Hart Ely, "Another Such Victory: Constitutional Theory and Practice in a World Where Courts Are No Different from Legislatures," 77 *Va. L. Rev.* 833 (1991) (lamenting the modern tendency to conflate law and politics). Cf. Erwin Chemerinsky, "The Supreme Court, 1988 Term—Foreword: The Vanishing Constitution," 103 *Harv. L. Rev.* 43 (1989) (faulting the Court for making value judgments in constitutional cases but purporting to be neutral).

91. See the text accompanying notes 1–2 supra.

92. Chemerinsky, "Parity Reconsidered," supra note 2. See also Howard Fink & Mark V. Tushnet, *Federal Jurisdiction: Policy and Practice* 20 (1984).

93. Chemerinsky, "Parity Reconsidered," supra note 2, at 300–301.

94. For now, let me say that Chemerinsky may make too much of the formal ability of litigants to choose the state courts. There will be occasions when plaintiffs may prefer the state system—perhaps to get their cases before a particular judge thought to be sympathetic, to avoid a federal judge thought to be hostile, or for a host of other tactical reasons. See Steven H. Steinglass, "The Emerging State Court §1983 Action: A Procedural Review," 38 *U. Miami L. Rev.* 381, 413–424 (1984). But those occasions will not be many. In practice, moreover, the busy scheme that Chemerinsky contemplates might aggravate friction between the two court systems. In accordance with the litigant-choice principle in the pure form in which Chemerinsky presents it, litigants who are sued in state court and have federal claims to raise in defense would be entitled to snub the state forum and, with noses upturned, transfer the lawsuits filed against them to federal court for trial. Likewise, litigants who are sued in federal court and prefer to litigate federal defenses in the state courts would be able to snub the federal courts and prance off to the state courts. If, as Chemerinsky appears to anticipate, the flow of cases proves to be nontrivial in both directions, there will be considerable snubbing going on. That, together with the costs of such an active, crisscrossing scheme, makes it appear awkward and cumbersome. Our fundamental commitment to the maintenance of two parallel sets of courts necessarily assumes some inefficiency. But a scheme promising all these comings and goings is difficult to defend on the ground that it enhances federalism—at least in the real world in which such schemes must operate. When I return to the litigant-choice principle later, I will offer a less pure, but more feasible, formulation.

95. Redish, himself scarcely a conservative, has made this point. Martin H. Redish, "Judicial Parity, Litigant Choice, and Democratic Theory: A Comment on Federal Jurisdiction and Constitutional Rights," 36 *UCLA L. Rev.* 329, 342 (1988).

96. Id. at 341. Judith Resnik has linked an accommodation of plaintiffs' litigation choices to individual dignity and the utilitarian value of fostering satisfaction with the judicial system. Judith Resnik, "Tiers," 57 *So. Calif. L. Rev.* 837, 846–847 (1984). Yet autonomy is not an absolute; Chemerinsky identifies it as one goal among many.

97. Chemerinsky, "Parity Reconsidered," supra note 2, at 308–309, relying on Akhil R. Amar, "Of Sovereignty and Federalism," 96 *Yale L.J.* 1425, 1428 (1987). The state courts can also promise independent state substantive grounds for relief. Yet I am here considering the availability of the federal and state courts to litigants with *federal* claims. The availability of independent state-law claims may have implications for the forum choices litigants ultimately make (assuming they are given a choice). But it has nothing necessarily to do with the narrow question of which court system, if either, is superior for federal claims alone. See note 3 supra.

98. On the values served by concurrent jurisdiction, see Robert M. Cover,

"The Uses of Jurisdictional Redundancy: Interest, Ideology, and Innovation," 22 *Wm. & Mary L. Rev.* 639 (1981).

99. Again, I lay aside occasional instances in which state courts have invoked their own local constitutions to protect individuals against state power. See note 3 supra.

100. See Richard Faust, Tina J. Rubenstein & Larry W. Yackle, "The Great Writ in Action: Empirical Light on the Federal Habeas Corpus Debate," 18 *N.Y.U. Rev. of L. & Soc. Change* 637 (1991).

101. See Michigan v. Long, 463 U. S. 1032 (1983) (rejecting any suggestion that the state courts may adopt more generous local interpretations of federal rights than the Supreme Court prescribes for the nation as a whole).

102. Chemerinsky, "Parity Reconsidered," supra note 2, at 302.

103. Id.

104. Chemerinsky does not say that *everyone* agrees that it is desirable to maximize the likelihood that individuals will succeed in constitutional cases. He says that "most" commentators take this view and that "[m]any" concede the point. Yet he cites only Solimine and Walker. Of course, those two observers can afford to be generous to their adversaries in light of their presumptuous conclusion that they have empirically proved that parity exists. That conclusion has now been so thoroughly discredited (by Chemerinsky's own hand) that it is hard to comprehend how Solimine and Walker can be cited for much of anything. See note 2 supra.

105. Chemerinsky concedes that "some *may* challenge" the premise that federal rights should be interpreted expansively, and he cites Bator. Chemerinsky, "Parity Reconsidered," supra note 2, at 303 (emphasis supplied). Given Bator, he then offers some thoughts about why, at all events, it "makes sense" to "maximize the opportunity for protecting constitutional rights." The operative term here is "opportunity." Chemerinsky disclaims any intent that individuals "should always win." Id. at 304.

Chemerinsky first contends that if we have only three choices—to maximize the opportunity for vindicating rights, to minimize the opportunity, or to be neutral—then it "makes sense" to maximize. If these were the only choices, Chemerinsky might be right that the first option is preferable to the other two. Yet his categories leave too little room for the value that Bator presses with equal zeal— the authority of elected legislatures and executive officers to make public policy, subject only to unquestioned rights embedded in the hard core of the Constitution.

Next, Chemerinsky dismisses the notion that rights can be overly protected against majoritarian power, citing Mark Tushnet's clever gambit that, if rights could be given too much protection, it would follow that statutes extending entitlements beyond the constitutional minimum would be suspect. Tushnet & Fink, *Federal Jurisdiction,* supra note 92, at 21. As Martin Redish has explained, the two cases can be distinguished. When courts give federal rights an outsized interpretation, they limit democratic authority; when legislatures establish rights over and above the constitutional floor, they exercise democratic power. Redish, "Judicial Parity," supra note 95, at 337–338 n.29. Nor is Bator logically bound to deny that rights can be overprotected. Since Bator insists that results must be accepted if they fall within reasonable limits, it follows, according to Chemerinsky, that he must accept judicial outcomes that stretch (within reason) the scope of rights. If he, Bator, does not, then he must surrender his position that decisions cannot be right or wrong in some absolute sense, but can only be acceptable within the bounds of tolerance. This, too, fails, I am afraid. Bator's Legal Process approach can accommodate *both* an objective that courts should pursue acceptable results, not by inclining toward the individual but by balancing competing interests and values, *and* the view that the outcomes duly reached *in that way* should stand.

106. Wells, "Parity Debate," supra note 46, at 611.

107. Cf. Chemerinsky, "Ending the Debate," supra note 4, at 604–606.

108. In Henry Friendly's words, "the inferior federal courts now have more work than they can properly do—including some work they are not institutionally fitted to do." Henry J. Friendly, *Federal Jurisdiction: A General View* 3–4 (1973).

109. Judge Friendly endorsed Hart's call for a "full-dress re-examination . . . of the use to which [the federal courts] are being put." Henry M. Hart, Jr., "The Relations between State and Federal Law," 54 *Colum. L. Rev.* 489, 541 (1954), quoted in Friendly, *General View,* supra note 108, at 4.

110. Federal Judicial Center, "Report of the Study Group on the Caseload of the Supreme Court," 57 F.R.D. 573 (1972) (recommending the creation of a new National Court of Appeals to shoulder some of the burden). See also Commission on Revision of the Federal Court Appellate System, "Recommendations for Change," 67 F.R.D. 195 (1975). See generally Note, "Of High Designs: A Compendium of Proposals to Reduce the Workload of the Supreme Court," 97 *Harv. L. Rev.* 307 (1983). To date, the Congress has addressed the congestion problem in the Supreme Court only by eliminating nearly all the Court's obligatory appellate jurisdiction. 28 U.S.C. §1257.

111. American Law Institute, *Study of the Division of Jurisdiction between State and Federal Courts* 1 (1969).

112. *Report of the Federal Courts Study Committee* 3 (1990).

113. *Annual Reports of the Director of the Administrative Office of United States Courts* (1986, 1987 & 1988).

114. E.g., Ruggero J. Aldisert, "Judicial Expansion of Federal Jurisdiction: A Federal Judge's Thoughts on Section 1983, Comity, and the Federal Caseload," 1973 *L. & Soc. Ord.* 557; James C. Hill & Thomas E. Baker, "Dam Federal Jurisdiction!" 32 *Emory L.J.* 3 (1983).

115. 28 U.S.C. §1332.

116. The conventional explanation for diversity jurisdiction is that out-of-state litigants may not receive fair treatment in the courts of the state in which their adversaries reside, or that local state legislatures may enact statutes favorable to their own. Historians also point out that an effective system of federal courts was needed in the late eighteenth century to undergird national economic development. Cf. Thomas D. Rowe, Jr., "Abolishing Diversity Jurisdiction: Positive Side

Effects and Potential for Further Reforms," 92 *Harv. L. Rev.* 963 (1979) (noting desiderata that would accompany abolition of diversity).

117. *Report,* supra note 112, at 38. For unsuccessful abolition bills, see H. R. 6691, 97th Cong., 2d Sess. (1983); H. R. 9622, 95th Cong., 2d Sess. (1978).

118. The Federal Courts Study Committee's proposal to delegate routine claims under the Social Security Act to a new Court of Disability Claims is more troublesome. It was not so long ago that the federal courts were desperately needed to halt the Reagan Administration's efforts to strike Social Security beneficiaries from the rolls on what turned out to be wholly illegitimate grounds. The Study Committee's proposal regarding state prisoners' *constitutional* claims is more troubling still.

119. Tracy Thompson, "Drug Case Avalanche Buries Federal Courts," *Washington Post* (Dec. 24, 1990).

120. *Report,* supra note 112, at 35.

121. Accord Jack M. Beermann, "Crisis? What Crisis?" 80 *Nw. U. L. Rev.* 1383, 1389 (1986).

122. *Report,* supra note 112, at 6. Justice Frankfurter linked our ability to attract "lawyers of the highest quality" to become federal judges to the "psychology and prestige" that attend the federal bench. Judge Friendly agreed, as have others, including Judge Newman. Frankfurter, "Distribution," supra note 11, at 515–516, quoted in Friendly, *General View,* supra note 108, at 28–29. See Jon O. Newman, "Restructuring Federal Jurisdiction: Proposals to Preserve the Federal Judicial System," 56 *U. Chi. L. Rev.* 761 (1989).

123. *Report,* supra note 112, at 7.

124. Michael Wells, "Against an Elite Federal Judiciary: Comments on the Report of the Federal Courts Study Committee," 1991 *B.Y.U. L. Rev.* 923, 937. Cf. J. Skelly Wright, "The Federal Courts and the Nature and Quality of State Law," 13 *Wayne L. Rev.* 317, 319 (1967) (protesting outsized concerns about "appointing a few additional judges").

Two. Of a Judiciary Nature

1. American Civil Liberties Union v. Rabun County Chamber of Commerce, 678 F.2d 1379 (11th Cir. 1982).

2. Gene R. Nichol, Jr., "Rethinking Standing," 72 *Calif. L. Rev.* 68, 77 (1984).

3. Marbury v. Madison, 5 U. S. (1 Cranch) 137, 166 (1803).

4. Ilustrations include some questions regarding the conduct of foreign affairs, U. S. Const., art. II, §2; see Goldwater v. Carter, 444 U. S. 996 (1979) (Rehnquist, J., concurring); the duty of the United States to guarantee a "republican form of government" in the states, U. S. Const., art. IV, §4; see Luther v. Borden, 48 U. S. (7 How.) 1 (1849); and the "sole" authority of the Senate to "try" cases of impeachment, U. S. Const., art. I, §3; see Nixon v. United States, 113 S.Ct. 732 (1993). See generally J. Peter Mulhern, "In Defense of the Political Question Doctrine," 137 *U. Pa. L. Rev.* 97 (1988).

5. In the classic example, Chief Justice John Jay declined to answer questions about treaties with France that President Washington sent to the Court. Paul M. Bator & Daniel J. Meltzer et al., *Hart and Wechsler's The Federal Courts and the Federal System* 65–67 (3d ed. 1988).

6. Marbury v. Madison, 5 U. S. (1 Cranch) 137, 177 (1803).

7. See Robert M. Cover, "The Uses of Jurisdictional Redundancy: Interest, Ideology, and Innovation," 22 *Wm. & Mary L. Rev.* 639, 643 (1981).

8. Many modern Supreme Court opinions in this context begin by listing the standing rules I summarize here. E. g., Lujan v. Defenders of Wildlife, 112 S.Ct. 2130 (1992); Whitmore v. Arkansas, 495 U. S. 149 (1990); Allen v. Wright, 468 U. S. 737 (1984); Warth v. Seldin, 422 U. S. 490 (1975). For secondary literature, see Erwin Chemerinsky, *Federal Jurisdiction* 35–145 (1989); Nichol, "Rethinking," supra note 2, at 71–72.

9. Henry P. Monaghan, "Third Party Standing," 84 *Colum. L. Rev.* 277 (1984); Robert A. Sedler, "The Assertion of Constitutional *Jus Tertii*: A Substantive Approach," 70 *Calif. L. Rev.* 1308 (1982); Robert A. Sedler, "Standing to Assert Constitutional *Jus Tertii* in the Supreme Court," 71 *Yale L.J.* 599 (1962).

10. Flast v. Cohen, 392 U. S. 83 (1968). The "zone of interest" standard derives from Assoc. of Data Processing Svc. Org. v. Camp, 397 U. S. 150 (1970), which drew it from the Administrative Procedure Act. See the text accompanying note 29 infra. Cf. note 45 infra (noting that this aspect of standing doctrine may be limited to APA cases).

11. See generally Gene R. Nichol, Jr., "Ripeness and the Constitution," 54 *U. Chi. L. Rev.* 153 (1987); Richard K. Greenstein, "Bridging the Mootness Gap in Federal Court Class Actions," 35 *Stan. L. Rev.* 897 (1983).

12. I rely in this section on Joseph Vining, *Legal Identity* 20–27 (1978).

13. Raoul Berger, "Standing to Sue in Public Actions: Is it a Constitutional Requirement?" 78 *Yale L.J.* 816 (1969).

14. Louis L. Jaffe, "Standing to Secure Judicial Review: Public Actions," 74 *Harv. L. Rev.* 1265 (1961). The availability of writs to compel adherence to law was complemented by *qui tam* statutes, both in England and in this country, which offered bounties to citizens who identified some breach of duty by a public official, sued to establish wrongdoing, and won a judgment enhancing the public treasury. See Berger, "Standing," supra note 13, at 825–826; Steven L. Winter, "The Metaphor of Standing and the Problem of Self-Governance," 40 *Stan. L. Rev.* 1371, 1406–09 (1988). For background, see Ann Woolhandler, "Judicial Deference to Administrative Action—A Revisionist History," 43 *Admin. L. Rev.* 197 (1991); Evan Caminker, "The Constitutionality of *Qui Tam* Actions," 99 *Yale L.J.* 341 (1989); Harold J. Krent, "Executive Control over Criminal Law Enforcement: Some Lessons from History," 38 *Am. U. L. Rev.* 275 (1989).

15. See Richard B. Stewart, "The Reformation of American Administrative Law," 88 *Harv. L. Rev.* 1669, 1679–80, 1717–18 (1975).

16. Wesley N. Hohfeld, "Some Fundamental Legal Conceptions as Applied in Judicial Reasoning," 23 *Yale L.J.* 16 (1913).

17. Louis L. Jaffe, "The Citizen as Litigant in Public Actions: The Non-Hohfeldian or Ideological Plaintiff," 116 *U. Pa. L. Rev.* 1033 (1968).

18. Henry P. Monaghan, "Constitutional Adjudication: The Who and When," 82 *Yale L.J.* 1363, 1369–70 (1973). The classic article is Abram Chayes, "The Role of the Judge in Public Law Litigation," 89 *Harv. L. Rev.* 1281 (1976). My discussion in the following paragraphs draws heavily on Cass R. Sunstein, "Standing and the Privatization of Public Law," 88 *Colum. L. Rev.* 1432 (1988).

19. Chapter One, the text accompanying notes 18–29. When the Old Court's Formalists felt called upon to meet the claims of regulatory beneficiaries on the merits, they typically responded that workers who were protected by regulation had no *rights,* but were merely the recipients of statutory *privileges.* Inasmuch as the courts could hear only claims of right, these new privileges were not judicially enforceable.

20. Cass Sunstein argues that reformers in the early twentieth century hoped to discard the common law system for arranging human affairs, which accepted the existing distribution of wealth and power and stubbornly resisted reform. In its place, they meant to establish a new framework, featuring affirmative governmental efforts to redress economic inequalities and foster a more just and humane social order. Progressives expected regulators to treat citizens properly, bringing technical expertise to bear on the nation's problems. They distrusted not the new regulators, but the federal courts, which already threatened to frustrate regulation on the theory that it violated private liberty. Sunstein, "Privatization," supra note 18.

21. Fairchild v. Hughes, 258 U. S. 126, 129 (1922), explored in Winter, "Metaphor," supra note 14, at 1376–79 (noting that the Court had entertained five similar taxpayer suits prior to *Fairchild*). The more famous case on the point is Frothingham v. Mellon, 262 U. S. 447 (1923).

22. Jaffe found no English case discussing a plaintiff's standing before 1807 and no square treatment of standing to file a public action until 1897. See Louis L. Jaffe, "Standing to Secure Judicial Review: Private Actions," 75 *Harv. L. Rev.* 255, 256 (1961), quoted in Berger, "Standing," supra note 13, at 818. Accord Vining, *Identity,* supra note 12, at 55–56. A computerized search by my colleague David Seipp reveals that the Court at least used the term "standing" on numerous occasions in the nineteenth century.

23. Coleman v. Miller, 307 U. S. 433, 464–468 (1939). For the Frankfurter treatise, see Felix Frankfurter & James Landis, *The Business of the Supreme Court: A Study in the Federal Judicial System* (1928). Winter notes that later materials by Frankfurter and Henry Hart also failed to mention standing. See Winter, "Metaphor," supra note 14, at 1376 & n.26.

24. Joint Anti-Fascist Refugee Comm. v. McGrath, 341 U. S. 123, 152 (1951) (Frankfurter, J., concurring).

25. See Chapter One, the text accompanying notes 34–37.

26. Sunstein, "Privatization," supra note 18, at 1444–45.

27. E.g., 42 U.S.C. §1973bb (the Voting Rights Act); 42 U.S.C. §§2000e-6 (the Civil Rights Act). See *Hart & Wechsler,* supra note 5, at 137 n.16.

28. For Judge Frank's characterization, see Assoc. Industries v. Ickes, 134 F.2d 694, 704 (2d Cir. 1943), vacated as moot, 320 U. S. 707 (1943). For Justice Frankfurter's formulation, see Scripps-Howard Radio v. FCC, 316 U. S. 4, 14 (1942). See also Jaffe, "Citizen as Litigant," supra note 17, at 1035–36.

29. 5 U.S.C. §702. Clearly, §10(a) was meant to prescribe standing rules for cases in which would-be litigants seek federal judicial relief from actions taken by administrative agencies covered by the Act. Yet while the statute refers only to statutory claims, i. e., claims that agencies have violated the statutes they are charged to enforce, it is widely agreed that §10(a) also applies when citizens raise constitutional claims against formal agency action.

30. Louis L. Jaffe, *Judicial Control of Administrative Action* 528–530 (1965). By Jaffe's account, the first line merely restated the private-rights basis for standing. Then, in the second line, §10(a) acknowledged that, as in the case of the Federal Communications Act, Congress had enacted special standing rules for lawsuits attacking actions by particular agencies. Accordingly, when such a "relevant" statute conferred standing on persons "aggrieved" or "adversely affected" within the meaning those terms were given in such a statute, then, too, §10(a) recognized that such persons were entitled to seek federal judicial relief. Some observers, including Justice Scalia, continue to insist on this construction. E. g., Antonin Scalia, "The Doctrine of Standing as an Essential Element of the Separation of Powers," 17 *Suffolk U. L. Rev.* 881, 887–888 (1983); Richard B. Stewart, "Standing for Solidarity," 88 *Yale L.J.* 1559, 1569 (1979).

31. 3 Kenneth C. Davis, *Administrative Law Treatise* §22.06, at 232 (1958). Professor Davis relied on a congressional committee report which explained that the statute was meant to confer standing on any person "adversely affected *in fact* by agency action or aggrieved within the meaning of any statute." This becomes a little tricky, but it's amusing to follow Davis' reasoning. The fun is in the second "or" in the second line of §10(a). Is this "or" a disjunctive between "affected" and "aggrieved," indicating that if there is a difference between being "aggrieved" and being affected "adversely," that difference doesn't matter for standing purposes? If so, then "within the meaning of a relevant statute" would seem to modify *both* "adversely affected" *and* "aggrieved by agency action." This is the meaning others took from the vital "or." Alternatively, might the "or" be a connecting article setting off two elements in a series of terms? This is to say, does the second "or" perform essentially the same function as the first? If so, there are not *two* ways to establish standing—the private-rights way and the way prescribed for persons "aggrieved" or "adversely affected" within the meaning of statutes fixing standing rules for particular agencies. Rather, there are *three* ways. To Davis, the committee's addition of the words "in fact" after "adversely affected," together with its placement of "by agency action" after "affected in fact," indicated that "within the meaning of any statute" does not modify "adversely affected," but only modifies "aggrieved." According to Davis, then, when §10(a) refers to persons "adversely affected" by agency action, it cannot mean to incorporate independent standing statutes governing particular agencies. In the end, by his account, §10(a) allows standing based solely on a litigant's "injury in fact,"

occasioned by the agency action under attack. See also Kenneth C. Davis, "The Liberalized Law of Standing," 37 *U. Chi. L. Rev.* 450, 466–467 (1970).

32. Assoc. of Data Processing Svc. Org. v. Camp, 397 U. S. 150 (1970).

33. Flast v. Cohen, 392 U. S. 83 (1968). See Kenneth C. Davis, "Standing: Taxpayers and Others," 35 *U. Chi. L. Rev.* 601 (1968). Writing separately in *Flast,* Justice Harlan expressed doubt that injury in fact should be sufficient to establish constitutional standing without congressional help. Yet in cases in which Congress acts affirmatively to confer standing on would-be federal litigants, Harlan thought that injury in fact should be unnecessary.

34. Davis asserts that the "zone" test was all but abandoned within a few years. Sunstein does not dismiss the test entirely, but he understands it to exclude only would-be litigants whose interests are "entirely afield" of the federal standards they seek to enforce. Sunstein, "Privatization," supra note 18, at 1450. The test seems to have seen some resurgence in recent cases. See note 45 infra.

35. Air Courier Conf. v. Amer. Postal Workers Union, 498 U. S. 517, 523 n.3 (1991). There is an unfortunate tendency in the cases and in the secondary literature to use the label "cause of action" to describe private citizens' entitlement to sue for the enforcement of federal standards. The cause-of-action rubric carries too much baggage to be invoked with clarity. It was originally used by David Dudley Field to identify the prerequisites for suit under the Field Code in New York. By 1938, the cause-of-action notion had become so cumbersome that the drafters of the new Federal Rules of Civil Procedure abandoned the phrase altogether and substituted "claims for which relief can be granted." To resurrect the cause-of-action language in this context is to invite confusion. Cf. Davis v. Passman, 442 U. S. 228, 229 (1979) (making clear that the Field Code meaning is not intended). See Henry P. Monaghan, "Federal Statutory Review under Section 1983 and the APA," 91 *Colum. L. Rev.* 233, 249 (1991). See also Chapter Three, notes 41–43 and the accompanying text.

36. Chapter One, note 42 and the accompanying text.

37. This syllogism is far from compelling. It is not at all clear that only one power is at work here—the power to create rights—and that the provision of remedies is merely a subset within that power. But let me defer discussion of this "the greater power includes the lesser" business until later. It arises in other, more controversial contexts. Chapter Three, the text accompanying notes 26–27; Chapter Four, the text accompanying note 81.

38. For decisions inferring rights of action from substantive rights themselves, see Carlson v. Green, 446 U. S. 14 (1980) (eighth amendment claims of "cruel and unusual punishment"); Davis v. Passman, 442 U. S. 228 (1979) (fifth amendment due process claims); Bivens v. Six Unknown Named Agents of Federal Bureau of Investigation, 403 U. S. 388 (1971) (fourth amendment claims of "unreasonable search and seizure"). See Walter E. Dellinger, "Of Rights and Remedies: The Constitution as a Sword," 85 *Harv. L. Rev.* 1532 (1972). On Congress' authority to foreclose private lawsuits in favor of alternative enforcement mechanisms, see Wilder v. Virginia Hosp. Ass'n, 496 U. S. 498 (1990); Middlesex County Sewerage Auth. v. Nat'l Sea Clammers Ass'n, 453 U. S. 1 (1981). The

Court wisely hesitates to read federal statutes to preclude judicial review entirely. E. g., McNary v. Haitian Refugee Center, 498 U. S. 479 (1991). But see id. at 499 (Rehnquist, C. J., dissenting) (insisting that Congress is free to foreclose judicial review even of constitutional claims).

39. 28 U.S.C. §2201. Henry Monaghan takes the view that this Act does not create a right of action. Monaghan, "Statutory Review," supra note 35, at 238; see also Chapter Three, notes 71–80 and the accompanying text. I accept what I think is the better view that it clearly does. In Golden State Transit Corp. v. City of Los Angeles, 493 U. S. 103 (1989), the Court held that the statute next to be discussed in the text, 42 U.S.C. §1983, established a right to sue for compensatory damages when the substantive claim was a violation of the National Labor Relations Act. In dissent from that judgment, Justice Anthony Kennedy insisted that the right of action created by §1983 was available only to enforce a federal statute securing some "right, privilege, or immunity"—none of which he found in the NLRA. *Golden State* at 113–119; see note 44 infra. The inapplicability of §1983 did not end the matter for Justice Kennedy, however, inasmuch as he recognized that the plaintiff could sue for declaratory relief pursuant to §2201. Id. at 455 (joined by Rehnquist, C. J. & O'Connor, J.). That understanding must have depended, in turn, on an understanding that the Declaratory Judgment Act is, indeed, a right-of-action statute.

40. Howlett v. Rose, 496 U. S. 356 (1990); Monroe v. Pape, 365 U. S. 167 (1961). The Court held in Maine v. Thiboutot, 448 U. S. 1 (1980), that §1983 plaintiffs may enforce both federal constitutional and *statutory* rights. See Cass R. Sunstein, "Section 1983 and the Private Enforcement of Federal Law," 49 *U. Chi. L. Rev.* 394 (1982). But the Court has also held that plaintiffs who wish to enforce a federal statute bear the burden of demonstrating congressional authorization of private litigation. Cort v. Ash, 422 U. S. 66 (1975). Whether §1983 can supply a right of action for a statute that does not itself contain such a litigation right can present hard questions of statutory interpretation. E. g., Middlesex County Sewerage Auth. v. Nat'l Sea Clammers Ass'n, 453 U. S. 1 (1981). Justices John Paul Stevens and Harry Blackmun maintain that §1983 is presumptively available and that Congress must say something clearly to *foreclose* private §1983 lawsuits. Id. at 22 (Stevens, J., concurring and dissenting); Suter v. Artist M., 112 S.Ct. 1360, 1370 (1992) (Blackmun, J., dissenting). Yet theirs may be a rearguard action. In the end, this Court seems likely to require a clear statement from Congress affirmatively *authorizing* private enforcement suits in any particular instance. That, of course, would make the availability of §1983 suits superfluous.

41. On the relationship between §1983 and standing generally, see Mark V. Tushnet, "The New Law of Standing: A Plea for Abandonment," 62 *Cornell L. Rev.* 663, 673–674 (1977). The Court follows the same pattern in so-called implied right-of-action cases, in which Congress has not enacted legislation permitting private suit, but the Court has inferred such a right from the Constitution itself. Occasionally, however, individual justices appear to recognize that a congressional grant of standing is practically indistinguishable from a decision to authorize a private right of action. Lujan v. Defenders of Wildlife, 112 S.Ct. 2130, 2147 (1992) (Kennedy, J., concurring).

42. See Karahalios v. Nat'l Federation of Federal Employees, 489 U. S. 527 (1989) (declining to read a federal statute to create a private right of action in the absence of clear evidence of congressional intent). Cf. Bray v. Alexandria Women's Health Clinic, 113 S.Ct. 753 (1993) (giving the right of action established by 42 U.S.C. §1985(3) a narrow construction).

43. In Lujan v. Defenders of Wildlife, 112 S.Ct. 2130 (1992), for example, the Court found a provision of the Endangered Species Act, 16 U.S.C. §1540(g), to be ineffectual to the extent it purported to confer standing on "any person" who wished to sue a governmental agency for an injunction to enforce the Act despite an "inability to allege any discrete injury flowing from" the agency's allegedly unlawful action. There are lots of similar "citizen standing" statutes on the books, and *Lujan* may have invalidated them all. Cass R. Sunstein, "What's Standing after *Lujan?* Of Citizen Suits, 'Injuries,' and Article III," 91 *Mich. L. Rev.* 163, 165 & n.11 (1992). There is no open-ended statute allowing suits by "any person" to enforce the Constitution itself. Yet if the Congress were to write such a statute, the same problem would presumably arise.

44. As to standing, we already have illustrations. E. g., Havens Realty Corp. v. Coleman, 455 U. S. 363, 372–384 (1982) (holding that the Fair Housing Act authorizes anyone with Article III standing to sue in federal court and raise any argument). As to the necessity of a right of action, however, the Court insists that §1983 is available only to protect (somebody's) "rights, privileges, or immunities" and not to test defendants' actions generally for "violations of federal law." Golden State Transit Corp. v. Los Angeles, 493 U. S. 103, 106 (1989). The meaning the Court attaches to this is a bit cloudy. Justice Brennan's opinion for the court in Wilder v. Virginia Hosp. Ass'n, 496 U. S. 498 (1990), held that by referring to "rights" §1983 merely restricts itself to the enforcement of statutes intended to "benefit" the plaintiff and excludes claims grounded in precatory statutory language or "vague and amorphous" statutory standards "beyond the competence of the judiciary to enforce." Id. at 509, quoting Wright v. Roanoke Redevelopment and Housing Auth., 479 U. S. 418, 431–432 (1987), and *Golden State* at 106. See Pennhurst State School and Hosp. v. Halderman, 451 U. S. 1 (1981). Yet in the hands of more conservative justices, the "rights" limitation in §1983 may be a more serious barrier—preventing plaintiffs from suing over alleged violations of statute unless some rather clear individual "right" can be discerned. See, e.g., Suter v. Artist M., 112 S.Ct. 1360 (1992) (opinion of Rehnquist, C.J.). But see Dennis v. Higgins, 498 U. S. 439 (1991) (opinion of White, J.) (managing to hold that private businesses have the necessary "right" under the commerce clause to conduct their affairs free of state regulations that are invalid only because imposed without congressional approval). Cf. United States v. Munoz-Flores, 495 U. S. 385 (1990) (opinion of Marshall, J.) (explaining that "individual rights" of a certain order are implicated even when citizens advance separation-of-powers arguments—because the Constitution "diffuses power" not for its own sake but to "secure liberty"), quoting Morrison v. Olsen, 487 U. S. 654, 694 (1988).

Cass Sunstein resists (as I do) the Rehnquist Court's insistence that Congress' power to confer standing on citizens is limited constitutionally by the injury-in-fact test. He argues (as I do) that Congress is constitutionally free to permit a citizen who is not injured in the sense of that test both to sue government officials to enforce federal law and to do so in an Article III court. Curiously, however, he contends not merely that a statutory right of action is *sufficient* to satisfy Article III, but also that such a congressionally established right to sue is *necessary* to the existence of an Article III "case" or "controversy" and, accordingly, standing. Sunstein, "Standing after *Lujan*," supra note 43, at 170. I fail to see why that should be so. When Congress decides to bar private suits to enforce some federal statute, it follows that a citizen cannot sue in federal court. But that is only because such a citzen cannot sue in *any* court (Congress having exercised its authority to choose another means of enforcing the statute), not because Article III independently demands a congressionally established right of action. If I understand him correctly, Sunstein principally criticizes the Court for holding that Congress' ability to confer standing is constitutionally limited by a factual injury requirement. That, again, is all well and good. I think, though, that Sunstein wanders onto dangerous ground when, after discarding one constitutional test (the Court's injury-in-fact rule), he substitutes another of his own creation (a required private right of action—either established by Congress or, presumably, inferred from the substantive legal standard to be enforced). A right of action does have "constitutional status," id., but, in my view, that is true only inasmuch as the existence of a right to sue satisfies Article III. I see no reason to think that such a right is itself a *constitutional* prerequisite.

Elsewhere, Sunstein appears to conceive of a right (or "cause") of action as the substance of a litigant's claim—the kind of "legal right" that Justice Frankfurter contended was essential to Article III standing. Id. at 181; see the text accompanying notes 24–25, 31–33 supra. In this, there may be some of the confusion that inevitably accompanies the cause-of-action rubric. See note 35 supra. In the next chapter, I will argue that (in a different context) Justice Holmes said "cause of action" when he meant "claim of right." Chapter Three, the text accompanying notes 41–45. If, indeed, that kind of substantive right is what Sunstein thinks is constitutionally required for standing, then his argument in this respect is evidently in aid of a more general effort to unseat the bifurcated standing doctrine we have had for generations and to press the alternative theories that William Fletcher and others have propounded. Sunstein, "Standing after *Lujan*" at 166 n.15; see notes 90–91 and the accompanying text infra. In my view, the Warren Court was perfectly correct in holding that the existence of a substantive right goes not to standing, but to the merits. I will have something to say about Fletcher's thesis later. See the text following note 91 infra.

Much of this is quintessentially academic; a right of action is, after all, a *practical* prerequisite. Indeed, my little difference with Sunstein is the very kind of debate that engages specialists, but needlessly adds complexity to legal doctrines that make a real difference in the world—doctrines I am trying in this volume to clear up. Suffice it to say that if Congress were to enact the proposal I offer later in this chapter, I *think* my difference with Sunstein would dwindle to insignificance, and only our parallel differences with the Rehnquist Court would remain.

45. E.g., Valley Forge Christian College v. Americans United for Separation of Church and State, 454 U. S. 464 (1982); United States v. Richardson, 418 U. S. 166 (1974); Schlesinger v. Reservists Comm. to Stop the War, 418 U. S. 208 (1974). See Gene R. Nichol, Jr., "Injury and the Disintegration of Article III," 74 *Calif. L. Rev.* 1915, 1923 (1986). On the rule against third-party claims in death penalty cases, see Ann Althouse, "Standing in Fluffy Slippers," 77 *Va. L. Rev.* 1177 (1991). The "zone" test has not presented a serious practical barrier in most instances. See Clarke v. Securities Industry Ass'n, 479 U. S. 388, 400 (1987) (suggesting that the test is ordinarily fairly easy to satisfy and "most usefully understood as a gloss on the meaning of [§10(a)]"). Yet the Court has recently invoked it to deny standing on grounds presumably ascribable to Congress. E. g., Air Courier Conf. v. Amer. Postal Workers Union, 498 U. S. 517 (1991).

46. Lujan v. Defenders of Wildlife, 112 S.Ct. 2130 (1992); Warth v. Seldin, 422 U. S. 490, 498–501 (1975) (dictum).

47. In 1963 and 1965, Senator Ervin introduced amendments to larger bills that would have permitted taxpayers to enforce the establishment clause. In 1966, Ervin and Senator Morse proposed even more open-ended taxpayer and *citizen* standing rules for establishment clause claims. See *Hearings before the Subcommittee on Constitutional Rights of the Committee on the Judiciary,* 89th Cong., 2d Sess. (1966).

48. The Citizens' Right to Standing in Federal Courts Act, S. 680, 96th Cong., 1st Sess. (1979).

49. E.g., Allen v. Wright, 468 U. S. 737 (1984).

50. United States v. Students Challenging Regulatory Agency Procedures, 412 U. S. 669 (1973).

51. Cf. Lujan v. National Wildlife Federation, 497 U. S. 871 (1990) (concluding that a trial court had properly granted a motion for summary judgment in another environmental case in which the defendant challenged the sufficiency of the allegations in the complaint).

52. Aberdeen & Rockfish R. R. Co. v. Students Challenging Regulatory Agency Procedures, 422 U. S. 289 (1975).

53. Sierra Club v. Morton, 405 U. S. 727 (1972).

54. See Sierra Club v. Morton, 348 F. Supp. 219 (N.D. Calif. 1972). Cf. Lujan v. Defenders of Wildlife, 112 S.Ct. 2130, 2138 (1992) (concluding that plaintiffs' allegations that they would "some day" return to foreign countries in an attempt to observe endangered animals were insufficient).

55. In Allen v. Wright, 468 U. S. 737, 753 (1984), the Court conceded that it demands "judicially cognizable" factual injury. See Nichol, "Disintegration," supra note 45, at 1942. Indeed, in Lujan v. Defenders of Wildlife, 112 S.Ct. 2130, 2136 (1992), the Court appeared to say that "injury in fact" actually means "legally-protected interest." It would be wrong to think, however, that in this the Court means to return to the "legal interest" test for standing championed by Justice Frankfurter and rejected by the Warren Court. See the text accompanying notes 24–25, 32–33 supra. Cf. Sunstein, "Standing after *Lujan,*" supra note 43 (criticizing *Lujan* for *failing* to revive a version of Frankfurter's framework). At

least, it seems premature to read a single line in one case to discard something so well established as the injury-in-fact model—in the same breath that the phrase "injury in fact" is used. By the same token, it would be a mistake (just yet) to read an (acknowledged) revival of Frankfurter into the Court's insistence that a factual "injury" must be "caused" by the action under attack (and therefore must be linked in some way with the plaintiff's legal theory). See notes 66, 90 infra. As a practical matter, the standing doctrine this Court purports to be using does, indeed, often reach the results we might expect from Frankfurter's analysis. That is a matter to which I will return. See note 91 and the accompanying text infra. For the moment, however, the Court seems still to respect the Warren Court's great achievement in this field, namely, the separation of standing from the merits. See notes 31–34 supra. The most one can safely say is that a determination of "injury in fact" demands normative judgment of some ilk. See Gene R. Nichol, Jr., "Justice Scalia, Standing, and Public Law Litigation," 42 *Duke L.J.* 1141 (1993).

56. U.S. Const., art. I, §9.

57. United States v. Richardson, 418 U. S. 166 (1974).

58. U.S. Const., art. I, §6; Schlesinger v. Reservists Committee to Stop the War, 418 U. S. 208 (1974).

59. Lea R. Brilmayer, "The Jurisprudence of Article III: Perspectives on the 'Case or Controversy' Requirement," 93 *Harv. L. Rev.* 297 (1979).

60. Lujan v. Defenders of Wildlife, 112 S.Ct. 2130, 2145 (1992). See also id. at 2147 (Kennedy, J., concurring) (insisting that an "independent" judiciary is obliged to keep its proceedings and judgments "open" so that the public can know "what persons or groups are invoking the judicial power, the reasons that they have brought suit, and whether their claims are vindicated or denied").

61. Cf. Mark V. Tushnet, "The Sociology of Article III: A Response to Professor Brilmayer," 93 *Harv. L. Rev.* 1698 (1980). We should not rely on economic costs to discourage frivolous litigation. While it may be true in some instances that pecuniary considerations can deter worthless lawsuits, it is equally true that financial barriers can frustrate meritorious litigation by the poor. We need a federal judicial system that screens for frivolous claims in an economically neutral fashion.

62. Duke Power Co. v. Carolina Envtl. Study Group, 438 U. S. 59, 74 (1978). See also Warth v. Seldin, 422 U. S. 490, 505 (1975) (stating that plaintiffs must allege that their injuries are the "consequence" of the defendant's action "or" that the relief they seek will "remove the harm").

63. Simon v. Eastern Kentucky Welfare Rights Org., 426 U. S. 26 (1976).

64. Warth v. Seldin, 422 U. S. 490 (1975) (also invoking various standing rules to box off a host of other potential plaintiffs).

65. Allen v. Wright, 468 U. S. 737 (1984). See Gene R. Nichol, Jr., "Abusing Standing: A Comment on *Allen v. Wright*," 133 *U. Pa. L. Rev.* 635 (1985).

66. While the Court actually used the old "legally-protected interest" formulation in Lujan v. Defenders of Wildlife, 112 S.Ct. 2130, 2136 (1992), I do not (yet) understand that the Court means forthrightly to resurrect Justice Frankfurter's analysis. See note 55 supra.

67. Lujan v. Defenders of Wildlife, 112 S.Ct. 2130 (1992).

68. City of Los Angeles v. Lyons, 461 U. S. 95 (1983).

69. Richard H. Fallon, Jr., "Of Justiciability, Remedies, and Public Law Litigation: Notes on the Jurisprudence of *Lyons*," 59 *N.Y.U. L. Rev.* 1 (1984).

70. Honig v. Doe, 484 U. S. 305, 329 (1988) (Rehnquist, C. J., concurring).

71. Monaghan, "Who and When," supra note 18, at 1384. See, e.g., Renne v. Geary, 111 S.Ct. 2331 (1991); Lewis v. Continental Bank Corp., 494 U. S. 472 (1990). But see Evan Tsen Lee, "Deconstitutionalizing Justiciability: The Example of Standing," 105 *Harv. L. Rev.* 603 (1992) (elaborating an excellent argument for freeing at least mootness doctrine from its constitutional straightjacket).

72. Nichol, "Ripeness," supra note 11.

73. E.g., Renne v. Geary, 111 S.Ct. 2331 (1991); Babbit v. United Farm Workers, 442 U. S. 289, 297 (1979).

74. Richard Fallon also sees the exclusion of Congress as the primary consequence, if not the goal, of the Court's work in the choke hold case. Fallon, "Justiciability," supra note 69, at 23.

75. E.g., Valley Forge Christian College v. Americans United for Separation of Church and State, 454 U. S. 464, 484 (1982). See Erwin Chemerinsky, "A Unified Approach to Standing," 22 *Conn. L. Rev.* 677 (1990).

76. See Akhil R. Amar, "Law Story," 102 *Harv. L. Rev.* 688, 701 (1989).

77. 2 Max Farrand, *The Records of the Federal Convention* 430 (1966), cited in Nichol, "Disintegration," supra note 45, at 1919.

78. The Supreme Court did refuse to respond to Washington's request for advice regarding those treaties with France back in 1793. But the Court's letter referred not only to "the lines of separation drawn by the Constitution between the three departments of the government," but also to the provision in Article II, which gives the president the explicit authority to "require" written opinions about their offices from "principal" officers in the "*executive* department." U. S. Const., art. II, §2, cl. 1 (emphasis supplied). See Russell Wheeler, "Extrajudicial Activities of the Early Supreme Court," 1973 *Sup. Ct. Rev.* 123, cited in *Hart & Wechsler,* supra note 5, at 67 n.1.

79. 28 U.S.C. §1254, 1257 (making all the Court's appellate jurisdiction discretionary).

80. Baker v. Carr, 369 U. S. 186, 204 (1962). Accord Bender v. Williamsport Area School Dist., 475 U. S. 534 (1986).

81. Flast v. Cohen, 392 U. S. 83, 106 (1968).

82. Jaffe, "Citizen as Litigant," supra note 17, at 1037.

83. Scalia, "Essential Element," supra note 30, at 891. Accord Monaghan, "Who and When," supra note 18, at 1385.

84. See Lawrence G. Sager, "Insular Minorities Unabated: *Warth v. Seldin* and *City of Eastlake v. Forest City Enterprises, Inc.*," 91 *Harv. L. Rev.* 1373 (1978). See also Daniel J. Meltzer, "Deterring Constitutional Violations by Law Enforcement Officials: Plaintiffs and Defendants as Private Attorneys General," 88 *Colum. L. Rev.* 247 (1988) (treating cases on local law enforcement).

85. Carol F. Lee, "The Political Safeguards of Federalism? Congressional Re-

sponses to Supreme Court Decisions on State and Local Liability," 20 *Urban Lawyer* 301 (1988).

86. E.g., Valley Forge Christian College v. Americans United for Separation of Church and State, 454 U. S. 464, 474 (1982). The appointments clause, Art. II, §2, cl. 2, states that justices of the Supreme Court are appointed by the president, subject to approval by the Senate. That same selection process has always been used to choose the federal judges who staff the inferior federal courts allowed by Article III.

87. Allen v. Wright, 468 U. S. 737, 752 (1984). For the Warren Court's view, see Flast v. Cohen, 392 U. S. 83, 100–101, 107 (1968). The political question doctrine merely tells the courts to keep their noses out of matters regarding which executive and legislative officers have no constitutional obligations, but independent authority—e.g., the president's discretion whether to sign gun control legislation or Congress' discretion whether to enact national health insurance. If the Court needs a basis for withholding a federal forum for cases in which public officials *do* have legal duties, then something other than the political question doctrine must do service. At the moment, that something is standing.

88. Lujan v. Defenders of Wildlife, 112 S.Ct. 2130, 2137 (1992) (emphasis in original).

89. Id. at 2145: "Vindicating the *public* interest (including the public interest in government observance of the Constitution and laws) is the function of Congress and the Chief Executive. . . . To permit Congress to convert the undifferentiated public interest in executive officers' compliance with the law into an 'individual right' vindicable in the courts is to permit Congress to transfer from the President to the courts the Chief Executive's most important constitutional duty, to 'take Care that the Laws be faithfully executed'. . . ." (quoting U. S. Const., art. II, §3) (emphasis and quotation marks in original). See Sunstein, "Standing after *Lujan*," supra note 43, at 164–165 (tracing Justice Scalia's opinion for the Court in *Lujan* to his earlier academic writings protesting judicial interference with the executive power of the presidency).

90. Chapter One, the text accompanying note 16. On the last point in the text, see Sunstein, "Standing after *Lujan*," supra note 43, at 211. Recall that Justice Harlan took the view that the separation of powers would present no difficulty if Congress conferred standing by legislation. See note 33 supra. That position seems no longer to prevail. See New York v. United States, 112 S.Ct. 2408, 2432 (1992) (stating that the "governmental unit whose domain is . . . narrowed" cannot consent to a breach of the separation-of-powers principle). In *Lujan*, however, Justices Kennedy and Souter wrote separately to say that they think Congress can "define injuries and articulate chains of causation that will give rise to a case or controversy where none existed before." 112 S.Ct. at 2146–47 (concurring opinion). That is not to suggest that Congress can forthrightly confer standing on citizens without dealing in some way with the injury-in-fact test, but it is to suggest that there may yet be things that Congress can do to diminish the bite that the Court's primary standing rules take out of Article III judicial power.

Justice Scalia's opinion for the majority in *Lujan* indicates that Congress might create the necessary individual interest in plaintiffs by establishing bounties for winning public-rights lawsuits. 112 S.Ct. at 2143. It escapes me how such a device can sensibly be thought to be constitutionally necessary. Certainly, it cannot be that the Court thinks that money must be at stake to foster effective advocacy. See note 83 and the accompanying text supra. Moreover, I would be astonished if, after declaring that the constitutional heavens would fall if Congress were permitted to confer standing on citizens forthrightly, the Court would find it perfectly acceptable for Congress to accomplish the same ends by the artful dodge that a formalistic bounty scheme would most certainly be. True, the Court sometimes describes the interest required for standing as a "personal stake in the outcome" of a lawsuit. Yet recall that the injury must also be causally connected to the governmental behavior a litigant contends is legally invalid. Since the prospect of a bounty is unrelated to the defendant's actions, I tend to doubt that this Court would hold that a citizen's anticipation of that kind of financial gain alone would suffice. The regulars at the bar down the street from the local district courthouse may bet on the outcomes of federal lawsuits, but I would not expect this Court to say that they have standing on that account to appear themselves as litigants. Cf. Diamond v. Charles, 476 U. S. 54 (1986) (holding that an intervenor's desire to escape being assessed for attorney fees did not establish the injury required for standing to appeal from an unfavorable judgment on the merits).

In this vein, I am not at all sure that this Court would be persuaded by an analogy to the bounty-like schemes found in *qui tam* statutes. See note 14 supra. In part, at least, the theory of a *qui tam* arrangement appears to be that the federal government has been bilked out of public funds and needs an efficient means by which to recoup its losses. Congress thus deputizes private agents to sue other private parties on behalf of the government, promising a percentage of the take as a form of compensation. A more free-wheeling authorization to citizens generally to challenge the validity of governmental behavior in hopes of obtaining a prize is arguably different. Of course, most *qui tam* statutes have been repealed or have remained dormant for years. The recent revival of the idea in the False Claims Amendments Act of 1986 has ignited a vigorous academic debate over whether *qui tam* statutes can survive the modern Court's standing doctrine. Compare Caminker, *"Qui Tam,"* supra note 14 (contending that the scheme envisioned by the 1986 Act can be sustained), with James T. Blanch, "The Constitutionality of the False Claims Act's *Qui Tam* Provision," 16 *Harv. J. Law & Pub. Policy* 701 (1993) (arguing the contrary). One tends to think that when the Court takes up the matter, it will focus on the particular program established by that Act (a collection scheme that encourages private persons who are aware of fraudulent claims to come forward) rather than exploring the wider field of *qui tam* statutes in general. Indeed, at the end of the day a good share of the Court's concern with respect to standing statutes may be that Congress should consider standing questions in the context of specific programs, thus exercising judgment not in a blanket way but on a case-by-case basis. Of course, if the justices now sitting really would accept the bounty gimmick, perhaps by analogy to *qui tam* arrangements, then perhaps Cass Sunstein is right and Congress should frame a general statute in that way. See Sunstein, "Standing after *Lujan*," supra note 43, at 232. See also Nichol, "Justice Scalia," supra note 55, at 1165 (assuming that a bounty system would be a "cheap" way to bring a suit "clearly within the *qui tam* tradition" and thus "safely under the umbrella of the case or controversy requirement").

Alternatively, Justice Scalia might allow Congress to legislate new, substantive, private *rights* in all citizens, perhaps denominated as such, and then to ground anyone's standing to enforce those rights in federal court in the old private-rights model. See the text accompanying note 26 supra. In the *Lujan* case, for example, the statute might have purported to make all Americans the joint and several "owners" of endangered animals. Accordingly, the plaintiffs might have contended that they were entitled to go to federal court to enforce their own federal ownership rights in elephants threatened in Sri Lanka. Here again, it seems silly to conceive of any such statutory "rights" in millions of people as the kind of private entitlements that Justice Frankfurter had in mind, or to think that the Court's outsized regard for executive power could be satisfied on such a basis.

Finally, I note that Martin Redish condemns the practice of declining to entertain cases in which Congress has conferred standing as inconsistent with the principle of "representation" in American constitutional law. These private rights standing cases, in Redish's view, conflict with the competing "countermajoritarian" principle—also embedded in the Constitution. By refusing to adjudicate claims for want of standing, the Court fails to perform its function to check the political branches. In this sense, standing does not rest *on* the separation of powers, but abdicates the role that idea ascribes to the Court. See Martin H. Redish, *The Federal Courts in the Political Order* (1991).

91. I take the arguments in the text primarily from William A. Fletcher, "The Structure of Standing," 98 *Yale L.J.* 221 (1988), who builds upon earlier work by others. E. g., Lee A. Albert, "Standing to Challenge Administrative Action: An Inadequate Surrogate for Claim for Relief," 83 *Yale L.J.* 425 (1974); David P. Currie, "Misunderstanding Standing," 1981 *Sup. Ct. Rev.* 41. See also Chemerinsky, "Unified Approach," supra note 75 (embracing Fletcher's framework at least in part). The Supreme Court has cited the Fletcher article—see Primate Protection League v. Tulane Educ. Fund, 111 S.Ct. 1700, 1704 (1991)—but the Court has not adopted his approach to standing. See Sunstein, "Standing after *Lujan*," supra note 43 (criticizing the Court precisely for the reason that it has failed to do so). Just what Fletcher would do to avoid advisory opinions and decisions on political questions, he does not say. But he clearly finds it troubling that the Congress occasionally establishes special, expedited review procedures respecting questionable new legislation. E. g., Federal Election Campaign Act of 1971, 2 U.S.C. §§ 431–442 (authorizing voters to challenge the validity of the statute). Fletcher, "Structure" at 283.

92. See Chapter One, note 107 and the accompanying text.

93. For prior illustrations, see *The Citizens' Right to Standing in Federal Courts Act of 1978, Joint Hearings before the Subcommittee on Citizens and Shareholders' Rights and Remedies of the Committee on the Judiciary and the Committee on Governmental Affairs on S. 3005*, U. S. Senate, 95th Cong., 2d Sess. (1978); *The Citizens' Right to Standing in Federal Courts Act, Hearings before the Committee on the Judiciary on S. 680*, U. S. Senate, 96th Cong., 2d

Sess. (1979). The following findings would be useful as an introduction to new legislation:

(a) It is essential to preserve the ability of citizens of the United States to gain access to the courts of the United States to enforce federal law, to vindicate both their own interests and rights and the interests and rights of others, and of the public generally.

(b) Judicially created doctrines regarding the enforceability of federal law in private lawsuits and the standing of citizens to file and maintain such lawsuits have unduly restricted access to the courts of the United States for these purposes.

(c) A citizen of the United States who is committed enough to assume the burdens of suit has a sufficient personal stake in the outcome of litigation to be a proper party to maintain an action to enforce federal law in the courts of the United States. Such a citizen will present the facts and legal issues in an adversary context and in a form historically viewed as capable of resolution through the judicial process. Private civil actions brought by such citizens are cases or controversies within the meaning of the Constitution.

(d) Neither the principle of federalism, nor the principle of the separation of powers within the national government, nor the principle of democratic government requires or justifies denying such citizens access to the courts of the United States for private enforcement actions.

(e) Congress should and does exercise the full measure of its constitutional powers to establish the courts of the United States and fix their jurisdiction and to enforce the thirteenth, fourteenth, and fifteenth amendments and other provisions of the Constitution, to eliminate all judicially created or other barriers to the federal courts faced by citizens who seek to enforce federal law by way of private civil actions.

These findings would make it difficult for a recalcitrant Supreme Court to read the substantive provisions of the bill for less than they are worth. Subsection (a) states a sweeping purpose to open the federal courts to public-rights litigation pressed by private attorneys general; subsection (b) makes it clear that the bill is meant to overrule existing court decisions that bar access; subsections (c) and (d) assert Congress' view that it can constitutionally authorize citizens to enforce federal law without regard to the primary standing rules the Court applies in the absence of legislation; subsection (e) declares that Congress means in this bill to do whatever it constitutionally can to make the federal courts accessible.

The question remains whether the Court would accede to Congress' assertion of power not only to discard prudential standing barriers, but also to dispense with restrictive rules the Court now insists are constitutionally grounded. The declaration in subsection (c) that citizen suits are cases or controversies within the meaning of Article III amounts to a congressional interpretation of the Constitution at odds with the interpretation the Court itself has reached. At some point, the justices may relent, especially in light of the reminders in subsection (e) that Congress enjoys undisputed authority to establish the lower federal courts and to prescribe the jurisdiction they will exercise. The citation to Congress' power to enforce the Civil War amendments fortifies the claim that the legislative branch is operating within its own sphere, albeit near the boundaries.

94. Specifically, the bill provided that a federal court should not dismiss an action on the ground that the defendant's conduct is not the "primary cause" of the plaintiff's injury, or that the plaintiff's injury cannot be remedied after a favorable judgment on the merits (provided that some sort of judicial relief can "contribute in significant part to remedying or preventing the injury"), or that the plaintiff's alleged injury is "shared by a large class of persons." *Hearings on S. 3005,* supra note 93, at 125–126.

95. Id. at 5 (Metzenbaum statement quoting the Douglas letter).

96. E.g., 5 U.S.C. §701 (excepting actions committed to agency discretion); §704 (excepting actions not yet final). Nor is the bill meant to make all treaties with foreign nations enforceable through private litigation. If a treaty is not self-executing, then by the same token it would be excepted from the civil actions this bill would authorize.

97. Both the Department of Health, Education, and Welfare and the Justice Department objected to the Ervin bills on the ground that private suits were unnecessary in light of existing administrative enforcement machinery and inappropriate in that they might interfere with those efforts. *Hearings before the Subcommittee on Constitutional Rights of the Committee on the Judiciary,* U. S. Senate, 89th Cong., 2d Sess. 8–55 (Ellenbogen testimony); 75–102 (Douglas testimony).

98. Recall that §1983 is available only to vindicate federal "rights." See note 44 supra. The proposal in the text would authorize suits for alleged violations of federal law generally.

99. Proposals to amend the Federal Tort Claims Act to make the federal government liable for damages in suits charging that federal agents have violated plaintiffs' constitutional rights have been rejected in the past. See Clark Byse, "Recent Developments in Federal Administrative Law: Damage Actions against the Government or Government Employees," 4 *Admin. L.J.* 275, 282–287 (1990).

100. In this, I pass over the intricacies of legal practice under the rules governing motions for summary judgment, regarding which the parties must supplement allegations with affidavits that set forth the "facts" and thus reveal any dispute of fact that must be resolved by the court. When plaintiffs whose standing is questioned file such affidavits, the sufficiency of the facts they assert is open to immediate legal judgment. The court makes no attempt to assess the truth, however, until final resolution of the case. See Lujan v. Defenders of Wildlife, 112 S.Ct. 2130, 2137 (1992) (explaining that critical facts must be "averred" at the summary judgment stage and "proved" at the trial stage).

Three. Arising Under

1. Steffel v. Thompson, 415 U. S. 452 (1974).

2. Chapman v. Houston Welfare Rights Org., 441 U. S. 600 (1979) (§1983); Skelly Oil Co. v. Phillips Petroleum Co., 339 U. S. 667 (1950) (Declaratory Judg-

ment Act). Cf. Califano v. Sanders, 430 U. S. 99 (1977) (§10(a) of the Administrative Procedure Act).

3. Steffel actually relied on 28 U.S.C. §1343(3), another provision of the same Ku Klux Klan Act of 1871 that produced §1983, the right-of-action statute. At the time, §1331 was often unavailable, because it carried a minimum amount-in-controversy requirement. That requirement has since been eliminated.

4. See generally Paul M. Bator & Daniel J. Meltzer et al., *Hart and Wechsler's The Federal Courts and the Federal System* 1–34 (3d ed. 1988).

5. 2 Max Farrand, *The Records of the Federal Convention* 46 (1911), quoted in *Hart & Wechsler,* supra note 4, at 12.

6. Wythe Holt, "To Establish Justice: Politics, the Judiciary Act of 1789, and the Invention of the Federal Courts," 1989 *Duke L.J.* 1421.

7. See Robert N. Clinton, "A Mandatory View of Federal Court Jurisdiction: A Guided Quest for the Original Understanding of Article III," 132 *U. Pa. L. Rev.* 741, 769 (1984).

8. Wythe Holt, "Federal Courts as the Asylum to Federal Interests: Randolph's Report, the Benson Amendment, and the Original Understanding of the Federal Judiciary," 36 *Buffalo L. Rev.* 341 (1987).

9. U.S. Const., art. III (emphasis supplied). See also U. S. Const., art. I, §8 (giving Congress authority to "constitute tribunals inferior to the supreme court").

10. E.g., Gerald Gunther, "Congressional Power to Curtail Federal Court Jurisdiction: An Opinionated Guide to the Ongoing Debate," 36 *Stan. L. Rev.* 895 (1984); Herbert Wechsler, "The Courts and the Constitution," 65 *Colum. L. Rev.* 1001 (1965).

11. Marbury v. Madison, 5 U. S. (1 Cranch) 137 (1803). Despite the suggestion otherwise in *Marbury,* Congress can give the lower federal courts concurrent jurisdiction with respect to matters within the Supreme Court's original jurisdiction. See 28 U.S.C. §1251; Mississippi v. Louisiana, 113 S.Ct. 549, 553 n.1 (1992).

12. The standard citation for broad congressional power under the exceptions clause is Ex parte McCardle, 74 U. S. (7 Wall.) 506 (1869). Whether that case truly supports the proposition is problematic. See William W. Van Alstyne, "A Critical Guide to Ex Parte McCardle," 15 *Ariz. L. Rev.* 229 (1973).

13. Kentucky v. Dennison, 65 U. S. (24 How.) 66 (1861).

14. Sheldon v. Sill, 49 U. S. (8 How.) 441 (1850). For recent confirmations, see Ankenbrandt v. Richards, 112 S.Ct. 2206, 2212 (1992); Palmore v. United States, 411 U. S. 389, 401 (1973). For a defense of this conventional view, see Michael Wells, "Congress's Paramount Role in Setting the Scope of Federal Jurisdiction," 85 *Nw. U. L. Rev.* 465 (1991).

15. See Robert B. McKay, "Court, Congress, and Reapportionment," 63 *Mich. L. Rev.* 255 (1964); Arthur J. Goldberg, "The Administration's Anti-Busing Proposals—Politics Makes Bad Law," 67 *Nw. U. L. Rev.* 319 (1972); Ronald D. Rotunda, "Congressional Power to Restrict the Jurisdiction of the Lower Federal Courts and the Problem of School Busing," 64 *Geo. L.J.* 839 (1976).

16. Raoul Berger, *Congress v. the Supreme Court* 285–296 (1969); Henry J. Merry, "Scope of the Supreme Court's Appellate Jurisdiction: Historical Basis," 47 *Minn. L. Rev.* 53 (1962). Berger has apparently withdrawn his previous argument. See *Hart & Wechsler,* supra note 4, at 381 n.26, citing Raoul Berger, *Death Penalties* 153–172 (1982).

17. Martin v. Hunter's Lessee, 14 U. S. (1 Wheat.) 304 (1816) (dictum).

18. Bob Clinton reads some draft proposals at the Convention to take something of this view. Clinton, "Guided Quest," supra note 7, at 778–780.

19. Clinton, "Guided Quest," supra note 7. For follow-up work, see Robert N. Clinton, "A Mandatory View of Federal Court Jurisdiction: Early Implementation of and Departures from the Constitutional Plan," 86 *Colum. L. Rev.* 1515 (1986).

20. Akhil R. Amar, "A Neo-Federalist View of Article III: Separating the Two Tiers of Federal Jurisdiction," 65 *B.U. L. Rev.* 205 (1985). In this, Amar borrows from Story, who first noted the possible significance of the "all" term. For follow-up work, see Akhil R. Amar, "The Two-Tiered Structure of the Judiciary Act of 1789," 138 *U. Pa. L. Rev.* 1499 (1990); Daniel J. Meltzer, "The History and Structure of Article III," 138 *U. Pa. L. Rev.* 1569 (1990); Martin H. Redish, "Text, Structure, and Common Sense in the Interpretation of Article III," 138 *U. Pa. L. Rev.* 1633 (1990); Akhil R. Amar, "Reports of My Death Are Greatly Exaggerated: A Reply," 138 *U. Pa. L. Rev.* 1651 (1990).

21. Henry M. Hart, Jr., "The Power of Congress to Limit the Jurisdiction of the Federal Courts: An Exercise in Dialectic," 66 *Harv. L. Rev.* 1362 (1953). See Leonard G. Ratner, "Congressional Power over the Appellate Jurisdiction of the Supreme Court," 109 *U. Pa. L. Rev.* 157 (1960) (elaborating on Hart's "essential function" theme).

22. Lawrence G. Sager, "The Supreme Court, 1980 Term—Foreword: Constitutional Limitations on Congress' Authority to Regulate the Jurisdiction of the Federal Courts," 95 *Harv. L. Rev.* 17 (1981).

23. *Hart & Wechsler,* supra note 4, at 383.

24. Theodore Eisenberg, "Congressional Authority to Restrict Lower Federal Court Jurisdiction," 83 *Yale L.J.* 498 (1974).

25. See, e.g., Carl McGowan, *The Organization of Judicial Power in the United States* 25 (1976); Holt, "Invention of the Federal Courts," supra note 6, at 1509.

26. Chapter Two, the text accompanying note 37.

27. The Supreme Court has interpreted Article III's reference to controversies "between citizens of different states" to require no more than that any two adverse parties reside in different states. State Farm Fire & Cas. Co. v. Tashire, 386 U. S. 523 (1967). Congress has never purported to extend the general diversity jurisdiction so far. Strawbridge v. Curtis, 7 U. S. (3 Cranch) 267 (1806) (holding that the diversity jurisdiction conferred by statute requires that *all* adverse parties reside in different states). See also 28 U.S.C. §1359 (providing that the district courts cannot exercise diversity jurisdiction if a party "has been improperly or collusively made or joined to invoke the jurisdiction of the court").

28. *Hart & Wechsler,* supra note 4, at 961–962.

29. Osborn v. Bank of the United States, 22 U. S. (9 Wheat.) 738 (1824).

30. Id. at 823. Some passages in his classic opinion suggest that any action involving an instrumentality of the United States is, for that reason alone, an action arising under federal law within the meaning of the Constitution, such that the federal courts can be given power to protect entities like the bank even when litigation turns entirely on state law. The "protective" jurisdiction idea has been mooted in the law reviews, and there are forms of jurisdiction now in place that appear to be "protective" in this sense. Yet the modern Court has never formally embraced the idea. See Paul J. Mishkin, "The Federal Question in the District Courts," 53 *Colum. L. Rev.* 157 (1953); Carole E. Goldberg-Ambrose, "The Protective Jurisdiction of the Federal Courts," 30 *UCLA L. Rev.* 542 (1983). See generally *Hart & Wechsler,* supra note 4, at 983–989. For treatments in the Court, see Textile Workers Union v. Lincoln Mills, 353 U. S. 448, 473–477 (1957) (Frankfurter, J., dissenting) (resisting "protective" jurisdiction); Mesa v. California, 489 U. S. 121, 137–138 (1989) (indicating doubts about it).

31. E.g., Verlinden B. V. v. Central Bank of Nigeria, 461 U. S. 480 (1983) (opinion by Burger, C.J.). See generally Erwin Chemerinsky, *Federal Jurisdiction* 225–228 (1989); Martin H. Redish, *Federal Jurisdiction: Tensions in the Allocation of Judicial Power* 84–85 (2d ed. 1989).

32. See James H. Chadbourn & A. Leo Levin, "Original Jurisdiction of Federal Questions," 90 *U. Pa. L. Rev.* 639 (1942).

33. Paul M. Bator, "Congressional Power over the Jurisdiction of the Federal Courts," 27 *Vill. L. Rev.* 1030 (1982); Martin H. Redish, "Constitutional Limitations on Congressional Power to Control Federal Jurisdiction: A Reaction to Professor Sager," 77 *Nw. U. L. Rev.* 143 (1982). See Martin H. Redish & Curtis E. Woods, "Congressional Power to Control the Jurisdiction of Lower Federal Courts: A Critical Review and a New Synthesis," 124 *U. Pa. L. Rev.* 45 (1975).

34. The floor manager said that the bill would give the federal courts what the Judiciary Act of 1789 had failed to give them, namely, "the power which the Constitution confers—nothing more, nothing less." 2 *Cong. Rec.* 4987 (1874). See Ray Forrester, "The Nature of a Federal Question," 16 *Tul. L. Rev.* 362 (1942); Chadbourn & Levin, "Original Jurisdiction," supra note 32; *Hart & Wechsler,* supra note 4, at 995–997. Early decisions took Article III as a guide to the meaning of the statute. See Michael G. Collins, "The Unhappy History of Federal Question Removal," 71 *Iowa L. Rev.* 717 (1986).

35. McGowan, *Organization,* supra note 25, at 25. For a recent confirmation, see Franchise Tax Bd. of Calif. v. Constr. Laborers Vacation Trust, 463 U. S. 1, 8 n.8 (1983).

36. Marrese v. Amer. Academy of Orth. Surgeons, 470 U. S. 373 (1985); Migra v. Warren City School Dist. Bd. of Educ., 465 U. S. 75 (1984).

37. Allan D. Vestal, *Res Judicata / Preclusion* (1969).

38. 1B *Moore's Federal Practice* §0.405; "Developments in the Law—Section 1983 and Federalism," 90 *Harv. L. Rev.* 1133, 1333 (1977).

39. Paul A. Freund, *The Supreme Court of the United States* 16 (1961). See

Anderson v. Harless, 459 U. S. 4, 12 n.6 (1982) (Stevens, J., dissenting); Boag v. MacDougall, 454 U. S. 364, 368 (1982) (Rehnquist, J., dissenting).

40. See William Cohen, "The Broken Compass: The Requirement that a Case Arise Directly under Federal Law," 115 *U. Pa. L. Rev.* 890 (1967).

41. American Well Works Co. v. Layne & Bowler Co., 241 U. S. 257, 260 (1916).

42. See the text accompanying notes 1–3 supra.

43. In Merrell Dow Pharmaceuticals v. Thompson, 478 U. S. 804 (1986), the plaintiffs filed a tort action in state court, alleging that Merrell Dow's failure to label a product as required by federal law constituted negligence under state law. Merrell Dow attempted to remove the matter on the theory that by relying on an alleged violation of federal statute the plaintiffs had made their action one "arising under" federal law. The Supreme Court refused to allow the removal, primarily because it assumed that Congress had created no right of action to enforce the federal statute through private litigation. It would be a mistake to read *Merrell Dow* for the proposition that a case arises under the law that creates the plaintiff's private right of action and that, since Congress had established no such right to sue (in some court), subject matter jurisdiction was defeated under the Holmes formulation. Instead, the Court in *Merrell Dow* merely considered the absence of a congressionally created right of action to be relevant to the question whether Congress really meant that the suit at hand should come within a federal court's subject matter jurisdiction pursuant to §1331. Certainly, *Merrell Dow* did not suggest that jurisdiction and a right of action are (theoretically) identical; they clearly are not. In roughly this same vein, the American Law Institute hypothesizes a case in which Congress creates a "right to sue" in federal court, but leaves the substantive rule of decision to be provided by state law. See note 30 supra. American Law Institute, *Study of the Division of Jurisdiction between State and Federal Courts* 483–484 (1969). In any given instance, the question whether a statute creates a right of action or establishes subject matter jurisdiction (or both) is a matter of interpretation for the Supreme Court to resolve authoritatively. Cf. Osborn v. Bank of the United States, 22 U. S. (9 Wheat.) 738 (1824) (reading a statute giving the national bank authority "to sue and be sued" in a federal court to confer jurisdiction on such a court to entertain such an action).

44. Chapter Two, the text accompanying note 24.

45. Puerto Rico v. Russell, 288 U. S. 476, 483 (1933). Redish proposes to deal with the problems presented by *Merrell Dow*—see note 43 supra—by adopting the view (either judicially or via new legislation) that subject matter jurisdiction exists if "*either* the cause of action is itself federally-created *or* the decision of the case may turn on the interpretation or application of federal law." Martin H. Redish, "Reassessing the Allocation of Judicial Business between State and Federal Courts: Federal Jurisdiction and 'The Martian Chronicles,'" 78 *Va. L. Rev.* 1769, 1794 (1992) (emphasis in original) (footnote omitted). David Shapiro has responded that Redish underestimates the relevance of a federal "cause of action" to an understanding of the extent of federal interest in a case—and thus the need for federal subject matter jurisdiction. David L. Shapiro, "Reflections on the Allo-

cation of Jurisdiction between State and Federal Courts: A Response to 'Reassessing the Allocation of Judicial Business between State and Federal Courts,'" 78 *Va. L. Rev.* 1839, 1842 n.17 (1992). If when Redish and Shapiro use the cause-of-action formulation, they are talking about substantive federal claims for relief, it seems to me that Redish has the better of the argument. Federal rights are entitled to federal remedies. Similarly, if Redish and Shapiro are talking about federal litigation rights, what I call rights of action—see Chapter Two, note 35— then again the federal forum is appropriate. I have proposed a blanket right-of-action statute for the private enforcement of federal law, subject to express exceptions. Chapter Two, the text accompanying notes 92–99. Under that proposal, and the proposed substitute for §1331 I offer later, in the text accompanying notes 88–89 infra, the federal district courts would have jurisdiction in a case like *Merrell Dow,* unless Congress explicitly disclaims private lawsuits for the enforcement of the Food, Drug, and Cosmetic Act—the statute involved in that case.

46. Montana Catholic Missions v. Missoula County, 200 U. S. 118, 130 (1906).

47. United Mine Workers v. Gibbs, 383 U. S. 715 (1966).

48. See Ashwander v. Tennessee Valley Auth., 297 U. S. 288, 346 (1936) (Brandeis, J., concurring). On the precise point in the text, see Siler v. Louisville & Nashville R. R., 213 U. S. 175, 191 (1909).

49. E.g., Louisville & Nashville R. R. v. Mottley, 211 U. S. 149 (1908).

50. There are, of course, some troublesome cases remaining. In cases in which state law incorporates federal law, plaintiffs can express their claims entirely in state-law terms, but, in the end, the only real issues to be decided are federal. Compare Smith v. Kansas City Title & Trust Co., 255 U. S. 180 (1921) (finding "arising under" jurisdiction), with Moore v. Chesapeake & Ohio Ry., 291 U. S. 205 (1934) (declining to do so). See Merrell Dow Pharmaceuticals v. Thompson, 478 U. S. 804, 814 n.12 (1986) (attempting to explain *Smith* on the basis of the special federal interest involved); but see id. at 821 n.1 (Brennan, J., dissenting) (dismissing *Moore* as a sport). On the flip side, in cases in which federal law embraces state law, plaintiffs can articulate claims that are facially federal in character, but their cases will turn entirely on state issues—on which federal liability is piggybacked. E. g., Shoshone Mining Co. v. Rutter, 177 U. S. 505 (1900). Cases in which plaintiffs press state claims that are available only because Congress has allowed the states to make substantive law can also be problematic. E. g., Gully v. First Nat'l Bank, 299 U. S. 109 (1936).

51. Henry M. Hart, Jr., "The Relations between State and Federal Law," 54 *Colum. L. Rev.* 489, 520 n.108 (1954), cited in *ALI Study,* supra note 43, at 190.

52. Chapter One, the text accompanying notes 92–105.

53. Mishkin, "The Federal Question," supra note 30, at 164; Donald T. Trautman, "Federal Right Jurisdiction and the Declaratory Remedy," 7 *Vand. L. Rev.* 445, 460 (1954).

54. *ALI Study,* supra note 43, at 190–191.

55. See Donald L. Doernberg, "There's No Reason for It, It's Just Our Policy:

Why the Well-Pleaded Complaint Rule Sabotages the Purposes of Federal Question Jurisdiction," 38 *Hastings L.J.* 597, 650 (1987).

56. Herbert Wechsler, "Federal Jurisdiction and the Revision of the Judicial Code," 13 *Law & Contemp. Probs.* 216, 234 (1948).

57. For an exhaustive appraisal of the legislative history, see Collins, "Unhappy History," supra note 34.

58. Subsection (2) of §1443 provides for removal in cases in which defendants are prosecuted for "any act under color of authority derived from any law providing for equal rights, or for refusing to do any act on the ground that it would be inconsistent with such law." In City of Greenwood v. Peacock, 384 U. S. 808 (1966), the Court held that removal under subsection (2) is limited to federal or state officers, or persons acting in concert with them. Read this way, subsection (2) overlaps with another removal statute, 28 U.S.C. §1442(a) (1), which allows removal on behalf of an "officer of the United States . . . or person acting under him, for any act under color of such office." See Redish, *Tensions,* supra note 31, at 375 n.4.

59. Anthony G. Amsterdam, "Criminal Prosecutions Affecting Federally Guaranteed Civil Rights: Federal Removal and Habeas Corpus Jurisdiction to Abort State Court Trial," 113 *U. Pa. L. Rev.* 793, 843 (1965).

60. *Annual Report of the Director of the Administrative Office of the United States Courts* 213–217 (1965), cited in Georgia v. Rachel, 384 U. S. 780, 788 n.8 (1966).

61. Georgia v. Rachel, 384 U. S. 780 (1966).

62. E.g., Strauder v. West Virginia, 100 U. S. 303 (1879) (allowing removal on behalf of an African American defendant because a state statute prohibited blacks from serving on the jury—in the teeth of a provision in the 1866 Civil Rights Act conferring on criminal defendants a federal right to be tried by jurors selected without discrimination on the basis of race).

63. Charles A. Wright, *Federal Courts* 151 n.26 (3d ed. 1976).

64. City of Greenwood v. Peacock, 384 U. S. 808, 828 (1966).

65. Chapter One, notes 1–2, 91–106 and the accompanying text. Redish contends that §1443 should be reinterpreted to allow criminal defendants to remove if they show that their federal rights will be denied in state court, either because of the procedures the state court will employ or because of prior state court rulings on the claims defendants assert. Redish, *Tensions,* supra note 31, at 391–392. Redish insists that this approach would not invite removal petitions in the run of cases and that the need to protect individuals from unfair state proceedings outweighs the costs. Moreover, according to Redish, his proposal is consistent with the general rule that state criminal prosecutions usually should be left where they are. Removal should be allowed only in exceptional cases, in which there are compelling reasons for transferring jurisdiction to the federal forum.

66. See Larry W. Yackle, "Explaining Habeas Corpus," 60 *N.Y.U. L. Rev.* 991, 1032–40 (1985).

67. There are exceptions to this. Some defendants challenge the validity of the state statutes under which they are charged or contend that trial in state court

would itself be invalid. In cases of that kind, it may be feasible to identify the federal character and merit of a claim before trial.

68. This does not mean that modern extensions of national power at the expense of state prerogatives are uniformly unwise or unconstitutional; it only means that decentralization is related to liberty. The task is to identify those matters for which national authority presents a serious danger and to allocate to the states decision-making authority regarding those matters.

69. Repression will not necessarily follow the assignment of authority for the criminal law to any government national in scope. Indeed, our decentralized scheme may be atypical; there are, after all, many centralized criminal justice systems in which individual liberty is respected. Nevertheless, federalism in this country is no historical accident.

70. See Peter Arenella, "Rethinking the Functions of Criminal Procedure: The Warren and Burger Courts' Competing Ideologies," 72 *Geo. L.J.* 185, 197 (1983).

71. See Willing v. Chicago Auditorium Ass'n, 277 U. S. 274 (1928) (opinion for the Court by Brandeis, J.). On the legislative history of the Act, see Donald L. Doernberg & Michael B. Mushlin, "The Trojan Horse: How the Declaratory Judgment Act Created a Cause of Action and Expanded Federal Jurisdiction While the Supreme Court Wasn't Looking," 36 *UCLA L. Rev.* 529 (1989).

72. Aetna Life Ins. Co. v. Haworth, 300 U. S. 227, 239–240 (1937).

73. Skelly Oil Co. v. Phillips Petroleum Co., 339 U. S. 667 (1950).

74. The analysis in the text, drawn from the *Skelly Oil* case, has recently been reaffirmed. Franchise Tax Bd. of Calif. v. Constr. Laborers Vacation Trust, 463 U. S. 1 (1983).

75. 10A Charles A. Wright et al., *Federal Practice and Procedure* §2767, 744–745 (2d ed. 1983).

76. Public Svc. Comm. of Utah v. Wycoff Co., 344 U. S. 237, 248 (1952) (dictum), quoted in Franchise Tax Bd. of Calif. v. Constr. Laborers Vacation Trust, 463 U. S. 1, 16 n.14 (1983). See also Oklahoma Tax Comm. v. Graham, 489 U. S. 838, 841 (1989) (stating that "the existence of a federal immunity" does not "convert a suit otherwise arising under state law into one" that "arises under federal law").

77. Cf. Collins, "Unhappy History," supra note 34, at 771–772 n.239.

78. See, e.g., Gade v. Nat'l Solid Wastes Management Ass'n, 112 S.Ct. 2374 (1992); Shaw v. Delta Air Lines, 463 U. S. 85 (1983). In *Gade* and *Shaw*, the plaintiffs' federal claims were that federal statutes preempted state regulatory schemes that state authorities threatened to enforce in state court. If the plaintiffs in those cases were able to go immediately to federal court for a declaration that the state enforcement actions they anticipated were merely preempted by federal law, how much clearer can it be that plaintiffs who assert affirmative federal rights against threatened lawsuits in state court can equally have prompt access to the federal forum?

79. *Hearings on H. R. 5623 before a Subcommittee of the Senate Committee on the Judiciary*, 70th Cong., 1st Sess. 75–76 (1928), quoted in Steffel v. Thompson, 415 U. S. 452, 468 n.18 (1974).

80. Henry Monaghan suggests that the tension between the *Wycoff* dictum and *Shaw*—see note 78 supra—undercuts the latter. Henry P. Monaghan, "Federal Statutory Review under Section 1983 and the APA," 91 *Colum. L. Rev.* 233, 239 (1991). It is not clear why—unless it is because he conceives that the only function served by the Declaratory Judgment Act is to authorize the federal courts to issue a particular form of relief, i. e., a declaration of rights, in an action in which both subject matter jurisdiction and a right of action are established by other means. Id. at 238. It seems to me that by its express terms, §2201 itself establishes a right of action. Chapter Two, the text accompanying note 39. This does not mean that the Act authorizes a private suit for declaratory relief in cases in which Congress, by independent enactment, precludes private lawsuits in favor of other enforcement mechanisms. Cf. Merrell Dow Pharmaceuticals v. Thompson, 478 U. S. 257 (1986), discussed in note 43 supra. Yet if Congress permits such private actions, as it would if it were to enact the proposals I offered in Chapter Two, declaratory judgment actions would remain available.

81. Hart, "Relations," supra note 51, at 540.

82. Henry J. Friendly, *Federal Jurisdiction: A General View* 8–11 (1973).

83. Id. at 75.

84. *ALI Study*, supra note 43, at 168.

85. Richard A. Posner, *The Federal Courts: Crisis and Reform* 175–192 (1985).

86. Many of Judge Posner's writings consist of attempts to fasten a neoclassical economic template on legal phenomena and to generate results as guides for policy-making. Oversimplified, the analysis proceeds from a syllogism: All actors, human and institutional, maximize self-interest. They function well when they "internalize" the costs of their behavior, poorly when they can "externalize" costs by shifting them to others. The ideal arrangement checks authority when it is essential to thwart the export of "externalities."

87. I Federal Courts Study Committee, *Working Papers and Subcommittee Reports* 103–105, 134, 131, 132, 119–121 (1990). For an edited version, see Erwin Chemerinsky & Larry B. Kramer, "Defining the Role of the Federal Courts," 1990 *B.Y.U. L. Rev.* 67.

88. Accord Wechsler, "Revision," supra note 56, at 225.

89. The ALI considered, but ultimately rejected, a proposal to make federal-question jurisdiction exclusive. *ALI Study*, supra note 43, at 477.

90. Gully v. First Nat'l Bank, 299 U. S. 109, 112 (1936).

91. The existing statute needlessly provides for removal "by the defendant *or defendants*" and specifies that cases are to be removed not only to the local district court, but to the particular *division* of that court embracing the place where the state action is filed.

92. The ALI would state explicitly that no amount in controversy should be required for removal in this conventional kind of case. See *ALI Study*, supra note 43, at 25.

93. In this vein, I should note that the ALI proposal regarding removal was offered before Congress eliminated the amount-in-controversy requirement from §1331.

94. The ALI would insist that any defense sufficient for removal must be one that, if sustained, would be "dispositive of the action or of all counterclaims therein." I cover the same ground by mandating that a defense or counterclaim be one that "can resolve the dispute between the parties." The ALI would also create exceptions to the general rule allowing removal for nine categories of cases in which federal adjudication is not thought to be needed or appropriate. Congress may well wish to exempt claims by railroad workers or seamen, workmen's compensation claims generally, and similar specialized claims from the removal jurisdiction created by new legislation—and can do so expressly and largely without ideological controversy.

Four. Our Federalism

1. On the "Red Scare" and the legislation it produced, see Zechariah Chafee, Jr., *Free Speech in the United States* (1941). See Whitney v. California, 274 U. S. 357 (1927) (sustaining the California statute); Brandenburg v. Ohio, 395 U. S. 444 (1969) (invalidating the Ohio law); Dombrowski v. Pfister, 380 U. S. 479 (1965) (approving a federal injunction against the prosecution in Louisiana).

2. After the federal proceedings I am about to describe were concluded, the California state courts ordered the charges against Harris dismissed. In re Harris, 20 Cal. App.3d 632, 97 Cal. Rptr. 844 (1971).

3. Younger v. Harris, 401 U. S. 37 (1971).

4. Harris had been deprived of his liberty by the arrest alone, and he stood to lose his freedom entirely if convicted and sentenced to a prison term. Those injuries were clearly caused by the prosecution he insisted was unconstitutional, and the injunction he sought would, just as clearly, set things right. Others who attempted to join Harris' suit on the ground that they only *feared* that they might be prosecuted *were* found to lack standing. But Harris himself was a proper federal plaintiff. His right of action was assured by §1983, and since he asserted a constitutional claim on the face of his complaint, he met the prerequisites for jurisdiction under §1331.

5. For Marshall's statement, see Cohens v. Virginia, 19 U. S. (6 Wheat.) 264, 404 (1821). For the modern Court's (formal) adherence, see New Orleans Pub. Svc. v. Council of City of New Orleans, 491 U. S. 350, 358–359 (1989).

6. Massachusetts v. Missouri, 308 U. S. 1, 19 (1939).

7. Hawaii Housing Auth. v. Midkiff, 467 U. S. 229, 236 (1984), quoting Colorado River Water Conservation Dist. v. United States, 424 U. S. 800, 813 (1976) (majority opinion by Brennan, J.).

8. Pennzoil Co. v. Texaco, 481 U. S. 1, 12 n.9 (1987).

9. E.g., Siler v. Louisville & Nashville R. R., 213 U. S. 175 (1909).

10. Chapter Three, the text accompanying notes 47–48.

11. Railroad Comm. of Texas v. Pullman, 312 U. S. 496 (1941).

12. Id. at 500.

13. For a synopsis and citations to classic texts, see Donald H. Zeigler, "Rights Require Remedies: A New Approach to the Enforcement of Rights in the Federal Courts," 38 *Hastings L.J.* 665, 667–671 (1987).

14. Chapter Three, note 48 and the accompanying text.

15. Railroad Comm. of Texas v. Pullman, 312 U. S. 496, 501 (1941).

16. Since state-question abstention holds out at least the theoretical promise that the federal court may yet treat the federal question, the Court has said that it may be "preferable" to refer to it as a doctrine of "deferral" rather than "abstention." Growe v. Emison, 113 S.Ct. 1075, 1080 n.1 (1993). Some commentators contend that if state-question abstention is merited to avoid constitutional decisions, it is equally warranted to avoid determinations of federal nonconstitutional issues. E. g., Randall P. Bezanson, "Abstention: The Supreme Court and Allocation of Judicial Power," 27 *Vand. L. Rev.* 1107, 1112 (1974). So far, abstention has not been so extended. E. g., Propper v. Clark, 337 U. S. 472, 490 (1949).

17. Chapter Three, the text accompanying notes 71–74.

18. Michael Wells, "Why Professor Redish Is Wrong about Abstention," 19 *Ga. L. Rev.* 1097, 1110 (1985).

19. E.g., Fornaris v. Ridge Tool Co., 400 U. S. 41 (1970); Clay v. Sun Ins. Office, 363 U. S. 207 (1960).

20. Railroad Comm. of Texas v. Pullman, 312 U. S. 496, 501 (1941), quoting Di Giovanni v. Camden Ins. Ass'n, 296 U. S. 64, 73 (1935).

21. E.g., Lake Carriers' Ass'n v. MacMullan, 406 U. S. 498 (1972); Zwickler v. Koota, 389 U. S. 241 (1967).

22. Martin H. Redish, "Abstention, Separation of Powers, and the Limits of the Judicial Function," 94 *Yale L.J.* 71, 95 (1984). See Bezanson, "Abstention," supra note 16, at 1118. But see Baggett v. Bullitt, 377 U. S. 360 (1964) (stating that it must be apparent that a plausible determination of a state question will avoid federal constitutional issues).

23. The Warren Court occasionally referred issues to the states in circumstances that were at best questionable. When the Court hoped to cajole the courts in Virginia into compliance with the Segregation Cases, the Court insisted that the state courts be given a chance to construe state statutes that appeared to require race discrimination. On the question whether state law really was unsettled, the Court said only that it was "unable to agree" that the statutes were so clear (and clearly invalid) that there was "no reasonable room" for an interpretation that would save them. Harrison v. NAACP, 360 U. S. 167, 177 (1959).

More recently, Justice Sandra Day O'Connor has said that the "relevant inquiry" is not whether there is a "bare, though unlikely, possibility" that the state courts *"might"* decide state-law issues in a way that makes the resolution of constitutional claims unnecessary. Rather, the federal courts should postpone their own work only if state law is genuinely "uncertain" and "obviously susceptible" to a construction that avoids federal issues. Hawaii Housing Auth. v. Midkiff, 467 U. S. 229, 237 (1984) (emphasis in original), quoting Zwickler v. Koota, 389 U. S. 241, 251 & n.14 (1967). Abstention is not, by this account, a means of inviting state courts to rewrite state statutes to forestall federal constitutional questions. Houston v. Hill, 482 U. S. 451, 470–471 (1987).

The cases to watch are those in which plaintiffs claim that state statutes violate both the federal and state constitutions. If the federal courts stay their hand every time it appears that the state courts might interpret their own constitutions to give plaintiffs the relief they seek, abstention would be called for in virtually any case. And the federal adjudication of federal constitutional claims would be postponed routinely—perhaps for good. Thus far, the Supreme Court has resisted any such course. Examining Bd. of Engineers v. Flores de Otero, 426 U. S. 572, 597–598 (1976). It is worth noting, however, that Chief Justice Burger was convinced that abstention is generally appropriate in these circumstances. Wisconsin v. Constantineau, 400 U. S. 433, 440 (1971) (dissenting opinion). Accord Reetz v. Bozanich, 397 U. S. 82 (1970). Burger, indeed, would have required plaintiffs to press state constitutional claims in federal court—in order to position the federal courts to defer to the adjudication of those claims in state court. A policy of that kind would have the federal courts leafing through state constitutions, identifying state constitutional claims that plaintiffs *might* have raised, incorporating those claims into the lawsuits at hand, and then abstaining—on the basis of state-law claims that plaintiffs never actually presented. Here again, the full Court has declined to go along, preserving instead the conventional rule that litigants control for themselves the claims on which they wish to proceed.

24. See Paul M. Bator & Daniel J. Meltzer et al., *Hart and Wechsler's The Federal Courts and the Federal System* 1381–83 (3d ed. 1988). At least this is true in states that permit federal district courts to invoke the certification scheme—as provided by the model act developed by the American Law Institute. In states in which certified questions are accepted only from a federal appellate court, certification probably delays the final disposition of disputes. For a general discussion, see Ira P. Robbins, "The Uniform Certification of Questions of State Law Act: A Proposal for Reform," 18 *J. Legis.* 127 (1992).

25. Martha A. Field, "Abstention in Constitutional Cases: The Scope of the *Pullman* Abstention Doctrine," 122 *U. Pa. L. Rev.* 1071, 1087 (1974). Accord Zeigler, "New Approach," supra note 13, at 691–693.

26. The pressure is all the more significant inasmuch as plaintiffs who are sent to state court for the adjudication of state-law claims must alert the state courts to the federal constitutional issues in the background. Otherwise, the state courts may not appreciate the federal context in which state-law issues arise and thus may overlook an opportunity to deal with those issues in a way that avoids constitutional difficulties. Government & Civic Employees Org. Comm. v. Windsor, 353 U. S. 364 (1957).

27. England v. Louisiana State Bd. of Medical Examiners, 375 U. S. 411 (1964).

28. Barry Friedman, "A Revisionist Theory of Abstention," 88 *Mich. L. Rev.* 530, 535 (1989).

29. Other forms of abstention also have the potential to thwart federal consideration of federal claims. In a line of decisions dating back to another opinion by Justice Frankfurter, abstention has been found appropriate because the parties are simultaneously litigating the same issues in state court. The rationale for declining jurisdiction in duplicative litigation cases is not to allow the state courts to grapple with uncertain questions of state law, but to avoid "interference" with parallel

state proceedings and to forestall "uneconomical" litigation in both court systems at once. Brillhart v. Excess Ins. Co., 316 U. S. 491, 494–495 (1942). Abstention is thus justified as "a means of docket clearing." Linda S. Mullenix, "A Branch Too Far: Pruning the Abstention Doctrine," 75 *Geo. L.J.* 99, 101 (1986). Most recent decisions, some of them written by Justice Brennan, honor this kind of abstention primarily in the breach—especially when federal rights are implicated. Yet Chief Justice Rehnquist has indicated that he would make greater use of abstention for the purpose of docket control. Compare Colorado River Water Conservation Dist. v. United States, 424 U. S. 800, 813 (1976) (majority opinion by Brennan, J.), quoting Allegheny v. Frank Mashuda Co., 360 U. S. 185, 188–189 (1959) (finding abstention appropriate—but only in "exceptional circumstances"), with Will v. Calvert Fire Ins. Co., 437 U. S. 655, 663 (1978) (opinion for a plurality by Rehnquist, J.) (approving abstention and suggesting that a district court decision to abstain in favor of parallel state court proceedings should not ordinarily be examined on appeal). See Moses H. Cone Memorial Hosp. v. Mercury Constr. Corp., 460 U. S. 1 (1983) (a Brennan majority opinion affirming a circuit court decision not to abstain—and making it clear that abstention orders *are* appealable). See generally David A. Sonenshein, "Abstention: The Crooked Course of *Colorado River*," 59 *Tul. L. Rev.* 651 (1985).

Abstention also has been ordered in diversity cases, where only state-law issues figure and the (theoretical) purpose of federal jurisdiction is to protect out-of-state parties from local bias. E. g., Louisiana Power & Light Co. v. City of Thibodaux, 360 U. S. 25, 28 (1959) (emphasizing the "special and peculiar" state interests in eminent domain involved in the case). But see Meredith v. Winter Haven, 320 U. S. 228 (1943) (declining to abstain in a diversity action and thus to relinquish jurisdiction of state-law issues conferred by Congress). On diversity, see Chapter One, notes 115–117 and the accompanying text.

In a related development beyond the scope of this chapter, the Court has held that the eleventh amendment prevents the federal courts from granting structural injunctive relief against state authorities on the basis of state law. Pennhurst State School & Hosp. v. Halderman, 465 U. S. 89 (1984). Accordingly, in at least some §1331 cases in which plaintiffs seek injunctions against state officials, the federal district courts no longer have jurisdiction over pendent state-law claims and are thus unable to invoke state-question abstention. The practical result is that many plaintiffs are driven into state court for the treatment of both state and federal claims. For after *Pennhurst,* the state courts often provide the only tribunals in which plaintiffs can obtain judgment on all their claims in a single judicial proceeding. See Keith Werhan, "*Pullman* Abstention after *Pennhurst:* A Comment on Judicial Federalism," 27 *Wm. & Mary L. Rev.* 449 (1986). It should be clear, however, that *Pennhurst* does not eliminate this form of abstention entirely. The eleventh amendment is inapplicable when defendants are city or county officers rather than state officials. Moreover, in the typical abstention setting in which the federal courts defer only to state court determinations of state law, the prohibition on injunctions announced in *Pennhurst* is not necessarily implicated.

30. David P. Currie, "The Federal Courts and the American Law Institute, Part

II," 36 *U. Chi. L. Rev.* 268, 317 (1969). Accord Martha A. Field, "The Abstention Doctrine Today," 125 *U. Pa. L. Rev.* 605 (1977); Charles A. Wright, "The Abstention Doctrine Reconsidered," 37 *Tex. L. Rev.* 815 (1959).

31. American Law Institute, *Study of the Division of Jurisdiction between State and Federal Courts* 282–298 (1969).

32. Mitchum v. Foster, 407 U. S. 225 (1972). Legal historians debate the actual purposes behind §2283. See, e.g., William T. Mayton, "Ersatz Federalism under the Anti-Injunction Statute," 78 *Colum. L. Rev.* 330 (1978); Comment, "Anti-Suit Injunctions between State and Federal Courts," 32 *U. Chi. L. Rev.* 471 (1965).

33. Atlantic Coast Line R. R. v. Brotherhood of Locomotive Engineers, 398 U. S. 281, 286 (1970).

34. Younger v. Harris, 401 U. S. 37, 43–44 (1971).

35. Owen M. Fiss, *"Dombrowski,"* 86 *Yale L.J.* 1103, 1107 (1977). For criticism of Black's treatment of the historical instances in which the federal courts had refused to enjoin state proceedings, see Aviam Soifer & Hugh C. Macgill, "The *Younger* Doctrine: Reconstructing Reconstruction," 55 *Tex. L. Rev.* 1141 (1977).

36. Younger v. Harris, 401 U. S. 37, 44–45 (1971). For an account of how Black gleaned his notion of "Our Federalism" from "four decades worth of Frankfurter opinions," see Michael G. Collins, "Whose Federalism?" 9 *Const. Commentary* 75, 85 (1992).

37. Harry T. Edwards, "The Changing Notion of Our Federalism," 33 *Wayne L. Rev.* 1015 (1987).

38. Thomas E. Baker, "Our Federalism in *Pennzoil Co. v. Texaco, Inc.,* or How the *Younger* Doctrine Keeps Getting Older Not Better," 9 *Rev. Litig.* 303, 355 (1990).

39. Chapter Three, the text accompanying notes 66–70.

40. Soifer & Macgill, "Reconstructing Reconstruction," supra note 35, at 1141.

41. Martin H. Redish, "The Doctrine of *Younger v. Harris:* Deference in Search of a Rationale," 63 *Cornell L. Rev.* 463, 465–466 (1978).

42. Academicians have attempted to construct a rigorous scheme that *does* account for all four values. E. g., Robert Bartels, "Avoiding a Comity of Errors: A Model for Adjudicating Federal Civil Rights Suits That Interfere with State Civil Proceedings," 29 *Stan. L. Rev.* 27 (1976); Friedman, "Revisionist Theory," supra note 28.

43. Steffel v. Thompson, 415 U. S. 452, 462 (1974), quoting Lake Carriers' Ass'n v. MacMullan, 406 U. S. 498, 509 (1972). See Chapter Three, the text accompanying notes 1–3.

44. See Chapter Five; Michael Wells, "Habeas Corpus and Freedom of Speech," 1978 *Duke L.J.* 1307.

45. Hicks v. Miranda, 422 U. S. 332, 349 (1975). *Hicks* is plainly viable despite Justice White's more recent insistence in Ankenbrandt v. Richards, 112 S.Ct. 2206 (1992), that "[a]bsent any *pending* proceeding in state tribunals" the "ap-

plication" of *Younger* abstention is "clearly erroneous." Id. at 2216 (emphasis in original). After all, Justice White wrote for the Court in *Hicks*. See also Morales v. TWA, 112 S.Ct. 2031, 2036 n.1 (1992) (indicating that *Younger* is applicable with respect to an "already-pending *or* an about-to-be-pending" action in state court) (emphasis supplied).

46. It is possible to distinguish the shopping mall case as an action for a declaratory judgment rather than an injunction. Justice Brennan's opinion drew that distinction expressly, as though it supported his result, and the purpose of the Declaratory Judgment Act is to permit citizens who anticipate that they will be named as defendants to take the initiative as affirmative plaintiffs. Yet to the extent federal-question abstention is invoked solely to avoid disrupting state court proceedings, there is little to choose between injunctions on the one hand and declaratory judgments on the other. Injunctions are immediately effective—and coercive by their very nature. Declaratory judgments are not; yet they may be enforced by injunctions if necessary. The Court has held, moreover, that abstention is proper in cases in which *either* declaratory or injunctive relief is sought from the federal courts after state court proceedings are under way. Samuels v. Mackell, 401 U. S. 66 (1971). If the two forms of relief are treated the same when state court actions are pending, it would seem that they should be treated in the same way when state court proceedings are *not* pending. This is to say, it should make no difference whether a federal plaintiff seeks declaratory or injunctive relief in advance of an action in state court. Either way, the federal courts should proceed to the merits—there being no state court proceedings to disrupt. To date, the issue remains open, albeit Chief Justice Rehnquist has stated his view that federal injunctions should be denied even before state proceedings have begun. Steffel v. Thompson, 415 U. S. 452, 478 (1974) (concurring opinion). It is unclear whether this question is resolved in the affirmative by the *preliminary* injunction approved in Doran v. Salem Inn, 422 U. S. 922 (1975), and the *permanent* injunction allowed in Wooley v. Maynard, 430 U. S. 705 (1977). Compare Fiss, *"Dombrowski,"* supra note 35, at 1145 (taking this view), with Martin H. Redish, *Federal Jurisdiction: Tensions in the Allocation of Judicial Power* 313 (2d ed. 1989) (treating *Wooley* as a "bad-faith" case). See Erwin Chemerinsky, *Federal Jurisdiction* 638–640 (1989).

47. New Orleans Pub. Svc. v. Council of City of New Orleans, 491 U. S. 350, 370 (1989). Initially, the Court moved to situations in which state authorities were prosecuting public nuisance proceedings, said to be sufficiently *like* criminal actions to fit. Huffman v. Pursue, 420 U. S. 592 (1975). From there, the Court moved to cases in which state officials were pressing entirely different state interests in state court, e.g., Moore v. Sims, 442 U. S. 415 (1979) (proceedings to terminate parental rights); from there to situations in which state officials were vindicating the "regular operation" of the state judicial system, e.g., Juidice v. Vail, 430 U. S. 327 (1977) (contempt proceedings); from there to administrative processes of a judicial character, e.g., Middlesex County Ethics Committee v. Garden State Bar Assoc., 457 U. S. 423 (1982) (bar proceedings); and from *there* to disputes between private parties—at least when the state has a special interest—e.g.,

Pennzoil Co. v. Texaco, 481 U. S. 1 (1987). In *New Orleans,* however, the Court declined to invoke abstention with respect either to judicial proceedings reviewing state legislative action or to administrative proceedings not sufficiently judicial in nature to fall within *Middlesex County.*

48. Chapter Three, notes 36–38 and the accompanying text. As I will explain in Chapter Five, habeas corpus is an exception to the full faith and credit statute, §1738. The right of action on which federal plaintiffs rely in actions to which federal-question abstention applies, §1983, is not such an exception. Allen v. McCurry, 449 U. S. 90 (1980); Migra v. Warren City School Dist. Bd. of Educ., 465 U. S. 75 (1984).

49. In Hicks v. Miranda, 422 U. S. 332 (1975), the Court held that a federal district court should abstain if state proceedings are instituted after a complaint is filed, but before proceedings of substance on the merits. In Huffman v. Pursue, 420 U. S. 592 (1975), the Court held that state proceedings are pending for abstention purposes through the appellate stages. And in Allen v. McCurry, 449 U. S. 90 (1980), and Migra v. Warren City School Dist. Bd. of Educ., 465 U. S. 75 (1984), the Court held that state court judgments in federal-question cases are entitled to preclusive effect in subsequent proceedings in federal court. See Bartels, "Comity," supra note 42, at 29–30.

50. Ann Althouse, "The Misguided Search for State Interest in Abstention Cases: Observations on the Occasion of *Pennzoil v. Texaco,*" 63 *N.Y.U. L. Rev.* 1051, 1082 (1988).

51. Of course, the states have an interest in every state court action, if it is only the interest in providing a forum for the resolution of disputes. Some justices occasionally describe the abstention doctrine broadly enough to cover all state proceedings of a judicial nature. E. g., Pennzoil Co. v. Texaco, 481 U. S. 1, 13 (1987) (opinion of Powell, J.). The full Court has suggested, however, that there is a stopping place. New Orleans Pub. Svc. v. Council of City of New Orleans, 491 U. S. 350 (1989) (holding that a state judicial proceeding reviewing legislative action was not an action to which *Younger* applied); cf. Morales v. TWA, 112 S.Ct. 2031, 2036 n.1 (1992) (stating that *Younger* "imposes heightened requirements" for an injunction to restrain a "civil action involving *important* state interests") (emphasis supplied). Recall in this vein that the abstention doctrine fashioned by the Court in *Younger* provides the standard for federal court action in a sizable number of cases only because §1983 is an exception to the Anti-Injunction Act, which, were it applicable, would bar injunctions against *all* pending state court proceedings, civil or criminal. See the text accompanying note 32 supra. Actions under §1983, in turn, are available only against persons who act under color of state law. For that reason, the state proceedings as to which the Anti-Injunction Act allows an injunction (because the federal plaintiff sues under §1983), and as to which *Younger* prescribes the standard for federal court action (because it constitutes a judicially crafted doctrine that controls when the Anti-Injunction Act is inapplicable), must by hypothesis require more state involvement than a rudimentary state civil action between wholly private litigants. While a private citizen or entity can act under color of state law and thus be subject to

suit under §1983, the typical defendants in such actions are state officials. The state actions that §1983 plaintiffs seek to enjoin are therefore usually actions involving state agents, not lawsuits between private citizens. See *Hart & Wechsler,* supra note 24, at 1635–37.

52. The declaratory action that Richard Steffel was (properly) allowed to bring also interfered with prosecutorial decisions, albeit those decisions were not yet manifest in a formal charge.

53. Rizzo v. Goode, 423 U. S. 362, 378–379 (1976), quoting Cafeteria Workers v. McElroy, 367 U. S. 886, 896 (1961). See also O'Shea v. Littleton, 414 U. S. 488 (1974). In Allee v. Medrano, 416 U. S. 802 (1974), Justice Douglas' opinion for the Court recognized that there are instances in which early federal relief is warranted to avert systemic violations of federal rights. That, however, was the last time the Court expressed such a view.

54. Louise Weinberg, "The New Judicial Federalism," 29 *Stan. L. Rev.* 1191, 1219 (1977).

55. City of Columbus v. Leonard, 443 U. S. 905, 910 (1979) (Rehnquist, J., dissenting).

56. E.g., Monroe v. Pape, 365 U. S. 167 (1961).

57. There are other cases in which abstention has been ordered to permit state courts to determine *federal* questions bearing on especially important state concerns—oil in Texas, for example. Burford v. Sun Oil Co., 319 U. S. 315 (1943). See also Alabama Pub. Serv. Comm. v. Southern Ry., 341 U. S. 341 (1951) (local railroad rates). Abstention of that kind is not really controversial—or troubling. Powerful arguments can often be made against federal court involvement in particularly local affairs. William E. Ryckman, Jr., "Land Use Litigation, Federal Jurisdiction, and the Abstention Doctrines," 69 *Calif. L. Rev.* 377 (1981) (contending for routine abstention in land use cases).

58. Younger v. Harris, 401 U. S. 37, 46–49 (1971).

59. Michael G. Collins, "The Right to Avoid Trial: Justifying Federal Court Intervention into Ongoing State Court Proceedings," 66 *N.C. L. Rev.* 49, 62–63 (1987). In the Louisiana case, prosecutors were careful always to withdraw trumped-up charges just before the state courts had an opportunity to reach the defendants' first amendment claims. It is beyond question that Justice Brennan's decision was also based on the proposition that federal injunctions should be available whenever plaintiffs attack the facial validity of state statutes under the first amendment. Dombrowski v. Pfister, 380 U. S. 479, 486 (1965). See Fiss, *"Dombrowski,"* supra note 35. In the syndicalism case, however, the Court discarded that half of Brennan's analysis.

60. Inasmuch as some cases refer to "bad faith" and "harassment" in the disjunctive—e.g., Huffman v. Pursue, 420 U. S. 592, 611 (1975)—it is possible that a showing of *either* can get would-be federal plaintiffs past the abstention barrier. There is no reason, after all, why a single prosecution cannot be brought in bad faith. Redish, *Tensions,* supra note 46, at 351 n.111. It is probably true, however, that bad faith will rarely be present in the absence of harassment. See Fiss, *"Dombrowski,"* supra note 35, at 1118.

61. Chemerinsky, *Federal Jurisdiction,* supra note 46, at 653 (asking whether the "bad faith" exception is not an "empty universe"). For lower court cases, see C. Keith Wingate, "The Bad-Faith Harassment Exception to the *Younger* Doctrine: Exploring the Empty Universe," 5 *Rev. Litig.* 123 (1986).

62. Douglas Laycock, "Federal Interference with State Prosecutions: The Need for Prospective Relief," 1977 *Sup. Ct. Rev.* 193.

63. Chapter Two, the text accompanying notes 50–74.

64. Younger v. Harris, 401 U. S. 37, 53 (1971), quoting Watson v. Buck, 313 U. S. 387, 402 (1941).

65. E.g., Trainor v. Hernandez, 431 U. S. 434, 463 (1977) (dissenting opinion); Juidice v. Vail, 430 U. S. 327, 340–341 (1977) (concurring opinion). On remand in *Trainor,* the district court decided that abstention was inappropriate because the state procedure in question would not permit the plaintiff to raise a federal claim against the procedure itself. Surprisingly, the Supreme Court summarily affirmed. Quern v. Hernandez, 440 U. S. 951 (1979).

66. Redish, *Tensions,* supra note 46, at 355.

67. For the quotation, see Younger v. Harris, 401 U. S. 37, 53 (1971), quoting Watson v. Buck, 313 U. S. 387, 402 (1941). See Gibson v. Berryhill, 411 U. S. 564 (1973) (the bias case); Kugler v. Helfant, 421 U. S. 117, 125 n.4 (1975) (listing *Gibson* as an illustration of this exception).

68. Kugler v. Helfant, 421 U. S. 117, 124 (1975). See Collins, "The Right to Avoid Trial," supra note 59, at 56.

69. E.g., Moore v. Sims, 442 U. S. 415, 436 (1979), quoting Juidice v. Vail, 430 U. S. 327, 338 (1977).

70. Chapter One, the text accompanying notes 75–88.

71. Even this possibility is typically cited in cases in which the Court concludes that its requirements are not met. E. g., Juidice v. Vail, 430 U. S. 327, 337 (1977) (holding that it no longer suffices to show that a federal claim cannot be raised as a defense in state court); Moore v. Sims, 442 U. S. 415 (1979) (finding abstention appropriate even though the plaintiffs' federal claims against a state scheme for dealing with child abuse could not be treated in pending state proceedings in which the state was seeking custody of their children).

72. Chapter Three, notes 36–38 and the accompanying text.

73. For recent recitations of the "full and fair" standard with respect to preclusion, see Allen v. McCurry, 449 U. S. 90, 101 (1980); Haring v. Prosise, 462 U. S. 306, 313 (1983).

74. E.g., Kremer v. Chemical Constr. Corp., 456 U. S. 461, 481 (1982).

75. Chapter One, the text accompanying notes 83–85.

76. Redish, "Separation of Powers," supra note 22. See also Martin H. Redish, *The Federal Courts in the Political Order* (1991) (developing this theme).

77. Martin H. Redish, "Judge-Made Abstention and the Fashionable Art of Democracy Bashing," 40 *Case W. Res. L. Rev.* 1023, 1026 (1990).

78. Barry Friedman, "A Different Dialogue: The Supreme Court, Congress, and Federal Jurisdiction," 85 *Nw. U. L. Rev.* 1 (1990). Mark Tushnet once suggested that Congress has plenary power to decide federalism questions touching

both state judicial authority and state legislative power, but that Congress may, by legislation, delegate authority to the Court to effect refinements not inconsistent with Congress' principal judgments. Mark V. Tushnet, "Constitutional and Statutory Analysis in the Law of Federal Jurisdiction," 25 *UCLA L. Rev.* 1301 (1978).

79. Jack M. Beermann, "'Bad' Judicial Activism and Liberal Federal-Courts Doctrine: A Comment on Professor Doernberg and Professor Redish," 40 *Case W. Res. L. Rev.* 1053 (1990); see generally Alan A. Feld, "Separation of Powers: Boundaries or Balance?" 21 *Ga. L. Rev.* 171 (1986). There are, to be sure, recent instances in which the Court has been more rigid about the separation of powers. See Chapter One, note 28. But on those occasions the Court has been properly criticized for the kind of duplicity that characterized the Formalist period—when, you will recall, the Old Court purported to reason deductively from primary propositions of doubtful neutrality.

80. Beermann, "Activism," supra note 79, at 1057–58.

81. Martin H. Redish, "Text, Structure, and Common Sense in the Interpretation of Article III," 138 *U. Pa. L. Rev.* 1633, 1636–37 (1990). See Chapter Two, the text accompanying note 37; Chapter Three, the text accompanying note 26.

82. Cf. Wells, "Why Redish Is Wrong," supra note 18 (arguing that Redish's attack on the Court's restrictions on §1983 actions neglects the extent to which the scope of §1983 itself reflects considerable judicial creativity).

83. David L. Shapiro, "Jurisdiction and Discretion," 60 *N.Y.U. L. Rev.* 543 (1985).

84. Redish does not dismiss Shapiro's case; he meets it forthrightly and with some power. Martin H. Redish, "Judicial Parity, Litigant Choice, and Democratic Theory: A Comment on Federal Jurisdiction and Constitutional Rights," 36 *UCLA L. Rev.* 329, 351–360 (1988). In the end, however, even if we credit Redish's objections, Shapiro establishes that the Court has often postponed or relinquished jurisdiction that Congress has prescribed.

85. Congressional silence is by nature ambiguous, and the Court is not entitled to assume congressional acquiescence in every decision that is not promptly overruled legislatively. Donald L. Doernberg, "'You Can Lead A Horse to Water . . .': The Supreme Court's Refusal to Allow the Exercise of Original Jurisdiction Conferred by Congress," 40 *Case W. Res. L. Rev.* 997, 1007 (1990). Still, Congress' unwillingness (thus far) to attend to the specifics of federal court jurisdiction constitutes at least an implicit invitation to the Court to take up the responsibility.

86. E.g., Martin H. Redish, "The Anti-Injunction Statute Reconsidered," 44 *U. Chi. L. Rev.* 717 (1977); Redish, "Deference," supra note 41.

87. Redish, *Tensions,* supra note 46, at 77.

88. Ann Althouse, "The Humble and the Treasonous: Judge-Made Jurisdiction Law," 40 *Case W. Res. L. Rev.* 1035 (1990).

89. Redish means to say that the Court cannot tell the lower federal courts to refuse or postpone jurisdiction conferred on them by statutes enacted by the Congress, unless the Court is prepared to hold those statutes unconstitutional.

Yet his rhetoric, read out of context, sometimes suggests a more sweeping propo-sition: "[A] democratic system cannot function if the majoritarian branches are allowed to reach only those constitutionally valid results that some external source [i.e., the Supreme Court] finds pleasing." Redish, "Democracy Bashing," supra note 77, at 1034. See Beermann, "Activism," supra note 79. In an elabora-tion of his views, Redish posits that both a "representational" model and a "counter-majoritarian" model operate within American constitutional govern-ment and recognizes that it may not always be easy to reconcile the two—as is required if the distinction in the text is to be drawn. See generally Redish, *Political Order,* supra note 76, at 137.

It is worth considering whether outcomes on the merits will be satisfying if conservative justices are forced to recognize that the federal courts have jurisdic-tion and must exercise it, even when the justices themselves think it would be better if federal adjudication were delayed or barred outright. Some observers read the Court's decisions withholding federal jurisdiction as indirect rulings against plaintiffs on the merits. If the discretionary grounds on which decisions are now based were removed, the Court might pass on to constitutional claims of right and reject them forthrightly. I worried over this same kind of thing with respect to standing doctrine in Chapter Two.

90. Friedman describes this as only an "intuition." Friedman, "Different Dia-logue," supra note 78, at 7 n.30. Redish has treated the problem in some depth. See Martin H. Redish, "Congressional Power to Regulate Supreme Court Appel-late Jurisdiction under the Exceptions Clause: An Internal and External Examina-tion," 27 *Vill. L. Rev.* 900 (1982); Martin H. Redish, "Constitutional Limitations on Congressional Power to Control Federal Jurisdiction: A Reaction to Professor Sager," 77 *Nw. U. L. Rev.* 143 (1982); Martin H. Redish & Curtis E. Woods, "Congressional Power to Control the Jurisdiction of the Lower Federal Courts: A Critical Review and a New Synthesis," 124 *U. Pa. L. Rev.* 45 (1975). Erwin Chemerinsky also seems to credit the notion. Chemerinsky, *Federal Jurisdiction,* supra note 46, at 381.

91. Chapter Three, the text accompanying notes 21–23.

92. Chapter Three, the text accompanying note 15.

93. Althouse, "Judge-Made Law," supra note 88.

94. See, e.g., Shapiro, "Discretion," supra note 83, at 577–588.

95. *ALI Study,* supra note 31; S. 35, 95th Cong., 2d Sess. (1978). For con-structive criticism of S. 35, see Tushnet, "Statutory Analysis," supra note 78, at 1349–57. My effort here is to deal with the politically sensitive judgments that drive current judge-made doctrines and any reforms that Congress may devise. I lay aside the ALI's many valuable suggestions touching the noncontroversial, mechanical aspects of abstention and its proposals regarding other, similarly non-controversial, abstention doctrines that now occur occasionally in the Judicial Code—e.g., the Tax Injunction Act, 28 U.S.C. §1341, and the Johnson Act, 28 U.S.C. §1342. While S. 35 dealt with a range of other matters that were and remain contentious, particularly the defenses available in §1983 actions, I have excluded those questions from the scope of this volume. Justice Blackmun has

worried in print that the Rehnquist Court's decisions regarding §1983 jeopardize this key statute's continued viability. Harry A. Blackmun, "Section 1983 and Federal Protection of Individual Rights—Will the Statute Remain Alive or Fade Away?" 60 *N.Y.U. L. Rev.* 1 (1985). For a (deep) historical perspective, see Michael G. Collins, "Economic Rights, Implied Constitutional Actions, and the Scope of Section 1983," 77 *Geo. L.J.* 1493 (1989).

96. *ALI Study,* supra note 31, at 285.

97. Id. at 287.

98. Id. at 49.

99. S. 35, supra note 95.

100. *ALI Study,* supra note 31, at 297.

101. Again laying aside noncontroversial subtopics, I have not included in this proposal exceptions for requests by the United States or disclaimers regarding other forms of abstention. The ALI model does include such provisions.

102. *ALI Study,* supra note 31, at 52.

103. See note 1 and the accompanying text supra.

104. *ALI Study,* supra note 31, at 303.

105. S. 35, supra note 95. See note 45 and the accompanying text supra.

106. See Chapter Three, the text accompanying notes 58–70.

107. See note 32 and the accompanying text supra.

108. Michael Collins has explored the overlapping ways in which existing statutes, doctrines, and practices counseling noninterference with state court proceedings (e.g., the Anti-Injunction Statute, *Younger* abstention, and restrictive removal rules) recognize essentially the same exceptions—which boil down to cases in which federal interference is essential "to protect against the immediate and irreparable loss of federally protected rights." Collins, "The Right to Avoid Trial," supra note 59, at 104–105. I think the complexities that Collins uncovers can and should be cleared away by opening up the federal courts' removal jurisdiction and making do with that means of access to the federal forum in almost every instance. Cf. note 109 infra. If I am wrong, and my proposed amendment to the removal statute does not fully compensate for my proposal to bar injunctions against civil proceedings (except to safeguard a federal court's jurisdiction or judgments), then Congress should identify the additional instances in which injunctions should be permitted, and the proposal in the text should be adjusted accordingly.

At this juncture, when I mean only to advance my principal remedy for these problems (more removal jurisdiction and less authority to issue injunctions against civil actions), I am content to leave aside particularistic adjustments that may potentially prove appropriate. In a like manner, I lay aside any other adjustments that may be warranted in the exceptions that the Anti-Injunction Act currently allows to its general ban on injunctions against state proceedings. I hasten to say, however, that I do not quarrel with the case that Diane Wood has advanced for making those exceptions track more closely the Supreme Court's decisions purporting to give them effect. See Diane P. Wood, "Fine-Tuning Judicial Federalism: A Proposal for Reform of the Anti-Injunction Act," 1990 *B.Y.U. L. Rev.* 289.

109. Here, too, combined with the proposal in the last chapter to allow the removal of civil actions on the basis of a federal defense or counterclaim, this provision would clean up the currently confusing relationships between §2283, *Younger,* and §1983. See note 51 supra. Under present law, two lines are critical: (1) the line between §1983 actions in federal court (as to which the *Younger* cases prescribe the standard for federal court interference with state actions) and all other kinds of federal lawsuits (in which §2283 bars injunctions against pending state proceedings), and (2) the line between state civil or criminal actions (to which *Younger* applies) and other state proceedings (to which *Younger* is inapplicable). Under the proposal in the text, the key distinction is, once again, between pending state civil actions (which are immune from federal interference but may be removed to federal court on the basis of a federal defense or counterclaim) and pending state criminal proceedings (which may not be removed but may be enjoined in four specified situations).

Five. In Custody

1. I take this description of the events from the Court's opinion in Moore v. Dempsey, 261 U. S. 86 (1923), which assumed for purposes of review that the prisoners' allegations were true. See generally Richard C. Cortner, *A Mob Intent on Death* (1988).

2. These quotations and those further down in the text are from the petitioners' allegations and other documents in the record.

3. J. S. Waterman & E. E. Overton, "Federal Habeas Corpus Statutes and *Moore v. Dempsey,*" 1 *U. Chi. L. Rev.* 754 (1933).

4. Chapter One, note 84 and the accompanying text.

5. Moore v. Dempsey, 261 U. S. 86, 96 (1923) (dissenting opinion).

6. Chapter One, notes 82–84 and the accompanying text.

7. Moore v. Dempsey, 261 U. S. 86, 91 (1923).

8. See notes 160–195 and the accompanying text infra. In a previous article, I explored the political history of habeas corpus in more detail than I do here, but postponed a discussion of these further doctrinal problems. See Larry W. Yackle, "The Habeas Hagioscope," 66 *So. Calif. L. Rev.* 2331, 2333 n.4 (1993).

9. See Larry W. Yackle, *Postconviction Remedies* §§4, 5, 19 & 20 (1981), citing Robert S. Walker, *The Constitutional and Legal Development of Habeas Corpus as the Writ of Liberty* (1960).

10. Walker, *Writ of Liberty,* supra note 9, at 20.

11. See 9 William S. Holdsworth, *History of English Law* 111 (4th ed. 1926); Daniel J. Meador, *Habeas Corpus and Magna Carta* 12–13 (1966).

12. Rollin C. Hurd, *A Treatise on the Right of Personal Liberty and on the Writ of Habeas Corpus* 122–127 (1858).

13. Compare Dallin H. Oaks, "Habeas Corpus in the States—1776–1865," 32 *U. Chi. L. Rev.* 243, 258–261 (1965), with Fay v. Noia, 372 U. S. 391, 405 (1963).

14. Chapter Three, notes 36–38 and the accompanying text.

15. Smith v. Yeager, 393 U. S. 122, 124–125 (1968); see Kremer v. Chemical Constr. Corp., 455 U. S. 461, 485 n.27 (1982) (noting the writ's exemption from §1738). Historically, petitioners have also been able to request federal habeas relief on more than one occasion and thus to press issues that were, or might have been, adjudicated in previous habeas proceedings. Increasingly these days, however, second or successive petitions are disfavored. See notes 187–195 and the accompanying text infra.

16. William S. Church, *A Treatise on the Writ of Habeas Corpus* 601 (2d ed. 1893).

17. Cox v. Hakes, 15 App. Cas. 506, 527 (H.L. 1890).

18. Perhaps early decisions were considered adjudications only if they were positive in nature, and negative actions like denials of habeas relief were mere refusals to act that did not foreclose repeated petitions by unsuccessful applicants. Alternatively, the writ's freedom from preclusion rules may have followed from the understanding that the denial of habeas relief was a summary matter and thus not subject to review on writ of error. Since only judgments that *were* reviewable were entitled to preclusive effect, dissatisfied habeas corpus petitioners were able to file repeated petitions without concern that failure in one court would frustrate consideration in another. Paul Bator insisted that habeas was not fashioned into a general postconviction remedy until Brown v. Allen, 344 U. S. 443 (1953). Paul M. Bator, "Finality in Criminal Law and Federal Habeas Corpus for State Prisoners," 76 *Harv. L. Rev.* 441 (1963). Gary Peller puts the development much earlier. Gary Peller, "In Defense of Federal Habeas Corpus Relitigation," 16 *Harv. C.R.–C.L. L. Rev.* 579 (1982). For more recent scholarship, see Marc M. Arkin, "A New Look at Antebellum Habeas Corpus: Revisiting the Relitigation Debate" (forthcoming); Ann Woolhandler, "Demodeling Habeas," 45 *Stan. L. Rev.* 575 (1993); James S. Liebman, "Apocalypse Next Time? The Anachronistic Attack on Habeas Corpus / Direct Review Parity," 92 *Colum. L. Rev.* 1997 (1992).

19. Sanders v. United States, 373 U. S. 1, 8 (1963). See D. M. Gordon, "The Unruly Writ of Habeas Corpus," 26 *Mod. L. Rev.* 520, 523 (1963); see generally "Developments in the Law—Federal Habeas Corpus," 83 *Harv. L. Rev.* 1038 (1970). See also Jordan M. Steiker, "Incorporating the Suspension Clause: Is There a Constitutional Right to Federal Habeas Corpus for State Prisoners?" (forthcoming) (mounting a new and creative argument that state prisoners have a constitutional right to seek the federal writ).

20. E.g., Hansen v. Circuit Court, 591 F.2d 404, 405 (7th Cir.), cert. denied, 444 U. S. 907 (1979); accord Ellis v. Dyson, 421 U. S. 426, 440 (1975) (Powell, J., dissenting). See Larry W. Yackle, "Explaining Habeas Corpus," 60 *N.Y.U. L. Rev.* 991, 1000 & nn.29–31 (1985).

21. Sanders v. United States, 373 U. S. 1, 8 (1963).

22. Id. at 8 (opinion of Brennan, J.); id. at 24 (Harlan, J., dissenting).

23. Chapter Two, the text accompanying note 8.

24. Chapter Three, the text accompanying notes 3, 35–50; Chapter Four, the text accompanying notes 6–8.

25. Cervantes v. Walker, 589 F.2d 424, 425 n.1 (9th Cir. 1978) (probation);

Jones v. Cunningham, 371 U. S. 236, 241–243 (1963) (parole); Hensley v. Municipal Court, 411 U. S. 345, 349 (1973) (bail). See Justices v. Lydon, 466 U. S. 294 (1984) (finding custody where the petitioner had been permitted to remain at large pending trial de novo); Peyton v. Rowe, 391 U. S. 54 (1968) (allowing a prisoner to attack a conviction scheduled to be served after the completion of his current term of confinement). Inasmuch as the Court has already diluted the custody requirement in the cases just cited, it may be argued that custody should simply be abandoned as a jurisdictional prerequisite. Other writs in the federal system, notably coram nobis, may be employed after judgment irrespective of whether the applicant remains under restraint. United States v. Morgan, 346 U. S. 502, 507 (1954). Retention of the custody requirement is scarcely essential to maintain the traditional relation between habeas and release from detention. Petitioners who win habeas relief from the conditions of parole or bail are not released from confinement. The officials responsible for their supervision are instructed to cease enforcing unlawful conditions. Habeas relief is in this way often indistinguishable from an injunction. See Yackle, "Explaining," supra note 20, at 1003–04.

26. Chapter Four, the text accompanying notes 34–35.

27. Minnesota v. Murphy, 465 U. S. 420, 430 (1984).

28. Brown v. Allen, 344 U. S. 443, 488 (1953) (opinion of Frankfurter, J.) (elaborating on the Court's holding that a state judgment on a federal claim is due only "the weight that federal practice gives to the conclusion of a court of last resort of another jurisdiction").

29. Sanders v. United States, 373 U. S. 1 (1963); Fay v. Noia, 372 U. S. 391 (1963); Townsend v. Sain, 372 U. S. 293 (1963). See Curtis R. Reitz, "Federal Habeas Corpus: Postconviction Remedy for State Prisoners," 108 *U. Pa. L. Rev.* 461 (1960); Curtis R. Reitz, "Federal Habeas Corpus: Impact of an Abortive State Proceeding," 74 *Harv. L. Rev.* 1315 (1961). Cf. William J. Brennan, "Federal Habeas Corpus and State Prisoners," 7 *Utah L. Rev.* 423 (1961).

30. Chapter One, notes 1–2, 91–106 and the accompanying text.

31. Brown v. Allen, 344 U. S. 443, 537 (1953) (Jackson, J., concurring).

32. Robert M. Cover & T. Alexander Aleinikoff, "Dialectical Federalism: Habeas Corpus and the Court," 86 *Yale L.J.* 1035 (1977); Peller, "Relitigation," supra note 18, at 663–669; Abraham D. Sofaer, "Federal Habeas Corpus for State Prisoners: The Isolation Principle," 39 *N.Y.U. L. Rev.* 78 (1964).

33. Walter V. Schaefer, "Federalism and State Criminal Procedure," 70 *Harv. L. Rev.* 1, 25 (1956). For success-rate figures, see *Hearings Concerning Fairness and Efficiency in Habeas Corpus Adjudication before the Subcommittee on Civil and Constitutional Rights of the Committee on the Judiciary, U. S. House of Representative,* 102d Cong., 1st Sess. (1991) (Curtin & Liebman testimony); Richard Faust, Tina J. Rubenstein & Larry W. Yackle, "The Great Writ in Action: Empirical Light on the Federal Habeas Corpus Debate," 18 *N.Y.U. Rev. L. & Soc. Change* 637, 681 (1991).

34. Chapter One, notes 75–86 and the accompanying text.

35. Chapter Three, the text accompanying notes 66–70.

36. Chapter Three, the text accompanying notes 35–40.

37. Townsend v. Sain, 372 U. S. 293, 311–312 (1963). For proposals to establish an appellate jurisdiction to replace habeas corpus, see Paul D. Carrington et al., *Justice on Appeal* 103–114 (1976); Daniel J. Meador, "Straightening Out Federal Review of State Criminal Cases," 44 *Ohio St. L.J.* 273 (1983); Shirley M. Hufstedler, "Comity and the Constitution: The Changing Role of the Federal Judiciary," 47 *N.Y.U. L. Rev.* 841, 852–854 (1972). For powerful arguments on behalf of an appellate model that I (still) find unconvincing, see Barry Friedman, *"Pas De Deux:* The Supreme Court and the Habeas Courts," 66 *So. Calif. L. Rev.* 2467 (1993); Barry Friedman, "A Tale of Two Habeas," 73 *Minn. L. Rev.* 247 (1988). Of course, I am speaking here of the facts underlying federal constitutional claims of right, which must be determined by the trial court when it passes on a defendant's objection to the proceedings in state court—not the facts going to guilt or innocence, which are typically matters for the jury. On the limitations affecting federal fact-finding, see notes 62–63 and the accompanying text infra. Cf. Herrera v. Collins, 113 S.Ct. 853 (1993) (wrestling with whether a prisoner's persuasive evidence of actual innocence supports a constitutional claim that the imposition of a death sentence would violate the eighth amendment ban on cruel and unusual punishment). See Jordan M. Steiker, "Innocence and Federal Habeas" (forthcoming) (contending that claims of factual innocence should be cognizable in federal habeas corpus).

38. See generally Welsh S. White, *The Death Penalty in the Eighties: An Examination of the Modern System of Capital Punishment* (1987); Michael Mello, "Facing Death Alone: The Post Conviction Attorney Crisis on Death Row," 37 *Am. U. L. Rev.* 513 (1988).

39. Gideon v. Wainwright, 372 U. S. 335 (1963) (felony trials); Douglas v. California, 372 U. S. 353 (1963) (first appeal as of right); Pennsylvania v. Finley, 481 U. S. 551 (1987) (state postconviction proceedings in noncapital cases); Murray v. Giarratano, 492 U. S. 1 (1989) (capital cases); cf. Ross v. Moffitt, 417 U. S. 600 (1974) (denying counsel for purposes of seeking certiorari review in the U. S. Supreme Court); Norris v. Wainwright, 588 F.2d 130 (5th Cir.), cert. denied, 444 U. S. 846 (1979) (repeating the general rule that counsel need not be appointed for federal habeas corpus).

40. For the statutory right to counsel in capital habeas cases in federal court, see 21 U.S.C. §848(q). For a recent bill offering the states incentives to supply counsel to indigents facing capital punishment, see S. 1441, 103rd Cong., 1st Sess. (1993), other aspects of which are discussed in notes 151–152 and the accompanying text infra. For the federal courts' authority to appoint counsel in their discretion, see 28 U.S.C. §1915; 18 U.S.C. §3006A. Rule 8(c) of the habeas corpus rules underscores the district courts' power to supply counsel at any stage of federal proceedings and requires an appointment if a hearing is scheduled. Beyond Rule 8(c), nothing has been done to provide lawyers in noncapital federal habeas corpus proceedings.

41. Faust, Rubenstein & Yackle, "Great Writ," supra note 33, at 660. On counsel's functions, see Larry W. Yackle, "Form and Function in the Administra-

tion of Justice: The Bill of Rights and Federal Habeas Corpus," 23 *U. Mich. J. L. Ref.* 685, 708–710 (1990); Gary S. Goodpaster, "The Trial for Life: Effective Assistance of Counsel in Death Penalty Cases," 58 *N.Y.U. L. Rev.* 299 (1983).

42. Louis Michael Seidman, "Factual Guilt and the Burger Court: An Examination of Continuity and Change in Criminal Procedure," 80 *Colum. L. Rev.* 436, 438–439 & n.11 (1980), quoting *Wall St. J.* (Oct. 22, 1968).

43. Attorney General's Task Force on Violent Crime, Final Report, Recommendation #42 (1981).

44. See note 55 and the accompanying text infra.

45. Chapter Three, note 60 and the accompanying text.

46. E.g., Daniel E. Lungren, Attorney General of California, et al. to the President (Nov. 21, 1991), quoted in 137 *Cong. Rec.* S18672 (Nov. 27, 1991) (a letter from ten state attorneys general urging Bush to veto a bill meant to retain habeas corpus in streamlined form).

47. In part, the justices' concerns may be rooted in the "hurry-up-and-wait" nature of capital litigation. Eleventh-hour petitions for stays of execution sometimes require hastily called evening sessions or deliberations by telephone. Once stays of execution are issued, years can be required for the litigation of complex legal issues. Remarks of the Chief Justice, American Law Institute Annual Meeting, Washington, D. C. (May 15, 1990).

48. Ad Hoc Committee on Federal Habeas Corpus in Capital Cases, *Report and Proposal* (Sept. 1989). If a state supplies counsel to capital petitioners in state postconviction proceedings, the committee recommended that stays of execution should be automatic (in order to eliminate unseemly midnight deliberations), that prisoners should be required to file their federal petitions within a fixed time period, that the federal courts should not ordinarily entertain claims that were not properly raised in state court, and that second or successive petitions from the same prisoner should usually be dismissed and should never be accepted in the absence of a claim going to the prisoner's guilt of the offense for which the death penalty was imposed. The Conference adopted two amendments. In place of the committee's proposal that the states be invited to provide counsel in postconviction proceedings in exchange for procedural advantages in federal court, the Conference substituted a recommendation that all death penalty states should be required to appoint qualified counsel at all stages of state proceedings. In addition, the Conference rejected the committee's proposal to restrict successive petitions to claims going to prisoners' guilt and substituted a recommendation allowing for claims going to the appropriateness of a death sentence. See Administrative Office of United States Courts, News Release (March 14, 1990).

49. American Bar Association, Criminal Justice Section, "Report to the House of Delegates," 40 *Am. U. L. Rev.* 9 (1991).

50. On this Court's criminal cases, see Peter Arenella, "Rethinking the Functions of Criminal Procedure: The Warren and Burger Courts' Competing Ideologies," 72 *Geo. L.J.* 185 (1983).

51. Sumner v. Mata, 449 U. S. 539, 543–544 (1981). See also Snead v. Stringer, 454 U. S. 988, 993–994 (1981) (Rehnquist, J., dissenting) (observing

that "[i]t is scarcely surprising that fewer and fewer capable lawyers can be found to serve on state benches when they may find their considered decisions overturned by the ruling of a single federal district judge on grounds as tenuous as these").

52. E.g., Spalding v. Aiken, 460 U. S. 1093, 1093–94 (1983) (statement of Burger, C.J.) (complaining that federal habeas permits prisoners to press "stale claims" that have been "fully ventilated in state court"); Braden v. 30th Judicial Circuit Court, 410 U. S. 484, 501 (1973) (Blackmun, J., concurring) (complaining that the "common-law scholars of the past hardly would recognize" the modern writ); Barefoot v. Estelle, 463 U. S. 880, 887 (1983) (opinion of White, J.) (insisting that the federal habeas jurisdiction is "secondary and limited" and that the federal district courts are not "forums in which to relitigate state trials"); Engle v. Isaac, 456 U. S. 107, 126–128 (1982) (opinion of O'Connor, J.) (insisting that habeas corpus "degrades the prominence of the trial itself" and frustrates "both the States' sovereign power to punish offenders and their good-faith attempts to honor constitutional rights").

53. H.R. Rep. No. 1471, 94th Cong., 2d Sess. (1976). The rules are codified at 28 U.S.C. §2254 foll.

54. For the Nixon plan, see S. 567, 93d Cong., 1st Sess. (1973). See also Richard G. Kleindienst, Attorney General of the United States, to Emanuel Celler, Chair, House Judiciary Committee (Jan. 21, 1973), quoted in 119 *Cong. Rec.* S1307 (Jan. 26, 1973) (explaining that the bill would limit claims to those going to the reliability of the fact-finding and appellate processes). For the Reagan program, see *Hearings on S. 2216 before the Senate Committee on the Judiciary,* 97th Cong., 2d Sess. (1982). See also Larry W. Yackle, "The Reagan Administration's Habeas Corpus Proposals," 68 *Iowa L. Rev.* 609, 612–613 (1983). The Reagan plan was severed from the President's crime package in the 98th Congress, S. 829, 98th Cong., 1st Sess. (1983), reported out of committee as S. 1763, and passed by the full body. 130 *Cong. Rec.* S1854–72 (Feb. 6, 1984). The House failed to act on it.

55. For the Bush Administration bill, see H. R. 2709, 101st Cong., 2d Sess. (1989). For a defense of it, see *Hearings on H. R. 4737 before the Subcommittee on Courts, Intellectual Property, and the Administration of Justice of the Committee on the Judiciary,* 101st Cong., 2d Sess. 279–320 (1990) (Maloney testimony). A Republican substitute for H. R. 4737, offered in the House Judiciary Committee in the summer of 1990, also reproduced the same program—as did yet another bill introduced by Senator Thurmond. S. 88, 101st Cong., 1st Sess. (1989). All pending bills reflecting the Reagan-Bush scheme died at the end of the 101st Congress. Bills embracing the same proposals were introduced in the 102d Congress. S. 635, 102d Cong., 1st Sess. (1991); H. R. 1400, 102d Cong., 1st Sess. (1991). The program was adopted by the Senate, but rejected in the House in favor of an alternative plan advanced by Rep. Don Edwards. A conference committee formed to reconcile the Senate and House bills adopted the Edwards program, and the House again approved it. 137 *Cong. Rec.* H11756 (Nov. 26, 1991). In the Senate, by contrast, a Republican filibuster prevented further action on the

bill. 137 *Cong. Rec.* S18615–16 (Nov. 27, 1991); 138 *Cong. Rec.* S3926–44 (March 19, 1992); 138 *Cong. Rec.* S16226–303 (Oct. 2, 1992) (reporting unsuccessful cloture votes).

56. See generally Yackle, *Remedies,* supra note 9, at 90–92 (cataloguing criticisms and attempts to curb habeas corpus by judicial decision or new legislation). It may be argued that the tenant farmer case itself actually fit McReynolds' model. A mob-dominated trial may be no trial at all, so that the "court" in such a case is without jurisdiction. Justice Holmes himself apparently took that view. Cf. Frank v. Mangum, 237 U. S. 309, 348 (1915) (dissenting opinion). See "Developments," supra note 19, at 1054 n.82; cf. Paul M. Bator & Daniel J. Meltzer et al., *Hart and Wechsler's The Federal Courts and the Federal System* 1500 (3d ed. 1988). During the New Deal period, the Court engaged the fiction that a state court *did* act without jurisdiction whenever it committed constitutional error. But in the early 1940s, the Court held flatly that habeas was available to raise constitutional claims, irrespective of any flaws in state proceedings that could be said to be "jurisdictional." Waley v. Johnston, 316 U. S. 101 (1942).

57. People v. Defore, 242 N. Y. 13, 21, 150 N. E. 585, 587 (1926).

58. On the establishment of the exclusionary rule, see Mapp v. Ohio, 367 U. S. 643 (1961). On this Court's position, see United States v. Peltier, 422 U. S. 531 (1975).

59. Stone v. Powell, 428 U. S. 465, 481–482 (1976).

60. E.g., Castaneda v. Partida, 430 U. S. 482, 508 n.1 (1977) (Powell, J., dissenting) (suggesting the applicability of *Stone* in a race discrimination case); Brewer v. Williams, 430 U. S. 387, 422 (1977) (Burger, C. J., dissenting) (arguing that *Stone* should control in a sixth amendment case); Withrow v. Williams, 113 S.Ct. 1745, 1765 (1993) (Scalia, J., concurring & dissenting) (joined by Thomas, J.) (arguing that a federal court should invoke "equitable discretion" to deny habeas relief on the basis of any claim a prisoner had a "prior opportunity to litigate" in state court—unless the claim "goes to the fairness of the trial process or to the accuracy of the ultimate result").

61. Allen v. McCurry, 449 U. S. 90, 98 (1980); accord Kimmelman v. Morrison, 477 U. S. 365 (1986); Yackle, "Reagan," supra note 54, at 623–628; Philip M. Halpern, "Federal Habeas Corpus and the *Mapp* Exclusionary Rule after *Stone v. Powell,*" 82 *Colum. L. Rev.* 1 (1982). See Rose v. Mitchell, 443 U. S. 545 (1979) (squarely rejecting an analogy to *Stone* in a race-discrimination case); Withrow v. Williams, 113 S.Ct. 1745 (1993) (rejecting the same analogy in a *"Miranda"* claim case). But see id. at 1756 (O'Connor, J., concurring & dissenting) (joined by Rehnquist, C.J.) (contending that *"Miranda"* claims *are* analogous).

62. Townsend v. Sain, 372 U. S. 293, 313 (1963) (opinion of Warren, C.J.). For the "vital flaw" rule, see Brown v. Allen, 344 U. S. 443, 506 (1953) (opinion of Frankfurter, J.).

63. For an elaboration, see Yackle, *Remedies,* supra note 9, at §133.

64. Brown v. Allen, 344 U. S. 443, 506–507 (1953) (opinion of Frankfurter, J.).

65. Henry P. Monaghan, "Constitutional Fact Review," 85 *Colum. L. Rev.* 229, 235 (1985).

66. Chapter Three, the text accompanying note 39; see the text accompanying notes 62–63 supra.

67. See Yackle, *Remedies,* supra note 9, at §133.

68. This, of course, follows from Brown v. Allen, 344 U. S. 443, 458 (1953), which §2254(d) does not change, but incorporates. See Charles D. Weisselberg, "Evidentiary Hearings in Federal Habeas Corpus," 1990 *B.Y.U. L. Rev.* 131, 156.

69. Townsend v. Sain, 372 U. S. 293, 309 n.6 (1963).

70. See Miller v. Fenton, 474 U. S. 104 (1985).

71. Brown v. Allen, 344 U. S. 443, 500, 507–508 (1953) (opinion of Frankfurter, J.).

72. E.g., Sumner v. Mata, 455 U. S. 591, 597 (1982).

73. Miller v. Fenton, 474 U. S. 104 (1985) (voluntariness); Cuyler v. Sullivan, 446 U. S. 335 (1980) (effectiveness); Patton v. Yount, 467 U. S. 1025 (1984) (partiality); Wainwright v. Witt, 469 U. S. 412 (1985) (bias); Maggio v. Fulford, 462 U. S. 111 (1983) (competency).

74. Miller v. Fenton, 474 U. S. 104 (1985).

75. Wright v. West, 112 S.Ct. 672 (1991). Without opinion, Justices Blackmun and Stevens noted their dissent from the Court's special order.

76. Brief for the Respondent in Wright v. West, 112 S.Ct. 2482 (1992). See also Brief Amicus Curiae on Behalf of the American Bar Association; Brief Amicus Curiae on Behalf of the American Civil Liberties Union; Brief Amicus Curiae on Behalf of Benjamin R. Civiletti, Nicholas Katzenbach, Edward H. Levi, Elliot L. Richardson, et al.; Brief Amicus Curiae on Behalf of Gerald Gunther, Philip B. Kurland, Daniel J. Meltzer, Paul J. Mishkin, Martin H. Redish, Frank J. Remington, David L. Shapiro & Herbert Wechsler. Readers should know that I consulted on all these briefs and served as counsel of record for the last.

77. Brief for the United States in Wright v. West, 112 S.Ct. 2482 (1992).

78. Cf. Weisselberg, "Hearings," supra note 68.

79. Critics' contention that the full-and-fair program amounts to such an extension of *Stone v. Powell* emphasizes the process-model doctrine the Court established for handling fourth amendment claims, namely, that the federal courts must decline to consider such claims unless the state courts fail to provide an opportunity for "full and fair" adjudication, rather than the theoretical basis that has now been identified for the decision—an elaboration of the fourth amendment exclusionary rule itself. See notes 59–61 and the accompanying text supra. No one suggests that the full-and-fair plan means to revise the content of all federal rights, rendering them by nature inapplicable in habeas corpus. Rather, critics point out that by barring federal relief on the basis of claims that were "fully and fairly" adjudicated in state court, the plan would amend the Habeas Corpus Act in a way that forecloses all claims in general in the same, practical way that *Stone* now forecloses exclusionary rule claims.

80. In cases in which prisoners are found to have passed up "opportunities" to litigate federal claims in state court, however, Supreme Court decisions already

typically foreclose federal consideration of the merits. See notes 177–186 and the accompanying text infra.

81. S. Rep. No. 98–226, 98th Cong., 1st Sess. 25 (1983). See *Hearings on S. 2216,* supra note 54, at 16 (Rose testimony).

82. Id. In a clarifying amendment in 1991, Rep. Henry Hyde proposed that state adjudication would not be entitled to respect if the state proceedings were "conducted in a manner inconsistent with the procedural requirements of Federal law," if the state judgment "involved an arbitrary or unreasonable determination of the facts," or if the outcome in state court was "contrary to or involved an arbitrary or unreasonable interpretation or application of clearly established Federal law." 137 *Cong. Rec.* H7996 (Oct. 17, 1991).

83. The Hyde amendment's references to "arbitrary" state judgments that conflict with "clearly established" federal law suggested an extremely high tolerance threshold. No surprise, then, that when Hyde offered these refinements to reassure his colleagues, he failed to bring the House round to his side. Rep. Hamilton Fish, the ranking minority member of the Judiciary Committee, answered that Hyde's proposed definition of "full and fair" adjudication made it clearer than ever that the adoption of the full-and-fair program very well *would* mean the end of habeas corpus for state convicts. 137 *Cong. Rec.* H8001 (Oct. 17, 1991).

84. Chapter One, the text accompanying notes 31–33. See James S. Liebman, "More Than Slightly Retro: The Rehnquist Court's Rout of Habeas Corpus Jurisdiction in *Teague v. Lane,*" 18 *N.Y.U. Rev. L. & Soc. Change* 537, 544 (1991).

85. In fairness, I should say that the Department of Justice under Reagan and Bush resisted this assessment. E. g., *The Administration's Proposed Reforms in Habeas Corpus Procedures* (1982).

86. ALI Remarks, supra note 47 (explicitly referring to Senator Thurmond's version of the full-and-fair proposal). See Remarks of Justice O'Connor, The Attorney General's Crime Summit, Washington, D. C. (March 4, 1991). The Conference of (State) Chief Justices endorsed the plan. "Resolution XVI" (Aug. 8, 1991).

87. ALI Remarks, supra note 47.

88. Id.

89. The same organizations of state's attorneys that have typically supported the full-and-fair plan have also contended that the availability of the federal writ frustrates implementation of the death penalty and, in this vein, have resisted proposals to overrule the Court's decisions on "new rules" in habeas corpus— next to be discussed in the text. E. g., National Association of Attorneys General, Criminal Law Committee, *Substitute Resolution Opposing Federal Habeas Corpus Reform Legislation That Undermines Finality and Promotes Delay and Relitigation* (June 23–26, 1991).

90. Teague v. Lane, 489 U. S. 288 (1989).

91. E.g., Graham Hughes, *The Decline of Habeas Corpus* 10–14 (1990); Susan Bandes, "Taking Justice to Its Logical Extreme: A Comment on Teague v. Lane," 66 *So. Calif. L. Rev.* 2453 (1993); Liebman, "Slightly Retro," supra note 84; Vivian O. Berger, "Justice Delayed or Justice Denied—A Comment on Recent

Proposals to Reform Death Penalty Habeas Corpus," 90 *Colum. L. Rev.* 1665, 1701–02 (1990); Joseph L. Hoffmann, "The Supreme Court's New Vision of Federal Habeas Corpus for State Prisoners," 1989 *Sup. Ct. Rev.* 165. But see Patrick E. Higginbotham, "Notes on *Teague*," 66 *So. Calif. L. Rev.* 2433 (1993) (defending the Court's work).

92. Chapter One, the text accompanying note 18.

93. See generally Linkletter v. Walker, 381 U. S. 618, 622–629 (1965). Cf. note 99 infra (discussing Justice Scalia's attempt to revive Formalist fictions regarding law—outside the context of habeas corpus).

94. Desist v. United States, 394 U. S. 244, 248 (1969). For the argument that the possibility of "prospective overruling" under *Linkletter* made it "easier to overrule prior precedents," see Harper v. Virginia Dep't of Taxation, 113 S.Ct. 2510, 2522 (1993) (Scalia, J., concurring).

95. Stovall v. Denno, 388 U. S. 293 (1967).

96. Linkletter v. Walker, 381 U. S. 618 (1965); Johnson v. New Jersey, 384 U. S. 719 (1966); Pickelsimer v. Wainwright, 375 U. S. 2 (1963). There were hitches in the Warren Court's framework. Litigants whose circumstances were difficult to distinguish were sometimes treated differently, depending on whether they were fortunate enough to get to the Supreme Court ahead of others. In addition, the past event that counted for retroactivity purposes varied with the claim: the date of an unlawful search in exclusionary rule cases, the date of trial in right-to-counsel cases, etc. These subtleties have been superseded in the Court's more recent decisions and need not detain us.

97. Desist v. United States, 394 U. S. 244, 258–259 (1969) (dissenting opinion).

98. Mackey v. United States, 401 U. S. 667, 692–693 (1971) (Harlan, J., concurring in the judgment), quoting Palko v. Connecticut, 302 U. S. 319, 325 (1937). As an illustration of the first of these exceptions, Harlan offered a "new rule" declaring that the very behavior that a state statute condemned as criminal was constitutionally protected. As an illustration of the second exception, he offered a "new rule" announcing a "bedrock procedural" element necessary to a fair conviction—e.g., the rule announcing the right to counsel at felony trials.

99. Griffith v. Kentucky, 479 U. S. 314 (1987) (direct review in criminal cases); Harper v. Virginia Dep't of Taxation, 113 S.Ct. 2510 (1993) (direct review in civil cases); Teague v. Lane, 489 U. S. 288 (1989) (habeas corpus cases). But see *Harper* at 2524 (Kennedy, J., concurring in the judgment) (indicating that "it is sometimes appropriate" to give civil decisions only prospective effect); id. at 2526 (O'Connor, J., dissenting) (defending a more ad hoc approach in civil cases). It is defensible (but I will argue misguided) to treat habeas corpus cases differently as a class—on Harlan's theory that the purpose of habeas is only to deter state authorities from flagrantly violating federal rights. It must be said, however, that Justice Scalia's rhetoric in the two kinds of cases (direct review cases and cases arising in habeas corpus) is oddly schizophrenic.

When cases reach the Supreme Court on direct review, Scalia has it that the Court's duty is to reach an accurate determination of federal law. He acknowledges that that function often requires the justices to "make" law, but (here following the Old Court's Formalists) Scalia insists they do it *"as though"* they don't and instead as though they only search for it and "find" it as it *"is"* and evidently always was. See Chapter One, the text accompanying notes 18–20. It follows, by Scalia's account, that in direct review cases the Court never announces "new rules" of law about which any question of retroactive effect can arise. For this reason, whatever the Court decides in a given case necessarily holds as well for others—past, present, and future. James B. Beam Distilling Co. v. Georgia, 111 S.Ct. 2439, 2451 (1991) (Scalia, J., concurring in the judgment).

When cases reach a federal district court in habeas corpus, by contrast, Justice Scalia (now following Harlan) has it that the court's function is merely to deter egregious state court violations of federal rights. To Harlan himself, the writ's limited function was best served by holding the state courts only to the federal legal standards existing at the time they acted. Of course, that approach recognizes that legal rules do change. One might have thought that Scalia's commitment to the fixed, Formalist understanding of constitutional law would prevent him from going along. Surprisingly, however, he does go along—with reckless abandon. Indeed, in habeas corpus cases Scalia concludes that virtually everything a district court may decide is "new" (here following the most radical of the Legal Realists). E. g., Penry v. Lynaugh, 492 U. S. 302, 350 (1989) (Scalia, J., dissenting).

One need not puzzle long over the way Justice Scalia's erratic behavior serves his conservative agenda. In direct review cases, he hopes that by insisting that *nothing* is "new" (and thus that *everything* applies retroactively) he can discourage judicial "activism." For if the other justices know that if they depart from previous interpretations in order to reach the best result in a case (and future cases like it) they must pay the price of upsetting judgments in other cases already settled, they will have an incentive to hold back. *James B. Beam* at 2451 (Scalia, J., concurring in the judgment); accord *Harper* at 2520 (Scalia, J., concurring). In habeas corpus, by contrast, he hopes that by insisting that almost *everything* is "new" (and thus that almost *nothing* applies retroactively) he can largely eliminate the federal courts' jurisdiction by indirection. See generally notes 116–123 and the accompanying text infra.

100. Teague v. Lane, 489 U. S. 288, 313 (1989). Cf. Butler v. McKellar, 494 U. S. 407, 417 (1990) (Brennan, J., dissenting).

101. Desist v. United States, 394 U. S. 244, 263 (1969) (dissenting opinion).

102. Teague v. Lane, 489 U. S. 288, 301 (1989).

103. Liebman, "Slightly Retro," supra note 84, at 578–579.

104. Sawyer v. Smith, 497 U. S. 227, 234 (1990).

105. Butler v. McKellar, 494 U. S. 407, 417 (1990) (Brennan, J., dissenting).

106. See Robin West, "The Supreme Court, 1989 Term—Foreword: Taking Freedom Seriously," 104 *Harv. L. Rev.* 43, 57 (1990).

107. Teague v. Lane, 489 U. S. 288, 301 (1989) (emphasis in original).

108. This, of course, is the vital difference between questions that are purely legal (or changes in the content of a legal principle) and mixed questions (or

differences of opinion regarding the result that the application of an unchanged legal principle should generate in a particular instance).

109. Sawyer v. Smith, 497 U. S. 227, 234 (1990).

110. Butler v. McKellar, 494 U. S. 407, 415 (1990).

111. In this situation, the prisoner is said to be asking the federal district court itself to announce and apply a "new rule," as defined in *Teague, Butler, Sawyer,* and similar decisions. E. g., Saffle v. Parks, 494 U. S. 484 (1990).

112. Stringer v. Black, 112 S.Ct. 1130, 1132 (1992), quoting Butler v. McKellar, 494 U. S. 407, 414 (1990).

113. See the text accompanying note 75 supra.

114. Brief for the Respondent, supra note 76, at 44–49.

115. Brief for the Petitioner in Wright v. West, 112 S.Ct. 2482 (1992), at 14–22; Brief for the United States, supra note 77, at 7–8.

116. Wright v. West, 112 S.Ct. 2482 (1992) (opinion of Thomas, J.) (joined by Rehnquist, C. J. & Scalia, J.). Justice Thomas insists that "if a state court has reasonably rejected the legal claim asserted by a habeas petitioner under existing law," the claim "seeks the benefit of a new rule." Id. at 2490, quoting Butler v. McKellar, 494 U. S. 407, 415 (1990). In his mind, this does indeed mean that a federal court "must defer to the state court's decision rejecting the claim unless that decision is patently unreasonable." *West* at 2490, quoting *Butler* at 422 (Brennan, J., dissenting). Responding to Justice O'Connor's argument that the federal courts must still determine whether the state courts decided prisoners' claims "properly" under the precedents then in existence, Thomas contends that, by definition, any "reasonable" state judgment based on old precedents must be accepted—because a federal court would have to establish a "new rule" in order to come out differently. *West* at 2490 n. 8. In his view, it is enough if the federal courts retain authority to decide "independently" whether the state courts reached such a "reasonable" judgment. Id. at 2488 n. 5. For a trenchant criticism of Justice Thomas' opinion in *West,* see Liebman, "Apocalypse," supra note 18.

For all practical purposes, I am afraid, Justice White must also be counted in this camp. While he expressed doubts about the Court's new analysis in *Teague* itself—see 489 U. S. at 317 (concurring opinion)—and while he was thunderously silent in *West,* 112 S.Ct. at 2493 (concurring opinion), White consistently joined majority opinions finding "new rules" in subsequent cases. His own opinion for the Court in Graham v. Collins, 113 S.Ct. 892 (1993), was couched as though he continued to understand *Teague* and its progeny to be addressed to changes in the law. Still, his bloodless reliance on *Butler* for the definition of what counts as a "new rule" revealed that Justice White was content with the practical implications everywhere apparent. He read the opinions filed by the other justices (and *amicus* briefs sounding the alarm); he knew perfectly well what he was doing.

117. Wright v. West, 112 S.Ct. 2482, 2497 (1992) (O'Connor, J., concurring in the judgment) (joined by Blackmun & Stevens, J.J.) (emphasis supplied); id. at 2495 (insisting that the federal courts continue to adjudicate prisoners' claims in light of the legal standards in place when the state courts acted "without any hint

of deference to the state courts"). To determine whether a state decision *was* correct at the time, according to Justice O'Connor, a federal court must undertake an "independent evaluation" of the precedents in place at that time. Much "time and effort" may be spent "scrutinizing" the relevant body of "federal law." The standard for this evaluation is "objective." The existence of conflicting authorities is not conclusive. Nor is it decisive that previous opinions have characterized a case as either establishing a "new rule" or simply applying a settled legal standard to different facts. Id. at 2497. I take all this only to acknowledge that courts and judges, members of the Supreme Court included, sometimes make mistakes about an existing rule of law. And a federal habeas court does not ineluctably create "new" law for *Teague* purposes when it later identifies and applies the correct, settled standard. Moreover, courts and judges typically insist that the results they reach are supported by precedent, the better to parry dissenters who typically argue that "new" law is being forged. It would be unrealistic to attach decisive import to such characterizations when they probably reflect disagreement about whether a legal standard is substantively sound rather than about whether, whatever its strengths or weaknesses, it is "new." See, e.g., Graham v. Collins, 113 S.Ct. 892, 903 (1993) (Thomas, J., concurring) (insisting that *Penry* was not only "new" law, but bad law as well). Surely what other judges have said about a legal standard is only evidence to be considered by the court charged to make its own, independent judgment on a "new rule" question. See Butler v. McKellar, 494 U. S. 407, 415 (1990) (concluding that a rule was "new" despite previous statements suggesting it was not); cf. Forsyth County v. Nationalist Movement, 112 S.Ct. 2395, 2406 (1992) (Rehnquist, C. J., dissenting) (pointing out that "a mistaken allusion in a later case to the facts of an earlier case does not by itself undermine the holding of the earlier case").

118. Wright v. West, 112 S.Ct. 2482, 2498 (1992) (Kennedy, J., concurring in the judgment) (emphasis supplied). Justice Kennedy has also said that the procedural obstacles the Court has placed in the way of habeas petitioners stop short of abridging the federal courts' authority to determine the merits. E. g., Coleman v. Thompson, 111 S.Ct. 2546 (1991) (elaborating the forfeiture standards for procedural default in state court); McCleskey v. Zant, 111 S.Ct. 1454 (1991) (applying those standards in cases in which prisoners file multiple federal petitions). See notes 177–195 infra. If a petitioner successfully clears the barriers that cases like *McCleskey* and *Coleman* establish and thus presents a federal district court with a claim "in a proper procedural manner," Justice Kennedy is content that the federal court can adjudicate "all dispositive constitutional claims." *McCleskey* at 1462. In a like manner, Justice Kennedy suggests that *Teague* constitutes a threshold condition for merits adjudication in federal habeas and does not limit the ability of the federal courts to enforce the proper legal standard in any case. A claim that can succeed only if the federal habeas courts bring to bear a "new rule" of law is simply not properly presented for decision on the merits. Claims that depend only on previously established legal standards *are* properly presented, however, and may be adjudicated in the ordinary course.

Justice O'Connor joined this chorus in Keeney v. Tamayo-Reyes, 112 S.Ct.

1715, 1721 (1992) (O'Connor, J., dissenting), and, importantly, managed to line up three others behind her—Justices Blackmun, Stevens, and Kennedy. Initially, O'Connor identified *Teague,* together with *McCleskey* and *Coleman,* as "hurdles" that habeas petitioners must negotiate in order to present a claim for consideration on the merits. Next, she explained: "Once [*McCleskey, Coleman, Teague,* and other threshold obstacles] have been surmounted—once the claim is properly before the district court—a habeas petitioner, like any civil litigant, has . . . a right to a hearing where one is necessary to prove the facts supporting his claim." *Tamayo-Reyes* at 1722 (dissenting opinion).

In his own separate opinion in *Tamayo-Reyes,* Justice Kennedy seemed to go along: "Our recent decisions in [*Coleman, McCleskey,* and *Teague*] . . . protect the integrity of the writ, curbing its abuse and insuring that the legal questions presented are ones which, if resolved against the State, can invalidate a final judgment. So we consider today only those habeas actions which present questions federal courts are bound to decide in order to protect constitutional rights." Id. at 1727–28.

It may be pressing the point a bit, but even Justice White's majority opinion in *Tamayo-Reyes* was at least arguably open to the notion that *Teague,* like the procedural bar cases, is merely a door-keeping device that identifies claims for consideration on the merits. In critical part, Justice O'Connor's dissent drew a distinction between rules for determining when a claim is properly before a federal court for decision on the merits (regarding which forfeitures are legitimate) and rules for determining the manner in which a federal court actually determines the merits (regarding which, in O'Connor's view, forfeitures are impermissible). Justice O'Connor put the rule at stake in *Tamayo-Reyes* (touching the establishment of primary facts in state court) in the second category. Justice White did not reject Justice O'Connor's distinction between the two kinds of rules. Indeed, he seemed to concede that *Coleman, McCleskey,* and *Teague* are "precondition[s] to reaching the merits." Id. at 1719 n.3 (majority opinion). Arguably at least, White disagreed with O'Connor only in that, in his opinion, rules governing procedural default with respect to the development of primary facts fall in the same category as procedural bar rules—and not (where Justice O'Connor would put them) in the (forbidden) category of rules that undermine the federal courts' jurisdiction to determine properly presented claims independently. Cf. Collins v. Youngblood, 497 U. S. 37, 40–41 (1990) (holding that an argument that *Teague* bars a claim in habeas corpus will not be noticed by the Court itself and must be raised by the respondent—as is the case with procedural bar rules). Accord Parke v. Raley, 113 S.Ct. 517, 521 (1992) (reaching the merits in a case in which the respondent had not argued that the prisoner was relying on a "new rule" of law).

Finally, it is worth recalling that, under *Teague,* a federal district court must determine the novelty of the legal standard on which a claim rests as the first order of business and can actually decide whether the claim has merit only if the legal standard is deemed to be sufficiently settled or the claim fits within one of *Teague*'s narrow exceptions to the general ban on retroactive application. That also arguably indicates that *Teague* is a "threshold question" and does not undermine a federal habeas court's subject matter jurisdiction to adjudicate properly presented claims on the merits. See Wright v. West, 112 S.Ct. 2482, 2500 (1992) (Souter, J., concurring in the judgment).

119. Justice Souter explicitly disavows any thought that, in order to defeat a "new rule" argument in habeas, a petitioner "must be able to point to an old case decided on facts identical to the facts of his own." Wright v. West, 112 S.Ct. 2482, 2502 (1992) (concurring opinion); accord Graham v. Collins, 113 S.Ct. 892, 917 (1993) (dissenting opinion). Moreover, speaking generally of retroactivity law (in the civil context), he has confirmed that "[i]t is only when law changes in some respect that an assertion of nonretroactivity may be entertained." James B. Beam Distilling Co. v. Georgia, 111 S.Ct. 2439, 2443 (1991). Thus in "ordinary" cases, in which courts are "in the business of applying settled principles and precedents of law to the disputes that come to bar," it follows that "no question of retroactivity arises." Id. at 2442. Still, Justice Souter finds "new rules" where even Justices O'Connor and Kennedy would not think to look. E. g., Stringer v. Black, 112 S.Ct. 1130, 1140 (1992) (Souter, J., dissenting); West at 2500 (concurring opinion). Accordingly, his case-by-case record, too, is less than reassuring.

I must say that it is scarcely insightful to point out, as Souter does, that everything turns on the level of generality in which a rule is stated. That, of course, is self-evident. If a prisoner were permitted to articulate the rule of law on which he bases his pursuit of federal relief in the most open-ended manner, e.g., a denial of fair process, then no case would call for the announcement of a "new rule." The problem we face in these cases is that the Court insists on articulating legal rules in extremely narrow, case-specific terms. That, in turn, transmutes factual distinctions between cases seemingly governed by the same settled legal standard into variations of the standard itself. Each such variation begets an entirely different rule, and the sum total of such "new rules" fills up the universe of the possible cases that can reach the federal courts in habeas corpus. For a more thorough examination of the views expressed by Justices O'Connor, Kennedy, and Souter, see Yackle, "Hagioscope," supra note 8.

Finally, I am reminded of Justice Scalia's contention that when, in substantive due process cases, the Court derives the content of protected liberty from American cultural history, it should confine its search for sources to the most specific level at which a relevant tradition can be said to exist. E. g., Michael H. v. Gerald D., 491 U. S. 110, 127–128 n.6 (1989). That argument has the purpose and effect of preventing the Court from taking account of overarching societal values (expressed in understandings articulated at a higher level of generality) and, instead, focusing the Court's attention on fact-centered applications of abstract ideas. The practical result, of course, is to defeat individual claims of right. The lower the level of generality at which a societal tradition (or a legal standard) must be identified, the less likely it is that any such tradition (or legal standard) will be found. Fortunately, Justice Scalia's approach to substantive due process cases has been rejected. Planned Parenthood v. Casey, 112 S.Ct. 2791, 2805 (1992) (joint opinion of O'Connor, Kennedy & Souter, J.J.) (stating that Scalia's position is "inconsistent with our law").

120. E.g., Richmond v. Lewis, 113 S.Ct. 528 (1992); Stringer v. Black, 112 S.Ct. 1130 (1992); Estelle v. McGuire, 112 S.Ct. 475 (1991); Lewis v. Jeffers, 497 U. S. 764 (1990). But see *Richmond* at 537 (Thomas, J., concurring) (insisting that the claims in both *Richmond* and *Stringer* depended on "new rules" and therefore should not have been considered on the merits). See generally Liebman, "Slightly Retro," supra note 84, at 588–593.

121. The dispositions in Graham v. Collins, 113 S.Ct. 892 (1993), and Gilmore v. Taylor, 113 S.Ct. 2112 (1993), illustrate this point. The prisoner in *Graham* attacked the Texas death penalty statute on grounds almost identical to the grounds asserted previously by the petitioner in Penry v. Lynaugh, 492 U. S. 302 (1989). In *Penry,* the Court had squarely held that the claim did not depend on a "new rule" of eighth amendment law and thus was not foreclosed by *Teague.* Accordingly, the parties in *Graham* set any retroactivity argument to one side and briefed only the merits. In the Supreme Court, however, a five-member majority opinion by Justice White switched to *Teague* anyway, distinguished *Penry* on its facts, and found the prisoner's claim *Teague*-barred. Similarly in *Gilmore,* the Court concluded that in the circumstances of the case at bar, the petitioner could succeed only by establishing a "new rule"—and thus refused to consider his claim in habeas corpus. The implications of this incremental evisceration of habeas could scarcely be more sobering. Readers should know that I prepared an *amicus curiae* brief on behalf of the American Civil Liberties Union in *Gilmore*—and contributed ideas and language originally developed for this chapter and a related article, Yackle, "Hagioscope," supra note 8, to that brief and another *amicus* brief filed in *Gilmore* by George H. Kendall and George N. Leighton on behalf of Nicholas Katzenbach, Edward H. Levi, and forty-three other individuals.

122. Wright v. West, 112 S.Ct. 2482, 2497 (1992) (O'Connor, J., concurring in the judgment).

123. Id. at 2499 (Kennedy, J., concurring in the judgment), quoting Stringer v. Black, 112 S.Ct. 1130, 1135 (1992). Justice Kennedy occasionally offers some hope. He acknowledges, for example, that some rules are by their nature general—meant to guide judgment in the examination of primary facts in a variety of patterns. Rules of that kind, he explains, infrequently yield results so novel as to forge a "new rule" of law, i. e., "one not dictated by precedent." Id. Nevertheless, Kennedy's formulations, too, are sufficiently fact-sensitive that they draw into question the conventional scope of the federal courts' authority to determine the merits of federal claims in habeas. In Graham v. Collins, 113 U. S. 892 (1993), for example, he gave Justice White the fifth vote necessary to hold that a petitioner's claim rested on a "new rule," notwithstanding that the Court had previously held, in Penry v. Lynaugh, 492 U. S. 302 (1989), that virtually the same claim could rest on preexisting decisions. Of course, both Kennedy and White had joined Justice Scalia's dissent on the "new rule" issue in *Penry.* Accordingly, we might have expected that if *Graham,* too, was to be recast as a "new rule" case, Justice Kennedy would vote to bar the prisoner's claim from habeas corpus. In the end, though, Justice White's majority opinion was loaded with boilerplate regarding "new" rules from Butler v. McKellar, 494 U. S. 407 (1990), and from Justice

Kennedy's own opinions for the Court in Saffle v. Parks, 494 U. S. 484 (1990), and Sawyer v. Smith, 497 U. S. 227 (1990). Kennedy's more recent (and more moderate) formulations in Wright v. West, 112 S.Ct. 2482 (1992), showed up only in Justice Souter's dissent in *Graham.*

In this vein, Justice Kennedy's generalizations for the Court in *Stringer* are unnerving. In that case, he said that "new rule" cases present not one question, but two. In a case in which a prisoner "seeks federal habeas relief based upon a principle announced after a final judgment," the district court must decide, first, whether "the decision relied upon announced a new rule." If so, the claim is barred, unless the case falls within one of *Teague's* exceptions. If not, the court must turn to a second question: "whether granting the relief sought would create a new rule because the prior decision is applied in a novel setting, thereby extending the precedent." Id. at 1135. If Justice Kennedy genuinely conceives of this second "application" question as qualitatively separate, rather than merely a more fact-sensitive version of his first question, the practical implications may be significant. Prisoners now contend that their claims rest on settled rules and that, to invoke *Teague,* state's attorneys must demonstrate that they are trying to apply such an established rule so far out of its bailiwick as to alter its substantive content. Justice Kennedy's discussion in *Stringer* threatens to change the terms of the debate by permitting state's attorneys to concede that a prisoner is relying on an unchanged substantive legal standard and *still* to argue that a fact-focused application of that rule is *Teague*-barred.

124. Chapman v. California, 386 U. S. 18, 24 (1967). See generally Tom Stacy & Kim Dayton, "Rethinking Harmless Constitutional Error," 79 *Colum. L. Rev.* 79 (1989).

125. E.g., Rose v. Clark, 478 U. S. 570 (1986).

126. Brecht v. Abrahamson, 113 S.Ct. 1710, 1714 (1993), quoting Kotteakos v. United States, 328 U. S. 750, 776 (1946).

127. Brecht v. Abrahamson, 113 S.Ct. 1710, 1722 (1993), quoting United States v. Lane, 474 U. S. 438, 449 (1986).

128. See the text accompanying note 75 supra.

129. Something of this sort is already done with respect to the "prejudice" prong of the test for ineffective assistance of counsel, e.g., Strickland v. Washington, 466 U. S. 668 (1984); and it should surprise no one if *Brecht* produces essentially the same effect across the board with respect to all claimed errors at trial. Still, a distinction might be drawn between backing into a case in this way when some showing of an effect on outcome is an element of the substantive claim (as is the case with the "prejudice" requirement in ineffective assistance cases) and doing so when the effect is to avoid the merits altogether. It seems to me that either approach abdicates the subject matter jurisdiction that Congress has conferred, but the latter does so more vividly than the former.

130. See the text accompanying note 19 supra.

131. Brecht v. Abrahamson, 113 S.Ct. 1710, 1717–18 (1993). The Chief Justice concedes that during the Nixon Administration, Congress considered, but failed to enact, legislation that would have relaxed the standard for harmless error in

habeas along the lines now accomplished in *Brecht*. For a discussion of that legislative history, see Yackle, "Hagioscope," supra note 8.

132. There may be some gaps in what Chief Justice Rehnquist has wrought. He leaves undisturbed the Court's longstanding view that some "structural defects" in criminal trials cannot *be* harmless on any standard, either on direct review or in habeas corpus. Brecht v. Abrahamson, 113 S.Ct. 1710, 1717 (1993), quoting Arizona v. Fulminante, 111 S.Ct. 1246, 1264–65 (1991) (opinion of Rehnquist, C.J.). Moreover, he does not "foreclose" the possibility that in an "unusual" case, even a trial error might justify habeas relief without a finding of a substantial effect on the verdict. He has in mind, however, a "deliberate and especially egregious" trial error or "one that is combined with a pattern of prosecutorial misconduct" that infects the "integrity" of the trial. *Brecht* at 1722 n. 9. That kind of case *would* be unusual, and one tends to think that Rehnquist mentions it not because he genuinely anticipates that it might arise, but to justify some choice quotations from a previous opinion by Justice Stevens. Greer v. Miller, 483 U. S. 756, 769 (1987) (concurring opinion). The question in *Brecht* was also presented in *Greer,* and when the majority failed to address it, Stevens attached a separate opinion to say that, in his view, the "beyond a reasonable doubt" standard for harmless error should not always be applied in habeas. I have to think that since Stevens' vote is essential in *Brecht,* the Chief Justice is merely trying in this instance to keep him satisfied.

133. Brecht v. Abrahamson, 113 S.Ct. 1710, 1724 (1993) (concurring opinion).

134. Id. In the main, then, Justice Stevens insists that the Court's articulation of a different standard for harmless error in habeas corpus may come to little more than a shift in labels—so long as the federal courts perform their function of judging actual cases in a way that transcends the "formula or precise rule" that guides them. Id. at 1725, quoting Kotteakos v. United States, 328 U.S. 750, 761 (1946).

135. Compare Brecht v. Abrahamson, 113 S.Ct. 1710, 1722 (1993), with id. at 1723 (Stevens, J., concurring). Justice Stevens acknowledges that the *Kotteakos* case on which the Chief Justice relies actually allows the burden to shift according to the nature of the claim: the prosecution has the burden with respect to a claim whose "natural effect is to prejudice a litigant's substantial rights," but the accused has the burden regarding a claim deemed to be "technical." Kotteakos v. United States, 328 U. S. 750, 760–761 (1946) (referring to congressional committee reports in point). To Stevens, however, it is perfectly clear that "a constitutional violation . . . would never fall in the 'technical' category." *Brecht* at 1723–24 (concurring opinion).

136. If reasonable minds could differ over the claim when the prisoner presented it to the state courts, then the prisoner was even then seeking the establishment of a "new rule." That was acceptable at trial in state court or on direct review, but under the Rehnquist Court's recent cases it is no longer acceptable in federal habeas corpus.

137. See the text accompanying notes 126–135 supra.

138. See the text accompanying notes 79–85 supra.

139. *Hearings on S. 1314 before the Subcommittee on Improvements in the Judicial Machinery of the Committee on the Judiciary,* 95th Cong., 2d Sess. (1978).

140. Writing separately in Teague v. Lane, 489 U. S. 288 (1989), Justice White said that while the decision in Griffith v. Kentucky, 479 U. S. 314 (1987), to make "new rules" announced on direct review fully retroactive to other cases also pending on direct review "appear[s] to have constitutional underpinnings," the decision in *Teague* to limit the applicability of "new rules" in habeas corpus constitutes an interpretation of the habeas corpus statutes and therefore can be changed by Congress. *Teague* at 317.

141. Readers should know that I consulted with the congressional staff members responsible for drafting this provision. Of course, it did not become law. For the details, see Yackle, "Hagioscope," supra note 8.

142. Recall that when in cases arising on direct review the Warren Court handed down decisions changing the law, that Court did not always extend the benefits of its "new rules" to other cases also pending on direct review at the time of the relevant decision. See notes 94–95 and the accompanying text supra.

143. A substitute offered on the House floor by Reps. William Hughes and Butler Derrick attempted to mollify the opposition by incorporating the Rehnquist Court's two exceptions in place of the Warren Court standards reflected in H. R. 5269. Inasmuch as that substitute retained H. R. 5269's definition of "new rules," however, it compromised only something of marginal signficance.

144. E.g., Desist v. United States, 394 U. S. 244, 248 (1969) (defining a "new rule" as a "clear break" from the past); Allen v. Hardy, 478 U. S. 255, 258 (1986) (referring to an "explicit and substantial break with prior precedent"). In an opinion by Justice White in Solem v. Stumes, 465 U. S. 638 (1984), the Court intimated that only a decision that overrules prior precedents is a "clear break," but did not make the definition of a "new rule" for retroactivity purposes contingent on explicit overruling.

145. A further subsection of the provision in the text would redefine the point at which a petitioner's sentence becomes final as the "conclusion of State court appellate and collateral (or unitary) litigation on the claimant's conviction and sentence and any review in the Supreme Court of the United States of that litigation." That would postpone the critical date from which "new rules" are measured from the end of the appellate process, as the Court's doctrine has it, to the conclusion of postconviction proceedings.

146. I also consulted with the drafters responsible for this provision. It, too, failed to pass. Again, for the details, see Yackle, "Hagioscope," supra note 8.

147. Memorandum distributed on the floor.

148. See note 55 supra.

149. See note 144 supra.

150. The limitation of "new rules" to breaks from precedent "announced by the Supreme Court" is chimerical in this same way. On its face, this limitation restricts the scope of "new rules" (and thus preserves the scope of federal habeas corpus) in that it eliminates from a federal district court's concerns the possibility

that a prisoner is asking the district court itself to establish (as well as to apply) a "new rule." Since by definition under this provision a rule can be "new" only if it is created by the Supreme Court, a district court need be concerned only with Supreme Court decisions handed down since a prisoner's case left the state system. Nevertheless, the reference to Supreme Court action *seems* (at least to the uninitiated) to cut the other way—by dealing explicitly with the problem the Court's definition of "new rules" is said to address, namely, prisoners' use of habeas corpus to gain the benefits of "new" Supreme Court interpretations of the Constitution in general and the eighth amendment in particular.

151. S. 1441, 103rd Cong., 1st Sess., 139 *Cong. Rec.* S10923 (Aug. 6, 1993).

152. Senator Biden explained on the floor that he and his staff had developed S. 1441 in negotiations with the National District Attorneys Association, which formally endorsed the bill on introduction. 139 *Cong. Rec.* S10926 (Aug. 6, 1993), quoting William C. O'Malley, President of the NDAA, to Joseph R. Biden, Chair, Senate Judiciary Committee (Aug. 5, 1993). In a memorandum distributed to the NDAA membership, one of the negotiators explained that the bill would "codif[y] the core of *Teague*" and thus frustrate attempts by "criminal defense lobbyists" to "gut current law." Ronald Eisenberg, "Federal Habeas Corpus Reform Talking Points" (Sept. 10, 1993). If the "core" of current law is the different treatment that "new rule" claims receive in habeas corpus as against direct review, then, of course, S. 1441 does embrace that central premise—as have all other bills in recent years. The "change in the constitutional standard" definition of "new rules," however, plainly is more confining than the Court's sweeping formulations. On this point, Senator Biden himself reassured his colleagues that his bill would retain *Teague*'s general policy of denying retroactive effect to genuine changes in the law, but explained that the bill clearly would reject the Court's capacious definitions of "new rules"—for the express purpose of forestalling deference to "reasonable" state court decisions:

> Over the years, the Supreme Court has come up with a variety of different definitions of a "new rule." These definitions have created much confusion, controversy, and conflicting interpretations—among scholars, litigators, the lower courts, and even among the Justices themselves. And these various definitions have created another problem: if you read some of the definitions literally, they can be used to create a virtual role of deference to State courts on questions of Federal constitutional law. For example, in one case, the Supreme Court defined a new rule as any rule about which State court judges could reasonably disagree. But, as we all know, lawyers—even reasonable lawyers—can disagree about anything and everything. So if we define a rule as "new" just because there is disagreement about it, every rule is a new rule. And if every rule is a new rule, we foreclose even the one chance for Federal habeas review that should be open for claims concerning constitutional error. In other cases, the Supreme Court has defined a new rule as one not dictated or compelled by precedent. Strictly speaking, this definition also can be read to capture virtually any rule on which a prisoner might rely. For again, as we all know, any case

can be distinguished in at least some small way from the cases that came before. So this definition can also be used to create a rule of deference and to undermine the Federal courts' ability even to apply well-settled legal standards to the unique facts of a particular case. That is not right. And it is not necessary to assure that State court decisions are not unreasonably overturned by the Federal courts. . . .

The definition in my proposal embodies a mainstream view of the proper role of habeas corpus: the Federal courts should independently apply prevailing legal standards to the facts of a particular case; they should not upset State sentences based on intervening decisions that change that [*sic*] prevailing legal standards and they should not defer to judgments that rest on incorrect—although reasonable—interpretations of Federal law. This definition protects State courts from being blindsided by the award of habeas relief, while at the same time ensuring that Federal habeas corpus continues to exist as a check on incorrect State decisions. 139 *Cong. Rec.* S15815 (Nov. 17, 1993)

Critics of the Biden bill objected to it precisely because it *would* displace the Court's definitions of "new rules" and thus restore the federal courts' authority to exercise independent judgment on legal and mixed issues. E.g., Larry EchoHawk, Attorney General of Idaho, and Frankie Sue Del Papa, Attorney General of Nevada, to All Attorneys General (Sept. 9, 1993) (insisting that the definition of "new rules" in S. 1441 is "vague" at best and that it would overrule the differently phrased formulations in *Teague* and *Butler*); Daniel E. Lungren, Attorney General of California, to Dianne Feinstein, United States Senator (Aug. 13, 1993) (explaining that the S. 1441 definition is more "narrow" than the Court's formulations and thus insisting that the bill would frustrate the purpose of the Court's decisions, namely, to forge a system in which the federal courts are constrained to "follow reasonable state court rulings").

153. Richard H. Fallon, Jr. & Daniel J. Meltzer, "New Law, Non-Retroactivity, and Constitutional Remedies," 104 *Harv. L. Rev.* 1733, 1736 (1991).

154. Desist v. United States, 394 U. S. 244, 260–262 (1969) (Harlan, J., dissenting).

155. Chapter Three, the text accompanying notes 64–70.

156. Cf. Liebman, "Slightly Retro," supra note 84, at 613; Joseph L. Hoffmann, "Retroactivity and the Great Writ: How Congress Should Respond to *Teague v. Lane*," 1990 *B.Y.U. L. Rev.* 183. Inasmuch as I attack the Court's premise that the purpose of habeas corpus is to deter the state courts from ignoring federal law, I do not pursue the different argument that, even given that premise, the Court should make the federal courts more accessible. See Evan Tsen Lee, "The Theories of Federal Habeas Corpus" (forthcoming) (elaborating such an argument).

157. Chapter Three, the text accompanying 91–94. This proposal would retain the longstanding requirement that petitioners in habeas corpus must be attacking some form of "custody." I have argued that the custody requirement might well be jettisoned, so that anyone who suffers a criminal conviction should be able to

apply for federal habeas relief, whether or not the sentence imposed contemplates some form of restraint. See note 25 supra. Dan Meltzer has called me to account for that view. He fairly points out that by conditioning the availability of habeas corpus on a petitioner's custody, current law screens out convicts whose need for a federal forum for relitigating federal issues is comparatively weak—for example, people who are merely fined for violating minor traffic regulations. Daniel J. Meltzer, "Habeas Corpus Jurisdiction: The Limits of Models," 66 *So. Calif. L. Rev.* 2507, 2510 n.17 (1993). I am not yet fully persuaded. For while it is true that discarding the custody doctrine would formally open federal habeas to citizens who think their federal rights were violated in the neighborhood traffic court, it seems extremely unlikely that many of those people would be *so* litigious as to act on the opportunity. And if anybody *did,* it might well be because her treatment in traffic court raises a serious constitutional issue worthy of federal judicial attention. Cf. Wooley v. Maynard, 430 U. S. 705 (1977) (sustaining a claim that a citizen's religious liberty had been violated when a traffic court fined him $25 for failing to display the state's "Live Free or Die" motto on his license plate). For the moment, however, I have left the custody requirement intact.

158. See note 99 and the accompanying text supra.

159. It may be that some judicial remedies can properly be withheld on account of shifts in the applicable legal standards. But habeas corpus is not one of them. It is one thing, for example, to hold that state *executive officers* sued *personally* for *damages* in a §1983 action should be heard to respond that they acted in good-faith reliance on existing precedents and did not violate any "clearly established" legal standard. Anderson v. Creighton, 483 U. S. 635 (1987). By allowing such officials to escape liability for damages, a federal court does not suggest that their "reasonable" judgments about federal law were correct (or in any fashion acceptable as correct). Indeed, the court assumes that the plaintiff's federal rights were violated—i.e., that the state officers' judgment was erroneous. Moreover, exacting damages from such defendants on a more demanding standard might discourage them from doing their jobs properly or, indeed, from taking government jobs in the first place. It is quite another thing to propose that federal claims should be boxed out of federal habeas corpus on the theory that state *judges* acted in good faith when they reached decisions that were reasonably close to the mark. On the differences between the *Teague* line of cases and suits for damages and other forms of relief, see Fallon & Meltzer, "New Law," supra note 153; Kit Kinports, "Habeas Corpus, Qualified Immunity, and Crystal Balls: Predicting the Course of Constitutional Law," 33 *Ariz. L. Rev.* 115 (1991).

160. 28 U.S.C. §2254(b)–(c); see Ex parte Royall, 117 U. S. 241, 252 (1886); accord Strickland v. Washington, 466 U. S. 668, 679 (1984).

161. Most prisoners attempt to comply with the doctrine; still, roughly half the habeas actions filed in federal court are dismissed on this ground. Faust, Rubenstein & Yackle, "Great Writ," supra note 33, at 684. On the intricacies of the exhaustion doctrine, see, e.g., Picard v. Connor, 404 U. S. 270 (1971) (dismissing a habeas application because the petitioner had not articulated his claim clearly

enough in state court); Pitchess v. Davis, 421 U. S. 482, 486–487 (1975) (citing *Picard* for the proposition that the exhaustion of state remedies is a firm "precondition" or "prerequisite" to federal habeas corpus; Duckworth v. Serrano, 454 U. S. 1 (1981) (insisting on exhaustion even when the prisoner was clearly entitled to relief on the merits); Anderson v. Harless, 459 U. S. 4 (1982) (finding a petitioner's exhaustion inadequate notwithstanding his effort to place the substance of his claim before the state courts); Rose v. Lundy, 455 U. S. 509 (1982) (holding that the district courts should ordinarily dismiss a petition containing multiple claims in its entirety if state remedies have not been exhausted with respect to a single claim). See Larry W. Yackle, "The Exhaustion Doctrine in Federal Habeas Corpus: An Argument for a Return to First Principles," 44 *Ohio St. L.J.* 393 (1983). But see Vasquez v. Hillery, 474 U. S. 254 (1986) (finding it unnecessary to send a prisoner back to state court to press factual matters developed in a federal evidentiary hearing); Granberry v. Greer, 481 U. S. 129 (1987) (apparently permitting state officials to concede or waive compliance with the exhaustion doctrine).

162. Parker v. Ellis, 362 U. S. 574, 582 (1960) (dissenting opinion).

163. See 137 *Cong. Rec.* S8661–65 (June 26, 1991).

164. *Report and Proposal,* supra note 48.

165. See Robb v. Connolly, 111 U. S. 624, 637 (1884).

166. Chapter Three, the text accompanying notes 66–70.

167. Arguably, we might choose a rule that disallows a habeas petition until state authorities are satisfied that they have convicted and sentenced a prisoner appropriately and thus cease to be the moving party in any further litigation. Rigorously understood, that rule would permit a habeas petition immediately after trial. Even initial appeals to the state appellate courts are at the instance of the convict who objects to the judgment, not the prosecutor who successfully obtained it. State law does not ordinarily require appellate review, and if a convict chooses to bypass the state appellate courts and seek immediate federal adjudication in habeas corpus, a rule permitting prompt access to the federal forum would seem to make theoretical sense. Still, the state appellate courts exist to do more than review prisoners' federal constitutional claims. Those courts also superintend state trial courts in the processing of criminal cases under local standards and, more important for my purposes, they elaborate on the meaning and reach of state criminal law. Accordingly, if federal habeas corpus were routinely available immediately after trial, so that ordinary appellate review in the state court system were neglected in an appreciable number of cases, the values associated with local control of the criminal law would be jeopardized.

168. For background, see Larry W. Yackle, "The Misadventures of State Postconviction Remedies," 16 *N.Y.U. Rev. L. & Soc. Change* 359 (1988).

169. Vasquez v. Hillery, 474 U. S. 254, 265 (1986).

170. See Robert N. Clinton, "Rule 9 of the Federal Habeas Corpus Rules: A Case Study on the Need for Reform of the Rules Enabling Acts," 63 *Iowa L. Rev.* 15 (1977); Judith Resnik, "Tiers," 57 *So. Calif. L. Rev.* 837, 929–930 (1984); Yackle, *Remedies,* supra note 9, at §114.

171. E.g., Vasquez v. Hillery, 474 U. S. 254, 280 (1986) (Powell, J., dissenting); Spalding v. Aiken, 460 U. S. 1093 (1983) (opinion of Burger, C.J.).

172. See S. 1441, 103rd Cong., 1st Sess. (1993), other aspects of which are discussed in notes 151–152 and the accompanying text supra.

173. Remarks of the Chief Justice, American Bar Association Mid-Year Meeting (Feb. 6, 1989). I have argued elsewhere that death row prisoners have ample incentives to proceed as soon as they are able, but that other constraints may cause delays—principally lack of professional counsel. Yackle, "Form and Function," supra note 41, at 706–710.

174. *Report and Proposal,* supra note 48; ABA "Report," supra note 49.

175. The federal courts were not presented with an excessive number of such petitions even prior to that rule's adoption in 1977. More recently, the rate of timely filing has increased. Faust, Rubenstein & Yackle, "Great Writ," supra note 33, at 686–687.

176. Filing deadlines may be established for all cases, capital and noncapital. Yet the time periods allotted should not be so brief as those proposed to date and, certainly, should be no *shorter* for capital cases than for noncapital cases. Since 1990, civil actions under new federal statutes have been subject to a four-year limitations period. 28 U.S.C. §1658. That would seem to be an appropriate baseline. Moreover, suspending the time period during the pendency of state postconviction remedies would not be inconsistent with abandoning the requirement that such remedies be exhausted before federal relief is sought. Petitioners should not be forced to pursue state postconviction relief on the misguided theory that the state courts must be given the initial opportunity to address federal claims. Yet so long as the states maintain postconviction procedures, it only makes sense to allow time for willing petitioners to invoke them if they wish. Senator Specter's proposal to preserve both state postconviction procedures and federal habeas corpus, but to allow time only for one or the other, would needlessly pressure prisoners to contend with alternatives that are available only in form.

177. Smith v. Murray, 477 U. S. 527, 533 (1986) (dictum).

178. Fay v. Noia, 372 U. S. 391, 438–439 (1963).

179. Wainwright v. Sykes, 433 U. S. 72 (1977). Under longstanding precedents, state procedural grounds of decision bar direct review in the Supreme Court, provided they are "adequate" to support the state courts' results and "independent" of any federal issue. The Warren Court's waiver rule for procedural default cases in habeas corpus made that feature of Supreme Court jurisdiction irrelevant. Whether or not a state's refusal to consider a claim because of default would prevent the Supreme Court from addressing the claim on direct review, a federal habeas court could entertain it in the absence of a waiver. The Rehnquist Court's forfeiture rule resurrects the "adequate and independent state ground doctrine" for application in habeas corpus. In a default case, the first federal question is whether the state courts' refusal to consider a claim because of default constitutes a state procedural ground that would bar direct review in the Supreme Court. If so, the district court passes on to the further questions noted in the text.

A petitioner can show "cause" only by proving some objective impediment to the timely presentation of a claim in state court. The only examples the Court has offered are cases in which the factual or legal basis of a claim was not reasonably available when the case was in state court and cases in which counsel's performance was constitutionally ineffective. In the latter instance, "cause" is demonstrated not because counsel's performance was so dismal that he or she ceased to be the client's agent, but because responsibility for constitutionally deficient proceedings can be ascribed to the state and is thus "external" to the defense. Murray v. Carrier, 477 U. S. 478, 488 (1986). In United States v. Frady, 456 U. S. 152 (1982), the Court said that the "prejudice" question is whether the constitutional error about which the prisoner complains "so infected the entire trial that the resulting conviction violates due process." Id. at 169. But see Yackle, *Remedies,* supra note 9, at §87 (1992 Supp.) (faulting the *Frady* opinion for running the "prejudice" idea with respect to procedural default into the merits of underlying claims). For other decisions following *Sykes* and elaborating the meaning of "cause" and "prejudice," see Coleman v. Thompson, 111 S.Ct. 2546 (1991); Dugger v. Adams, 489 U. S. 401 (1989); Amadeo v. Zant, 486 U. S. 214 (1988); Smith v. Murray, 477 U. S. 527 (1986). A "fundamental miscarriage of justice" is presented only in an "extraordinary" case in which a constitutional violation "probably resulted in the conviction of one who is actually innocent." *Carrier* at 479. See Sawyer v. Whitley, 112 S.Ct. 2514 (1992).

180. Keeney v. Tamayo-Reyes, 112 S.Ct. 1715 (1992).

181. Yackle, "Misadventures," supra note 168, at 379.

182. Wainwright v. Sykes, 433 U. S. 72, 89 (1977).

183. See the text accompanying note 124 supra. On "sandbagging," see Graham Hughes, "Sandbagging Constitutional Rights: Federal Habeas Corpus and the Procedural Default Principle," 16 *N.Y.U. Rev. L. & Soc. Change* 321 (1988). Counsel's strategy could embrace these possibilities. If conviction is inevitable on the basis of other evidence, if a currently withheld claim could be constructed from a barren record, if the harmless error doctrine could be avoided, and if retrial would be troublesome or particularly expensive for the prosecution—then counsel might be in a position to negotiate a better settlement. Cases in which such scheming is plausible must be extremely rare and scarcely the stuff from which routine doctrine is or should be fashioned.

184. Resnik, "Tiers," supra note 170, at 896–897.

185. With the shift away from the bypass rule, the argument that default should foreclose federal habeas adjudication became a much more potent weapon in the hands of state's attorneys. Faust, Rubenstein & Yackle, "Great Writ," supra note 33, at 667.

186. *Hearings on S. 1314,* supra note 139; *Hearings on H. R. 4737,* supra note 55.

187. Smith v. Yeager, 393 U. S. 122, 124–125 (1968).

188. Sanders v. United States, 373 U. S. 1 (1963). On the codification of *Sanders* in §2244(b), see Paprskar v. Estelle, 612 F.2d 1003, 1005 n.11 (5th Cir.), cert. denied, 439 U. S. 843 (1980). The Supreme Court itself originally said that Rule 9(b) also incorporated *Sanders.* E. g., Rose v. Lundy, 455 U. S. 509, 521 (1982).

189. Sanders v. United States, 373 U. S. 1, 15 (1963). See Richard A. Williamson, "Federal Habeas Corpus: Limitations on Successive Applications from the Same Prisoner," 15 *Wm. & Mary L. Rev.* 265 (1973) (reviewing the decision in *Sanders*).

190. Sanders v. United States, 373 U. S. 1, 17–18 (1963). The original draft of Rule 9(b) as it came from the Judicial Conference would have omitted any reference to an "abuse of the writ" and, perhaps, the linkage to the waiver standard. That draft would have allowed dismissal if a petitioner's failure to raise a claim in a prior petition was "not excusable." The ostensible departure excited controversy in Congress, where the "abuse" standard was reinserted. H. R. Rep. No. 1471, 94th Cong., 2d Sess. 5 (1976). See Clinton, "Rule 9," supra note 170.

191. In Kuhlmann v. Wilson, 477 U. S. 436 (1986), Justice Powell said (on behalf of a plurality) that the "ends of justice" would be served by reconsidering a claim that had been raised and rejected previously only if the prisoner made out a "colorable showing of actual innocence." In Rose v. Lundy, 455 U. S. 509, 521 (1982), Justice O'Connor said (on behalf of a plurality) that petitioners may withdraw claims regarding which state remedies have not yet been exhausted from a current petition and thus obtain immediate treatment of claims the state courts have seen. If they do so, however, she said they risk dismissal under Rule 9(b)— if and when they exhaust state remedies with respect to currently "unexhausted" claims and file later petitions raising those claims. While the withdrawal of known claims already in a current petition is surely deliberate, there is a substantial question whether such an action (driven by the prisoner's understandable desire to litigate other claims while they are fresh) should be taken as a waiver within the meaning of the *Sanders* and *Noia* decisions.

192. E.g., Stephens v. Kemp, 464 U. S. 1027, 1030 (1983) (separate opinion of Powell, J.) (joined by Burger, C. J. and O'Connor & Rehnquist, J.J.); Woodard v. Hutchins, 464 U. S. 377, 379 (1984) (opinion of Powell, J.) (joined by Burger, C. J. and Blackmun, O'Connor & Rehnquist, J.J.).

193. McCleskey v. Zant, 111 S.Ct. 1454 (1991).

194. News Release, supra note 48.

195. See S. 1441, 103rd Cong., 1st Sess. (1993), other aspects of which are discussed in notes 151–152 and the accompanying text supra.

Index